Penguin Literary Biographies
DENTON WELCH:
THE MAKING OF A WRITER

Michael De-la-Noy was born in 1934 in Hessle, Yorkshire and was educated at Bedford School, where he won the Lord Luke History Prize and the Philpotts English Literature Prize twice. After active service in Egypt he worked for three years on the *Bedfordshire Times* as a reporter and feature writer, and spent a further year on the *Brighton and Hove Herald*. He began reviewing books and plays for a variety of publications at the age of twenty, and his freelance journalistic career included some time as a feature writer for the *Guardian*. In 1965, with the photographer Clay Perry, he published *Young Once Only*, an account of an experiment with boys on probation, and in 1968 he edited *The Fields of Praise*, an anthology of poetry. In 1983 he published his first biography, *Elgar: The Man*. *Denton Welch: The Making of a Writer* followed in 1984, to wide critical acclaim. He has also edited the first unexpurgated edition of *The Journals of Denton Welch*, together with *Best Short Prose of Denton Welch*, both published by Penguin. His most recent book is *The Honours System*. He works in London during the week and escapes to the country at the weekends, where he goes for very short walks and admires other people's gardens.

By the same author

Elgar: The Man

·DENTON WELCH·

THE MAKING OF A WRITER

MICHAEL DE-LA-NOY

PENGUIN BOOKS

Penguin Books Ltd, Harmondsworth, Middlesex, England
Viking Penguin Inc., 40 West 23rd Street, New York, New York 10010, U.S.A.
Penguin Books Australia Ltd, Ringwood, Victoria, Australia
Penguin Books Canada Limited, 2801 John Street, Markham, Ontario, Canada L3R 1B4
Penguin Books (N.Z.) Ltd, 182–190 Wairau Road, Auckland 10, New Zealand

First published by Viking 1984
Published in Penguin Books 1986
Copyright © Michael De-la-Noy, 1984

Made and printed in Great Britain by
Richard Clay (The Chaucer Press) Ltd,
Bungay, Suffolk
Filmset in Palatino

FOR JUNE

Contents

List of Plates

Introduction

Denton Welch's first ambition, conceived while at school at Repton and consolidated as a student at the Goldsmith School of Art, was to be a painter. He never lost this ambition – indeed, he more than adequately fulfilled it, developing into an artist of extraordinary imaginative power and technical skill – but in 1935, when he was twenty, the course of his life was changed in such a way that he discovered another talent, one which turned out to be even more potent. As he was cycling one day from his lodgings in Greenwich to visit an aunt and uncle in Leigh, near Reigate, he was run over by a car. He sustained appalling injuries from which, thirteen years later, he was to die.

His instinctive response to the accident, and the way in which he managed to face up to his blighted youth and extremely uncertain future, was to turn inwards on himself and to live, in his imagination, almost entirely in the past. In doing so – in refining and recording his memories – he discovered his genius as a writer. Had it not been for the accident and his subsequent confinement, often for weeks at a time, to the claustrophobic atmosphere of the sick-room, it is unlikely that he would ever have written a word. Like the accident itself, this would have been a tragedy for, as Edith Sitwell so precisely noted, he was a born writer. Instead of remaining in the ranks of the many thousands of potentially creative people who never discover their gifts, Denton Welch, through the misfortune of a terrible disaster, was presented with the very conditions under which his hitherto untapped talents could develop.

In 1940, when he was twenty-five, he began work on his first book. Entitled *Maiden Voyage*, it was partly about his schooldays at Repton and partly about an extended holiday spent in China when he was sixteen. Like everything he was to write, it was based exclusively on actual events and real people. The first edition, published in 1943, was an instant success. During the five remaining years of his life, as he became progressively more ill, he went on to write another two autobiographical novels, *In Youth is Pleasure* and *A Voice Through a Cloud*, some two dozen short stories, hundreds of poems and more than two hundred thousand words of a journal which he kept between July 1942 and August 1948. *In Youth is Pleasure*, which tells the story of a school holiday he spent in England when he was fifteen, repeated the success of his first book when it was published in 1945. Had he lived he would have seen *A Voice Through a Cloud*, an account of the accident and the months he spent in hospital, also published to widespread critical acclaim. This, the book by which he set greatest store and which he understandably found the hardest to write, lay unfinished beside his bed when he died on 30 December 1948. Arguably his finest work, it was published, incomplete by a dozen or so pages, in 1950.

From the age of twenty-one until his death at thirty-three, Denton Welch lived in Kent, in and around Tonbridge and often in cramped, unsatisfactory conditions. Because of his relative immobility, a visit to London became an event, and even after he had made his name his access to the literary world was negligible. Edith Sitwell was the only established writer of serious repute with whom he was ever on first-name terms, and his friendship with painters was restricted to lady amateurs in the villages where he lived.

When in his first two novels and some of his best short stories he had exhausted the material available from his itinerant childhood and unhappy adolescence, he was compelled to fall back for inspiration on the parochial dramas provided by his immediate circle of friends and neighbours. From most of these people he seems to have detached himself behind a conventional screen of camp humour, for he was at every level a deeply isolated and lonely person, insecure in his affections and in his standing as a writer. He frequently wrote to strangers, he encouraged letters and visits from his fans, and he became heavily reliant on what one might term second-rate relationships, with people whom a part of him despised yet who at least provided companionship and contact with the outside world.

In his seclusion his thirst for news became insatiable yet, paradoxically, he remained comparatively unaware of the eventful – and in literature prolific – times through which he lived. Only in the privacy of his journals, for example, did he touch upon the war, which he loathed, and among the books that he is known to have read there feature practically none by his contemporaries, even though his own work was appearing in literary magazines to which a host of major writers of the period also contributed. Henry Green, George Orwell, William Plomer, V. S.

Pritchett, William Sansom and Lionel Trilling are just a handful of those whose work was appearing alongside his in *Penguin New Writing*, one of the leading literary magazines of the forties; and in *Horizon*, where he made his début as a short-story writer, perhaps the most gifted novelist of his generation, Angus Wilson, was making his name with stories reflecting wartime and post-war social change which were later incorporated into *Such Darling Dodos* and *The Wrong Set*. Denton Welch seemed to care nothing for social or political inspiration. Indeed, he had no concrete philosophy. He was quite simply a lone experimenter in literary technique, a wholly original writer guided solely by instinct.

First and foremost a reporter, he had an astonishing ear for remembered dialogue and a razor-sharp recollection of things seen, smelled and touched. That he was not in the broadest sense an inventive or creative writer becomes apparent whenever one compares events described in his novels and short stories with the same events recorded in his journals and in his delightfully garrulous letters. On the whole one can take it for granted that everything in his 'fiction' is a more or less exact record of experience. Had he ever exhausted his autobiographical material it is doubtful whether he could have achieved a successful novel set outside the narrow limits of his own sphere. Unlike most writers of autobiographical fiction, he was interested more in the fabric than in the drama of human experience. '*This* is what life is really like,' he seems to be saying, and in his short stories he analysed what he saw of life with an understanding of human motivation that sets him apart as such an interesting writer. At first sight these narratives seem almost too simple in construction and ideas, too restricted in action and characterization, and when one reaches the end of a story one marvels that he has managed to capture and hold one's attention. He does so simply by enhancing the impact of small events and by exploiting the fact that life is often – indeed almost always – about things that do *not* happen.

But if Denton Welch was not strictly speaking a creative writer, he was certainly a compulsive one, and his letters, recording every detail of his domestic life and his literary fortunes and misfortunes, are a biographer's dream. Nevertheless, while often lengthy and almost invariably entertaining, they are concerned usually with trivia. References to the war are confined to accounts of 'doodle-bugs' landing near by, with the occasional expression of concern for the safety of his brother Paul, while politics, literature, indeed the entire world outside his bedroom window, scarcely existed when he was writing to friends. For that reason he cannot be considered among the top flight of letter writers. As a poet, too, it has to be said that he failed at a public level. He wrote hundreds of poems, but by and large they are trite and poorly finished, and it is doubtful whether he seriously thought them worth publishing. It was in the prose work that he did intend for publication that he refined his gifts as an honest and careful craftsman, and developed that aesthetic fastidiousness for which, above all, he deserves to be praised and remembered. Many of the incidents he records are erotic, and in his day he blazed a trail of frankness about homosexual yearnings that alarmed his publishers and excited and delighted his readers, yet always he refrained from labouring a point or seeking to titillate for the sake of it. Now that our palates have become jaded with fantasy and dulled with sensationalism, his writing, with its refusal to compromise with the truth and its constant reassessment of perspective, strikes us as both original and refreshing.

Because of his accident and his early death, Denton Welch came to embody to perfection the romantic image of the doomed young artist, and for a decade after his death his writings acquired something of a cult following. One consequence of this was that his gifts as a painter, which he continued to develop throughout his life, have been largely ignored, and as far as his best work is concerned, grossly under-estimated. In contrast to his writings, his paintings, of which there number some two score mature canvases, are astonishingly inventive, evoking an exotic world of wide-eyed girls wearing monstrous hats adorned with birds and shells, of surrealistic hands clasping vases of flowers, of rabbits and cats entwined in a nightmare jungle of foliage. Sometimes, in the ample arms and bosoms of an imaginary girl figure, for example, there is an obvious similarity with the style of Stanley Spencer; more often, in his handling of shapes and his elaborate detail, he retreats to an almost medieval concept of art as a symbolic form of expression. As an illustrator, too, he excelled, creating fantastic and contrived jackets and endpapers for his own books. Portrait painting, on the other hand, he found difficult, and one of the few portraits he ever conceived with affection (although it is poorly drawn) was of his brother Paul, reclining on a sofa.

The years between the ages of twenty and thirty-three, which ought to have been his heyday, were for Denton Welch his only adult years, into which he had to cram not only the experience of growing to maturity but also his entire creative life. Only during his last seven years did he learn and exercise his craft as a writer. As a painter his progress is less easy to map because it is far less adequately documented. What is certain is that throughout his last years of illness and pain, at the same time as he was writing so prolifically, he was also painting with consummate skill, and it is not until one examines closely the records he left of this period that one is able to appreciate the physical courage and iron self-discipline that were required to produce such a body of outstanding work.

While one may indulge in the luxury of laughing at many of Denton Welch's personal absurdities, and at the amazing tangle of domestic dramas which he created around himself – his candid self-awareness gives us licence to do so – one cannot at the same time remain unmoved by the realization that through all the frippery and pettiness there struggled a man with a mission – a burning need to fulfil himself as an artist. Had this not been the case he would surely have died long before he did, for to say that he kept himself alive through little more than will-power is not, in the face of his medical history, stretching the evidence too far. In this ambition he was sustained by a high degree of moral courage, and it was perhaps his ability to be so frank about himself which, against all the odds, saw him through. He was under no illusions about his difficult temperament, and he would always have found life, even without the accident, a frustrating and complex business. Fortunately he did not have any serious doubts, other than those that beset all writers, about the quality of his work, and such was his belief in it that he became tenacious in his pursuit of publishers and critics to endorse it. Those who rejected or scorned it he saw as crass incompetents.

Though he never saw in print his finest work – his last novel and his journals – he did enjoy high critical acclaim and encouragement from the literary establishment, and he also had the satisfaction of knowing that several of his best paintings had found appreciative buyers, two of whom, John Lehmann and Rose Macaulay, were fellow writers who in addition admired his literary work. In spite of his success, however, he remained below the surface immensely vulnerable, not least because on top of his other difficulties his accident had left him incapable of sexual fulfilment. Frequently attracted to the most improbable and unsuitable people, and burdened with a damaged body and the shame of partial impotence, he nevertheless did manage to salvage his integrity and self-respect sufficiently to be able to recognize and respond to an offer of true friendship when it came just a few years before he died. While his relationship with Eric Oliver was to some extent one-sided, it was crucial to the final development of his sensitivity and understanding of human nature, not least of his own. Through it the cynical voyeur, much to his own surprise, came at last to rest.

There can be few people whose lives have ended in their thirties who merit a biography, and I am very aware of the peculiarities of this one. Much of what is known about Denton Welch is supplied by himself in his writings, while other documentary records are unfortunately fragmentary. Because of this I have deliberately allowed him to tell his own story, though in doing so I am conscious that there is a marked difference in texture between the earlier and the later years, the later years being illuminated by a galaxy of letters and by contemporaneous journal entries. These I have relied upon heavily, making greater use of quotations than is perhaps usual in a biography. I have been tempted to do so, particularly in the case of the letters, because in them is contained the narrative of his daily life, his work and his states of mind in a form which is far more entertaining than a straightforward summary of mine would have been. I have also deliberately tended to stand back, not just from elaborating on the facts but from evaluating the intricacies of his personality and behaviour, since few could judge him more astutely than he did himself. If I have not praised him highly enough for some, it is because I have wished to preserve him from extravagant claims which he would have been the first to denounce. He was an exceptional person and a unique writer. I have been prepared to leave it at that.

My interest in Denton Welch goes back to 1951, when I first read *A Voice Through a Cloud*. In 1973 Kay Dick gave me a copy of *The Denton Welch Journals*, which sent me in search of other books by him and suggested to me, in 1975, the idea of interviewing for the *Guardian* the companion of his last four years, Eric Oliver. Though the man and his work continued to intrigue me, it was not until 1982, when Kay Dick again took a hand by giving me the confidence to contemplate writing a biography of him, that I was finally spurred to satisfy my curiosity about his life. For her timely and continued encouragement I am most grateful.

While writing this biography I have received further and sometimes astonishing acts of kindness. Mr W. J. Reed presented me with a set of Denton Welch's books, including a first edition of *Maiden Voyage*, a gift of incomparable value. Mr Benjamin Whitrow made available to me, before I was able to examine the original journals in the University of Texas, a typescript copy of the unpublished portions, formerly in the possession of Francis Streeten, together with letters from Francis

Streeten to himself. Mr Richard Adeney and Mrs Charlotte Forman lent me no less than one hundred and thirty letters from Denton Welch to their mother, Noël Adeney, as well as photographs and her unpublished commentary on the letters. It is impossible to exaggerate the debt I owe to these four benefactors.

Denton Welch's manuscripts, some of his early paintings and much of his correspondence including, most importantly, his letters to Eric Oliver, are now preserved in the Denton Welch Collection in the Humanities Research Center at the University of Texas in Austin. While I was researching there I received from Mrs Ellen Dunlap, research librarian at the Center, and from all the members of her staff, unfailing friendliness and help. Dr Charlotte Laughlin's catalogue, compiled in 1975, was useful, as were the previous excavations made by Jean-Louis Chevalier among biographical material in the Center's archives. My visit to Austin was enhanced beyond measure by the generous and often hilarious hospitality I received from Professor Ernest Mossner and his wife, Carolyn.

I owe a major debt of gratitude, but sadly one I cannot now repay, to the late Miss Beatrice Kane, Denton Welch's cousin, who made available photographs from her private collection and who, without in any way attempting to influence my judgement, generously gave me her sharp and sympathetic memories of Denton Welch and of his relationship with his family. It is a matter of the deepest regret to me that she died before this book was completed. Her sister, Mrs Phyllis Timberlake, kindly consented to my retaining family papers on loan from Miss Kane. Although she never met Denton Welch, his sister-in-law, Mrs Judy Welch, passed on to me during a visit to England much interesting information about family matters. To Dr John Easton, Denton Welch's physician and mentor, who features so honourably as 'Dr Farley' in *A Voice Through a Cloud*, I am especially grateful for medical information, for unstinted and immensely warm-hearted recollections, and for permission to quote from letters. To have received his cooperation I regard as a singular privilege. Lady Fisher, whose husband, Bishop Geoffrey Fisher, was Denton Welch's headmaster at Repton, was able to give me not only her recollections of Denton Welch as a boy but also her memories of his two brothers, Bill and Paul Welch. Mr John Walker, secretary of the Old Reptonian Society, has provided further information about Denton Welch's days at school, and Mr Guy Willatt, who shared a study with Denton Welch, has kindly sent me his memories. Others who knew him and have written to me or talked to me about him, to all of whom I am most grateful, include Mrs Nancy Carline, Mrs Brenda Cobb, Professor Maurice Cranston, Mr John Hesketh, Miss Helen Roeder, Mrs Charles Terrot and Mrs Igor Vinogradoff.

The following have also been kind enough to offer assistance or information of one kind or another: Mr W. H. Boomgaard, Mr Neville Braybrooke, Mrs Sally Brown of the British Library, Mrs Bunny Cantor, librarian of Condé Nast Publications, Professor J. Stewart Cameron, Miss Isobel English, Mr Stephen Francis, Mr P. N. Furbank, Mr J. A. Glover, bursar of Tonbridge School, Miss Caroline Goodfellow, research assistant at the Bethnal Green Museum of Childhood, Miss Patricia Hann, senior assistant at Broadstairs Library, Mr Andrew Kemp of Boosey & Hawkes, Mr George Lawson of Bertram Rota Ltd, Dr John Lehmann, Mr Francis King, the late Mr Roger Machell of Hamish Hamilton Ltd, Mr Charles Monteith, senior editorial consultant at Faber & Faber, Mr Nigel Nicolson, Mr Patrick O'Connor, Mr Peter Parker, Mr Alan Robinson, Mr John Sharp, Mr Tom Sargant, the late Lord Vaizey, and Mr George Summerfield, whose enthusiastic cooperation enabled me to discover, among much other valuable material, a mysteriously concealed hoard of forty-two letters from Denton Welch to Marcus Oliver.

In addition to the majority of Denton Welch's letters, previously un-published material includes letters from Lord Berners, Rose Macaulay, Harold Nicolson, Margot Oxford, Herbert Read, Vita Sackville-West, Edith Sitwell and Frank Swinnerton. For permission to quote from copy-right material in their possession I am indebted to the University of Texas. Letters from Lord Berners are quoted by kind permission of Mr Robert Heber-Percy, from the Hon. Sir Harold Nicolson and the Hon. Vita Sackville-West by kind permission of Mr Nigel Nicolson, from Margot Lady Oxford and Asquith by kind permission of the Hon. Mark Bonham Carter, from Frank Swinnerton by kind permission of Miss Olivia Swinnerton, from Dame Rose Macaulay by permission of the Rose Macaulay Estate, from E. M. Forster by permission of the provost and scholars of King's College, Cambridge and from Dame Edith Sitwell by permission of Mr Francis Sitwell. Family photographs appear by permission of the late Miss Beatrice Kane. The photograph of Noël Adeney was taken by Mr Richard Adeney and is reproduced with his permission.

It remains for me to try to express the debt I owe to Eric Oliver, Denton Welch's closest friend. It was not until I began my research at the University of Texas that I came to realize to what extent this biography would rely on the use of the many extremely personal letters

Denton Welch wrote to him, some of them so personal that he was asked to destroy them. He did not destroy them, and today they form a vital part of the archives relating to the life and work of his friend. Eric Oliver's immediate reaction to my discovery of the letters was to consent to their publication. I have therefore not hesitated to make use of them, because without them it would not be possible to appreciate the full range of Denton Welch's personality, and in particular his extraordinary generosity of spirit. Eric Oliver's attitude towards my use of those letters was in fact only one instance of the patient, courteous and enthusiastic way in which he has endeavoured to share with me his experience of living with Denton Welch. It can be taken that where any information is directly attributed to Eric Oliver it has been imparted in the course of conversation with him or by letter. I need hardly say that he shares no responsibility for any inaccuracies, or opinions other than his own. Far from attempting to interfere or to influence me, he has consistently gone out of his way to be as helpful and cooperative as possible.

Michael De-là-Noy
London NW1

ONE

Childhood

Maurice Denton Welch was born on 29 March 1915 in Shanghai, where both his grandfathers had settled to make their fortunes – his maternal grandfather, Thomas Bassett, in shipping, and his paternal grandfather, Joseph Welch, as a tea merchant – and where his father, Arthur Joseph Welch, was a partner in a firm of rubber estate managers called Wattie & Co. In this cosmopolitan city he spent the greater part of his childhood, interspersed with visits to England, before being sent to school there at the age of nine. In later life he was to recall his grandfathers' 'great houses of grey and red rubbed brick' that gave 'a notion of their wealth, their love of comfort and show', and his own childhood home, at 585 Avenue Foch, with its 'long, heavy arched verandas aflame with Virginia creeper'.[1] Here, in the garden, he built make-believe houses with his brother Paul and hid in the branches of a camphor tree. The two boys had a swing shaped like a boat, that would 'fly up at one end and into the scented bushes and one was lost for a second in the pink froth, to be torn out again like a rushing wind'. At the bottom of the garden was a coach-house and stables, and even after the First World War a coachman was employed to drive an antique carriage that 'used to stand next to the cars, one open and one closed, looking like a broken-down aristocrat trying to keep pace with two smart parvenus'.

The family's wealth had been built up following the rapid expansion of Shanghai from an isolated, walled city of less than 300,000 inhabitants in 1832 into one of the most prosperous trading centres of the East by the middle of the nineteenth century. During the Opium War of 1839–42 a British fleet had bombarded the fortifications, but after the Treaty of Nanking, which ended the war, Western merchants were

---

1. One of a number of autobiographical fragments quoted here which are to be found in the Humanities Research Center at the University of Texas in Austin. Many of them have been published in the *Texas Quarterly*.

allowed in to trade and lease land on the west bank of the Hwangpu River. The combination of an ideally situated port and an unlimited supply of cheap labour soon resulted in a proliferation of trading houses, banks and consulates, and Shanghai developed into an international centre of commerce and vice, its glamorous reputation as a haven for smugglers, speculators and fortune-hunters resulting from the fact that instead of remaining under the authority of the central government in Peking it became a self-governing city, and one where corruption and graft were allowed to flourish in the highest quarters. Divided into a British-dominated International Settlement, a French Concession, the Chinese city itself and the Chinese suburbs, it was the least Chinese city in China, and it was possible for Englishmen such as Arthur Welch, although born there, to retain an entirely English outlook and way of life.

Arthur's father, Joseph Welch, had been married in Shanghai in 1876 when he was thirty-one, to a girl from London named Edith Bois. Joseph's middle brother, John St Vincent Welch, settled and married in Sydney, Australia (his three sons, all born in Sydney, became doctors), and his youngest brother, Edward Welch, followed the same family tradition by emigrating to South Africa. Arthur, born on 26 September 1880, was exceptionally good-looking as a boy (many of the Welch family were) though in later life he is seen with his hair parted firmly down the middle and swept straight back, the oval shape of his face and his rimless spectacles giving him a rather severe, Germanic appearance. By nature taciturn and, like his brother and sisters, emotionally reserved, his conversation and interests were confined almost entirely to business matters.

Of Arthur's four sons, Maurice Denton was the youngest. He was given the name Denton in honour of his maternal grandmother, Katherine Denton, who came from New England; his pride in this ancestry, bolstered by his inordinate devotion to his mother, who was also American, led him to adopt the name Denton to the exclusion of the patrimonial Maurice. Denton tells us that his father would call him 'Microbe', 'Maggot', or sometimes 'Flea', clearly with reference to his diminutive stature, which was in marked contrast to the athletic physique of his older brothers. The use of these nicknames may well be seen as an attempt by Arthur Welch to establish some sort of intimacy with his sensitive, precocious, perhaps precious youngest son, but that there was no genuine rapport between the two may be deduced from a short story Denton was to write, called 'The Coffin on the Hill',[2] in which he seems to

2. First published in *Life and Letters* in June 1946 and reprinted in *Brave and Cruel*.

go out of his way to emphasize the barrenness of their relationship. The story is set when he was at the age of eight, and he makes a point of mentioning that he bid good night to his father 'without kissing him'. On the few occasions that his father flits in and out of Denton's writings he does so as a colourless figure with no real connection to events, people or places.

With his frizzed-up hair, bulging forehead and sharply tapering face, Denton as a little boy gives the distinct impression of a startled Easter chick, and his appearance and personality, differing so radically from those of his brothers, must have disconcerted his strait-laced, conventional father. It was Denton's eldest brother, William (always known as Bill), whom Arthur Welch most loved. Bill was seven years older than Denton (he was born in Shanghai in 1908), and when he grew up he flew aeroplanes, drove expensive cars, and went, like his father, into business. Denton notes that his father was always rather excited when he received Bill's unpaid accounts 'from shops or professional men in Oxford and London'; secretly, he thought, his father was most fond of Bill 'because of his dashing extravagance and unreliability'.

Denton's mother, Rosalind, whose father Thomas Bassett had come to Shanghai from Boston in Massachusetts, was six years younger than her husband (she was born in 1886). At the time of their marriage she was almost plump, though when Denton knew her she had exchanged a handsome face for a beautiful one, and a well-proportioned figure for a slim one – but at a dreadful price. She was a victim of Bright's disease, or nephritis, a wasting disease of the kidneys which results in renal failure. Though not necessarily a hereditary condition it was the cause of death also of her third son, Paul, born in 1913, at the early age of forty. Her second son, Tommy, a beautiful little boy with flaxen hair, died in childhood, a family tragedy that Denton seems to have entirely erased from his mind; although he may have been too young to remember Tommy his brother Bill would certainly have done, and he and his parents might well have been expected to speak of him, yet nowhere in Denton's writings is there any reference, at first or second hand, to his dead brother.

Paul, closest to Denton in age, was not only startlingly good-looking but was endowed with a natural and unaffected charm, physical courage, and a kind and gentle personality. Denton idolized him, looking up to him rather than to Bill for protection and companionship. His relationship with Bill, on the other hand, was complex, and is described in detail in his writings. In *A Voice Through a Cloud*, his last novel, he remembered that Bill had the power to make him feel 'petty, spinsterishly careful, really rather contemptible in my concern for pennies and shillings'. For most of his childhood he had little to do with Bill, though at the age of fifteen it seems that Denton did try to make contact, as we learn from his second novel, *In Youth is Pleasure*, in which he described one day laying out Bill's evening clothes and offering to minister to him as he had a headache. On that occasion Bill responded, pulling Denton down beside him on the bed and making an effort to find some topic of conversation that would interest his introspective young brother. Denton recorded that this was one of the rare moments when he had felt no hatred or fear of him. Denton in fact became obsessed with the sense of inadequacy that Bill, almost certainly without intention, produced in him, writing about him mercilessly in print and suffering agonies worrying about his reaction. Bill seems not to have turned a hair; on the contrary, he always treated Denton with as much fraternal concern as could be expected given their difference in age and their quite different natures.

Denton's paternal family was a large one. His father's elder sister, Edith, who married a navy chaplain, the Reverend Thomas Kane, had produced no less than nine children with whom Denton frequently stayed in England after his mother's death in 1927. He was later to spend much time and trouble looking up these and more distant relatives, as though in pursuit of the illusory security of family connections, yet he was all too aware that it was a quirk of fate that had set him down in a conventional, wealthy, upper-middle-class background. 'I bitterly regretted the family I had been born into,' he wrote in *A Voice Through a Cloud*. 'It was not that they were wrong or that I was wrong. It was the connection that was freakish, invalid, arbitrary.' In another passage in the same book in which he described taking tea with the family of a boy of his own age, he wrote, 'There was no place for me there, or in any family. My life must shape itself alone.'

If one single family influence was to direct that life, however, it was surely that of his mother, with her strict adherence to the teachings of Christian Science. She encouraged him to love her possessively, teaching him petit point, taking his advice about what clothes to wear and still bathing him when he was nine. He would have escaped some of this maternal suffocation up to the age of six, for with only nineteen months between them he and Paul spent most of their early childhood together, but once Paul followed Bill to school in England, Denton had only his mother for company.

'All my childhood was spent in travelling backwards and forwards from China to England and England to China,' he recalled. 'In this way my mother divided her time equally between my father and my brothers.' When he was three he spent time in the Diamond Mountains in Korea. The next summer found him at Frinton-on-Sea in Essex, and visits followed to a Canadian ranch and again to England to stay at Whaphams, the house in Henfield, Sussex to which his grandfather Joseph Welch had retired in 1910 and where Denton was to make his home for a time after his mother's death. One result of this unsettled life was that his formal education was severely disrupted (he was still unable to read at the age of nine), necessitating the engagement of a governess to help him catch up at the time he was sent to school in England.

Such schooling as he did receive in Shanghai began with a spell in a kindergarten. 'I shuddered when I heard the sentence,' he remembered, 'and implored my mother not to send me, but she said she was sure I would like it and it would be so nice to learn something. So one morning I was taken by my brother into the Jaws of Hell. There I was left with some other children, and a woman with pale hair wrote strange signs in my new book; she said that they were numbers up to nine and would I copy them very nicely underneath? I began laboriously to copy, my heart swelling with the feeling of captivity. When I had got to five I noticed the little dash at the top and feeling sure that she had made a mistake I carefully copied it out several times leaving the stroke out. The teacher came up a little later and put them all in, but I hardly believed it to be correct even then.'

Another school he attended was run by a lady named Mrs Paul, who always gave him the impression 'that she had been cooking in front of a kitchen range, or that she had just had a hot bath and dressed in the steamy bathroom or else had been sitting on a terrace in the sun gulping down cups of hot coffee. She had that fatigued, pale, damp look, with tails of greying hair that had strayed from its place.'

One of his more sinister introductions to the adult world took place at a Christmas party in Shanghai. 'We started with a Punch and Judy show. I had never seen one before and thought Punch the most disgusting criminal type. When he began hitting the baby with hard wooden thuds I felt its skull crack and knew that none of us were safe while grown-ups thought that this sort of thing was funny.' To another children's party he went dressed in a blue suit with knee-breeches and powdered hair, and was given a 'richly bound book of Greek Myths. I turned the pages idly for I could not yet read, until my eyes fell on a picture of Prometheus chained to a rock, a vulture hovering over him.

He was nearly naked, his athlete's chest and arms pinned to the rock, his powerful legs straddled apart, his perfect features contorted with pain. He gave me the same feeling that crucifixes did. I felt shame and admiration. I shut the book quickly. I did not want anyone to see me looking at the picture.'

His schooling did not, however, release him entirely from the attentions of his mother, who continued to turn to him to compensate for the undemonstrative nature of her husband and her separation from her two other sons. A glimpse of their extravagantly dependent relationship is found in a short story Denton wrote called 'At Sea',[3] which is set on an ocean liner when he was about seven, and in which he gives himself the name 'Robert', one of his favourite pseudonyms:

'Robert thought for the thousandth time "My mother is young and pretty, most people's mothers look old and ugly." Always he felt this when he looked at her; especially if, as now, she were a little bedraggled and unwell. When in the morning she asked him to kiss her before she was absolutely awake, when her eyes were still heavy and she felt almost damp from the warmth of the bed, he would have the curious proud feeling mixed with distaste. And sometimes he would not kiss her until she was quite awake and smiling, with her curly, fried-bread-crumb-coloured hair fluffed out and pretty.'

His mother's craving for affection may be explained by what Denton later learned of her own mother, Katherine Denton, from his mother's friend, Irene Dallas, who described his grandmother as 'stiff and fierce and snobbish and seemingly stern and unlovable', and his mother, by contrast, as 'so pretty with her child's face looking up between the gold brown curls, and her nose and the eyes that almost turned into slits when she laughed', adding that she thought it greatly to his grandmother's credit that she could produce a child so different, so lovable, so uninhibited and so unworried by life. His mother's education had been a fairly sophisticated one – she had been sent to a convent in Florence – and this may account for her unexpectedly adult attitude towards him when she was not molly-coddling him. For example, on a visit to a distant relative in England when Denton was only six, his mother took it into her head to buy him a decanter and a set of tiny goblets on a round glass tray. 'They were painted with red and black dots,' he recorded in *A Voice Through a Cloud*, 'and the minute stopper and the decanter was a great delight to me. As soon as we came to an old horse trough,

3. First published in *English Story* in 1944 and reprinted in *Brave and Cruel*.

I insisted on filling the decanter, then pouring from it into the thimble goblets. It was the perfect present for that hot day.'

In the summer of 1924, when he was nine, his father took him and his mother to England, renting a house in the village of Benson in Oxfordshire, in the garden of which Denton noticed gnarled little fruit trees trained against the walls, 'hung in a crucified way, as if the nails were supporting them, not restraining them'. Bill, then sixteen years of age, was half-way through his time at Repton, his father's old school near Derby, and Denton was taken to see him on Speech Day, gaining his first, rather favourable impressions of the institution from which he was later to run away. He remembered how he loved 'the salmon mayonnaise and claret cup we had in the huge marquee. I only was allowed to sip the claret cup but I loved the very thought of it.' Auspiciously, he paid a visit to the art school in the old priory ox stables, which he thought 'very romantic'. His early introduction to architecture and furnishings occurred also at this time through visits to Haddon Hall in Bakewell, Hardwick Hall in Chesterfield, and to Chatsworth House, and while being whisked around on this cultural tour he stayed at the Lygon Arms in Broadway and the Peacock Inn in Naseby.

One of the incidents which took place during his stay in Benson was vividly recreated in a short story called 'The Barn'.[4] An excellent example of his literary technique, it is interesting, too, for the light it throws on his sexual development, always a strong ingredient in his writing. The story, in which he appears under his own name, describes how he climbed up on some boxes in the barn, caught hold of a beam and swung there 'like a monkey'. Then, he tells us, he sank down on the boxes and thought how miserable and lonely he was:

'As I lay there I decided to be a slave who had to sweat and labour in the barn all day. But slaves had to be naked. I put my hand inside my flannel shirt and felt the flesh on my chest. Slowly I leant forward and began to pull the shirt over my head. It was straining work, for I was sitting on the tails. When my body was free of the shirt and my arms were imprisoned in it above my head, I looked down at the vague whiteness of my skin. I thought of the men I had seen, with

4. First published in *New Writing and Daylight*, Winter 1943–4, and reprinted in *Brave and Cruel*. Denton named the location Brook House, possibly with his Repton school house in mind. A Brook House had in fact existed in Benson but had been demolished some time before 1924, and the house the Welchs rented may have been called Brookside or Brook Lodge. There was also a Brook House opposite his grandfather's house in Henfield.

tufts of strong hair on their chests and under their arms. It was ugly and beautiful at once, I thought.

'I caught hold of the beam again and swung about fiercely, hurting my arms, straining the muscles as I pulled myself up. I swore not to stop pulling until I had rested my chin on the top of the beam. At last, with a shudder of pain and pleasure, I brought it to rest there on the rough, beetle-eaten oak. The harsh wood grazed the soft skin of my throat.

'Then slowly and gently I felt my trousers slipping. They slid carelessly over my hips and fell with a soft plop to my ankles, where they caught in bunched up folds. I still hung there, supported by my chin and my tingling arms. Soft draughts of air blew deliciously against my complete nakedness.

' "Now I am a criminal whose feet have been tied together, and whose body has been stripped by the hangman," I told myself. "I shall be swinging here till late at night, when my friends will come and cut me down."

'I hung there not moving, living passionately my idea of a criminal on a gibbet; while the rain beat against the great barn door, and drops fell from the roof.

'Gradually, as my strength gave out, I sank nearer to the ground, until my arms were stretched out agonizingly. There were still some feet to fall to reach the ground. I decided to drop, although I knew that my feet were trapped in the trousers. I fell in a crumpled mass, and lay on the barn floor with the short pieces of hay pricking me. I felt the smooth, satiny mounds of bird-droppings against my flesh. Slowly and wearily I put on my shirt, pulled up my trousers, ran my fingers through my hair, and went in to tea.'

The association in Denton's mind between pain and pleasure which this story so clearly illustrates was a characteristic which remained with him throughout his life, at times amounting to a strong tendency towards masochism. The genesis of the story demonstrates, too, a typical fusion in his writing of his real and his fantasy life, for another version exists, almost certainly written before 'The Barn' was brushed up for publication, in which the sequence of events is rather different. In this version he goes outside the barn, naked, to dance in the rain, when suddenly Paul appears:

'He seemed to show hardly any surprise and followed me into the barn where I began to swing like a monkey again from the beams. Soon he had no clothes on too and we were dancing and swinging like mad mice. We sang and shrieked, we were so excited and then as suddenly we subsided and began to put our clothes on again. I thought it all the greatest fun especially as I felt that the grown-ups would be horrified. Suddenly, desperately, I thought I would tell my mother. I was so vain about my wickedness.

'She laughed and smiled and I saw she had a far-seeing, inward look.'

More interesting than his initial suppression or later exaggeration — whichever it may be — of the masochistic element is the relative importance in his narrative of the appearance later on of a young tramp. In the earlier version we are simply told: 'One rainy night a tramp arrived at the back door and asked if he could spend the night in the barn. My mother said that he could and early next morning I got up and saw him go. He was grey and unwashed and quite young.' In the version elaborated for publication, Denton actually spent the night curled up in the hay beside the tramp who, having failed to dissuade the boy from staying out, conveniently fell asleep, whereupon Denton lowered himself gently beside him 'until we were in one nest'. Whatever the truth of the matter — the idea that a boy of nine could stay out all night unmissed by a solicitous mother seems, on the face of it, unlikely — what is perfectly believable is that the tramp did indeed make an appearance and that Denton dwelt for the next nineteen years on the thought of sleeping with him, perhaps even to the point of persuading himself that he had.

At the end of the summer of 1924, Bill returned to Repton and Denton learned, 'with horror', that he too was to be packed off to school, to an establishment in Queen's Gate, Kensington, that took mostly girls. He was to board for the Christmas term with the parents of one of the female pupils. 'I can remember the terrible day [my mother] took me to the door of the house,' he has written. 'I was crying bitterly and the horror of the long row of coloured brick houses almost overcame me. I had never lived amongst such dreariness and did not know what I should do.' In the end, however, he came to regard it as 'the only school I ever really enjoyed', where everything seemed to be done for the interest of doing it. 'Perhaps it was because it was a girls' school and so more or less civilized.' The mistress who taught him he found 'a charming woman. Tall, fair and kind. I admired her and felt completely safe.' He admitted, nevertheless, to having been bad at everything except handwork and drawing.

At some stage during that Christmas term his mother came to visit him and he stayed with her near the Queen's Gate school at the Van

Dyck Hotel, with rooms overlooking the gardens of the Natural History Museum. He wrote down his recollections of this visit many years later when he began to keep a journal in 1942.[5] In a passage which illustrates her dependence upon Christian Science, the faith in which Denton himself had been brought up, he describes how one day he had gone into 'our' room to find his mother lying on the bed, clearly unwell. She had been crying, and looking back on the scene some twenty years later, he realized that 'the illness which killed my mother was just beginning to show itself'.

'"Love me, darling," she says, turning towards me. "Love me, love me, and I shall be all right."

'I am terribly disturbed. Tears start to run down my cheeks and my mother sees them shining on my face.

'"Don't cry, darling; I didn't say cry." My mother laughs and teases me so that it is unbearably sad.

'"Sing to me," she says. "Sing 'O Gentle Presence, Peace and Joy and Power' or 'Saw ye my Saviour? Heard ye the glad sound?'"

'I try to sing the Christian Science hymns, but break down completely and hug my mother fiercely. Gradually she seems to get better. At last she sits up and says laughingly, "How silly to behave like that! It's only Error trying to get hold of me!"'

In view of her family's New England connections it is likely that Rosalind Bassett came from Evangelical stock, though her education in a Florentine convent might, on the other hand, suggest a Roman Catholic background. However that may be, it was perhaps more than coincidental that the Mother Church of Christ Scientist had been founded, just a year before she was born, in the very town from which her family had moved to Shanghai; and though it is not known precisely when her conversion to the doctrines of Mrs Mary Baker Eddy took place, she was certainly among the first generation to succumb to the idea of total dependence upon the power of prayer to heal the wounds of illness and accident. Based upon the belief that pain and diseases are caused solely through the existence of evil, the doctrine had revived in some measure the established church's traditional but at that time neglected ministry of healing, and had spread with remarkable rapidity. Many of

5. The journals, like all his writings, were written by hand, sometimes in pencil, in school exercise-books, and often he would decorate the covers; sometimes, when half-way through an exercise-book, he would turn it upside down and begin again from the other end. The journals occupy nineteen such books.

Rosalind's friends, whom Denton was to know for the rest of his life, were Christian Scientists, and the most formative years of his childhood were spent in the company of a fervent believer – his mother – struggling with an incurable illness. He was later, through intellectual scepticism, to discard any formal allegiance to the faith, but its influence, perhaps because it was so strongly associated with his mother, never entirely left him; on the whole, while making use of doctors in later life, he disliked and distrusted them.

When he was eleven he was sent to a preparatory school in Uckfield, Sussex. Typical of English prep schools designed for middle-class boys going on to middle-class public schools, St Michael's was different in one respect which dictated its choice for Denton. While the headmaster, a remarkable eccentric who rejoiced in the name of Harold Hibbert Herbert Hockey, and was known to the boys as Mr Bean, was an Anglican clergyman, his wife, a harridan with bright orange hair (according to one of Denton's contemporaries), was a devout Christian Scientist. The school had not been founded exclusively for the patronage of boys from Christian Scientist homes, but they were particularly welcome since their families – of which the Astors were an illustrious example – tended to be rich, and Mr Hockey's finances tended to be shaky; indeed, it is said that he left money matters entirely in the hands of his butler, and when the butler robbed him Mr Hockey took, not at all successfully, to backing horses. When things got completely out of hand he committed suicide. In order to attract those rich parents Mr Hockey had engaged three Christian Scientist masters who were, unfortunately, otherwise unqualified to teach; there were also two matrons, one to administer castor oil, the other silent prayer. Mr Hockey conducted an Anglican form of school prayers each morning, attended by all ninety boys, and it may be imagined that religious instruction at St Michael's took on a decidedly schizophrenic character.

The Astors had already sent their son David to St Michael's, and he was followed there by Michael, an exact contemporary of Denton. In a performance of *The Mikado*, Denton sang the role of Peep-Bo and Michael took the part of one of his fellow Wards, Pitti-Sing. After the performance Lady Astor helped unpin Denton's costume. It was, like many of Mr Hockey's enterprises, a somewhat accident-prone perform-ance, and Denton left an account of it, and of his meeting with the formidable Lady Astor, in an unpublished story with the title 'A Child Meets Church and State and Poetry in Strange Places'.

Of Mr Hockey a vivid description is given by Michael Astor in his

book *Tribal Feeling*,[6] a portrait described by another of Denton's contemporaries, John Hesketh, as 'first class'.[7] Michael Astor writes that
Hockey possessed both selflessness and imagination, but by the time
he and Denton were in his care, 'his physiognomy and manner were
showing signs of stress'. He resembled 'more than anything else a large
and kindly monkey with sad but trusting eyes and a troubled brow'.

Another of Mr Hockey's pupils, seven years Denton's senior, had
been the writer Jocelyn Brooke, who gave a brief account of his time
there in his memoir *The Military Orchid*,[8] in which the school is named
'St Ethelbert's'. Yet another writer who was at St Michael's at the same
time as Denton was Charles Terrot, whose mother was a Christian
Scientist and a friend of Lady Astor, and whose family Denton was
to visit when he was fifteen, later writing about them in *In Youth is
Pleasure*. Terrot remembers Denton as introverted, kind, good at tennis
and 'very good-looking, indeed a beautiful boy, which is why he got
on so well with the masters'. The school itself he recalls as 'a downright
madhouse, run by a charming lunatic', staffed either by 'very old masters
or very young failed undergraduates'. The standard of education, he
says, was 'quite simply terrible'.[9]

Mr Hockey had a passion for producing plays (many of his pupils
believe that he missed his true vocation by taking holy orders instead
of going into the theatre), and *The Mikado* would not have been the
only school entertainment staged at St Michael's during the three years
Denton was there. In one of the earliest entries in his journal, he was
reminded of his first Christmas at the school by hearing on the wireless
Gilbert and Sullivan's *H.M.S. Pinafore*. The sound wafted him back to
a time when he was so tense with life and unhappy that he could
remember 'every flavour of those trivial, tuneful songs'. He was amazed
that the actors were singing 'so glibly, so lightly, not with all the fear,
sorrow, hope and beauty that I felt'. They were singing it 'for what
it is – silly stuff that perfectly expresses late Victorian England, and
I am singing it to myself as the language of all my life as a boy of

6. John Murray, 1963.

7. Letter to the author dated 15 February 1983. John Hesketh was to introduce Denton
to a family friend, Mrs Hayes-Jackson, who became 'Fanny Seaton-Leverett' in Denton's
short story 'Evergreen Seaton-Leverett', published posthumously in *Orpheus 2* in 1949
and reprinted in *A Last Sheaf*. Hesketh, in the same story, is named 'Alec Gale'.

8. The Bodley Head, 1948; reissued in 1981 by Secker & Warburg and Penguin
Books in *The Orchid Trilogy*.

9. In conversation with the author.

eleven. It spells out now how I was afraid of what life could do to me; how I was alone among wild animals.

'And now I see myself as I was then, running up to the cold dormitory, hiding myself in the bed-clothes, imagining my cubicle transformed with precious stones and woods. Praying, always praying for freedom and loveliness.

'Hearing the masters laughing downstairs and thinking of their horse-play.

'Then I would sing:

> O joy, O rapture unforeseen,
> For now the skies are all serene,
> The God of joy, the orb of love
> Has set his standard high above,
> The sky is all ablaze.

until I wanted to cry at the heartless, wicked words.'

He had particular reason to look back on his days at St Michael's with a shudder, for his first year there spelt not only a wrench from the cosseted, cosmopolitan life he had known in Shanghai and on board luxury liners, surrounded by servants both on land and at sea, but it also saw the death of his mother. Having been in increasingly poor health for two years, she died, at her home in Shanghai, on 3 March 1927. She was forty-one, and Denton was not quite twelve. Referring to this time years later when, in response to a note of congratulation from an old schoolfriend, Basil Jonzen, on the publication of his first book, *Maiden Voyage*, he wrote on 16 June 1943, 'I think you are right about St Michael's; there is a dramatic quality about my memories of it. It is the religious foundation of course, and then the complete (in my case) ignorance of all sex matters. This all mixes up with the death of my mother. (I remember that yours died at this time too – and that we walked round and round the field talking of our bereavements, our gardens, and our anxiety about passing the common entrance!)'

This letter is interesting, too, because in it he went on to indicate as clearly as he ever would the exclusively autobiographical basis of his writing: 'I am now going to say that life is very peculiar, and that I am always pressing back into the past remembering these things and pondering on them. They seem to be only just round the corner still. I think I shall always write about myself – so I am warning you!

'Perhaps my next book may be broader, fuller, but it also may not be. The one thing I have learned from this book is to select and manipulate my material a little, that is all. This, it seems to me, may lead to even more narrowness and elimination!'

Indeed, when he came to write that next book – *In Youth is Pleasure* – both the revised manuscript and the typescript bore the subtitle, 'A Fragment of Life Story with Changed Names', though this revealing statement, perhaps not surprisingly, was to be deleted by his cautious editor from the published edition.

Towards the end of his life he again recalled the effect on him of the news of his mother's death when memories of that bleak day were prompted by the death in 1947 of one of her wealthy friends, a painter and fellow Christian Scientist, Cecilia Carpmael: 'I went into the headmaster's drawing-room. I didn't cry. I was very stiff and still and smiling. I held my gloves, straightened my coat and waited to be taken out to the car.' Mrs Carpmael had come to take him home with her for a few days. That night, however, he did begin to 'cry and gulp', and Mrs Carpmael tried to soothe him with 'Christian Science truisms and words of comfort'. She did it very well, he wrote, 'with great conviction', but when he went to bed he 'cried and cried again and thought that I was lost'.

Following his mother's death, and with his father living permanently in Shanghai, Denton made his home in Henfield with his grandfather and his father's unmarried sister, Dorothy, who kept house for her father. He spent his school holidays there for the next four years. Though his father made the occasional visit to England, from now on Denton was in every practical sense an orphan. His grandfather appears to have felt nothing more than family affection for him, and his aunt Dorothy he found too distant and reserved for his liking. In any event, no one could take the place of his mother. When he came to write *A Voice Through a Cloud*, he remembered how at the age of twelve he had tried to maintain contact with his dead mother by writing letters to her: 'I used to take these letters out with me into the fields. There I would post them in rabbit-holes, under the overhanging cornices of streams, amongst the tangle of roots and stones and earth, in empty birds' nests, in old tins and bottles and the pockets of ragged clothes on rubbish dumps, down waterfalls and mill-races and a deep forgotten well in the garden of a ruined cottage.

'Once I posted a tiny note in a fat bunch of grass which I gave to a cow. As I watched her munch my message and take it down into her huge body, I pretended to believe that this note at least would reach its destination; it would live in her blood, be emptied on the ground, where it would make leaves and flowers grow. It would open like a fan, shooting out calls in all directions.'

By the age of thirteen, despite two years at boarding school, the 'complete ignorance of all sex matters' to which he referred in his letter to Jonzen does not seem to have been enlightened. While on a trip to Switzerland during the Christmas holidays with his brother Bill – by then an undergraduate at Hertford College, Oxford – and the Oxford University ski team of which Bill was a member, Denton made friends with another undergraduate, whom he names 'Archer' in a short story called 'When I Was Thirteen'.[10] He had brought along as holiday reading Tolstoy's *Resurrection*, in which he had encountered the phrase, 'illegitimate child', and had plucked up courage to ask Archer what it meant. Archer matter-of-factly told him it meant, 'Outside the law – when two people have a child although they're not married'. Convinced that this explanation was wrong, though not saying so in order to spare Archer's feelings, Denton was adamant that it was quite impossible to have a child unless one was married. 'The very fact of being married produced the child. I had a vague idea that some particularly reckless people attempted, without being married, to have children in places called "night clubs", but they were always unsuccessful, and this made them drink, and plunge into the most hectic gaiety.'

This passage is a good example of his brilliant ability as an adult to catch exactly the nuance of the child's mind; had Daisy Ashford attempted a sequel to *The Young Visiters* she could not have recorded adolescent thoughts more faithfully. 'When I Was Thirteen' is notable, too, for the portrait of Archer himself: 'He had broad shoulders but was not tall. He had a look of strength and solidarity which I admired and envied. He had rather a nice pug face with insignificant nose and broad cheeks. Sometimes, when he was animated, a tassel of fair, almost colourless, hair would fall across his forehead, half covering one eye. He had a thick, beautiful neck, rather meaty barbarian hands, and a skin as smooth and evenly coloured as a pink fondant.' (Food, with which Denton was obsessed throughout his adult life, occurs frequently in his imagery; another story, 'The Trout Stream', describes a character who, though named Mr Mellon, had a face which 'looked like a very large, scrubbed, kind potato'.[11])

10. Published in *Horizon* in April 1944 and reprinted in *Brave and Cruel*.
11. 'The Trout Stream' was first published in the *Cornhill* magazine in 1948 and was reprinted in *Brave and Cruel*. 'Mr Mellon' was in reality Mr Wattie, the retired senior partner in Denton's father's firm.

For much of the holiday Bill seems to have left Denton behind at the hotel for days and nights on end while he went off on skiing expeditions with his friends, not that Denton, immature in many ways but an independent boy, minded in the least. 'I was slightly afraid of my brother,' he wrote, 'and found life very much easier and less exacting when he was not there.' During one of Bill's absences he spent a carefree day with Archer. After taking the ski train to the slopes they ate a picnic lunch and afterwards Archer produced from his pocket some 'black, cheap Swiss cigarettes', placed one between Denton's lips and lit it. 'It was wonderful to be really smoking with Archer,' Denton wrote. 'He treated me just like a man.'

They then took to their skis, and Denton thought he had never enjoyed himself quite so much before; he thought Archer 'the most wonderful companion, not a bit intimidating, in spite of being rather a hero'. On their way to Denton's hotel they stopped off at the chalet annexe where Archer was lodging. Archer suggested that they have a bath and asked Denton to pull off his boots. 'When the ski boot suddenly flew off,' Denton recalled, 'my nose dipped forward and I smelt Archer's foot in its woolly, hairy, humid casing of sock.' Archer said he had cramp, and got Denton to massage his leg. While Archer bathed Denton hurried back to the hotel to fetch his dinner-jacket (it had once belonged to Bill and Denton had been so ashamed of the fact that he had taken his brother's name from the inside of the breast pocket and had written in his own 'in elaborate lettering'). As soon as he returned to the annexe Archer called to him to come and scrub his back. '"It gives me a lovely feeling," he said. He thrust a large stiff nailbrush into my hands and told me to scrub as hard as I could. I ran it up and down his back until I'd made harsh red tramlines. Delicious tremors seemed to be passing through Archer. "Ah! go on!" said Archer in a dream, like a purring cat. "When I'm rich I'll have a special back-scratcher slave." I went on industriously scrubbing his back till I was afraid that I would rub the skin off. I liked to give him pleasure.'

They then swapped places in the bath and afterwards, while Denton was getting dressed, Archer helped him with his tie. 'Archer gave the bows a little expert jerk and pat. His eyes had a very concentrated, almost crossed look and I felt him breathing down my face. All down the front our bodies touched featherily; little points of warmth came together. The hard-boiled shirts were like slightly warmed dinner-plates.'

They both drank Pilsner with their meal that evening, followed by crème de menthe. 'To be ordered a liqueur in all seriousness was a thrilling moment for me. I sipped the fumy peppermint, which left such an artificial heat in my throat and chest, and thought that apart from my mother, who was dead, I had never liked anyone so much as I liked Archer. He didn't try to interfere with me at all. He just took me as I was and yet seemed to like me.'

Later they drank a white wine cup at the buffet bar, and Denton soon began to feel tipsy. Standing beside Archer in the lavatory he asked, '"Do I look queer?"'

'"No, you don't look queer; you look nice," he said simply.'

Denton remembered that he had left his skiing clothes in the annexe, and Archer suggested fetching them there and then. 'We set out in the moonlight; Archer soon took my arm, for he saw that I was drunk, and the path was more slippery than ever. Archer sang "Silent Night" in German, and I began to cry. I could not stop myself. It was such a delight to cry in the moonlight with Archer singing my favourite song; and my brother far away up in the mountain.'

Archer made Denton a cup of coffee, loosened his clothes, and before long the inebriated boy fell asleep. In the morning he folded his dinner-jacket into a neat bundle, tied it to his toboggan, and he and Archer made their way to the hotel for breakfast. 'There on the doorstep we met my brother with one of the guides. They had had to return early, because someone in the party had broken a ski.' Bill was in a temper. He asked Denton what he had been doing, but Denton was too un-nerved to offer any explanation. '"Your brother's just been down to my place,"' Archer volunteered. '"We went skiing together yesterday and he left some clothes at the chalet."'

'"It's very early", was all my brother said.'

When Bill went up to Denton's room he saw that the bed had not been slept in.

Denton said, '"The maid must have been in and done my room early." I could not bear to explain to him about my wonderful day, or why I had slept at the chalet.

'My brother was so furious that he took no more notice of my weak explanations and lies.

'When I suddenly said in desperation, "I feel sick" he seized me, took me to the basin, forced my fingers down my throat and struck me on the back till a yellow cascade of vomit gushed out of my mouth. My eyes were filled with stinging water; I was trembling. I ran the water in the basin madly, to wash away this sign of shame.

'Gradually I grew a little more composed. I felt better, after being sick, and my brother had stopped swearing at me. I filled the basin with freezing water and dipped my face into it. The icy feel seemed to bite round my eye-sockets and made the flesh round my nose firm again. I waited, holding my breath for as long as possible.

'Suddenly my head was pushed down and held. I felt my brother's hard fingers digging into my neck. He was hitting me now with a slipper, beating my buttocks and my back with slashing strokes, hitting a different place each time, as he had been taught when a prefect at school, so that the flesh should not be numbed from a previous blow.

'I felt that I was going to choke. I could not breathe under the water, and realized that I would die. I was seized with such a panic that I wrenched myself free and darted round the room, with him after me. Water dripped on the bed, the carpet, the chest of drawers. Splashes of it spat against the mirror in the wardrobe door. My brother aimed vicious blows at me until he had driven me into a corner. Then he beat against my uplifted arms, yelling in a hoarse, mad, religious voice: "Bastard, Devil, Harlot, Sod!"

'As I cowered under his blows, I remember thinking that my brother had suddenly become a lunatic and was talking gibberish in his madness, for, of all the words he was using, I had not heard any before, except "Devil".'

There are, if one is to take this account at its face value, a number of possible explanations for Bill's insanely violent behaviour: acute anxiety over the boy's disappearance and guilt at having left him alone; disgust, if he suspected Archer of being homosexual, at his brother's association with him; perhaps even a deep uncertainty within himself causing him to lash out on the suspicion of his brother's sexual involvement. A less obvious though no less likely one, that Bill was in a confused way himself attracted to his younger brother, is strongly hinted at in a passage in *In Youth is Pleasure*, in which Denton appears as 'Orvil' and Bill as 'Charles':

'He [Orvil] was very much afraid of his eldest brother. Charles was always able to make him feel small, young, effeminate, inferior, cowardly and disgraceful. Charles would lavish a curious love on him sometimes – in the privacy of a bedroom in the early morning, or in a car at night – but by the light of day, with other people present, he was mocking and contemptuous. And his rages were so terrible. For no apparent reason he would suddenly pour out a stream of shaming words which seemed to shrivel up Orvil's soul for days afterwards. The uncertainty of his temper was the most terrifying thing about him.'

Whatever the truth may have been about Denton's relations with his elder brother — to what degree, if any, he exaggerated the situation is not known — Bill never bore any grudge for these lurid accounts of what passed between them. If the story is not a true record, however, then something must have gone sadly amiss for Denton, an essentially honest person, to have portrayed Bill in this way. The only light that Denton himself throws on the matter, though in a general comment which referred perhaps more to Archer's role in the story than to Bill's, is contained in a typically high-spirited letter to a friend, Marcus Oliver, which he wrote on 19 April 1944: 'A frightfully chi-chi story of mine has just come out in "Horizon". Read it if you ever see that mag. I think it'll make some people's hair stand on end, as it's not a bit cloaked really.'

Repton

In September 1929, when Denton was fourteen, he joined Paul at Repton; Paul had entered the school two years before, arriving the term after Bill left. A reading of Kipling's *Stalky & Co.* at the age of nine had filled Denton with the awful realization that one day he might have to 'live with such barbarians in some such slum called a public school'. The 'slum' to which he followed his father and brothers was eight miles from Derby, contained four hundred and fifty boys and was still staffed by house-boys and maids, for it was assumed that the boys who went there would be accustomed to the luxuries of at least a middle- and probably an upper-middle-class home. Repton, established in 1557 during the great heyday of grammar school foundations, is centred around an eleventh-century priory and cloister. Denton's new headmaster, like his prep-school headmaster, was an Anglican clergyman, the Reverend Geoffrey Fisher; he had been appointed to Repton at the early age of twenty-eight, and he had already been there for fourteen years by the time Denton arrived at the school. (In 1932, shortly after Denton's departure, Fisher also left, to become Bishop of Chester. In 1945 he became the 99th Archbishop of Canterbury.)

Following in the footsteps of two popular and successful brothers – Bill had won his colours for hockey and had been a prefect; Paul was to win his colours for football – did not make things any easier for Denton. Apart from the company of friends of his own, and the painting and singing lessons which he enjoyed, there were few compensations for a regimented life made unendurable by petty rules, legalized brutality, unappetizing food and, for Denton almost certainly the greatest trial, a total lack of privacy. He seems to have enjoyed practically nothing that the cloistered, homo-erotic atmosphere had to offer except, surprisingly, the chance of seeking refuge in the gymnasium when he did not have to play games. 'I used to go down and let myself in quietly,' he recorded in *Maiden Voyage.* 'Nobody was there at this time. It seemed to me a sort of temple of freedom.' After he had taken off his 'hateful butterfly collar, tailcoat and straw hat,' he would run round, jump over the horse, climb up the wall-bars and shin up the ropes and, on reaching the top, 'a climax of excitement' would pass through him. There was a grand piano in one corner of the gym on which he used to play one of three pieces he knew by heart, a Bach gigue, a Mozart 'waltz' and a Beethoven sonatina. He also sought solitude in a field behind the gym which was pitted with deep holes that the boys called the 'Witches' Cauldrons', where illicit smoking used to take place and in which Denton would sit alone, thinking, with only 'a small sheet of sky' overhead.

All his life he relished what he called 'a love of horror', and the only lesson at Repton he ever remembered enjoying was one in which he had to write a chapter of a ghost story.[1] In it he borrowed a phrase from the Bible, 'The hair of my flesh stood up', which of course reduced the other boys to fits of laughter when he read it out in class. The story went on to describe red damask walls, silver sconces and 'a great bed crowned with mouldy ostrich feathers'.

'Horribly unhappy and lonely' was how he otherwise described his days at Repton when talking about them, after he had left, to a fellow student at art school. Whether or not he realized that one of the ways in which he had sought to escape from this unhappiness and loneliness had demonstrated his continuing taste for masochistic fantasy is not clear, but his description of his behaviour is unambiguous enough. He told the student, 'I used to go down to the end of the field and chain myself up to the old horse-roller; then I'd pretend to be a slave dragging stones to build the Pyramids. You have to symbolize and dramatize your unhappiness in some way, then it almost gives you pleasure. I can also remember how frustrated I felt when a boisterous, rather likeable prefect let me off my first beating. I had so keyed myself up for the awful event that the reprieve came as a jarring anti-climax. I felt washed-out, grey, humiliated, nondescript, when I had expected to feel thoroughly sore and full of burning indignation. You see, the ending was wrong, inartistic, a flop.'[2]

Writing to the poet and novelist Alex Comfort on 5 January 1943, in connection with the publication of *Maiden Voyage*, Denton noted, 'Early adolescence was, to me, what I can only describe as a *sordid* and fearful

1. This story was the first he ever wrote, as he recorded in another short story, called 'Ghosts', published in *A Last Sheaf*.
2. 'A Novel Fragment', begun in a blue school exercise-book on 19 January 1943 and published in *A Last Sheaf*.

time. I was frightened of everything and everything seemed sullied and "slimed-over" with this fear.' In the physical encounters at school, such as they were, that he records, fear certainly seems to have been the dominant element, frequently compelling him to withdraw from physical contact once his interest had been aroused. Indeed, he was a classic example of the boy who longs for sexual adventure while being held back through fear engendered by guilt. By no means conventionally good-looking, he was nevertheless attractive to other boys, but his image of himself was imbued with self-disgust, as can be clearly seen in the grotesque caricatures of some of the self-portraits he painted in later life, notably in one executed some time in his mid-twenties,[3] with its almost negroid exaggeration of his high forehead, its swept-back, curly 'gingerbread' hair (as he described it in a poem called 'Will it Twine at Last'[4]), upturned nose, slightly flared nostrils and pixy ears.

Like many small men who dislike their own looks, he was to take much trouble over his clothes and to go out of his way to attract attention and admiration through his conversation. Mrs Nancy Carline, an acquaintance who recalls meeting him several times in 1937, when he was twenty-two, has described him as 'extremely witty and amusing', always elegantly dressed and 'very charming and good-looking'.[5] His delight in dress is evident in a letter written in April 1940 to his friend Marcus Oliver to thank him for a sartorial gift: 'I was enchanted with the lovely tie, so diaphanous and fairy-like; I'm going to wear it with a brown striped shirt and shall be very disappointed if I'm not quite the belle of the Bull.' In the same letter he censures a mutual friend for his lack of interest in clothes: 'Gerald's been down here on and off for several days and we had several heart-to-heart talks and quarrels. He really is getting more and more like a complacent pussy every time I see him. I do wish he'd brighten up his wardrobe because he'll only be young once and there'll be plenty of time for him to wear galoshes and raincoats later on. I've been telling him all this but with not much effect.'

When recounting his abortive sexual adventures, Denton excelled in conjuring up for his readers the smell, the taste, the touch, indeed every physical detail of his experiences. In Maiden Voyage, for example, he described an incident at Repton when he went out beagling with some other boys one day. While sitting on a stile 'to wait and rest', an older boy from another house came towards him. 'He had a large rent in

3. Now in the National Portrait Gallery.
4. Published in A Last Sheaf.
5. Letter to the author, 24 September 1982.

his shirt and I could see his bare shoulder through it. He stopped when he saw me and said, "Is anything sticking in my shoulder, Welch? It hurts like hell."

'I jumped off the stile and went up to him. He was as big as a man and I suddenly felt very puny. He turned his back to me and pulled the shirt off his shoulder. There was a long, red scratch on the white flesh. Beads of blood were dropping from it, so I wiped it with my handkerchief and then tried to look into it.

'I found two broken-off thorn heads and gradually worked them out. I held on to his other shoulder and he bent down so that I could reach. He was still trembling from running and his breath came in gasps.

'"There, I've got them out!" I said at last.

'He swung round quickly and pressed hard against me, rubbing his cheek against mine. I could feel how warm and moist his body was, and the touch of his eyelashes was like feathers. He spoke harshly and yearningly and shut his eyes.

'I was suddenly alarmed and made a movement away from him, but he grasped me tightly and dug his fingers into my flesh until I gave a short gasp of pain. When he heard it he dropped his hands to his sides and laughed softly.

'"Was I suffocating you?" he asked. Then he hitched up his shorts and ran on.'

Even while in the throes of adolescent homosexuality it is normally obligatory for boys at least to pretend to an interest in girls, but such was Denton's individualism that he seems, at an early age, to have shut his mind to the possibility of heterosexual experimentation – for reasons that seem to have been perfectly apparent to his schoolfriends. One afternoon, Denton and a boy called Brophy went off, somewhat half-heartedly, in search of three local ladies who lived near Repton, at a place called Findern, and who had become known to the boys as the 'Findern Fillies'; 'not', as Denton explained in *Maiden Voyage*, 'because we were at all attracted to girls but because, I think, we wanted to appear knowing and vicious'.

During the course of their walk, Denton told Brophy that he would never send any of his children to a public school. 'Not that I shall marry or have any children,' he added as an afterthought.

'"Don't you ever want to marry, Welch?" he asked.

'"Not unless I found a very old woman with plenty of money."

'"What a swine you are, Welch. Besides, you'd have to go to bed with her."

'"No, I shouldn't. There'd be an agreement that we only met at meals or when other people were there."

'"Then what do you think she'd marry you for?" he jeered.

'"She might like to have young life about the place," I answered weakly.' A friend called Geoffrey (in reality, Geoffrey Lumsden, later in life an actor) met them on their return:

'"What have you sissies been up to?" he screamed hysterically, rolling his eyes. "Why don't you go toboganing?"

'"We've been looking for the Findern Fillies," I answered. I thought the wickedness of it might satisfy him.

'"A lot of good they'd be to you!" he sneered. Then he chased me into the drying-room, which was full of steaming, muddy, sweaty clothes. I ran behind the boiler and pressed hard against the wall to get away from him; but it was too hot and I had to come out. He was ready for me.

'"You can pretend I'm one of your Findern Fillies," he shouted as he pounced on me and knocked me down. When he had me on the floor his head swooped down like a bird and slobbered on me, biting my ear viciously in his pretended kiss. I pushed my hand in his face and he bit my finger; then he got up and trod on me, knocking all the air out of me.'

When Denton came to record his first summer holiday away from Repton in *In Youth is Pleasure*, he wrote of his autobiographical hero, 'Orvil Pym', that 'His first year at public school had been so alarming and disintegrating that he found himself longing all the time for a very quiet room where he could go to sleep.' Denton in fact spent the holiday in a hotel in Surrey with his father (whom he now saw about once every three years and who wrote so seldom 'that his letters were an event') and his brothers, sharing a bedroom with Paul.[6] Orvil called his father 'Daddy', though he 'hardly meant more ... than black cars and exciting restaurant meals'. What Denton called the 'one subject of deep interest to them both' – his mother – was banned: 'Orvil knew that if he even so much as mentioned her, his father's face would freeze and harden, and his voice become abrupt and cruel and contemptuous. She had never to be thought of or considered again – because she had

6. It is possible that part of this school holiday – it would have lasted two months – was spent in Belgium; Denton once began an account of a summer holiday he spent when he was fifteen in Zoute, in the company of Paul and an aunt, but he abandoned it after covering one and a half pages of an exercise-book. The Surrey hotel was Oatlands, near Weybridge, once one of Queen Elizabeth I's palaces.

been loved so much. It was disgusting to show that you knew that such a woman had ever existed. She was so unmentionable that it was necessary to use elaborate circumlocutions in speaking about the past.'

And yet, of course, Denton did think about and consider his mother. 'If only,' he wrote of Orvil, 'his fascinating sunburnt mother could rise out of the grave and come back to him in her curious, ugly, red-and-tartan dress with the shiny belt ... If he could put her rings on for her once again, and make her eyebrows up at night, just as he used to do so cleverly, with the tiny black brush.' (It is small wonder that during an adolescent shop-lifting phase he should have chosen to steal, of all things, a tube of lipstick from a chemist's shop.)

His writings are, inevitably, strewn with evidence of sexual frustration, and only once does he describe, overtly, a consummated sexual encounter.[7] More often, as in *In Youth is Pleasure*, he resorts to language reminiscent of Boy Scouts' literature; there, for instance, we are told that 'The temptation to do something bad came many times, but he had withstood it, and had felt very powerful and good, as if God were on his side.' The challenge to resist the urge to masturbate in order to feel a sense of achievement is not uncommon among adolescent boys, but Denton's use of the word 'temptation' may justly be regarded as implying a sense of guilt, and it is reasonable to surmise that the thought of his mother's, just as much as God's, disapproval would have been the cause. Certainly it seems that whenever he indulged in conduct of which he felt ashamed, someone would come unexpectedly upon the scene as though sent on purpose to catch him out, as happens in another incident described in the same book. Aroused by watching for a long time two boys of his own age canoeing with a London youth-worker, Orvil 'fiercely desired some very solitary place; for the frustration and excitement inside him were becoming unbearable.

'He climbed up the broken steps [of a garden in the hotel grounds] and hid himself in the deep overgrown laurels.

'When, after some minutes, he pushed through the hole and stood on the tow-path again, a man, who had evidently been waiting, jumped out at him from behind one of the stucco pillars.

'"What are you doing on private property?" the man snapped, his eyes behind his glasses seeming to swell, and then to grow smaller, as some people's do when they are lusting.'

7. In a short story called 'The Fire in the Wood', in which Denton casts himself as a woman. It was published in *Brave and Cruel*.

Then the man betrayed himself completely by shouting at Orvil, '"I saw you! You devil! You filthy little devil! You'll go mad. Your eyes will drop out. And serve you right too. God is not mocked! God is not mocked!"'

Orvil later gets to know the youth-worker, and his encounter with the man in his hut in the woods is one of the most brilliantly written episodes in the book.[8]

Another fine passage describes Orvil's stay for part of the holiday with a former prep-school friend, 'Guy', and his family in Hastings; it evokes perfectly the dislike so many children experience for treats they are expected by adults to enjoy, such as staying with schoolfriends, when embarrassment so often lurks around every unfamiliar corner. Orvil even found himself given a bedroom through which Guy's parents, 'Sir Robert and Lady Winkle', had to pass to reach their own. 'This,' Denton wrote, 'was an added anxiety.'

On the way to Hastings to stay with Guy, Orvil sat in the train near 'an old, grand-looking man in a long tweed overcoat with an Inverness cape. Orvil had never seen one of these old-fashioned coats before, and he stared at it. He lifted his eyes and saw that one of the old man's ears was swathed in bandages. They crossed through his pewter-coloured hair, making a sort of coronal for him. He had an acid, bird-like face, the colour and texture of cooked sweetbread. He was ordering special food from the cowed and still truculent waiter. He seemed to be insisting and dominating with almost fanatical zeal.

'Orvil felt that anyone with so many whims and fancies must be of great importance.

'Suddenly the old man looked away from the waiter and caught Orvil staring at him. His eyes flashed; one of his eyelids twitched; his mouth set into a rigid snarl. He seemed about to say something terrible. But just as Orvil expected the words to come pouring out, the old man started to his feet and left the carriage. The tails of his long coat and the Inverness cape swished out behind him.

'Orvil became alarmed. He now imagined that the old gentleman was a lunatic.

'When, some few minutes later, he saw the tall figure standing in the

8. It was, indeed, a section singled out for special praise by Herbert Read of Routledge when he wrote to Denton on 17 January 1944 to accept the book for publication: 'Incidentally, I would say that your ability to write quite objectively is indicated by your portrait of the scout-master, which seems to me quite the most vivid and substantial piece of writing you have yet done.'

doorway again, he turned deep red and darted his glance away.
The old man went to another seat and sat down pointedly with his
back to Orvil.'

Later, when he got off the train, 'Orvil turned his head and was just
in time to see the fierce old man swirl into the crowd, driving a porter
in front of him. Before he disappeared, he jerked his head round abruptly
and once more caught Orvil staring at him. The look of malevolence
that crossed his face was so exaggerated that it was almost funny; but
when Orvil turned to Constance [Guy's sister] to make her laugh by
telling her about this strange old man, a sudden superstitious dread held
him back. He decided never to mention him again.'

The 'old, grand-looking man' who had so alarmed the fifteen-year-old
Denton Welch was Lord Alfred Douglas, but because Douglas was still
alive when In Youth is Pleasure went to press in 1944 (he died the
following year), the publishers did not dare allow Denton to identify
him – Douglas was far too fond of taking people to court. In fact, Denton
had originally intended this adventure for Maiden Voyage, published the
previous year, but at that time, on the advice of their solicitors, the
publishers deleted the entire episode. What he originally wrote was:

'I was going to stay with some friends in Folkestone. I had been put
into a Pullman so that I could have lunch on the way. I sat at my little
table, pleased with the comfort and novelty, looking at the other
passengers. One especially I noticed. He seemed very old, and one of
his ears was heavily bandaged. I remember his pointed nose and the
greyness of his face. He was impatient with the porter and I thought
he must feel very ill. After giving the waiter some instructions he turned
to leave the carriage, saying, so that I could hear, "My name's Douglas.
Lord Alfred Douglas."

'I was thrilled. I had just read all about Oscar Wilde. I waited
impatiently for him to come back. I hoped he had only gone to the
lavatory. While he was away I heard the waiter talking to someone
in the kitchen. He spoke slowly, as if he were in a trance. "Fellow ordered
coffee," he said. Then, after a long pause, "Says he's a Lord." The long
tweed coat swished in again, and I tried to watch without looking up.
He sat down and read a book, and I thought he looked like a fierce
bird. When he saw me staring his scowl went deeper, and I did not
dare to look again.'[9]

In this version it will be noted that Orvil was on his way to stay

9. Autograph final manuscript in the British Library (Additional MS 49062).

with friends in Folkestone, whereas in the version ultimately published the destination becomes Hastings. Hastings was simply part of the camouflage, as was the name 'Winkle'; his hosts were in reality Brigadier and Mrs Charles Terrot, who normally lived outside Eastbourne but who had taken a holiday flat in Folkestone, and 'Guy' was Charles Terrot, with whom Denton had been at St Michael's and who was now at Harrow. Denton's virtually true-to-life description of an old schoolfriend and his family in this book – especially as his portrait of Charles as a boy is not a particularly flattering one – is typical of the unashamed use he made of his friends in his writing. Terrot, who had himself written a book (called *Young Colt's Diary*, published in 1936), did not baulk; on the contrary, he has said[10] that he went into 'hysterics of merriment' when he first read the book, and on publication he wrote generously to Denton, on 25 March 1945: 'I could make a guess where you got your material for Chapter VI but since I myself have drawn on real-life characters for material on numerous occasions it would be rather a case of "throwing stones in glass houses" were I to raise a finger of admonition.' Shortly after receiving this letter, while recording mostly favourable reviews of *In Youth is Pleasure*, Denton wrote in his journal on 9 April, 'Even Charles Terrot, who is made use of in it, has written a smooth letter.' Denton had already replied to Terrot, addressing him as 'Dear Boy', on 4 April: 'It is good of you to say that you've liked things of mine you've seen. I was afraid the second book would be objected to, if only because it *was* a second book, but so far people have been rather encouraging, which is a relief.'

Back at Repton after the summer holidays life went on much as before. On Speech Day no one came to visit him, as he recorded thirteen years later in his journal, and so he stood 'rather forlornly by the school shop ... wondering whether to go on staring at the cricket match or to slip away and hide myself either in the library or the fields'. Then he realized he was being watched, by two prefects from another house and two other boys who had only recently left. They were talking in subdued voices. His embarrassment grew acute, and he began to think that he must have transgressed some unwritten rule, or behaved in some horribly gauche way. It was in fact the two prefects who were planning to transgress an unwritten rule, one which forbade fraternizing between boys of different ages. The four conspirators managed to enveigle him into a motor car, the plan being for one of the old boys to seduce him

10. In conversation with the author.

in a wood, but after sitting on the older boy's knee and nervously fluttering his eyelids, Denton's ordeal seems to have petered out.

Still smitten a week later, the old boy sent him a letter, 'quite elaborately romantic − the sort of letter that only generous, unwise people write', as Denton remembered it. 'Through it all ran a nostalgia to be back at school ... I saw in a flash that leaving school was not freedom for this sort of person.' Obviously thrilled and flattered, during a mid-morning break one day he could not resist stealing a moment to re-read this dangerous missive, but in such a way as to arouse the curiosity of his friend Geoffrey:

'"What are you so engrossed in?" he jeered, rolling the "r" stagily. "A tart-note I bet. You've had a tart-note."

'He snatched the piece of paper and read it avidly. He had not expected anything like it. He seemed hardly able to believe it.

'"Christ, what an absolute marvel," he said, handing it back to me. "But the only trouble is that now you'll think you're Cleopatra, or the Face that Launched a Thousand Ships or something. There'll be no holding you."'

Geoffrey then gave his ankles a vicious little kick to quell his pride in advance, and before long the note was wisely destroyed.

Denton was to sum up his days at Repton when, after watching a party of army officers in a crowded tea-room on 9 November 1944, he recorded in his journal, 'It reminded me so much of school. No ease, or grace or enjoyment, only anxiety.' It was this anxiety which, festering within him without any means of release, finally drove him to desperation. On his way back to Repton after the summer holidays at the end of his second year, in 1931, he gave his brother Paul the slip in London, and ran away. *Maiden Voyage* gives an account of this adventure, opening with the poignant sentence, 'After I had run away from school, no one knew what to do with me.' No one ever knew what to do with him − no member of his family at any rate. He took a train to London and at Waterloo station he saw another train going to Salisbury. He had been there once before, with his mother. Lying about his age (he was small for his sixteen years) he bought a half-fare ticket, and once on the train he locked himself in the lavatory. He knew that nobody would be looking for him yet, but he felt safer there. He had £5.

When he arrived in Salisbury he went first to the cathedral. Finding it closed, he then went to a hotel called The George where he plucked up the courage to ask for a room. As he had no luggage the receptionist made him pay in advance; 12s. 6d. for the room and 5s. for a four-course dinner. While he was drinking coffee after dinner, an old lady smiled and asked if he was staying long. '"I think I shall be going tomorrow,"' he told her.

'"Are you all alone, then?" she asked, looking interested.

'"Yes, but my mother's picking me up here and we're going to Devonshire,"' he replied. 'I was suddenly able to lie very easily,' he recorded. 'It made itself up almost as I talked.'

After breakfast he returned to the cathedral where he began to pray, and grew 'more and more unhappy'; he longed for someone to talk to him, but 'they were all too busy looking at the sights or praying'. He then went to the station to buy a ticket to Exeter, only to find the train crowded with boys going back to Sherborne. As he passed a group of three of them, one called out to the others, 'in a mocking voice, "There's a pretty boy for you!"' Again he locked himself in the lavatory, and stayed there until he reached his destination.

At Exeter he took a room at The Royal Clarence, bought a postcard and went to the cathedral where he addressed the card to his aunt Dorothy in Sussex. 'I hope you have not been worrying about me,' he wrote. 'I am quite all right but I will never go back to school. I have a very nice room here with hot and cold water. The cathedral is lovely, I have been wandering all over it.' As the card was adorned with a picture of the hotel, this note was clearly a cry for help, for someone to come and rescue him before the £5 ran out.

At The Royal Clarence he again found it easy to lie. Asked by the receptionist whether he had any luggage he answered, '"Oh, my mother's bringing that in the car tomorrow."' Again he was asked for payment in advance, this time for 17s. 6d. 'I knew that I should have found cheaper lodgings, but the dread of squalor was too strong.' He bought toothpaste and a toothbrush and, feeling desolate, went round exploring the antique shops. After sleeping for a second night in the same shirt, and by now beginning to feel 'as if I had never been young and fresh', he tried to clean it in the morning by rubbing the cuffs and collar with a wet towel.

He left the hotel as quickly as he could in case his aunt telephoned on receiving the postcard, and sat down under some trees near a pond. 'It was,' he wrote, 'a damp, misty day and I felt I wanted to die.' He began to hate Exeter so much that he decided to leave, setting off on foot for Budleigh Salterton and crossing the road every time he saw a policeman, for he felt sure that they would all be searching for him by now. At Budleigh Salterton he booked in to the first inn he came to, pulled off his clothes and got into bed. Soon he realized that his room was directly over the bar. 'The sound of talking and of glasses being knocked came up through the floor. It maddened me, I could not go to sleep. I lay awake long after the noises had stopped, watching the faint square of light from the window and listening to the sea rustling the stones on the beach.'

Although he had eaten nothing since lunch-time the previous day, he left his bacon untouched at breakfast the next morning. As he left the inn he remembered that some people he had met in Switzerland lived in Budleigh Salterton. He called on them, saying that he was staying with an aunt in Exeter, and got a lift back to the city. 'I was in a fever,' he wrote. 'I had no money left. I thought of writing for some, but I could not wait three days until I had an answer. I knew that I must go back to London, and I was almost glad.'

He pawned his watch for 6s. and managed, after some difficulty, to persuade the station clerk to sell him a half-fare ticket to Salisbury. He had 10d. left.

Back in Salisbury, standing hopelessly in the city centre at midnight, he was approached by two policemen. He told them he was travelling alone to London and had lost a 10s. note, and he asked them where he could get a bed for 10d. The police were friendly, letting him sleep in a cell at the police station and giving him a cup of tea in the morning. Again, by extraordinary luck, he remembered some other people living in Salisbury whom he had also met on holiday in Switzerland, and from them he boldly borrowed £1. 'Tired of lying and contriving,' he paid the full fare for a ticket back to London. Rather than turn to Bill, who now lived there, he decided to enlist the support of his 'second cousin', May Beeman. 'Although I knew her so little,' he wrote, 'I felt that she must be clever and wise. I hailed a taxi and drove to the Boltons.'[11]

He was greeted by May's maid, Wills, who had 'the sour, grudging look that faithful maids often have', and was left standing in the hall while she went to announce the unexpected visitor. May gave him lunch and afterwards sent telegrams to Bill and Aunt Dorothy. 'DENTON SAFE WITH ME MAY,' they read. 'That'll bring them down on me,' he thought. That afternoon, over tea, May asked him what he wanted to do in life.

11. May Beeman, who lived at 33 The Grove, since renamed the Little Boltons, was actually Denton's first cousin once removed. He asserted in *Maiden Voyage* that she had once refused a D.B.E. on the curious grounds that she had better things on which to spend £25 than the insignia she would have needed for the ceremony; she did in fact accept the C.B.E. for her work as honorary secretary of the Alexandra Fund Flag Day.

He said he was interested in history and architecture, and that he liked drawing and painting. (He had been given oil-paints and an easel when he was nine, and at Repton he had attended advanced art classes, exhibiting 'some good paintings and a competent pencil portrait'.) In the evening he had to sit through dinner with a man he had never met, a soldier from India called Stanley. He knew that May would tell Stanley about him, and later he heard Stanley laughing softly. 'I hated it,' he wrote. 'I knew he was laughing at me. It was like laughing at someone who had tried to commit suicide, I thought.'

May, not only clever and wise, seems also to have been practical and kind, for the next morning, before Aunt Dorothy and Bill were due, she took Denton round London to inspect a variety of art schools, in Chelsea, Bloomsbury, Holborn, Westminster and Kensington. When Bill and Aunt Dorothy arrived, however, the question of which art school he would attend was set firmly in the future since they had decided that he must first go back to Repton, 'as everyone expected it'. His aunt and Bill then proceeded to discuss Denton in the third person, as though he was absent, and eventually May asked him if he would go back just for that one term.

'"There isn't any point in going back just for this term,"' said Denton, fighting. '"Why can't I leave now?"'

'"Because,"' replied the resourceful May, '"they'd think you were afraid."' Denton felt betrayed, and 'slowly and miserably' he agreed.

Next morning Aunt Dorothy undertook to refund the £1 and to redeem the wrist-watch. At St Pancras station Denton experienced an odd mental aberration when he saw a Frenchwoman buying a basket of fruit. 'She was annoyed because the girl behind the counter could not understand her. She gave me an imploring look and I wanted to help, but I suddenly thought that she might be a prostitute, so I hurried away.'

At Derby, where he had to change trains, he bumped into a boy called 'Taylour', who had left Repton to take up engineering. Taylour told Denton how much he hated his work:

'"What a lucky devil you are," he said, "to be going back!"'

'I would have given almost anything to have changed places with him. A part of me suddenly whispered, "Why not run away again?" but I put it away and got into the carriage.

'As it moved out of the station I looked back and saw Taylour standing forlornly amongst the trucks and engines.'[12]

12. 'Taylour' was in fact William Roscoe-Taylor, who became an assistant superintendent with British Rail.

On arriving at the station for Repton, Denton decided to walk to the school rather than take a taxi, even though it was raining, because to walk would take longer. He returned to a spate of rumours: that he had got hold of £40 and had gone off to France, or that he had been taken to Italy by a boy called Iliffe who had a reputation for preferring the company of boys younger than himself. Summoned by the house-boy to report to his house-master, Denton's 'movements were not well joined together' as he made his way up to the master's room, took a plunge for the door and stood in front of Mr Snape, 'smiling but feeling burnt out and gutted inside'.

Snape was 'a small man with a manly voice and dog's lips. His head was thick and round.'

'"Look here, Welch,"' he said to Denton. '"I'm never going to mention this again. You've had a brainstorm, that's all, and there's no reason why we shouldn't carry on just as if nothing had ever happened. I shall never hold it against you."'

One of the new boys that term, Guy Willatt, who in spite of the difference in their ages shared a study with Denton, remembers wondering, 'but not daring to ask', why Denton's place at table had been empty. All was revealed after prayers one evening, when Mr Snape explained to the house that Welch had had 'a brainstorm' ('the word had stuck in my memory', says Willatt) and would be returning the next day. But, 'under dire threats', no one was to ask him why he was returning late.[13]

It was then discovered that Denton had a temperature of 100° so, without further ado and to his absolute delight, he was packed off to the sanatorium for a rest. 'So I left the house again,' he wrote, 'without speaking to a single boy.'

It was not until two days later, when he was back in his house, that he learned that Paul had been dispatched to London by the house-master to hunt for him and had spent three anxious days telephoning hospitals and police stations. Denton also found himself moved up two forms because one of the rumours circulating about the cause of his truancy had it that he had been frightened of his form-master. The Remove, where he was now placed, was 'quite peaceful', and Mr Ward, his new form master, whose 'flat face dominated it like a placid, soapstone sphinx',

13. Letter from Guy Willatt to the author, 5 October 1982. Two other boys who shared a study with Denton, Kenneth Blackburn and Gordon Wilkie, appear in *Maiden Voyage* as 'Bradbourne' and 'Wilks'.

would regale his class with improbable gastronomic tales of the Siege of Paris, of wealthy Parisians eating rats stewed in green chartreuse and of mice swimming in Benedictine. 'Everywhere,' Denton wrote, 'I met with more tolerance than I had ever known before.'

With the certain knowledge that he had only ten more weeks of school life to endure, he seems at last to have allowed himself to savour some of the more enjoyable activities, spending time, for example, on Sunday mornings singing with a few other boys in Miss Fenwick's room ('Miss Fenwick' was the headmaster's sister-in-law, her real name being Miss Penny Forman), where the atmosphere was freer than anywhere else in the school, for the boys who congregated there were all of different ages and from different houses, so that 'the caste system was broken down'. And on Sunday afternoons — 'Sunday was the most civilized day of all' — he generally went for a walk with the ebullient Geoffrey, who would recite Shakespeare while flourishing his umbrella (although permitted, after two years at Repton, to carry one himself, Denton never did). 'If I showed no pleasure,' Denton recalled in *Maiden Voyage*, 'he would begin to shout, "You little sissy, you can't think about anything but yourself."' Then he would poke Denton with his umbrella, and once he tried to tie him to a tree with his scarf. Sometimes, when not trying to deflate Denton's vanity, Geoffrey would sing to him. 'He would set his face very carefully, then begin "Hark, hark, the lark at Heaven's Gate sings" or "Who is Sylvia, what is she?" It always seemed to be Schubert.'

Geoffrey, too, lost his mother while at school. 'One day he came to me while I was in the lavatory (all the doors had been removed from the compartments) and told me that his mother was dead. He leant forward as I sat there and said, "She's dead, Bird's just told me." He spoke in an excited way and his eyes sparkled.' That afternoon he took Denton with him to tea with an aunt of his. 'She wore a tight little turban and she looked like a monkey,' Denton remembered. 'She kissed Geoffrey and grinned at me with her wide, prehistoric mouth.' In an effort to make bright conversation, Denton said to the aunt, '"What a nice lustre pot!"' and felt Geoffrey trying to kick him under the table. Afterwards, Geoffrey remonstrated with him. '"Why did you talk to her about lust at tea-time?"' he demanded to know. '"I thought you were mad — muttering something about lust."'

That night Denton 'lay awake after the lights were out wondering if Geoffrey was very unhappy. I could just see his bed in the corner, but there was no sign from it. The cold air swept round the floor and the iron beds creaked.

'I fell asleep after the last person had stopped talking, and did not wake till several hours later. It was still dark; nothing could be heard but the trains shunting two miles away. Suddenly I thought I heard deep intakes of breath from the corner where Geoffrey's bed was. He must be snoring, I thought. Then I imagined that he was crying under the bed-clothes. I listened for some time, trying to decide.'

Denton was always to remember that dormitory, with its red blankets and white chamber pots gleaming beneath the beds, with particular distaste. 'Every morning when I woke up and remembered where I was, I felt something draining out of me, leaving me weak.' The dormitory was 'the grimmest part of the house. It was so lofty and cold that it seemed to make people heartless.' A vivid account of an initiation ceremony, so typical of public schools, that took place there is given in *Maiden Voyage*:

'Two lips had been painted on one of the beams and all the new boys had to pull themselves up by their arms, to kiss them. I remember straining up, and at last reaching the yellow pitch-pine and the two crimson lips. They looked indecent, for some reason; as if they were the drawing of another part of the body.

'When I kissed them, the taste of varnish and dust came as a shock. I imagined that they would somehow be scented.

'I thought of this now as I watched other people trying to kiss them. If they were not quick or could not reach them, they were flicked with wet towels as an encouragement.

'I had been told that you could lift the skin off someone's back in this way. I always waited, half in horror, to see a ribbon of flesh come off.'

Denton describes, too, a first-hand experience of the public-school mania for beatings. On this occasion he had gone on an expedition to Chatsworth House with his art-master, quite forgetting to obtain permission from the captain of house games, Newman, who had put him down that day to play in the Third Eleven. The reckoning came that night after prayers. When Newman came into the study to beat him, Denton thought 'he looked really nice, with his powerful body and springy, uncoloured hair.

'"Why the devil didn't you let me know, before you went to Chatsworth, Welch?" he began.

'"I didn't think I had to. I had Bird's permission," I answered anxiously.

'"How can I make the games lists out if I don't know who's available?"

'"I'm afraid I forgot that."

'"Well, it's no good forgetting. You've got to learn that. Bend over the desk, please."

'The moment had come. I held my tongue between my teeth, biting on it, trying to make it hurt; then I put my hands over my eyes and burrowed inwards to myself, shutting everything outside away. My eyes bored down long passages of glittering darkness as I waited.

'I heard Newman's feet shuffle slightly on the boards, then the faint whine of the cane in the air.

'There were two bars of fire eating into ice, then nothing. Only two strokes, but the room was quite different when I opened my eyes. The light was thick like milk and it seemed to float cloudily about the room.'

After the obligatory charade of bidding a courteous good night to the boy who had just inflicted pain and humiliation upon him was over, 'Through the pain that was biting into me I felt a surge of admiration for Newman, yet I hated myself for liking him. The other part of me wanted to smash his face into pulp. My mind was rocking about like a cart on a rough road.'

Back in the dormitory he was asked if he had had a nice beating, and was told to show his marks, but then for some reason was left alone. So he got into bed, and 'lay, hot and sore, between the cold sheets'.

No less unsatisfactory than every other aspect of his life at Repton was the progress his formal education had made. 'I realize how terribly my education has been neglected,' he was to write in his journal in 1942 just a month after learning that his first book had been accepted for publication, 'firstly by submitting to orthodox, traditional schooling; then by rebelling against it and spending all my energy in trying to escape – ties and obligations of every sort. I am almost resigned to being nearly illiterate, but sometimes I have a sharp regret that nearly all my schooldays were wasted days!'

Towards the end of the Christmas term, out of the blue he received a letter from his father asking if he would like to come out to Shanghai with his brother Paul, who had already arranged to leave the school at Christmas to travel to China. 'I leapt up and walked about, giving small jumps and screwing up my eyes as climaxes of excitement swept over me,' Denton recorded. 'I could not believe that my father was suggesting that I should leave school and go to China. I was so full of joy that I ran down the lane and over the fields until I was exhausted. I felt like a person full of power and skill ... I could bear anything now till the end of term.'

His academic attainments, like those of so many gifted people, had indeed been less than distinguished. The only subjects that had ever really interested him at school were history and art, and at the end of his last term he came fourteenth in his class. When he called in at the art school for the last time the art-master said, 'Well, good-bye, Welch. Go on with your drawing. Don't let them make you do anything else.' Denton felt flattered, and decided there and then that he wanted to be a painter. He gathered up his drawings and 'went out feeling warm and comfortable'.

The term ended with a house supper to which old boys were invited. Each boy who was leaving had to make a speech, and Denton, being the youngest to leave that term, was due to speak last. He went from boy to boy imploring suggestions for a suitable text, and at last one old boy told him what to say: '"Everything I wanted to say has been said, so like the humble onion I will not repeat myself, since brevity is the soul of wit."' It was, as Denton realized, horrible, but he learnt it by heart. 'I was a drowning man clutching at anything.' The speeches followed the meal, and just as his turn came he saw Mr Bird rise, evidently to say grace, so he quickly sat down again, 'confusion and relief racing through me, and somewhere, the remotest resentment that he should have ignored me'. But he was not to escape after all. The head of the house bent towards Mr Bird, whispered something to him, and voices called out, '"We haven't heard from young Welch yet, Sir!"'

Mr Bird smiled patronizingly and waved his hand at Denton 'with a shade of impatience.

'I stood up and began the speech, very falsely and loudly. I tried to imagine that I was alone in a wood, miles from anywhere. I dissociated myself from my words.

'At the mention of the "humble onion" I saw Mr Bird's face crumple up, like an affected music-master's when his pupil plays a discord.

'I knew the dreary, matey vulgarity of my speech. It was sickening; but I resented his face.

'People were clapping and laughing, and I was pulled down on to the bench again by my neighbours and fed with dates and raisins. They hit me on the back and shouted, "Well done, Welch, well done!"

'I felt comforted. At least they knew what I had been through.'

He had one further ordeal to endure before he could leave – the ritual interview with the headmaster, and it would seem that this fare-well was also his first proper meeting with Dr Fisher. As he waited to go into the study he smoothed his hair and ran the palms of his hands down his trousers. 'I wanted to be calm when he saw me, not mad with anxiety, like a cat let out of a basket.'

He entered the study to find Dr Fisher busy writing. 'There was only a gleam from the top of his spectacles as he said, "Sit down, Welch, I won't be a minute."

'I looked round the room; I had never seen it before. It was in the medieval tower round which the Hall had been built. The walls were newly and roughly plastered, and little coats of arms had been fastened to the bosses of the ceiling. Two new wrought-iron fire-dogs held up the logs in the worn Tudor brick fireplace. Wine-coloured carpet, studded leather chairs and leaping flames completed the club-land "luxury".

'When I had made my inventory, my eyes came back to the man at the desk. He was soon to be a famous bishop, but I would never have suspected it. In spite of his dog-collar, I never thought of him as clerical. He lifted his head and I saw the little piece of cotton-wool stuck to his chin to stanch a shaving cut. The skin round it seemed purply black and uneven like rusticated granite.

'"So you're the one who went to visit cathedrals instead of coming back to school!" he began. He knew me slightly; he had seen me sketching the priory ruins and had noticed that I was left-handed. He seemed amused now. I blushed. To have my escape explained as an architectural holiday sounded silly. I said nothing, so he went on talking.

'"My experience is that one must accept one's environment and fit into it as best one can; otherwise life is nothing but beating one's head against a brick wall."

'I felt his sincerity apart from his ordinary words. Schoolmasters generally never show it. I had never had three words of deeply felt advice before. It had always been argument or parrot-rule. I knew the difference now. I got up, warm inside and admiring.

'"Good-bye, Welch. You ought to have an interesting time in China." He shook my hand; my fingers curled round and I felt the black hairs on his wrist.'

Anxious as Denton was to leave Repton, even he was not to be immune from the magnetic attraction exerted on so many old boys by their public schools, whether they have been happy there or not, which urges them to revisit the scene of their inhibitions and fantasies, their deep, grinding fears and moments of exhilaration and achievement, and to recall the time when they were able to complain and conform, free of personal responsibility and thoughtless of the future. So it was that two years later he was to return for an old boys' reunion. His first worry was about what to wear, but when he asked a friend whether his blue checked shirt would be too conspicuous for the occasion, and the friend said that perhaps it was, he became all the more determined to wear it. 'I was always defiant,' he wrote, 'feeling it cowardly not to persist, if surprise was expressed at my clothes.' When he arrived at Brook House he let himself in to the boys' part, for clearly he still thought of himself as a schoolboy rather than as an adult and on equal terms with the house-master and his wife. 'When I smelt that mixture of scrubbed wood, sweaty football socks and shirts from the "Dryer" and hair-oil and toast, I was back again in a moment, dressed in an Eton suit, frightened, stifled, full of revolt, feeling that I would never be young and happy again.'

He seems to have had no desire to mix with the other old boys. He was, in any case, only eighteen, the same age as the senior boys still at school, most of whom he would have known. The head of the house invited him into his study, 'and I tasted the privilege which had been denied me as a schoolboy. He told his fag to make me two pieces of buttered toast for tea and I remembered how I had had to do this every night.' Denton watched the fag at work: 'His face was crimson from the heat. And he looked curiously pleasant and attractive, because, although he seemed strong and sensible, yet he was submissive.'

After a drunken dinner Denton repaired to the school sanatorium where he was to sleep that night. He found the place 'buzzing with an extraordinary glamour. The old boys, rather the worse for wear, were indulging in horse-play. Very exuberant and rather peculiar in some cases.'

It was not long before a 'plump drunk' had come up to him 'and made a curious suggestion in mockery and fun'. Then, in the room where he was to sleep, he found Riley, 'who had in some ways been the evil genius of my schooldays'. Denton was reminded of the last day of his first term at Repton, when Riley had dragged him on to his knee and he had burst into tears, 'which seemed to please him all the more'. Denton also remembered 'the awful nights in the dormitory when he ordered me to come and stand by his bed after I had come up from practising for the House Singing Competition. I would stand by his head and he would reach out with his rather "hungry" hand and grip hold of me. How I disliked him!'

It seems always to have been Denton's fate to have attracted people who did not appeal to him, and to be rejected by those that did. He admitted in his journal that he had disliked Riley not so much 'because of his acts, which were bad enough, but because of his body and face.

He was well built, but his skin had a repulsive tone and touch and all the features of his face seemed thickened, like those coarse black-eyed portraits of Alexandrine mummy-case lids.' After the lights had been turned out that night, Denton 'could still feel the alertness of Riley in his bed. He turned and let out sighs of breath. I waited with dread for what might happen. Everything was wiped away of the last two years and I, now at his mercy again, a fag in the dormitory of which he was the head.'

Nothing did happen then, but early the next morning he heard Riley tiptoe across to him and say, '"Let's go to the bathroom before the others wake up; there'll be a terrible crush."

'I was most unwilling to do this, but I had to be amiable.

'"Shall I go first?" I said firmly, "or will you?"

'This was clearly not his idea, but he appeared to fall in with it.

'"All right, you go first, if you're quick."

'I got up hastily, taking my clothes with me to the bathroom.

'As I stood up in the bath naked (for the water had not yet warmed the cold enamel), I heard the door being tried.

'"Let me in, let me in," Riley said. "I want to get some water for shaving, while you're bathing."

'I turned the key reluctantly and jumped back into the bath. He came in, muffled up in his dark camel-hair dressing-gown, and bent over the can as he held it under the tap. Something was going on within him and he would not talk, but seemed to be fuming and fretting. He spent far too long over filling the can and still would not go. At last the situation petered out in complete anti-climax. Something went quite hard and stern and loathing within me. I would not even look at him until he gradually, weakly withdrew from the room.

'Then I became quite sorry for poor Riley who must be hated quite as much, now that he was at Sandhurst, as he had been at Repton.'

Reflecting nine years later on what had prompted him to attend the reunion, Denton wrote in his journal, 'It seems perhaps a curious thing for me to have done and yet not curious at all. Although I ran away and hated it so much, my eyes and my heart often look that way. At any moment of the day a picture may flick up in my mind of the street outside Brook House with the high wall of the games yard and the little gate piercing it. The high wall looks like a prison wall and the little gate is wicked too, yet they still hold their sort of frightening glamour.'

THREE

China

Like many schoolboys, Denton's first act on leaving school was to discard his uniform. He had always been irked by the 'tightness and blackness' of Repton clothes, and by his straw hat in particular, and what he most longed to wear were 'soft, loose, bright clothes' with no hat at all. But while he had occupied his last days at school thinking about what he would wear in China, he had known, too, that the choice would be made for him by his aunt Dorothy. She had written to Paul, in a letter which he intercepted (he seems to have shared with W. H. Auden a penchant for quite casually reading other people's correspondence), to say how glad she was that he was to be removed from the bad influence of his friends, from the influence, moreover, of one particular friend of whom he was especially fond. He dashed off a furious letter to his aunt, to which she retaliated by telling Paul that she would have nothing more to do with Denton until he apologized; since he had no intention of doing so, the warmth of the reception awaiting him at his grandfather's house must have been in some doubt.

The train journey that carried him away at last from Repton was 'too happy to be remembered well', he recorded in *Maiden Voyage*. 'I only know that it was the most delightful feeling of escape that I have ever had.' To celebrate their freedom, Paul and Denton decided to splash out on a sophisticated lunch at Scott's, at that time a famous landmark in Piccadilly Circus, where they ate hors-d'oeuvres, steak-and-kidney pudding stuffed with oysters, and green figs and cream. Afterwards they decided, 'without much enthusiasm' on Denton's part, to call on Bill, who was living in rooms in Adam Street,[1] off Baker Street. They found him sitting by the fire 'in a small, fresh sitting-room', staring at a bottle of brandy someone had given him for Christmas. Denton drank some – he hated the taste but 'loved the idea of drinking it' – and then they all had

1. Now Robert Adam Street.

tea with the tenant upstairs. In her flat Denton immediately noticed, suspended from the ceiling, a gilded flying angel carrying a torch in its arms. The tenant saw him looking at it.

'"Do you like my angel?" she asked.

'She lit it up, switching the light on and off as if she were a spy signalling the enemy.

'Having been brought up to like "artistic" Tudor cottages, I thought it rather vulgar.

'"It's very nice," I said.'

When he and Paul eventually arrived at Whaphams they found Aunt Dorothy waiting to meet them at the foot of the stairs. 'She held her glasses in one hand and her book in the other. She kissed us quickly, her lips seemed dry and cracked, then she led us into the drawing-room where our grandfather was sitting by the fire. He wore his thin, oval spectacles and was reading Herodotus.

'"What a liar this man is! What an imagination!" he ejaculated. Then he saw us and said:

'"Well, how are you? Neither of you seems to have changed much."

'He never mentioned my running away, nor did my aunt. I realized that it was to be forgotten and not talked about.'

Of his visits to Whaphams, Denton remembered always being the one to fetch and carry, his grandfather, a slightly stooped old man of eighty-six with bushy white eyebrows and a calm, benign face, saying, with mock ceremony, '"Will the youngest bachelor ring the bell"', or '"shut the door"', or '"open the window"'. The house itself was old-fashioned, though over the years it had acquired many additions and alterations. 'There was,' Denton wrote, 'a miniature grand staircase as there is on ships from the deck to the saloon. I thought the furniture very ugly but I loved the coloured window at the top of the stairs; every pane was a different colour and one looked through each one in turn at a garden transformed. This last was trim and intimate with lawns and roses, and a wonderful tree called Black Jack's apple tree, after a famous local smuggler. It was hung with mistletoe and my mother told me that this was the Druids' sacred plant and how they cut it with their golden sickles. Then there was the hothouse for the early grapes and the greenhouse for the grapes and peaches. How I loved the hot scented steam that passed for air in these houses.'[2]

Before sailing for China he had first to endure an English Christmas

2. Many years later Whaphams was bought by Adam Faith.

in the country, which meant going to parties given by neighbours whose sons and daughters were of his own age. He managed to escape from one such gathering, on Christmas Eve, in order to attend midnight mass in a Roman Catholic chapel, where all was a 'maze of lighted candles, frothing lace and incense'. He was thrilled by the deadness and silence before the birth of Christ, 'and then by the coming to life of the congregation again as they moved about uneasily on their hassocks and made coughing, human noises'.

So long as he remained an outsider – a non-believer – the ritual manifestations of religion always fascinated him. An outsider in so many respects, all his life he would find himself mesmerized by the private activities of other people. Indeed, voyeurism became almost an addiction with him, one of his earliest experiences of it occurring at about this time. After supper one day, he slipped out into the garden:

'The leaves and bushes smelt strong and aromatic. I felt the light film of dust on the laurels under my fingers. I walked over the bricks in the stable-yard and stood by the gate. A young man passed me with a cigarette between his lips. I walked behind him up the road and saw him climb over a stile. It only led into the fields and down to a spring. I wondered what he was going to do; I decided to follow.

'When he stopped underneath the elms I hid behind the corner of a shed. The little red tip of his cigarette still glowed like a button on a switchboard. His shoulders were very broad as he hunched them. He seemed to be holding his hands in his pockets, against his thighs. He hummed a little tune and threw his weight from one foot to another. Then he stopped suddenly and came forward. Someone else had arrived from across the snowy fields.

'He drew her underneath the trees and I saw him throw down the cigarette impatiently, so that it fell like a small rocket. Then his arms went round her and I saw them moving nervously up and down her back like black shadows on a wall. He bent her backwards, curving her like a bridge until he lost his balance and fell and lay on her, a long, dark, trembling line in the snow.

'I left them to their bliss, running away with my face on fire. Back in the lighted drawing-room I could not concentrate on the pictures in the *Illustrated London News*. I went to bed and lay in the dark, thinking of what I had seen.'

The next morning he returned to the clump of trees, bent down and looked at the shape in the snow made by the two bodies. He saw 'the sickly, yellow patch' of the man's cigarette, where it had melted and stained the snow, and he picked up the remains. 'The paper was grey and wet now, falling away from the sodden strands of tobacco. I thought of it lighted and glowing, stuck between his teeth the night before.'

A year previously, again while on holiday, he had indulged in a similar inquest, this time inside a country church. Along one wall hung the cassocks and surplices belonging to the choir. 'Orvil [as he called himself, for the incident is recounted in *In Youth is Pleasure*] began idly to ferret in the pockets, to find evidence of the personalities of the wearers. He found that a hole had been made in the bottom of one of the pockets; in another was a stiff old handkerchief; a third held a shiny snapshot of a nearly bald woman clasping a fat baby in her arms.' Before relinquishing the scene, 'Orvil buried his nose in the cassocks, wanting, fastidiously, to be disgusted by their smell.'

At last the time came for Aunt Dorothy to take Denton to London to buy the clothes he would need for China – grey flannels and palm-beach suits. She also made him purchase a hat, which he refused to wear as it gave him a headache. The night before he and Paul sailed, they stayed in a 'politely fly-blown' hotel of a kind which his aunt, he noted, had a talent for finding. Bill joined them for dinner, and the next morning they took a long taxi-ride to the docks through a part of London that horrified Denton, to whom it looked 'like a back-cloth of an early pantomime with all the colour left out'.

'"God, how I envy you,"' Bill said to his brothers as they sat chatting in the ship's cabin. His aunt turned her head slightly, for she did not like God to be mentioned. When the siren blew, she kissed Denton quickly, giving him 'a sort of sincere peck'. And then, not yet having learnt that to travel is far better than to be left behind, he 'suddenly hated leaving England. I wished impatiently for them to go. I felt that I was going to cry.'

Every image and incident of this trip, as of all his experiences, was stored in his memory, to emerge in vivid detail when he came to write *Maiden Voyage*. On his first visit to the dining-saloon, for instance, he observed a man he was to describe ten years later as middle-aged, 'with a very fine nose. It was small and straight with no lumps. The skin was thick, not delicate, so that no veins and blood showed underneath.' And that same evening, the two brothers met up with another boy who had just left Marlborough, whom Denton took against when the boy came out with his hackneyed definition of a gentleman: '"A person who uses his butter-knife when he's alone." The boy looked at us triumphantly and we tried to force a laugh. My growing dislike crystallized. It was degrading to have to laugh at anything so suburban and BBC. It wasn't even improper, and I'd been preparing my face for something dirty.'

To pass the time during the voyage, Denton decided to do some sketching on deck, but was immediately importuned by a middle-aged lady whose silk scarf fluttered in the wind. 'Her head and neck were like the Roman symbol of an axe embedded in a bundle of sticks. The neck was all broken up into wrinkled skin and corded muscles, and the head jutted out at the top.' He judged by the colour of her scarf — puce and peacock-blue — that she was 'interested in Art. She was persistent as a bird, swooping down to peck at my drawing every moment.' At last he gave in and consented to talk to her, disliking her more and more as she contrived to prise from him details about his life. That evening, as he passed the porthole of her cabin, he spotted, on the sill, an unopened box of chocolates. '"The greedy bitch," I thought to myself. I thought of her sitting up in her bunk, wearing, perhaps, a boudoir cap with lace and blue ribbons; reaching for the chocolate without taking her eyes from the page of her novel.'

He tried to imagine the expression on her face if she were to discover them gone. Reaching through the porthole, he picked up the chocolates and walked away. Standing safely at the stern of the vessel, he tore the wrapping off the box and began to eat. 'It was like a communion feast. I was eating Mrs Wright. Not for love but for hate, so that later she should be ejected from my body to go swimming down with the rest of the ship's sewage. I put large pieces in my mouth and savoured them deliciously until the whole pound was finished.

'At dinner Paul asked me why I ate so little. He asked me if I felt seasick.'

En route to China the ship passed through the Red Sea where, in 1891, Denton's grandmother had died on board ship while sailing from Shanghai to England, and where she had been buried at sea. Now, passing the exact spot, Denton was inspired by the scene to write a poem, the first, he noted, that he had attempted since he was nine. As he came on deck he suddenly saw 'the burnt-up mountains ... crumbling in long lines to the sea'. He thought they looked like 'piles of brown sugar, everlasting and fierce, sticking up out of the sea'. The poem he wrote about them seemed to him almost perfect. 'I hugged it to me for the rest of the day, saying it over to myself.

'Other poems followed and I thought how good they were, but I told no one I was a poet. It was nothing to laugh at and I could not trust them to do anything else.'

When at last the two boys arrived in Shanghai they found their father waiting for them on the quay. He ferried them through the customs and then set off back to his office, saying to the chauffeur, '"Take young master home; by-and-by come catchy me Shanghai Club."' The pidgin-English 'sounded fresh and amusing' to Denton, and he did not in the least resent his father's immediate return to business: 'I was glad that we were going to be alone. I wanted to drink everything in.'

For the next few months he was intoxicated by all he saw. 'The houses were a dreary mixture of Western and Eastern styles,' he noted, 'but the smells were almost pure Chinese. Once when we stopped near a cook-house I caught the most complex smell of roasted meat and vege-tables.'

His father now lived in a luxury penthouse flat just outside the city, at 7a Rivers Court Apartments. The baroque, 'barley-sugar' columns of the porch reminded Denton of Oxford. 'I went quickly into the hall and found myself walking on deep blue carpets. Electric candelabra glowed softly against the rough-surfaced walls. Large Botticelli re-productions in silvered frames hung over the two fringed and tasselled Knole settees. Realizing that this was what was known as "quiet, good taste" I made hurriedly for the dull bronze lift.'

The door of the flat was opened by a Chinese Boy, 'who gave us a wide, mechanical, ballerina's smile'. He was deaf, and as he spoke he bent forward, cupping his ear with his hand, saying, '"No can hear, young master."' Surveying the flat with the patronizing self-assurance of youth, Denton remarked of his father's drawing-room, which ran the whole length of the building, 'It was a pleasant room, although a dis-criminating person would have found much to change.' A natural home-maker, he was always wanting to change people's rooms, to rearrange their décor and furnishings and sometimes to throw them out altogether. After the 'dull Sussex rooms' of his grandfather's house, however, he relished the brilliant surfaces and rich colours of his father's flat. He immediately went exploring, but just as he was undoing the leather straps of a dressing-case he found in his father's bedroom, which he remembered used to be full of Victorian jewellery, his father returned from the office for lunch. After lunch, as soon as the coast was clear, he was back on his hands and knees struggling with the straps of the dressing-case. Among a collection of bracelets, ornaments, necklaces, silver buttons, fans and perfume bottles, all of which had belonged to his mother, he discovered a silver disc bearing the inscription, 'Persevere to higher attainments. Awarded to Wm Pitt Denton, Dec. 31 1838. Fourth Prize. Chauncy Hall School. Industry secures its reward.'[3]

With his father and Paul both away every day at the office, he was alone in the house. He loved 'the feeling that swiftly settled down on me as the front door clicked behind them. With the servants shut away through double doors, I had every room to myself. The things seemed to be living for me especially.' He touched the furniture and china and looked into every cupboard. On a shelf in the kitchen he found two open-work Worcester baskets and two old powder-blue jugs. 'I took them down and studied them greedily; then I washed them and polished them and put them in my room.'

Many of the things he found in the flat made him think of his mother, and such was his preoccupation with her that he now went in search of a family she had known, who lived in the French Concession. He found their house, and at the end of his visit they invited him to return one day for lunch. Since it was, he tells us, the first time he had been asked out to lunch alone, he wanted to look nice, so when the day came he dressed carefully, in a grey flannel suit, and shaved using his brother's razor. Mr and Mrs Saunders (he named them 'Fielding' in *Maiden Voyage*) had three daughters, Pocetta (whom he named 'Vesta'), Enid ('Elaine') and Jane ('Ruth'), who was the same age as Denton and was mentally handicapped. Pocetta had married a man fifteen years older than herself, though they still lived at home because she had refused to marry at all if it had meant leaving her family. '"We were married in the garden – under the trees,"' she told Denton.

'And before I knew it I found myself stupidly saying, "I hope the weather was fine."'

Denton and Pocetta soon became friends, and she, clearly sensing that he presented no threat to a woman, would ask him to chaperone her to lessons with her Hungarian cello teacher because, she said, she was afraid he had designs on her.

One day, rather to Denton's surprise, his father asked him if he would like to go into the interior – to Kai-feng Fu – with a friend of his,

3. The silver disc, along with a miniature dating from about 1840 of his grandfather Thomas Bassett, was discovered after Denton's death in the lining of a battered old suitcase, held together by string, which also contained a collection of Denton's papers. The contents of the case, inherited by Denton's friend and literary executor, Eric Oliver, were sold, via the writer Hector Bolitho and an American dealer, John Fleming, to the University of Texas.

a Mr Butler, who was a former consul and who spoke Chinese. Although Denton was strangely apprehensive about it the trip was soon arranged. 'I felt very uncomfortable inside as we drove to the quay,' he wrote. 'I had never seen this Mr Butler before. I wondered what he would be like. My mental pictures shifted every moment from a delightful man to a horrible man and then back again; so that it was an anti-climax to be led across the deck and introduced to a mild, well-covered person, with crinkly hair and rather piggy eyes.'

On discovering that he was to share a cabin with Mr Butler, Denton 'hoped very much that he did not snore or have any peculiar tricks'.[4] So that he would not have to undress in front of Mr Butler – not, it can be assumed, because he seriously thought that that would somehow preserve him from Mr Butler's advances, but because he was by nature prim – he went straight to bed after dinner. He was still awake, however, when Mr Butler came in. 'His braces gave a squeak and slither as he unbuttoned them and drew them over his shoulders, and his false teeth tinkled as he dropped them into a tumbler of water.' Fortunately, Mr Butler did not snore; 'He only breathed deeply and let the air whistle out of his nostrils as if he were terribly unhappy.'

They stopped for a few days in Nanking with a friend of Mr Butler's who had 'pale moustaches and sagging, rather pink eyelids'. Denton, forever going off on his own, had a frightening experience the first day when he strayed across some trampled-down barbed wire and was confronted by a Chinese soldier. 'He waved a rifle uncertainly as he ran. I held my hands above my head and then, ashamed of the stagey gesture, dropped them to my sides again and waited.'

As the soldier came up to him, Denton saw that his face was distorted with rage. He seemed about to ram him in the stomach with his rifle. 'Short, sneering Chinese words cascaded out of his mouth. I looked as innocent and stupid as possible.

'"Me no savvy," I said, walking backwards slowly and deliberately. He followed me in fitful jerks, charging and then stopping to shake his gun at me. When he came to the trampled barbed wire he pointed to it and seemed to be asking how I could have neglected such a sign.'

Once on the road again, Denton walked away, trembling with anger and the reaction from his fear. 'I looked back once and saw the soldier's

---

4. The rather pointless phrase, 'any peculiar tricks', which appears in the published edition of *Maiden Voyage*, was in fact a substitution by the publishers' lawyers of Denton's original phrase, 'any homosexual tendencies'.

close-cropped, naked looking head above the parapet of the wall. He looked like a helpless baby vulture in a lonely nest.'

The train journey from Nanking to Kai-feng Fu offered new scope for Denton's never-tiring curiosity. The waiters in the dining-car seemed to him to be serving dirty grey rags and string out of cracked, steaming pudding-basins, while out of the window he could see 'the eternal hills and plains and cities of dried mud. Everything was the same, tawny, earth-brown. Even the city walls were of baked-gold mud which made them look imitation, like the scenery at a searchlight tattoo. Fields of poppies raged against the universal mud-colour. They were not only the scarlet poppies that we see in English cornfields, but pink, white, mauve, crimson and deep, dried-blood purple. They were as large as garden flowers.'

They were met at the station at Kai-feng Fu by a garrulous student called Li, and were taken to a former mission house where they were to stay. The mission had been closed down after the death of the missionary and his wife, and Denton hoped fervently that he had not been given the bed in which they had died: 'I tried to make myself believe that they had both died in the big double bed in Mr Butler's room.'

He was woken next morning by the sound of a bugle. Looking outside he saw a Chinese soldier, who spat violently when he noticed the boy watching him and then walked off, across a wide expanse of trodden mud, after giving him 'a last, evil look'. Mr Butler explained that foreigners were not welcome in that part of China and advised him not to go out alone. Curiosity soon got the better of him, however, and at the first opportunity he gave Mr Butler the slip and set off to explore the countryside. He quickly found cause to regret it, when he stumbled, to his horror, upon the fly-infested remains of a human head.

While he was in Kai-feng Fu he received an invitation from a young Canadian doctor with 'a pleasant, brown face with a little golden-red moustache' to spend a few days with him and his wife at their home in Yi-ching, which the doctor described as a real Chinese town with very few foreigners. It was agreed that Li would have to go too, in order to escort Denton back on his return journey to Kai-feng Fu. The train to Yi-ching was crowded with Chinese, 'eating, sleeping, quarrelling, laughing, crying, praying, breast-feeding their babies and making love. Li sat haughtily, looking straight in front of him. He made me understand that he was a student and these were cattle, mere grubbing peasants.'

'"I expect you're feeling kind of travel-stained," the doctor's wife said on their arrival at the mission bungalow. '"Jim, show your friend where the bath is."'

The doctor led Denton upstairs and opened the door. 'He turned the taps on and said, "You get in first while I have a shave."

'He pulled his limp shirt over his head and stood over the basin, lathering his chin. I undressed hurriedly and got into the bath. I lay back and watched the silky muscles running over his back as he moved his arms, scrubbing vigorously at his face. He had a fine body, smooth and hard and rounded. I admired it enviously, wondering if I could make mine like it by doing exercises every morning. The sweat and steam made his shoulders glisten and I thought he looked like a marble statue.'

Li was given the box-room in which to sleep. 'Like all the rest of the house, it was extremely neat and clean, but it was filled with boxes except for the corner where the bed had been put up. I thought of the dirt and untidiness of his own home.' But the room did not suit Li at all. '"It is not fit, Mr Welch,"' he said. '"It is not fit. I am student, not Chinese coolie."'

Li was in a more dignified mood when next Denton came upon him, in the sitting-room, reading a book. '"What dynasty does King Lear belong to in your history, Mr Welch?"' he inquired. '"Is he an ancestor of your present King?"'

'"Oh no,"' Denton explained. '"I don't think he was a real person at all."'

Li looked disappointed, and then his face brightened as he put Denton's reply down to ignorance. He began again.

'"Does Bernard Shaw write in English as well as Irish?"' he wanted to know.

'"So far as I know,"' Denton told him, '"he only writes in English."'

'"Yes?" His voice sounded scornful and patronizing. "It says here that he is Irish, so I think it more likely that he writes in his native language. You have no doubt read translations."'

Mr Butler now rejoined Denton and the impossible Li, and the three of them, together with Mr Butler's Boy, set out to return to Kai-feng. The journey swiftly developed into a memorable nightmare. The only available train was a cattle-truck, and even then they had to bribe their way on. They were later turfed out by some Chinese soldiers. Stranded, they had to pass the night in a filthy brothel which seems not to have catered entirely for heterosexual customers. Before making their escape Denton nearly managed to suffocate himself by setting fire to his old school blazer. The entire episode is one of the highlights of *Maiden Voyage*, and the description of the brothel, in particular, was to earn enthusiastic praise from Edith Sitwell, an early admirer of his writing.

The train journey back to Nanking, though less dramatic, was enlivened by an encounter with a colourful compatriot, the recently installed dean of Canterbury, Dr Hewlett Johnson, who innocently excited Mr Butler's indignation by travelling second-class. '"No Englishman travels second-class,"' Mr Butler expostulated. '"Why, even first-class is like a pigsty, and often the wagon-lits are not much better. It's a disgusting affectation, and I for one don't think any the better of him for it."'

Denton suggested to him that perhaps the dean did not realize the difference between England and China; as most people found third-class travel in England quite acceptable, he might have thought second-class in China 'perfectly possible'.

But Mr Butler was not having any of that. '"I don't expect he thought anything of the sort,"' he rapped out. '"It's just repulsive, mawkish sentiment. It's his way of demonstrating what a good Christian he is. It's far too theatrical for me."'

Denton thought that Mr Butler seemed to take it personally – as if the dean were travelling second-class especially to outrage him.[5]

Back in Shanghai, and as a welcome relief from the poverty of the Chinese peasants, Denton began to make the acquaintance of some of the British soldiers billeted in the public park. While he was chatting to one of them he heard himself saying, rather primly, '"Would you like to come to tea this afternoon? If you're at a loose end. I live quite near."

'He looked at me soberly, through the separating fence. "What would your Mum and Dad say to a stranger?" he asked.

'"I've only got a father and he won't be there," I answered.'

Denton returned home for lunch, and afterwards, with his father safely back at the office, he informed the Boy that '"one master"' would be coming for tea that afternoon, and then fussed about the drawing-room, putting cigarettes and small tables in convenient places. 'I had never

5. What Mr Butler clearly did not know was that Hewlett Johnson also happened to be a communist. He was fifty-eight when Denton met him in 1932 and did not retire from the deanery of Canterbury until he was eighty-nine, during which time he published two books on China, *China's New Creative Urge* in 1953 and *The Upsurge of China* in 1961. When he retired he went to live in a house he roguishly named The Red House; his widow, when she died in 1983, left £300,000 in her Will.

had a guest of my own before,' he wrote. Then he went back to the park to meet the soldier, who arrived on time and gave Denton a smart salute.

'"How punctual you are," I said, although, because I had been waiting, I really felt that he was late.'

When they arrived at Rivers Court Apartments the soldier hesitated, saying he thought the place looked a bit posh and wondering whether there were any officers about.

'"They might wonder what I was up to in there," he explained.

'"Couldn't you just say that you'd been out to tea?"

'"They might think it a bit queer."'

The door was opened by the Boy, wearing, as always, his ballerina's smile, but with a shrewd look in his eyes as he noted the rank of the soldier.

It transpired that the soldier could not stand China tea so in desperation Denton gave him a whisky and soda. As soon as the first glass was empty Denton offered him some more.

'"What'll your Dad say if he comes back and finds I've drunk all his whisky?"' he asked.

'"I can fill the decanter up from another bottle before he turns up." I wanted to appear cool and daring.'

Again, Denton replenished the soldier's glass.

'"I'll be tight if you go on like this,"' the soldier protested.

Then they both began to smoke.

'"You smoke like as if you thought it was going to blow up," he said, after watching me for some moments.

'"I don't smoke often," I admitted, turning red.

'"You come over here and I'll show you how to smoke."

'I went and sat on the arm of the sofa and looked down over his shoulder.

'"First you put it in the side of your mouth, not in the middle; then you breathe in deep." He demonstrated. "Now you take it right down inside you till it gets to your belly." He grabbed my hand, and scraping it down the buttons on his tunic, banged it at last on his stomach, which he had made tight as a drum. I imagined the smoke churning about inside.

'"Next you breathe out; but you've eaten most of it by then, as you can see."

'Only a little puff came out of each nostril.

'"Now you try," he said. He handed me his cigarette. My own had gone out while I watched. His was wet at the end and I did not want to put it in my mouth.

'"Put it in the corner," he ordered. "Don't have it sticking out like a bloody maypole. Now breathe in."

'I filled my lungs. The smoke began to choke me. I spluttered.

'"Go on sucking it in," he shouted wildly.

'My eyes filled with water. I gave two tearing gasps and all the smoke belched out.

'"Oh, you're no good," he said scornfully.

'I lay back, recovering my breath, while the soldier poured some more whisky into his glass and offered it to me. He held it under my nose, so that I had to breathe through my mouth to avoid the sickly smell.

'"Take it away," I groaned.

'He looked at his glass thoughtfully. "Seems a pity to waste it." He tipped the contents down his throat and gazed contentedly into the distance.

'There was a delicate rattle, like a mouse scraping. A key was being fitted into a lock. I looked wildly at the clock. It was nearly six. We should have left the flat at half-past five. I waited in fear for my father to open the door. I wondered what he would think when he saw the soldier and the half-empty decanter.

'I decided desperately to try to bundle my guest through the dining-room into the kitchen and so down the back stairs; but it was too late, the door-handle was turning, and the next moment my brother stood gazing at us in astonishment.

'"Oh, I thought you were Daddy!" I flopped into a chair, limp with relief.

'The soldier had jumped up, expecting some sort of encounter. He stood with careful steadiness, staring solemnly at Paul.

'"We've just been having some tea," I said gaily, trying to ease the situation.

'"It doesn't smell like tea," Paul muttered; then he said in a louder voice, "You'd better clear the mess up before Daddy comes in. He'll be back almost any minute now."

'I pushed the bell feverishly.

'"Have finish tea, Boy, can take away." I deprived the soldier of his glass and put it firmly on the tray, together with the soda-water bottles, their metal tops and the bottle-opener.

'"Paul," I said imploringly, "will you open another bottle of whisky and fill up the decanter while I show my friend the way out?" I thought how silly and schoolgirlish the word "friend" always sounded. One part of my mind began to wonder if people would soon stop using it, and if so, what other word would do instead.

'My brother said, "Damned if I will!" which brought me down to earth. I grabbed the soldier's arm and led him through the kitchen into the servants' quarters. I thought that the back stairs would be safer than the lift, where we might meet my father. I wondered if the soldier was drunk or not. He had seemed quite all right in the drawing-room, but now he was lurching rather queerly. I should have given him more soda-water, I thought. We reached the ground floor.

'"Will you be able to find your way back to the park?" I asked anxiously.

'"Yes, mate, don't you worry about me," he answered.

'I felt guilty as I watched his stately progress down the drive.

'"See you soon again," I shouted out. He waved his cane.

'I hurried upstairs to fill the decanter.

'Paul had already drawn the cork from the bottle. He tilted the spirit into the decanter savagely, so that it plopped and gurgled. He was furious.'[6]

The nights were so hot that Denton took to going to bed later and later, using the time after dinner to go off for walks on his own. One morning his father remarked that he would be kidnapped if he insisted on prowling about alone. '"God knows where you go,"' Mr Welch said, to which Denton innocently protested that he only went out for a little air before bed.

One evening his walk took him to the park where, as had happened there previously, he fell into conversation with a soldier:

'I sat down beside him on the bench and took in his smell. It was a mixture of Blue-Bell polish, tobacco, hair-oil and onions.

'"I know what you've been eating," I said archly and stupidly, to make conversation.

'He grunted. "What do you think of these Russian girls?" he asked.

'"I'm afraid I don't know anything about them," I answered awkwardly.

6. It seems that shortly after *Maiden Voyage* was published, Denton's friend Marcus Oliver reported having heard a shop-assistant express disappointment at the inconclusiveness of narratives such as this, which prompted an interesting reply from Denton on 19 May 1943: 'My dear, How amusing about girl in bookshop. She evidently knows how many beans makes five. Why was the poor thing disappointed? I'm sorry. Was it because things led to a climax and then rather petered out? But isn't this what life usually does? You must remember that my book is supposed to be true, not fiction.'

'"Ain't you started yet, then? I had my first when I was fifteen."

'"That was early," I said, beginning to feel rather desperate.

'"I wish you was a nice bit of skirt," he went on earnestly.

'"Yes-it's-a-pity-I'm-not-from-you're-point-of-view." In my embarrassment all my words ran together.

'"You got any sisters?" he asked in a yearning voice.

'"No."

'"What's your Ma like?"

'"My mother's dead," I said severely and repressively.

'I got up and threw away my cigarette.

'"You going, boy?"

'"Yes."

'"If you see anything, send it my way."

'"All right, good night."

'I walked over the misty grass. At the gates, two women were waiting. They might, or might not, have been prostitutes. As I passed them, something prompted me to shout, "Go into the rose garden." Then, horrified at my peculiar behaviour, I started to run. I wondered if they would follow my advice. I imagined them chasing the soldier over the rose-beds.'

There was, perhaps, a girlish look about Denton which the soldiers found appealing. That he recognized a strong feminine streak in himself can be seen from an incident which occurred one September evening when he was staying with the Saunderses. He had been given Pocetta's bedroom — she had gone to Peking with her husband — and while wandering around the room, looking at her jewellery, the temptation to dress up in her clothes came to him. First he put on a thin woollen dress, then he found a pair of high-heeled shoes and some make-up, and as a finishing touch he stuffed two bunched-up handkerchiefs into the bosom of the dress. He then decided to test the effect in the street, making his exit through the window and over the roof, nearly coming to grief when a clatter of loose tiles brought Mrs Saunders out to ask if everything was all right. Once in the street his self-confidence was such that he even managed to risk making eyes at a French policeman, but when a man riding in a rickshaw stopped alongside him to ask the way he panicked and, tearing off his shoes, ran back to the safety of the Saunders's house. At breakfast the next morning Mrs Saunders said, '"I hope you slept well, Denton."' She was, he wrote, looking straight at him.

'"Fairly well, thank you,"' he replied. In an attempt to explain the noises he added, '"I was rather restless, as it's hotter on the ground than up in the penthouse."' Mrs Saunders smiled sweetly and said no more.

As Christmas approached arrangements were made for Denton to stay in Peking with his mother's brother-in-law, Sir Percy Fox, and his second wife. He remembered this aunt for the high dog-collar of pearls she had worn as a young woman, and for her maid, whose name was Clutterbuck, which when he was a little boy he had mistaken for Clara Butt. He recalled, too, the day when he had been with her and his mother on board an ocean liner (she had come to see Denton and his mother off on one of their trips to England), and how she had allowed him to play with her scarab ring; he had accidentally dropped the ring, beyond reach, inside a cabin window-frame, and his aunt had vengefully tipped all his toys into the sea. He had thought her then the wickedest woman in the world, but now she was on the freezing platform at Peking, waiting to welcome and kiss him.

On Christmas Day, Lady Fox gave a lunch party at which everything on the table – crackers, napkins, china and glass – was blue, so that before the caviare was served Denton half expected to see blue food arrive. After lunch he was whisked off by a large lady in a large car, in which a spray of carnations bounced about in a cut-glass vase, to see her house and then to visit the Temple of Heaven. He arrived back at his aunt's house to discover that his uncle had meanwhile suffered a stroke. As if he was still a child, he was dispatched to neighbours for dinner. He changed into a dinner-jacket, and when he arrived he found only a boy and a girl of his own age.

'The girl was the first to jump up. She gave my evening clothes a swift, darting look.

'"Daddy and Mummy had to go out to dinner, so we're all alone. That's why we haven't changed," she said.

'Then her brother stood up and stared at me in a most discomforting way. I was thankful when we went into dinner, which was all that had been left from lunch, served up in a different way.'

Soon conversation dried up completely, and Denton kept wondering if his uncle would die. He hoped he would be able to leave before it happened, because he dreaded the thought of being left alone with his aunt. 'I would not know how to behave with death in the house,' he confessed.

After scrambling through a game or two of mah-jong, he made his escape, and hurried back through the icy air to his aunt's house.

'I went up to Clutterbuck's room and knocked on the door.

'"Come in," she said severely, to guard against being imposed upon. She was sitting on the bed, fully dressed, reading Baroness Orczy.

'"Oh, it's you, is it?" she said gruffly, but I saw how relieved she was by the way her face relaxed. I think she had a horror of being told to do something by a doctor or a nurse.'

She told Denton that his aunt wished him to return to Shanghai the next day, as she would be far too busy to have any time to spare for him.

'Clutterbuck,' he wrote, 'always liked making me feel small and insignificant.' She brought him up a steaming cup. 'I guessed before I smelt it that it was chocolate. It used to be chocolate when I was small, so it must still be chocolate. Nothing changed for Clutterbuck. It gave me a feeling of security and despair.'

Back in his own room, he wished that he could write a story, about his uncle's sudden stroke, Clutterbuck's sour philosophy and his aunt's 'childish, pleasant love of show and her longing for affection'.

On his return to Shanghai his father broached the subject of his future. He had, after all, spent nearly a year in China, and would soon be eighteen. He told his father that he wanted to go to an art school. 'I had to say it very quickly, because, for some reason, the words made me feel ashamed.

'My father made a face.

'"I don't think that's at all a good idea," was all he said. And after that we talked of other things.'

When he next went to see his friend Pocetta she advised him to go to a university or an art school. '"You can't just play around,"' she said. She showed him some poems she had written while he had been away, and he thought them very good, 'Almost better than my own.' On his way home from her house he again ran into the soldier who had come to tea. '"What, you going back to England!"' the soldier exclaimed. '"I don't expect I'll see you again, then."'

'Everyone seemed to be saying good-bye,' Denton wrote. 'I had an unhappy, mourning feeling which I nursed.' Within a few days his father had booked his passage back to England. 'But in spite of being ready for it, the words came as a shock. My thoughts buzzed and jumped about as if hot water had been poured on them. I would have to live in rooms in London or with relations who disapproved of me. Sometimes the English food would be horrible. There would be so little sun. I would belong again to my surroundings and would understand what people said. I would be able to go anywhere without fear, and I would see again the places I loved. The pros and cons darted one after the other; but, deep down under all my thinking, I knew that I was glad.'

He began to pack, collecting up all his silver, china and glass treasures, as well as ten of his great-grandmother's flower paintings, and silver forks and spoons that had come down from his mother's American family.[7] When his father discovered that he was planning to help himself to these he was furious, and unpacked them all again. What had angered him was Denton's failure to ask if he might have them. Denton well understood this, yet his possessiveness towards his mother had made him instinctively regard her family's things as his own; neither his father's nor his brothers' rights in the matter of his mother ever entered his head.

He decided to go out. 'I wanted to do something abandoned, to horrify my father. I slammed the front door to show that I had left.'

Out on the street, feeling desperate because he wanted to do something spectacular but could think of nothing, he started to run to give vent to the energy his anger had built up in him. Eventually he came home again after drinking more than was good for him, and the next day, having made it up with his father, he was allowed to take most of the things he wanted. By the time he had finished re-packing he had eight boxes.

He went to the kitchen to say good-bye to the cook, who never having been able to pronounce his name always called him 'Master Dung-dung'. '"I never more see you,"' he said to Denton. '"By and by, s'pose you come Shanghai, I makey die!"

'"What for talky so fashion, Cook?" I said. "You no very old!"

'"You no savvy how old; maybe I b'long one hundred years!" He laughed at the impossibility.'

Denton still thought pidgin-English charming, and regretted that he would never speak it again.

Paul and his father accompanied him to the quay. He found to his relief that he had a cabin to himself, with all his boxes stowed in it. Suddenly Pocetta, who had come with her husband to see him off, walked in, just as Denton was smoothing his hair in the glass.

'"How vain you are!"' she said.

'"Isn't going away awful!"' was all he could say.

7. The paintings, charmingly executed, are now in the Denton Welch Collection at the University of Texas.

Paul opened a miniature bottle of Cointreau and everyone drank little quantities of it from a tooth-glass, smacking their lips and saying how good it was.

When the hooter sounded they all jumped up to go, but as they were leaving, Pocetta ran back into the cabin. 'I knew suddenly that she was my greatest friend,' Denton wrote, 'and I had the grotesque idea that her husband might imagine us to be in love. It was so funny, I wanted to laugh.

'"Good-bye, darling," she said, kissing me desperately, half afraid, I think, that I might pull away. When she stepped back, her hat was a little crooked and some more tight curls had pushed out on to her forehead.

'We looked at each other for a moment, then she turned and ran away.

'I stood in the empty cabin, wondering what to do; then I too ran up on deck.

'She was already in the stern of the bobbing motor-launch. I waved to her, and I saw her face suddenly break into lines. She was crying now. Her mouth was open, showing her white teeth.

'Her husband stood behind her, looking embarrassed and upset. He took her arm and tried to calm her. The launch began to pull away.

'I felt my throat thickening and aching. Slow, heavy tears gathered in the corners of my eyes and glistened there until they dropped on to the scrubbed deck, where they made dark patches.

'I waved until her face was only a little pink blob; then I turned miserably away and went back to my cabin.

'It still smelt of Cointreau. I lay down on the bunk, feeling sick. The woodwork began to creak. I wanted to go to sleep for ever.

'There was a knock on the door. A steward poked his head in, saying "Lunch will be served in five minutes."

'Already it was "lunch", not "tiffin".'

FOUR

Art School

Denton's ambition to begin training as an artist was fulfilled just as soon as he returned to England in 1933. He enrolled at the Goldsmith School of Art in New Cross (now the School of Art and Design in Goldsmith's College, University of London). His aunt Dorothy, apparently, chose the school for him — it was not one that Denton and his cousin May had visited — because she had once bought a print from a man who taught wood-engraving there. The three years he spent at the school were, once he had settled down, probably the happiest of his life, for not only was he at last free to devote himself to something he really wanted to do, but he was able to choose friends of his own for the first time. There was Carel Weight, seven years older than Denton and destined to become Emeritus Professor at the Royal College of Art; Helen Roeder, a third-year student when Denton arrived, who became a life-long friend; Betty Swanwick, later a Royal Academician; and another student, Gerald, who was three years older than Denton and who appears under various guises in his writings.

Looking back on his first year at art school when writing up his journal in 1942, Denton recalled being in disgrace with Aunt Dorothy because he *'would not* "settle down"', and his aunt saying to him, '"If you want to study art, why don't you do some work? You should be sketching every day; instead of that, you wander in the fields doing nothing at all from morning till night."'

Aunt Dorothy, like the rest of his family, had little understanding of his personality or potential. Although anything but lazy, he was, as many adolescents are, afflicted by restlessness and an inability to concentrate on one objective. His lack of self-confidence is apparent in a passage in *A Voice Through a Cloud* in which he recalls at first knowing nobody at the art school, and returning in the evenings to his lodgings to throw himself down on his bed, 'sprawling out my legs and burying my face in the pillow'. He would, he wrote, be thinking of the pleasures and pains of the day that had just passed. 'Then, turning over, I would stare at the uneven ceiling and wonder how much longer my life would lack direction, how much longer I would be cut off yet searching for my true place in the world. I thought of the hours wasted at the art school, with the drawing-board in front of me and the pencil in my hand, the feeling of uselessness that came upon me as I sat there, staring into space.'

He remembered the relief and pleasure he always felt when classes were over, for then he could go to the refectory and take refuge in food, buying 'an enormous shortbread biscuit wrapped in silver paper' and 'a glass of very hot milky coffee'. But he found that 'there was a sadness, too, in coming to this point in the day, for it brought with it the realization that another precious piece of my life had melted away; and I had done nothing to catch it, to hold it, to *know* it'.

Eventually he did settle down to a routine of work, at the same time discovering some of the conditions for contentment. In an entry in his journal in 1946 he wrote, 'Thinking back to the times in my life when I have been happy, it has always been when I have been doing almost everything for myself, as when I was at Brixham in 1934 [when he was nineteen and on holiday in Devon] with the house full of other art students, but with me alone – bathing early every morning, making my own breakfast of cornflakes and cream and coffee, bicycling about the country, doing every day a little picture as my work, then gazing at the churches, the ruins and the antique shops, bathing and climbing and bicycling, till I was tired out. The quiet content came bubbling up, was with me every day then.'

The luxury of solitude without loneliness was an early need which remained strong. The same journal entry went on, 'It is most important to have people near one that one need hardly see. Without this consciousness of other human beings I think almost all of us are liable to be swamped by the power of matter. One's strength is not enough to bear this with no other help.

'But the waste that one should do everything to avoid is the pointless, joyless chatter, the dislocations of meeting and parting; worst waste of all, snarlings and frustration.

'I do not think that people want love most, they need the settled reverie, the calm testing and tasting of their past and the world's past.

'I am talking about "people" when I mean "me".'

On his return from China he had lived at first in the house in Adam Street where his brother Bill had rooms. The other occupants, as Denton described in his short story 'The Earth's Crust',[1] were 'a woman with a tightly held mouth and contemptuous eyes', and 'a curate viscount who ran up the stairs and usually carried a music-case stuffed with papers'. The owner of the house, who lived with her children in the basement, had a 'harsh, dry cough' which, whenever Denton heard it, made the back of his own throat tickle. Quite apart from the discomfort of his relations with Bill, the atmosphere of the house seemed to him to be charged with other tensions: 'In houses where people live behind closed doors, unknown to one another, some emanation broods in the passages and especially on the stairs. Perhaps it is just vague, diffused suspicion. This house had it in particular. The embittered woman, going to the bathroom with her sponge, moved almost furtively, as if afraid of eyes staring down from the top landing; and the curate, as he bustled past me with his papers, seemed to be escaping from someone or something. Even the landlady seemed to be affected by the atmosphere. She climbed up from her basement with a look of deep anxiety and secretiveness on her face.'

She nevertheless produced excellent breakfasts, served in the tenants' rooms, which Denton would eat while reading a book. At the last possible moment he would get up and, 'without even going upstairs to see my brother', rush out of the house to catch the bus to the art school. It was a long journey, and he would sit whenever he could on the top of the bus at the front, 'in order to see everything'. He thought that the people thronging the pavements were 'like bottles walking; their heads as inexpressive as round stoppers. What if some god or giant should bend down and take several of the stoppers out?' he wondered. 'Inside there would be black churning depths like bile, or bitter medicine.'

Sometimes when he entered the antique room at the art school there would be only two or three girls sitting at the donkeys, and they would continue chattering among themselves about men 'as if I were just another plaster-cast'. He was left to get down on paper 'something that looked a little like the Hermes of Praxiteles'. In the early days, instead of joining the other students in the refectory at lunch-time, he would go out and buy some rolls and liver sausage from a shop and eat them on the steps of a nearby church. At the end of the day, dreading having to go back to his lonely bedsitting-room, he would often go for a walk in Hyde Park and order tea and ice-cream at Fuller's.

One night when he went home he ran into Bill and a friend on their

1. Published in *Contact* in October 1950, and reprinted in *A Last Sheaf*.

way out for the evening. 'They asked me perfunctorily to join them, but I looked at the friend's rolled umbrella, at my brother's smartness, and I felt tousled and callow. Their age, their sleekness and assurance made them inhuman.' He excused himself by pretending he had plans to visit a friend of his mother's, then decided he would after all go in search of her, but when he reached her flat and rang the bell there was no answer. 'To find the door locked at that moment,' he wrote, 'was a catastrophe,' and he trudged back to his lodgings, 'feeling sick and empty'.

The strain of living so close to Bill, and the long journey he had to make each day to New Cross, decided him to find lodgings closer to the school. The house he settled upon was 34 Croom's Hill, close by Greenwich Park and within a short bus journey of the art school. The landlady was Miss Evelyn Sinclair. Describing the house in a letter dated 31 November 1945 to a friend, Noël Adeney, who was then planning to buy and restore the property, Denton wrote, 'I think the rough outline of the house's history is that it is an early eighteenth-century building with a few later eighteenth-century additions (like the Adam fireplace and I think the thin banisters, if not the whole staircase) and more important changes in the early nineteenth century, when the deep bows were added, the panelling taken out of the long rooms, the jutting-out piece stuccoed, and probably the rest of the front refaced and most of the window sashes changed from thick bars to thin. (The arched window and the one below are the only two early ones remaining.) Then of course there are the mid to late Victorian mantels in the two long rooms, and the grates put into the earlier mantels.

'It is delightful, I think, to have so many bits of different periods in the same house.

'I hope I don't sound too fancy about Croom's Hill, but I have always liked it *very* much, and I still imagine it in its freshness as I first saw it.'

The Adam fireplace mentioned in the letter was, as he recorded in 'A Novel Fragment', 'the chief glory' of the front first-floor room to which 'Miss Middlesborough' (Miss Sinclair) conducted him, and it was this that made him decide to move in.[2] 'The extreme refinement of its detail made one think that it was moulded in composition and not carved in wood. It looked a thoroughly commercial product of the late eighteenth century, but how attractive it was! How "elegant and chaste"!'

2. He later transferred to an attic room on the second floor, 'under the roof', as he wrote in his journal.

'A Novel Fragment', in spite of the title, is no less autobiographical than anything else Denton wrote, and contains his most comprehensive account of his days at art school (he appears in it under the pseudonym 'Robert'). In it he describes, for example, days spent drawing a more-than-life-size model called Madame David, whose arms and legs were like 'heavy tubes'. He tried in vain to respond to her 'swelling stomach and torso', and found particularly difficult her breasts, with their 'night-marishly large purple-pink nipples', as 'curved and globular as the breakfast-cups on the L.M.S. Railway'. Busily he would fall to drawing her head, the only part 'at all familiar to him'.

One day, while the class paused to allow Madame David to rest, she turned and looked at him disconcertingly, her gaze resting finally on his small feet. 'She could see the whole shape clearly, for he wore sandals which only consisted of straps and soles.

'"You ought to be a ballet-dancer," she said emphatically. "You could do springs like Nijinsky."'

Denton came to regard her, in spite of his incomprehension of her anatomy, as almost the only life-model who came to the school who was palpably alive. 'Many of the others seemed drugged, apathetic, enveloped in a mist.' But another exception was a 'fine-looking man', who made one girl student's eyes glisten 'quite simply with reverence and lust', and whose body 'Robert' envied 'almost painfully – the hard thighs and stomach, the pectorals, Greek in their clear-cut shape, the over-developed arms and legs with thin biceps and calves like hard rubber balls'. (This young Adonis represented the archetype to whom Denton was throughout his life attracted.)

'A Novel Fragment' also describes the birth of his friendship with Gerald, who appears in it as 'Gerard Hope'. One day Gerard noticed Robert reading Wilde's De Profundis and asked him what he thought of it. He then asked him what he did in the evenings, and Robert replied, '"Oh, I don't know; I read and go for walks over the heath."'

Hope told him, '"I have to spend most of my evenings going round to my various friends and cheering them up."' He showed, thought Robert, a 'little too much gaiety and brightness'.

Determined to cheer him up too, for Robert had confessed to some-times getting depressed, Hope asked where he lived. Reluctantly, Robert told him, and one evening, uninvited, Hope turned up at Croom's Hill. After listening politely to Hope's stories about public schools – 'always so fertile a field for anecdotes of the ridiculous and the sexy' – Robert, 'before he realized what he was doing', held his wrist out and looked at his watch.

'"It's frightfully late," he said gaily. "Do you think you've lost your last bus or tram or whatever you travel by?"

'He was to learn that Hope never missed buses or trains – unless he had planned to.'

It was not long before Hope had invited Robert to dinner one evening when his mother was out. As they were sitting side by side on a sofa after dinner, Hope produced his family photo-album. 'The stiff pages were turned, one by one, very slowly. Hope put one arm along the back of the sofa behind Robert's neck; then, when a particularly funny picture was discovered and they were both shaking with laughter, he placed his other hand over Robert's, under the book as if to steady him.

'Robert finished his laugh carefully; then, with a jerk, he jumped to his feet, saying with unnatural heartiness, "Christ, I'm hot! Sitting so close to the fire and all that laughing have made me sweat like anything!"'

With his 'small round head' and eyes 'that held a curious glittering expression which was too bird-like or lizard-like to be comfortable', Hope was no athletic model with Greek pectorals; but in spite of the evidently irritating aspects of his character and behaviour, he was typical of many people to whom Denton was drawn, people who could entertain him with macabre tales of their adventures, whether they were true or imaginary. Hope was also one of those people who could be played upon: '"I suppose we all have our fads,"' Robert had said to him in the course of conversation. '"Yours may be that you must get enough exercise, or that you must be 'regular', as the advertisements put it!"

'"But I am 'regular'!" Hope said almost angrily. And Robert knew that that was *his* fad.'

The appearance of the male model had been first discovered by two girls, sisters straight from school in Ramsgate, who 'in friendly derision' called Robert 'Sonny Boy', and confided to him the details of their love-lives. '"Let's go and see him,"' they had said. '"Sonny Boy, you're to show us the way and chaperon us."' When the class had a period of rest, 'the model, seeing Robert so close, put a hand on his shoulder and jumped down from the dais. As he jumped, his arms just brushed one of Robert's cheeks. Robert felt the hair on his forearm tickle, like a spider's legs. A shiver went through him; he looked up and smiled at the model.' The model also happened to be a wrestler, and Robert soon had him telling the gory details of tricks wrestlers used in the ring — 'Robert was pleased that the stories were getting horrific' — and before long 'the model had got him into some impossible position between his legs. Next, Robert found himself hanging over the model's back, being held by one leg.'

All his life, Denton had a natural gift for falling into conversation with strangers. 'Robert', of course, has the same gift. After playing a game of hockey one evening, he happened to go into the lavatory of a nearby public house. 'Someone was already in there. He could just see the dark shape against the glistening, discoloured tiles and the pink polished-copper pipes. The man turned his face towards Robert as he stood near, and said pleasantly, "Evenings are drawing out a bit now, thank God, aren't they? Let's say good-bye to bloody winter."' The young man, whose name was John Russell, had just been invalided out of the army, and he and Robert soon became friends.

Twelve years later, Denton wrote in his journal that a recent visit to Blackheath had made him think of the evenings 'I had walked there with John Russell when I was nineteen, how we had fooled and laughed and quarrelled as we took the air on the heath after work — I at the art school, he with his practising on the cor anglais'. The correspondence between events in 'A Novel Fragment', in which Russell appears under his real name, and those described in his journal thus offers further evidence of Denton's dependence upon real people and events for his writing; indeed, the parallels are often so close that it would appear that the fiction serves more as a garnish to the facts than the other way around.

On the day of their first meeting, after they had walked some way together across the heath, John suddenly asked Robert if he would go with him to a concert. Robert agreed to this, and when he said good-bye he held out his hand. 'Russell took the hand and held it for a moment, then, with a lightning movement, his head swooped down and he kissed it. For a moment he knelt before Robert in such a posture of mixed clumsiness, melodrama and sincerity that a cry of protest sprang to Robert's lips. He choked it; but he could not restrain the stiffening of his body. His hand went dead; then it was free and he saw Russell disappear in the darkness, running hell for leather down the hill.

'"He's not mad," thought Robert. "Only lonely and stagey. That's why he tried picking me up. I'll go to the concert next week."'

The tickets for the concert had been given to John by an older admirer of his, who on the night came up to the boys during the interval. 'He pushed towards them, smiling and showing the gold in his teeth. The short paunchy body and the fish-shaped head, covered with silvery bristles, repelled Robert. He hated the worn pin-striped suit, the watch-chain with the spade guinea and the Boy Scout's fleur-de-lis in the button-hole.

'"Introduce me to your friend, John," said the man, smiling ingrati-atingly and reassuringly at Robert.

'"It was very good of you to give us these tickets for the concert," said Robert after they had shaken hands.

'"Oh, I always give John tickets. He must hear good music, you know."

'There was a pause; the man slipped away and came back bearing two cups of coffee. He opened his arms dramatically and held out the cups to Robert and John.

'"Oh, you lucky young things!" he said with fervour. "What wouldn't I give to be right at the beginning of life again, with all youth's glorious chances and friendships before me!"'

No less embarrassing were his parting words, when the warning-bell sounded for the second half of the concert. 'The man caught Robert and John by the hand, linking both of them to him at the same time. "Well, this is where we have to part," he said; "enjoy yourselves, my children, and – be good!"'

One can well imagine Denton storing up his revulsion for the man for years.

Other opportunities for meeting people like Russell, scarce though they were, did occur from time to time. One of Denton's short stories, 'A Party',[3] describes a fancy-dress party to which he was invited by a fellow art student, Betty Swanwick, whom he unkindly named 'Fat Bertha Swan', during the course of which he found himself in the centre of a rather half-hearted orgy in the lavatory. Having 'wedged himself between the other bodies', he 'felt a hand exploring him. It ran tenta-tively down his arm, flickered over his stomach, one finger dipping for not more than an instant into the tiny cup of his navel before travelling on to his other arm. The hand had clutched his now, was kneading it excitedly in little rushes, rather as loving cats bite each other's necks.' Unsure whether the hand belonged to Bertha, or to a young man who had gone to the party dressed as a nun, or indeed to someone quite unknown, he was sure there was some mistake or intended cruelty. 'His

3. Published in *A Last Sheaf*.

own hand had gone quite stiff with discomfort and unhappiness. Yes, it was true; no one could ever love him.'

This feeling of isolation and loneliness was never far away, as he recalled in his journal on 21 January 1945: 'In the winter the fire [in the dining-room at Croom's Hill] would snap and I would long for the perfect friend who I knew could never exist. (For in those days even the possibility of a day-to-day friendship seemed utterly remote.) I lived young, alone, secret in my room or at the art school, walking over the dark heath at night, staring down at London and the puce glow it made in the sky.

'The river sirens hooted, the trams far away sparked and rocked down to Woolwich. I was lost in my own world, with no one to speak to. Then when I came home and fell down on the bed, covered with the brilliant wreck of my grandmother's Kashmir shawl, I would almost groan to think that nothing had come out of me that day, only the ghost of an effort to be great.'

Later on at that same party, finding that he had missed the last bus home, he had been offered a bed for the night by the male nun. 'It took a second for Ian [as Denton named himself in the story] to adjust himself to this idea, then he decided. "That is very good of you. Are you sure you don't mind?" Perhaps this was the friend he'd been waiting for, he must wait and see, he wanted so to talk to him alone.'

Unhappily, the nun – who was 'firmly and neatly built ... like a miniature navvy with all the edges polished' – turned out to have a girlfriend, though he and Ian did end up sleeping in the same double bed that night. Ian consoled himself with the thought that at least it was 'nicer sleeping in bed with someone else; one wasn't so lonely'. In the morning he borrowed a book, so that he would have an excuse to return.

Denton's quest for the illusory 'perfect friend' was in reality a desire to find someone who would make no demands upon him, emotionally or physically, for he was highly destructive of the veneer under which almost all human activities and relationships thrive; indeed, much of his writing, particularly in the journals, is concerned with probing beneath the surface of life in order to understand human motivation, needs and attainments.

Of another fancy-dress party, which he described in 'A Novel Fragment', he wrote that there was 'no joy, no love, no pleasure, no delight and no cohesion. Each little body had rushed about distractedly, alone.'

Now he knew 'why the very thought of ordinary "pleasure" filled him with despair'.

During the summer holidays in 1933, he decided to go on a tour in the west country, his plan being to walk from his grandfather's house in Henfield to Devon, staying on the way in youth-hostels. His account of this holiday, written ten years afterwards in his journal, ran to some 35,000 words and was eventually published separately, in 1958, under the title *I Left My Grandfather's House*.[4]

He stayed no longer than was necessary at his grandfather's 'ugly ivy and stucco house' ('it's better to sleep in the ditch ... than to thrust yourself on your relations', he wrote elsewhere), and his aunt seemed pleased to be rid of him. 'She speeded me on my way rather too gaily and quickly,' he thought. An early port of call was at the house near Petersfield of a not particularly agreeable great-uncle, Percy Bois, and his wife, Maggie, who later went mad. He was feeling very tired as he drew near to where they lived, the sun was hot on his back and he wanted a nice bed for the night. He rested on the grass at the edge of the road. 'Then I took my courage in my hands and walked up to their house, down the drive, till I found a building so like their last house that I knew the same mind had chosen it ...

'I knocked at the door rather desperately and rang. I was taken to my uncle who had just come in. I explained myself and brazenly asked to stay the night. He looked at me like an old turkey or vulture with a loose scrawny neck; then he said rather unexpectedly, gently, repressively, "Of course, there are buses."

'"I know, but I am tired," I said, determined to stay the night, determined to be made welcome, to reap the benefits of their comfortable home, to have a new experience, not always to miss new happenings and surroundings because of timidity and other people's dried, dead hearts.'

He got his way in the end, and was given a 'good, cold supper'. In the morning, after agonizing over whether to leave a tip for the maid, he said his good-byes, which he found 'so funny – so cold – so woolly'.

4. Two limited editions were published simultaneously; 150 copies were printed privately for James Campbell, an antiquarian bookseller who had acquired the copyright in Denton's writings, and 200 copies were published by the Lion and Unicorn Press at the Royal College of Art. In 1963 a copy of the book was available for £7 10s.; in 1982 one was offered for sale at £85. (A first edition of *Maiden Voyage* may currently fetch £75, and *In Youth is Pleasure*, £50.)

He had found his relations 'pleasant and distant and half dead', and he did not breathe freely again until he was on the road. 'How stuffed and stuck in the mud they are! I thought. They ought to have enjoyed having me and told me to come again.'[5]

He spent one night in the open in a farm out-building, having first tried to induce the farmer's sixteen-year-old son to join him. 'I told him I'd never slept out before and suggested, jokingly, that he should come out and join me in the hay as I was afraid of ghosts. He was shining the torch up in the air now and I could see his face in the dim light. It was a nice face – rather blunt and strong with a broad nose. He was seriously considering the suggestion; it was an adventure, and he wanted to be nice to me. But at last he said, "I'd better not; my old man wouldn't like it. I'll stay out here and talk to you a bit though."

'I was torn between wanting to sleep and not wanting to be left alone. I let him ask his questions and teased him a little by making startling remarks and joking with him. I remember him now as a person who was just emerging from his chrysalis; he seemed a little timid, but ready to try everything for himself.

'He said good night and got up to go. "Perhaps I'll see you in the morning," I said. "Perhaps. Have a good night. Don't let the fleas bite."

'He was nice,' Denton added. 'I liked him.'

Another night was spent in a youth-hostel in Winchester, where he was spoken to by a bald young man with a stutter, causing him to reflect, 'with rather a conventional pang of annoyance', that he always attracted rather dreary oddities and not the interesting people that he wanted to know.

When he arrived at Minehead, in Somerset, he was brought up sharply yet not unpleasantly with memories of school, for quite unexpectedly he bumped into Miss Forman, his old headmaster's sister-in-law, who

5. About ten years after this visit it became known that Denton's great-uncle Percy, as sole trustee of a capital trust fund of about £48,000 in the name of his sister, Aunt Bertie, had secretly helped himself to about £10,000 of her money. He had always been thought quite rich, but when Aunt Bertie died and the fraud was discovered – he was then ninety years of age, 'frail and a little senile' – he was found to be running the house at Petersfield and maintaining his deranged wife, an unmarried daughter, another widowed daughter and her children, all on a mere £200 a year. His deception left no less than sixteen nieces and nephews each with £1,000 less than they had been expecting.

A good deal of money circulated in Denton's family generally. His great-aunt, Mrs Frances Bois, who lived near Okehampton, left £37,685 when she died in 1936; and his grandfather, who also died in 1936, left £28,628.

had taught him the piano at Repton and who had felt sorry for him because he was, according to the recollections of her sister, 'very much a motherless little boy'.[6] Mrs Fisher and Miss Forman were two of a family of twelve. Their father had been a house-master at Repton from 1880 until his death in 1905, and had taken his large family every year to Minehead for their holidays; hence Mrs Fisher had known the town all her life, and after her father's death her husband, Dr Fisher, had continued the family's connections with Minehead by buying a holiday home there which was large enough for his own six sons and their innumerable cousins to congregate. It was to meet this formidable ménage that Miss Forman now invited Denton to tea; after protesting mildly that he did not think his former headmaster, now Bishop of Chester, would want to see him, he accepted.

Alas, he disgraced himself by spilling a cup of tea all over the tablecloth, whereupon Dr Fisher, to cover Denton's embarrassment, instantly seized a piece of bread and threw it down the table to his wife. 'She caught it deftly,' Denton remembered, 'still pouring out with the other hand.

'Now the whole table was laughing and gay and boisterous; my awful accident had been merged and incorporated into the bishop's wild breadthrowing. It really was the most charming and brilliant thing to do.'

The next day the Fishers took Denton part of his way across Exmoor in their car, and after he had waved them good-bye he met a young farmer 'on a huge horse', who apparently had managed to lose the local hunt. He asked Denton 'in his soft, sing-song voice' which way the horses had gone.

'I pointed down the road, but he seemed in no hurry. He asked me where I was heading for, and seemed generally curious about me.

'Suddenly he slapped the horse and said, "Wouldn't you like to jump up and have a ride on her? Aren't you tired, walking?"'

Denton decided he was, but instead of riding pillion he found himself sitting in front of the farmer. 'I could smell his clothes – the mingled tobacco, beer, horse and sweat that clung to them; and I could tell how hot he was, for I was pressed hard against him as he reached round for the reins. I could even feel his heart beating into my back ... I felt the hard press of his thighs and legs along my own.'

The farmer asked if he would like to go hunting, but then his manner began to unnerve Denton. 'Just as I thought we were about to turn

6. Letter from Lady Fisher to the author, 4 September 1982.

into a field, to catch up the hunt, the young farmer bent over me and said cajolingly but with a certain menace, "What are you going to give me for the ride, it's worth something to you, the ride, isn't it?"'

This was so new and unpleasant a turn of events that Denton could only answer, '"Oh, I didn't know you wanted money." I was very hurt, since I thought that he had picked me up entirely for fun and amusement; I was rather alarmed, for I now seemed to be in his power. I could not see myself escaping from between these two huge arms and throwing myself off that horse with any success. I decided to take up as light and indifferent an attitude as possible.

'"What do you want?" I said coldly. "I've got very little money, so perhaps I'd better get off at once."

'"No, don't do that," he said, holding on to me firmly. "You give me something," he wheedled. "It's worth it to you, isn't it?" The wheedling from the strong lusty man enraged me; everything had been spoilt by his trying to extract money, and I had been enjoying myself so much.'

No doubt feeling fairly desperate by this time, Denton began to bargain. '"Put me down now and I'll give you sixpence,"' he said. '"I want to go on walking."'

The 'lusty' farmer scorned the notion of taking the sixpence, but began to bargain too. '"Oh, come on,"' he said, '"give me a bit more than that and I'll take you a long way."'

Eventually the farmer took the sixpence, and Denton managed to get off the horse, falling backwards over a little bush in the process. As he picked himself up he held his hands out for his rucksack, but the farmer pretended not to notice. Denton thought for a minute that he was going to gallop away with it.

'Filled with horror (for it contained everything I needed for my journey) I ran after the horse and said, "Chuck me my rucksack, please." My voice sounded very firm and severe and artificial.

'At last he turned round; he was smiling. "Catch!" he said as he swung it out to me. I caught it by the straps. When I looked up again I was just in time to see him hit his horse, making it break into a fast trot. "Good-bye," he shouted jovially, as he disappeared across the fields. I did not answer; I was trying to understand the whole episode.'

Denton was almost twenty-eight when he wrote this account; by then, if not at the time, he can have been in no serious doubt when it came to understanding 'the whole episode'. Unless one regards this comment as an example of his extraordinary ability to recreate an event many years later with all the immediacy of adolescent naivety, one may be tempted to agree with E. M. Forster who, when he read a manuscript copy of the journals, commented, perhaps with this very account in mind, on Denton's 'funking of intimacy, the sham-innocence and cock-teasiness'.[7] Whichever view one takes, one cannot deny that such scrapes as these were the stuff of life for Denton, satisfying both his fascination with horror and providing a source of the sensual pleasure he derived from fear.

At last his holiday came to an end, and back at Croom's Hill life resumed its measured tread. He began to acquire antiques for his room, buying, for 17s., an early Victorian work-table, which he had to carry home across the heath on his shoulder, a seventeenth-century Flemish cabinet which he bought for 10s. in New Cross Road and an early eighteenth-century Indian miniature which cost him 8s. The meals in the house were served by a maid, and Miss Sinclair did not mind him bringing guests home for dinner. In the basement, her father played 'his great golden harp ... entirely according to his own whim and fancy, never having learnt to read music'. The strains, Denton recalled in 'A Novel Fragment', 'were unrecognizable as European melodies, but old Mr Middlesborough [Mr Sinclair] would have it that they were hymns and sacred airs. Sometimes he would sing in high, goatish falsetto; then the whole effect was almost overwhelmingly bizarre and strange; especially if he could be seen as well as heard; for it would be discovered that he dressed for his harp-playing in an old corded dressing-gown and curious woollen cap which, together with his little square beard, lent him a strikingly Jewish and Old Testament appearance.'

With Miss Sinclair, a former Methodist and now, like his mother, a Christian Scientist, Denton had formed a warm friendship, one which was to last, despite dramatic rows and experimental partings, until the end of his life. She was forty when he first went to live in her house. It is unlikely that the idea of marriage for herself had ever crossed her mind, and she was not the sort of landlady likely to trouble a young homosexual student with embarrassing questions or sidelong looks. Devoted to cats, she added to Denton's roll of nicknames by calling him 'Puss', or sometimes 'Pusky'; he, in turn, usually called her Eve or Evie, but sometimes also 'Lydia', and was not above defaming her in letters as 'the Harlot' or 'the Whore'.

Having brought with him from Sussex the bicycle he rode when on

7. Letter to John Lehmann, 17 July 1951.

holiday there, he decided to make use of it during the Whitsun weekend in 1935 in order to go to stay with his aunt Edith, his father's elder sister, and her husband, the Reverend Thomas Kane, who lived at Leigh Vicarage near Reigate.[8] He set off, without warning the Kanes, on 7 June, pushing his bicycle up the hill to Blackheath, past some 'charming, rather squalid old houses'. He mounted it when he reached the heath and began to pedal towards Lewisham. At the Roman Catholic church he got off his bicycle and went inside. He had been in the church twice before: once with a fellow student, when they had lit a couple of candles, and once on a saint's day, when he had watched a procession of pretty girls with wreaths in their hair. This time he encountered two nuns, 'kneeling in a curious, thrown-forward position, as if they had been naughty boys ordered to "bend over".' Then, feeling that he was trespassing, he hastily collected his bicycle and carried on to Catford.

Now he took the road to Beckenham. Most of his journeys from Croom's Hill to the art school had been made by bus, and most of his bicycling had been done on country roads during the holidays, so he was not used to traffic. He thought he was managing well, however, threading in and out between the lorries and buses so as to be at the head of the queue when the traffic-lights turned green. Near Beckenham he saw a sign advertising teas, so he turned into the long drive that led to a small eighteenth-century house, and although it was lunch-time he ordered only coffee and biscuits. The waitress who brought his coffee retired behind the counter again, 'and began to laugh and talk quietly with her companion'. Denton wondered whether she was laughing at him.

He lingered in what must once have been the drawing-room, trying to ignore the sizzling tea-urns, the Japanese crape table-cloths and the glossy plaques advertising Schweppes and Players cigarettes, enjoying instead the three huge sash windows and the deep, rich mahogany of the door set in a framework of plain, white-painted wood. He thought, too, about the Whitsun holiday, and about a picture he was painting, of a Corinthian capital 'with strange plants and weeds growing in the crevices'; some of the plants were imaginary, others he had copied from ones he had found in a playing-field behind the art school. He thought this was going to be his best picture so far, and thinking about it made him feel warm.

8. Thomas Kane was the vicar of Leigh from 1924 to 1938. The vicarage, where Denton frequently stayed as a boy and as a young man, was destroyed by fire in 1972.

As he left the house his head was full of ideas on how he would renovate it if it was his, 'ruthlessly sweeping away the waitresses, the laced parchment lamp-shades, the wicker furniture and the food counter'. He remounted his bicycle, pedalled down the drive, and took the road for Beckenham and Bromley. A summer heat-haze was beginning to shimmer on the grass and the trees, and he thought to himself as he cycled along a straight, wide road, 'keeping close to the kerb, not looking behind or bothering about the traffic at all', how very easy and pleasant the ride had been so far.

FIVE

The Accident

'A voice through a great cloud of agony and sickness' was the first thing Denton registered when he regained consciousness. A policeman was asking him his name, where he lived, where he was going. Denton could hear the fright in his voice, which sounded to him like the opening and closing of a concertina. 'The notes were loud, as the swelling notes of an organ, then they melted to the tiniest wiry tinkle of water in a glass.' He could feel the blades of grass on his neck, but he could not move. 'Everything about me seemed to be reeling and breaking up. My whole body was screaming with pain, filling my head with its roaring, and my eyes were swimming in a sort of gum mucilage.' He tried desperately to answer the policeman's questions – 'I told myself that I must give him the right answers at once' – but he had no real control over his voice, and as the shaken policeman bent over him, 'I felt the boiling and seething rise in me. It was drowning my brain, beating on it, plunging over it, shattering it. The earth swung, hovered, leaving my feet in the air and my head far below. I was overcome and drowned in waves of sickness and blackness.'

The account comes from *A Voice Through a Cloud*, Denton's third and last novel, which he began writing in 1944 and left unfinished at his death in 1948. In it he recorded the long months he spent in hospital and a nursing home, and his re-telling of the immediate circumstances of the accident itself is one of the most moving and painful episodes in autobiographical literature.

A car, probably going at some speed, had collided with him on the road. The extent of his injuries was so great that it is likely that the car wheels actually went over his body, for in addition to a broken ankle and extensive bruising, he sustained a fracture of the spine. The initial effect of the fracture was to render him for some months completely paralysed from the chest downwards. He retained the free use of his arms, and although he was eventually able to walk again, he did so

with a form of spastic paralysis. The most serious long-term effects of
the fracture, because of the resulting paralysis of the bladder, were
infections of the bladder and kidneys. These infections caused feverish
attacks, often of acute severity, accompanied by blinding headaches. His
blood pressure, too, became abnormally high; indeed, his death certificate
gave high blood pressure, coupled with pyelitis (inflammation of the
pelvis of the kidney), as the cause of death.

In the initial stages of paralysis he had no control over his bowels
or his bladder, though he was taught during convalescence to drain his
bladder reasonably satisfactorily by applying pressure to his stomach.
Later, he was condemned to wear a catheter. To add to his worries,
haemorrhaging developed in 1944, but perhaps the most emotionally
searing consequence, as it might be for any man, again resulting from
the paralysis, was partial impotence.[1] In spite of these appalling injuries
and the distressing complications that inevitably set in, he lived for
another thirteen years. That he survived for so long was not as a result
of any special medical treatment, but because through the vital
encouragement of his doctor, John Easton, and the love of his closest
friend, Eric Oliver, he was able to harness to a mind already possessed
of great moral courage a remarkable and previously untapped reserve
of physical stamina. Although he sometimes longed for death and
confidently expected it, until the very last moment he quite simply
refused to die.

The writing of A Voice Through a Cloud was a means of exorcizing
the trauma of the accident and of coming to terms with its effects. His
other references to his terrible fate, while fairly rare, show how bitter
he was to have had his life blighted by it. On 11 February 1944 he
wrote in his journal, 'Nothing can make up for the fact that my very
early youth was so clouded with illness and unhappiness. I feel cheated
as if I had never had that fiercely thrilling time when the fears of childhood have left one and no other thing has swamped one.' On the ninth
anniversary of the accident he simply wrote, 'What a day of aching
and giving up! The day nine years ago on which I was run over and
my health ruined for ever.' And on 7 April 1946 he wrote, with an
element of self-mockery which so often came to his rescue, 'If a silly

1. His friend Helen Roeder recalls Denton in 1941 saying, with some show of
vehemence, that although people said he was impotent it was not true; Eric Oliver,
who as his lover was in a unique position to know, reports that he could achieve an
erection but not an orgasm.

woman in a car ten years ago had driven straight instead of crooked I should not be whining till I'm stiff all through.'

On the day of the accident he had been taken to Lewisham Hospital, where no one seems to have appreciated the intensity of the pain he was suffering. 'I tried to tell myself that the agony was not real,' he wrote in *A Voice Through a Cloud*, 'that I would wake up to find it a dream. It seemed too violent and extraordinary to be real; but then I knew that it was real and that the comforting thought was the lie.' He very soon succumbed to the demands hospitals make upon their patients, to behave as if they are not ill at all, and when his aunt Edith and his cousin Bernard Kane arrived he told himself, 'I must behave normally, brightly, intelligently. The idea of proper behaviour obsessed me.' But the pain, when he was conscious, was real enough, and the sympathy of the nurses was almost non-existent. 'One pain inside me began to conquer all the others,' he wrote. 'I did not know what was happening. When I could bear it no longer, I cried out to the nurses, but they were as stern and unbending as Roman matrons. They told me not to be silly and not to make a fuss.'

The fact that it was his bladder that was the cause of the pain slowly dawned on one of the nurses, and after further intolerable delay a male orderly arrived to fit a catheter. 'It seemed an extraordinary thing to be doing,' Denton wrote. 'I felt that I ought perhaps to resent his taking such strange liberties with my body when I was defenceless.' But 'the relief, when it came, was so enormous that I forgot for a moment all my other pains; and in that moment I loved the man better than anyone else on earth and felt that I could never thank him enough for what he had done'.

When the pain grew intense again, 'like some huge grizzly bear' taking him between its paws, he screamed from the sheer shock of its sudden violence. '"Stop it,"' two nurses said together. '"You'll wake the others."' But there was nothing he could do to stop himself shrieking, feeling that if he bore the agony a moment longer it would split his skin. Eventually he became too much for them, and while one attempted to hold him down, the other gave him a pain-killing injection. At first Denton did not believe in the power of the syringe, 'but the moment she pricked me so heartlessly, pushing the needle right in with vicious pleasure, I had faith; I knew that it was magic'.

Next morning, when a nurse came to wash him, Denton began to realize the extent of some of his injuries. There were cuts on his chest and in his groin that had required stitching and dressing, one leg was in a splint from the knee downwards which, when the bandages were taken off, he could see was 'the deepest plum colour, with a sort of cerulean blue and a mustard yellow in it, too', and his ankle was swollen 'to the size of a young tree trunk'. He was unable to move either leg, 'but they were both filled with a biting, bristling tingle which never left them, and the pain in the broken ankle was like fire'.

When the nurse touched the flesh of his bruised leg, 'it yielded in just the way that a wine jelly yields to the pressure of a spoon'. Then began the ordeal of refitting the splint. 'I told the nurse that I could not bear so tight a bandage on my terribly bruised leg. She said that the splint had to be tied tightly and that I was not to try to teach her her own business.'

'"Don't,"' Denton implored. '"You can't, Nurse!"'

'"Can't what?"' she asked, affronted. '"This is the right way to do it. I've got too much to do to waste my time playing about. Just you show me what you're made of instead of creating."'

The next torture in store was a trip to the X-ray department. Denton was transported on a trolley by two porters, and he decided that there was nothing left for him to do but to yell if the pain became too strong. As the porters lifted him they said things to quieten him, 'for they saw that I was as raw as a piece of butcher's meat'.

Afterwards he asked if a friend of his could be telephoned from the hospital to come to see him, and while he waited for her he began to brood on his situation: 'I thought of eating delicious food, wearing good clothes, feeling proud and gay, going for walks, singing and dancing alone, fencing and swimming and painting pictures with other people, reading books. And everything seemed horrible and thin and nasty as soiled paper. I wondered how I could ever have believed in these things, how I could ever for a moment have thought they were real. Now I knew nothing was real but pain, heat, blood, tingling, loneliness and sweat. I began almost to gloat on the horror of my situation and surroundings. I felt paid out, dragged down, punished finally. Never again would my own good fortune make me feel guilty. I could look any beggars, blind people in the face now. Everything I had loved was disgusting; and I was disgusting, too.'

Clare, the friend for whom he had asked, was, like many of the people he knew, a Christian Scientist. His thoughts had fixed on her because he longed to be told to get up and walk, but now that she was standing by his bed, 'she said little or nothing to me, because she was so busy denying the power of evil'. After Clare had gone, the pain from the tightly bound splint on his leg became so unbearable that he decided to undo the bandages. 'I was delighted to see how quick and nimble my fingers were,' he wrote. 'All the rest of my body seemed spoilt, but these and my arms still acted perfectly.'

It was not long before his misdeed was discovered. '"Maurice, you are a naughty boy,"' the sister told him, using the name on the hospital records. '"I didn't expect this sort of thing from you. It's not good enough. We do all that work for you and this is your return!"'

The sister held the splint against his leg while another nurse bound it on again. 'I was past imploring,' he wrote. 'I bit my tongue hard, to give myself another pain to think of.'

As soon as she had gone he again worked loose the knots. 'I seemed to have no compunction left, nor did the thought of the consequences trouble me. My present pain was the only important thing.'

The scene that night, when his second disobedience was discovered, shook him. He was even made to cry. 'The matron herself was brought to stand over me and intimidate me. The nurse who readjusted the splint fixed it so that the knots were at the ankle, out of my reach; for I could not sit up or move my legs. She pulled fiercely on the knots, making them into balls as hard as oak-apples.'

Another pain-killing injection was administered, but long before dawn its effect began to wear off, and he experienced a strange sensation of departure from his body such as people on the verge of death have described. 'I was lost and obliterated,' he wrote. 'I seemed to be hovering in the air, looking down on the row of beds. I suddenly saw myself lying in one of the beds. I could tell myself perfectly, by the nose, the throat, and the tight-curled matted hair. I sailed through the air, so that I hovered directly above myself in the bed. Then began an extraordinary sort of elastic play between myself in the air and myself on the bed. It was like nothing so much as the bouncing and springing of a tennis-ball fixed to a long piece of rubber.'

When he came out of his trance he was comforted, briefly, by the night nurse, who came to him and held his hand. 'She bent closer and I saw her worried frown. She tried to withdraw her hand, but I clung to it desperately. She said, "Don't", and left her mouth half open after the words. She was uneasy.

'Suddenly she pulled away her hand, whispering at the same time, "I'll bring you some hot milk."

'While she was away I thought she must be a very new nurse; she had not yet become inhuman, but was trying to learn the trick.'

The night nurse brought the milk, telling Denton to try to sleep and not to make any more noise. '"You've got to think of the others, you know," she said mechanically. I waited, wondering how to make her more human and real.

'The next moment she had slipped away from me into the dark. I was left to face the blackness alone. I could trust no one and no one would help me. My fears and bewilderment came flooding back. I cried out many times. I cried madly again and again.'

The next day, the splint was taken off his leg and replaced with a cast. 'As I felt the plaster hardening, I became filled with a sort of panic,' he wrote. 'I would never be able to get at the leg again, never be able to ease the pain and tingle by undoing the bandages.

'Sister and nurse seemed pleased with their work. As if by echoing my thoughts, Sister said: "You won't be able to do anything about *that*."' Then, in accordance with hospital custom, which decrees that physicians require to be placated by cleanliness and obedience, she told him to keep himself tidy – because the doctor was coming to see him. The doctor arrived, accompanied by some students, and asked a few desultory questions without appearing much interested in Denton's replies. Some of the students scribbled notes on little pads while others picked their noses. 'They were stupid bullocks following a dispirited bull,' thought Denton.

His first cheerful moment in hospital came when he was visited by Betty Swanwick (in *A Voice Through a Cloud* she is called 'Betsy'), and another girl, Cora, from the art school, bearing books and a bunch of roses. The two girls failed to disguise their immediate shock at seeing his face, one of them exclaiming, '"Sonny Boy!"' with a mixture of horror and what he described as 'a peculiar sort of amusement' in her voice.

'I said, "What's it like, Betsy? What's wrong? Show me quickly in your mirror."

'I was all agog to see the damage to my face. I wasn't afraid, but interested and amused.'

'Betsy opened her bag to take out her mirror, then turned suddenly to Cora and said, "Do you think I ought to?"'

Denton snatched the mirror from her hand, and looked at his face. 'I was unrecognizable,' he wrote. 'My eyes, tiny and slit-like, were sunk in two bulging purple velvet cushions. A forked cut, like red lightning, spread right across my forehead and down my nose. On my head were cuts, surrounded by large bald patches where the hair had been snipped away. The rest of the hair stood up in isolated curls and jagged tufts.

The parts of my face that were not purple or red were dyed brilliant sulphur-yellow.'

The two girls boosted his morale, however. 'I felt very gay with Cora and Betsy,' he wrote. 'They brought back my active life so vividly that it seemed all wrong for me to be lying in bed, unable to move my legs. I refused to believe that I should be in this condition for long. I told myself with only the slightest hint of defiance that I would be up and about in a week or a fortnight.' If not quite up and about, he was soon feeling active enough to take up his sketching again, filling nineteen pages of a little brown sketch-book with pencil drawings.[2] He also had another visit from Clare, who now came bearing copies of the Bible and Mrs Eddy's *Science and Health* (in which are set out the teachings of Christian Science), having selected appropriate passages to incant over him. The words she had chosen seemed to Denton 'wonderful, deep, true, like poetry and music. She denied the reality of all physical ills with such a pugnacious determination, such violence of feeling, that I might have been alarmed if I had not been exalted.' When it occurred to him to question why he had not been healed at once, he thought it was because of his own laziness and disbelief; in later life, while rejecting Christian Science because he recognized that for him it did not work, he retained, so some of his friends believed, a vestige of loyalty to the faith, always feeling a little guilty about consulting doctors.

Bill, who had been away for the Whitsun weekend in the country, came straight to the hospital when he heard about the accident. Looking around the old infirmary 'with a sort of expressionless distaste', he kept saying, '"We'll get you out of this, we'll get you out of this"', though there was no question of moving Denton anywhere in his present condition. Bill told him of the intention of the police to prosecute the motorist, talking about solicitors and barristers in a way that half interested Denton and half repelled him; as he could not remember the accident he wanted to feel outside it and beyond it, free, at least in thought, from its grim sordidness.

What Bill was clearly trying to do was to tidy everything up, because that was the only way he knew how to behave. Although he did not love Denton, he felt it to be his duty to act the responsible older brother. For all his shortcomings in Denton's eyes, he did manage to obtain for Denton £8,000 in compensation which was to provide the basis of his

2. He later annotated the sketch-book, now in the Denton Welch Collection in the University of Texas, with the words, 'Done in my first days in the hospital, June 1935'.

modest income for the rest of his life. This was supplemented by an allowance of £300 a year from his father, though that was to cease on his father's death in Japanese hands in 1942, and later by fees and royalties derived from sales of his paintings, short stories and books.

It also fell to Bill to break the news to Denton that a bone in his spine – a little one, Bill said – had probably been bruised or fractured, and that a specialist was to be called in to examine him. 'He spoke lightly and hurriedly,' wrote Denton, 'as if my trouble were no more than a cold in the head. I knew that he was trying not to alarm me, doing all in his power to help.'

Next to visit him was Evie Sinclair – 'Miss Hellier' in *A Voice Through a Cloud*. 'She wore her tight black turban, her short shaggy black jacket made of astrakhan cloth. But she didn't look hot; her face was calm and pale. Her deep-brown eyes looked from side to side with unconcern; she might have been at a fruit and vegetable show, glancing at the marrows and the pears as she passed.' She had brought him some of his favourite foods, chicken essence, Ovaltine and chocolates, and as a Christian Scientist she too assumed not only that he would be hungry but that he would be up and about again in a few days' time.

Some weeks later, when the cuts had healed and the plaster-cast had been removed, the first stages of physiotherapy were introduced. 'I began to be massaged by a tall man with very large arms,' Denton wrote. 'His body and face were flat and broad. The great arms hung down loosely. When he set to work, he rolled up the sleeves of his starched white coat with a sort of lazy, bullying pride. He put lavender talcum powder on his hands before he began to knead me.'

He would start on Denton's arms, but as these were unharmed he soon passed to the back and legs. 'He would turn me over and rub and press and stroke my spine, my ribs, my shoulder-blades; then he would pummel me until my flesh shook.

'When he reached my still bruised and tingling legs, I held my breath. Sometimes he dealt roughly with them and I would be ready to cry out as he pressed down hard on the bone under the flesh; but the next moment I would be soothed by the rhythm of his movements. The pain itself became almost a sharp pleasure.'

This treatment after such a serious accident may seem drastic, but the fact remains that, in spite of relapses and periods of incapacity, and the inexorable deterioration of his condition over the remaining years of his life, he nevertheless recovered the ability at times to walk, run, cycle and drive a car. That he escaped the accident with his life was fortuitous; that he made a recovery, even if partial, such that many people who met him were unaware that he was semi-invalid, was little short of a miracle.

Like most patients who spend any length of time in hospital, he was in danger of becoming institutionalized. While he was being massaged he had to listen – perhaps not entirely unwillingly – to gruesome hospital tales, and in the wards at night he would sometimes be kept awake by the sound of people dying, so that finally, when the noise stopped, he would sink into a heavy sleep, 'free at last of the terrible human foghorn'.

He began to envy 'everything that moved on its own feet freely. To be able to walk and run with ease seemed the chief delight of life. Without this foundation nothing else seemed worth very much.

'Clare, who came to see me so often, and who insisted with such force that nothing but good had any real existence, filled me with some of her own fire, so that I found myself saying over and over again, "Today I shall walk. Nothing can stop me. I shall get up and amaze them all."'

Before he had time to fulfil this wish – it was barely a month since the accident – he was moved to the National Hospital for Nervous Diseases in Queen Square, Bloomsbury, so that he could receive specialist care more conveniently. On the way there, he wrote, 'I suddenly became greedy for the life of the streets,' wishing that the ambulance would go slower. He found a strange reception committee waiting for him when he arrived at the hospital, three girlfriends of Bill's who had been sent along to see him settled in. 'The fact that I hardly knew them, that they had come to please him, made the situation false to me,' Denton wrote. 'As the stretcher was carried out of the ambulance, the girls all smiled and called out gaily. I felt bound to respond, although I could only think of myself as a loaf of bread being lifted out of the back of a baker's van on a wire tray.'

His first impression of the new hospital was that the ward seemed much quieter, but he soon learned that the style of nursing was much the same as he had been used to. Still suffering dreadful pain, he began to drum wildly on his chest to distract his mind from it. 'The nurse who had come into the ward to take temperatures found me beating a mad tattoo and humming.

'"Well, and what's wrong with you?" She spoke disdainfully, as if she suspected all men of trying to take "liberties" with her.'

There was also 'a good Irish nurse ... plump and comely', whom

Denton soon came to like for her 'boisterous, easy-going efficiency'. One day, however, while washing him, she left him for a moment:

'While she was away, I decided to try and help by going on with the washing myself. I threw back the towel in which she had draped me and started to rub myself all over with the soapy flannel.

'In the middle of my washing she returned and saw me lying on the bed quite naked. This did not perturb me, I had long ago grown used to living in public; but the face of the Irish nurse stiffened. She seemed to bristle.

'She, who had always seemed so broad and lively and careless, now startled me by exclaiming; "Maurice! What is this? What do you mean by it? You must never appear like that before me again." She quickly threw the towel across and started to scrub me punishingly.'

At first he thought the nurse was having him on. Then it occurred to him, to his acute embarrassment, that she must have thought he had thrown the towel off for her benefit. 'She really believed that I enjoyed being washed, that I took pleasure in lying naked on a bed before her. If she could but know how, deep down, I hated to be touched.'

He was again X-rayed, this time for the benefit of the specialist under whose care he was now placed. Just as he was wondering how much longer he could bear the hardness of the table on which he had to lie, the woman radiologist came towards him 'purposefully, her eyes taking no notice of me except as part of her day's work.

'She stood beside me with a frown on her face. She seemed to be considering some problem.

'Suddenly, without any warning, she gave my body a sharp little jerk which sent such agony through me that I screamed out in distraction. Sweat broke out all over me; I lay there, wondering what the woman would do next. She had me there alone, I could do nothing but beg her not to jerk me again.

'The woman, after the first shock of my screams, said; "Oh, I never pinched you! Fancy making all that fuss! I never pinched you."

'Again she tweaked my body into the position she desired and again I yelled out uncontrollably.

'This time she said nothing aloud, but muttered under her breath as she went about her business. Her movements were fierce and flapping. I guessed that she was taunting me for my weakness, blaming me for adding to the difficulty of her day.

'Through my pain I remember wondering why she denied pinching me when I had made no mention of pinching.'

When he returned to the ward he was violently sick, and a male nurse called Hardy, the nurse he liked best, came to his assistance. 'How strangely the strong black bristles swept back behind his ears!' he noted. 'They were like thousands of tiny birds' legs tucked up for flight.'

In order to escape from the horror of the ward, which was inhabited mainly by patients with nervous conditions and was even swept by epileptic maids, Denton invented for himself a number of reveries, one of which consisted of imagining that he was sitting down to a table spread with delicious food: 'a large speckled brown egg, some thin golden toast, curls of fresh butter sprinkled with dewdrops and resting on ice, translucent jam made from white cherries, and a squat silver pot filled with a foaming mixture of milk and coffee'. He also made friends with a boy of about eighteen called Ray, who had been operated on for a brain tumour and was having difficulty articulating his thoughts. One day Ray asked Denton to help him re-learn the alphabet, so Denton spent part of each day with him, encouraging him to talk again and to recognize written language. When Ray left the hospital he gave Denton an address to write to. Denton did write but received no reply, and shortly afterwards one of the nurses told him that Ray had died.

'The futile ending of Ray's life dismayed me,' he wrote. 'We both had felt the savage change from fair to dark.' He thought of Ray all day, 'and hugged the dread and fear which my thoughts bred'. Ray's bed was now occupied by an old man who just lay there, staring at the ceiling, his hands plucking the sheets aimlessly. 'I thought of the many people who had said to me, "You're young; you've got plenty of time to recover." This seemed the coldest comfort, the grimmest fact of all.'

A new night nurse appeared on the scene, whose face 'was the colour of newspaper that has been spread on a shelf in the attic', and who was planning to leave the medical profession to become a Roman Catholic priest. One night, still suffering from disturbed sleep, Denton began to talk out loud. '"Shut that bloody row, do you hear!"' hissed the future ordinand.

'This sudden violence,' Denton wrote, 'instead of waking me properly, threw me into an even greater state of confusion. I must have called out again, for the next thing I knew was that the nurse had caught hold of my shoulders and shaken me, knocking me from one side of the bed to the other. He ended by slapping my face. In a still moment of realization, he stared down at me, savouring what he had done. There seemed to be a guiltiness and delight in his face. I stared back at it blankly, until I was swamped in rushes of pain and could see nothing.

'Once more I told myself always to expect evil. I had imagined human hearts as dried and shrivelled frogs before; now I thought of them as daffodil bulbs treacherously plump, full of black rottenness.'

The death one night of an old man in the ward gave him some cause for comfort. 'I saw that it was best to die at night – more beautiful in the darkness, with only the lamps; the traffic stiller in the city, and most people asleep, or cut off by the meltingly soft black veil.

'I found that my fear of the night had turned back into the love I used to have for it when I was well and free and could walk over the wind-bitten grass or bicycle for miles down lanes that were almost tunnels.

'As I watched the screens round the death-bed, I noted how much glowing green colour there was: green cloth screens with the light behind, the translucent green shade of the night nurse's lamp. I had had green all round me when first I found myself in hospital; so this unsubtle, luminous grass green has become associated in my mind with death and disaster.'

It was only after some months in hospital that it occurred to Denton to wonder why the student he had seen most of at art school, Gerald – in *A Voice Through a Cloud* he is named 'Mark Lynch' – had not been to see him. Then one day he turned up, and Denton noted 'the tenseness of his expression and the lizard-like darting of his eyes. There was a sort of fluttering alarm in them which I had never seen before. I had remembered them only as bright and rather penetrating.

'He was upon me, almost, before he had recognized me. I called his name, and he started; then he came straight up to the bed, caught hold of my hand rather desperately and began to pump it up and down.

'"I've been looking for someone with no face or only half a face, and all the time you've been lying here looking more or less the same!" he exclaimed, stringing all his words together.'

Mark had been so afraid that he might have to confront drastic disfigurement that he had wasted most of the visiting time walking round Queen Square before plucking up courage to enter the hospital. Now that he was here he had no idea what to talk to Denton about, and then he felt guilty when the bell rang for visitors to leave. 'Once more he grabbed my hand and jerked it up and down; he muttered something about coming to see me again; then he was away, hurrying down the ward as if the police were after him.'

By the autumn, although after months in bed Denton weighed less than five stone and still could not walk, he was at last thought well enough to use a wheelchair. 'At first,' he wrote, 'when I was stood on my feet, the blood roared into them. They were bursting. My head turned. Black shutters slid over my eyes.

'The male nurse Scott tucked me into the chair and wheeled me down the ward. I gazed at the other patients, so much closer to me now, and I could hardly believe in them or in the movement of the chair. Nothing was real. I was wrapped in a dream of warped images. Nurse Scott seemed hairier and swarthier than a monkey, and his starched coat seemed to be made of harsh plaster.

'"I can't sit up any more," I said, suddenly desperate to get back to bed, to lie flat and shut my eyes.

'"Nonsense," Scott said, "of course you can sit up; and whether you can or not, you're going to. You've got to begin some time."

'"Take me back!" I called out helplessly, with futile anger.

'"Don't be silly, now, Maurice. We don't want any fuss, so just make up your mind."

'I began to cry with rage. I longed to be able to get up, hit Scott, smash the chair to pieces and walk out for ever; but I was helpless and in his hands.'

Shortly after this the ward went into quarantine as a result of an outbreak of diphtheria, and Denton wrote a frantic letter to Bill asking him to try to make arrangements for him to leave as soon as the period of quarantine was over. Meanwhile, visitors were not allowed in and could only wave to the patients through the window. Denton had two unexpected visitors during this time, a distant cousin who brought crystallized fruits, 'and waved and laughed, as if the whole situation was outrageously droll', and a mysterious man, 'sleek and elderly and a little fanatical', who wore a carnation in his buttonhole. He scribbled a message on a piece of card: '"I have been specially sent by your mother,"' it read.

From Bill arrived a parcel containing a book on English china, three bottles of sherry and a letter, which Denton felt sure contained disappointing news, the presents being intended merely to soften the blow. When he forced himself to open the letter he learned that the book and the sherry were from a friend of Bill's of whom he had never heard, and that once he was out of quarantine he was to be moved 'to a town on the south-east coast where an uncle of ours lived'. The town was Broadstairs, and the uncle was Sir Percy Fox who, after suffering his stroke in Peking, had retired from the diplomatic service to live in England.

'With the first shock of pleasure,' Denton recorded, 'was mixed an uncomfortable fear of new surroundings, and a curious regret for things I did not care about.' He even began to regret that there would be no more visits from the hospital chaplain, who had intoned, '"Poor boy!"' while fondling Denton's hand 'with a sort of panic-stricken pity'. And he would never again see 'the rather mad visitor with her basket of everlasting flowers', in the heart of each posy a little flag bearing sacred words. '"That's for you," she had said, handing me one with much satisfaction. I had seldom seen a woman quite so certain of herself. She was gone without another glance or word. No human contacts for her. She was a quite impersonal well-doer.'

Several nights before the date of his departure he made his first efforts to walk. 'When I was first helped out of bed, I stood and willed my feet to move. Nothing happened; I just swayed and caught the nurse's hand. But on the second night I felt my slipper slithering over the floor. It soon stopped, but I had forced one foot forward one inch.'

At last the day came for him to leave the National Hospital and to travel by ambulance to the Southcourt Nursing Home in Broadstairs.[3] Clare came to accompany him, and they drove first to his lodgings in Croom's Hill. The ambulance men put him into what he described as a miniature sedan chair and carried him into the house, where he was able to revel in the rediscovery of his treasured possessions. By hanging on to the furniture he managed to get round his room, packing three pieces of his favourite china in a suitcase with his clothes. Then he was taken in the ambulance to Broadstairs, by the same road along which he had cycled that fateful Whitsun weekend.

The door of the nursing home, 'a grey, rough-cast house' with white balconies, was opened by the matron, Miss Widdop, one of two sisters who owned the home. Denton was carried in to a room with a high, white bed, beetroot-pink curtains, a french window 'as big as a garage door' and a log fire that scented the air with smoke. Although he found the room ugly, he at least appreciated having it to himself. After the public wards of the hospitals the stillness fascinated him: 'no footsteps in the ward, no calling, groaning, crying, swearing, snapping, laughing, joking – only the sound of the wind and the fire and perhaps the distant mumble of the sea'.

3. The Southcourt Nursing Home was situated on the corner of Ramsgate Road and Swinburne Avenue, not far from the railway station. It continued as a nursing home until 1951, when it became a National Sunday School Union Holiday Home. The building has now been converted into flats.

He found himself torn by conflicting emotions. 'The stillness in the room was balm,' yet it frightened him; he longed for the reassuring noise of the ward. He felt isolated, yet it was a feeling that he cherished. And, as ever, food was the great compensation for all his ills: 'Every other feeling was swallowed up in the importance of food. Nothing else mattered for the moment; the pleasantness of life seemed largely to depend on the goodness of the meals. I thought of the evil hospital food and enjoyed my shudders.'

Later that evening, a local G.P., Dr Hugh Raven, came to see him. He talked about religion, about 'lunch with the Archbishop' (Cosmo Lang), and about a poem he had written on Ethiopia, smiling to himself as he spoke, as if the memory of his lines pleased him. 'Then he whipped back the bed-clothes, examined me in a flash and was gone.'

Denton's first visitor at the nursing home was Lady Fox, who arrived on the first morning accompanied by her smoke-coloured chow and an invalid pekinese called Baby. (At home she had a collection of five hundred Chinese jade and glass dogs, many of which had come out of Christmas crackers.) Her visit transported him at once to his childhood, 'to the days when a visit from her meant everything delightful'. But her visits also tended to be fleeting, and no sooner had she and the dogs settled down than up she jumped, exclaiming, '"We two must have a long talk soon; we've got *so* much to say to each other!"' With that, and with Baby tucked under her arm, she disappeared.

His next visitor was the ubiquitous 'Mark', now employed giving drawing lessons to the daughter of an admiral, and in the course of his gossipy, lengthy visit (clearly he did not find the nursing home as inhibiting as the Bloomsbury hospital) he entertained Denton with a story of the kind they both relished. At lunch one day with the admiral and his family in their Kensington flat, the cook had burst into the dining-room and had given her notice.

'"But why, cook, do you want to go?"' asked the admiral anxiously. '"Don't you like it here? Is there too much to do?"'

'"No, it isn't that, sir,"' said the cook, breathing hard. She seemed, Mark told Denton, to be keeping back something which caused her great agitation.

'"Then what is it?"' the admiral asked.

'"I'd rather not tell,"' said the cook.

'"Oh, come, cook,"' said the admiral. '"You can't leave us without telling us why."'

'"Well, if you must know,"' said the cook, '"there's a couple of young lady lovers next door to me, down below in the servants' quarters, and the walls are that thin I can hear every word, and I don't know what all besides! I don't like it, I can tell you – not a bit!"'

The cook then made a stately exit, leaving behind her a terrible silence. Eventually the daughter jumped up and whisked Mark into her own room, where the two of them exploded, 'rolling about in agonies of laughter'.

When Mark was about to go, Denton, by now able to walk a little, suggested going outside with him through the french window into the garden. Mark warned him that he ought not to go out, but Denton insisted, and 'walked very slowly down the grass path'. By nature independent and fond of his own freedom, it was of the utmost importance to him to regain the means to enjoy it. 'I was going out into the garden in pyjamas,' he wrote, 'obeying my own whim, and nobody had interfered with me. It was almost a forgotten experience.'

His walk in the garden with Mark was to precipitate his first meeting with the nursing home's other visiting physician, Dr John Easton, who is named 'Dr Farley' in *A Voice Through a Cloud*.[4] Dr Farley was coming out of the front door just as Denton was making his way back to his room. 'I stood still,' Denton wrote, 'my muscles taut for a fight, my mood broken to pieces. What did he want? What was he going to say?'

Denton described the doctor as he appeared then as 'tall and dark and dressed in dark clothes. His body seemed elastic but not light.' As he came nearer, 'I saw that he was looking into me with eyes that could not pierce, because they were too brown and soft, too like a stag's eyes. His chin was cleft, his lips square and good; but a harshness from nose to mouth reminded me of Charles the Second's portraits. His expression was too concentrated and searching. He did not conciliate me. I thought of him as an inquisitor; and, smiling with anxiety and annoyance, I lifted my head to confront him and keep him at bay.'

Denton's defensiveness dissolved as Dr Farley said to him, '"Hullo, I'm coming to see you tomorrow. My partner's going away for a few days."' Having expected grimness, the doctor's friendliness came as a shock to Denton. Dr Farley began to ask him about himself, and about

4. Denton took the name 'Farley' from the village of East Farley in Kent, where the friend of his last years, Eric Oliver, once worked. Dr Easton also inspired the character of the anonymous doctor in 'A Fragment of a Life Story', published in *A Last Sheaf*, and that of 'Jack' in 'Alex Fairburn', which exists as a manuscript in the Denton Welch Collection, University of Texas.

the London hospitals, and then he said, '"Well, you *have* had a bad time,"' evoking in Denton a feeling of pure pleasure. Before going to sleep that night he kept saying to himself, 'I wonder why I didn't like the look of him. What was wrong with him? Or is there something wrong with me? Am I suspicious of everybody?'

When Dr Farley came to examine him the next morning he seemed more than anything concerned that Denton was so thin, and promptly prescribed cream. Denton so wanted him to stay for a while that he began to talk very quickly and animatedly, dreading the doctor's departure. The rest of the day seemed to threaten him: 'Empty and hollow, it stretched before me without end. I half wished that he had not made me more aware of his interest, his kindness, that I had been left in the shell I had grown.'

Dr Farley was popular with everyone. The matron, 'flicking her eternal ladylike duster', asked Denton one day, 'saucily over her shoulder', how he liked his new doctor. Later that day Lady Fox returned, and remarked, '"Oh, Dr Farley is a darling."'

As part of his treatment Dr Farley had suggested that Denton should practise walking, so every afternoon he went out with one of the nurses. Supported on two sticks, he made his slow progress along the pavement outside the nursing home.

Bill, who was staying with Lady Fox, came to visit him, but as usual their meeting was a dismal affair. Standing dejectedly by the window, Bill asked again and again if Denton had everything he wanted, if he liked the nursing home, if there was anything he could do for him in London. 'But all the time his eyes were fixed rather desperately on the dying stalks of the flowers, the scatter of yellow leaves over the grass and the beds, the holes in the thatch of the summer-house where the birds had nested.'

When a nurse brought in tea Denton thought, 'Now something may melt, something may happen; we may be able to talk', but seeing Bill hurry through his rock-cake and gulp down the hot tea, he realized that nothing could be done. 'I sat still, just dully waiting for him to go. Even my anger and sorrow at the failure were becoming clouded and submerged.'

Although Bill's visit at first left Denton feeling drained, it did galvanize him into a desire to escape the institutional world of hospitals. 'I saw all at once that visits, either pleasant or painful, were beginning to leave me with this sensation of power gone, of lack and dislocation. It was the sensation of the prisoner growing in me. I felt that the room, the house, the garden and the strip of road outside were as poisoning as iron-spiked walls. I must get out and away from them. I must go down to the front and see my aunt and brother again; for although we had only just parted and our meeting had come to nothing, I had a sudden longing to be with them, to stay with the people who had known me all my life. If I could do that, the rat that was gnawing me inside might stop. It seemed the only possible thing to do.'

And so he set out, on his own and with only one stick, and somehow dragged himself as far as Lady Fox's house. By the time he arrived he was on the point of collapse, and Bill immediately rang for a taxi to take him back. 'I felt like a present being posted back ungratefully before even the seal had been broken,' Denton wrote. Back at the nursing home he was put to bed in disgrace. 'My feet were walking still but burning, and my mind still desperate with the problem of reaching my goal. I was so tired that I had travelled far beyond rest. To lie down and be still was a torture, but to move about any more would have been impossible.

'I began to long, as I had before, for some special smell, some special music that would fill me and carry me away, float me off the rocks of my body and sweep me into some wideness, some vast expanse of blue-grey nothingness.'

The ill-effects of his excursion, which had given him a high temperature and had caused his ankle to swell again, making it impossible for him to have his usual massage, kept him in bed for a fortnight. Dr Farley merely commented, '"What a fool to overdo things like that!"'

The time in bed was whiled away by another visit from Mark and by the loan of a gramophone from Dr Farley. When the doctor seemed a little ashamed of liking Tchaikovsky, Denton 'felt sorry to see his uncertainty; it shook my confidence a little. I wanted someone who was sure of everything he said and did.'

As soon as he had recovered sufficiently, Dr Farley invited him out for a drive in his car. They drove down to the beach. 'How slowly I walked!' Denton wrote. 'My legs were hung with chains and I dragged my prisoner's iron ball behind me. I tried to breathe deeply and give no hints of gasping or panting.' The doctor noticed and took his arm, making him feel 'almost bitter at so much watchfulness and under-standing'. Denton collected some shells and then they went to Dr Farley's house, where the maid produced toast and dripping for tea.

It was Dr Farley who first encouraged Denton to face the prospect of recovery and to consider the future. Before the accident, as a student, he had been shielded from the necessity to earn a living, and since then he had been cocooned for several months in hospitals. Lady Fox had only recently told him that when he was twenty-one he would inherit a small sum from his mother's Will, so the question was not so much one of how he would support himself in the immediate future as of a choice between pursuing his ambitions or settling into the sedentary life of an invalid. He tried to appear indifferent about the future, but Farley, not to be deflected, told him that he thought he was gifted. Denton wondered why he said this: 'What part of me displayed my gifts? My face, hands, behind, feet, hair? I did not feel gifted. I felt bereft, fleeced, defaced.'

Since there was little tangible evidence at this time of the gifts that were to blossom over the next few years in Denton's paintings and writings – his early paintings show few signs of promise, and Dr Easton is unlikely to have seen any of his written work other than perhaps a few poems – the doctor's intuition of his potential was as remarkable as it was fortuitous. Though Denton felt that he was being pushed into making efforts he did not want to make, something nevertheless did begin to stir in him, 'to gain a little confidence and warm itself in his encouragement'. He at once began to paint the shells he had collected on the beach. It was the first painting he had attempted since his accident.

Soon afterwards, Dr Farley took Denton on another outing in his car, this time to visit an orphanage on his rounds. Denton waited in the car while the doctor went inside, and then saw him as he 'came out of the home smiling, as if all the boys had made him feel admired and waited for. I saw at once how delightful he would seem in a grim dormitory – really a golden person, warm and true all through, something that a child longed for, protection from matron, master or other orphans. His understanding and acceptance would enslave the boys, so that they talked of him until their keepers grew tired of the name. I thought of this charm, left behind in the home.'

At the same time as he was taking up painting again, Denton also began to write down some of his thoughts and observations, about the birds he could hear at night, the sounds of the sea and the lonely barking of a dog. 'I liked what I wrote in flashes; but something was wrong with it. There is always something wrong with writing. So I tore the paper up at last, liking the untouched memory much better, not wanting it forced into the insincerity of words.'

By now much better able to walk, he was soon venturing out on his own and going into the town by bus. On one occasion he paid a visit to Lady Fox's mother, Mrs Louisa Noott, who lived at Upton Lodge in Broadstairs. He had not seen her since he was six, and he now found her to be not only very rich (when she died the following year she left £126,858 in her Will) but down to earth and positive minded. She gave him tea and afterwards they smoked cigarettes. 'I was suddenly very pleased to be sitting there smoking with her,' he wrote. 'It was as if she had flattered me, treated me as a man with a great deal of good sense and experience. It was a very rare feeling, and I often wonder why it came. I suppose deep down she accepted me placidly, did not necessarily understand yet did not question; so this acceptance flowed out to me and I was warmed.'

As they walked across the lawn, Mrs Noott took Denton's arm in such a manner that he could not tell whether she was supporting him or he supporting her. She confided to him that she had been in touch with her dead son. 'I had not known,' Denton wrote, 'that my aunt's mother was in communication with the dead. Her conviction changed her for me. She seemed madder, less dignified, but more interesting.'

His response to this revelation was symptomatic of the nature of his interest in people generally, for he was particularly attracted to sane people who behaved eccentrically, and to the socially suave whose veneer could be scraped away to reveal the fascination even of phoneyness. Many of the people about whom he wrote were not only eccentric but often insincere or snobbish, and as he became more and more housebound through ill-health, anyone whose character was in any way suspect, or who appeared to be living dangerously or adventurously, became for him an object of interest as much for his writing as for his own vicarious experience of life. Indeed, in *A Voice Through a Cloud*, in a passage which most succinctly outlines this attraction, he wrote, 'It was to the outcasts and wanderers that I was attracted. I wanted to watch them without being seen. I wanted to know their thoughts without making close contact. I wanted to share without my body being present.' But he knew also that this desire was unrealistic, that he would have to compromise with the world of responsive human beings. In any case, as he says, 'Such cold, invisible spying was impossible; and so I found myself asked for cigarettes, asked for money, asked what I wanted and what I meant by staring.'

Now that he was out and about on his own again, he found that he was himself an object of interest once more, as he was reminded when, on one of his solitary promenades, he was approached by a tall young man who looked at him 'earnestly'. At first the man did not speak.

'Then he said slowly and impressively, "I'd do anything for a bob, I would."' Denton gave no hint in his account that he comprehended the meaning of that remark, even when the young man later told him how he liked life on the road, as '"You have some queer things happen to you. Had a woman ask me the other night to go down on the beach with her."

'"Did you go?" I asked.

'"Yus, and, what's more, she give me ten bob."'

At Christmas-time Mark came to stay, taking a room on the sea-front in a house mischievously named 'Lesbia'. He was due to go with Denton to lunch on Christmas Day with Sir Percy and Lady Fox, and he came first to the nursing home. He walked into Denton's room 'in his stealthy, off-hand way and said, "Here's a present for you."' It was a Victorian book of illustrated limericks. Oddly, Denton had not thought to buy a present for Mark, although he had purchased for Dr Farley a pair of hog-skin gloves lined with lamb's-wool, and it was rather unfortunate that the doctor should choose this moment to burst into the room and thank Denton for them.

All in all, the luncheon party could not be rated a success. For a Christmas present Lady Fox gave Denton a walking-stick which had a silver band with his initials engraved on it and, to his annoyance, also had a rubber ferrule on the tip. 'Did she imagine that I was to hobble and totter for the rest of my life?' he wrote. 'Even now, if I were careful, I could walk for short distances almost normally.' Then Mark, invited to inspect Lady Fox's youthful self-portraits, disgraced himself by saying, 'Of course they'd be very nice if they were at all like you.' The atmosphere at lunch was tense: 'The food had been good, but what of the human beings? We had all been dried up or dammed up, four *things* performing the ceremony of eating because it was one o'clock.' After lunch they drank their coffee 'in a sort of reverent silence' while they listened to the king's speech, 'afraid even that our spoons might make a distracting tinkle', and while the king was speaking, Sir Percy, confined to a wheelchair since his stroke in China, quietly began to cry. 'I wondered why we weren't all crying to relieve the strain,' Denton sagely noted. On his way out through the hall after lunch, he noticed a stick which was identical to the one his aunt had given him, except that this one had a gold band inscribed with his uncle's initials. 'As I stared at them a sort of cold hatred possessed me.' When he reached the sea-front he threw the offending ferrule out to sea, and not long afterwards left the stick, 'by mistake', on the top of a bus.

Christmas 1935 was a crossroads for Denton, 'a point at which I gazed but could not look beyond, a full stop to the year and my catastrophe'. There now developed a tug-of-war over him between the matron, who advised him to remain longer in the nursing home, and Dr Farley, whose aim was to encourage him to stand on his own feet again and to make positive plans for the future. The matron warned him that he would have to be extremely careful, otherwise the consequences would be very serious indeed; Dr Farley may be a clever doctor and a very nice man, she said, but Denton was not to imagine that he understood all the intricacies of nursing. '"What utter nonsense!"' exclaimed Dr Farley when he heard what the matron had said.

A further spur to Denton to leave the nursing home as soon as possible came when Dr Farley broke the news that he would shortly be moving to another practice, and such was Denton's dependence upon him – emotional as well as medical – that his first thought was to find a cottage or flat near Farley's new practice. '"Then you could keep an eye on me,"' he told Farley, '"and I wouldn't have to start again with yet another doctor; I should hate that. To get out of that nursing home and have a little place of my own would be a great step forward for me."'

To Denton's delight, Dr Farley responded enthusiastically, and even suggested that he might stay with him and his wife until Denton found somewhere else.

The matron, meanwhile, was unaware of the doctor's intended departure and of Denton's determination to follow him, and Denton enjoyed the feeling of superiority that this privy knowledge gave him. In the course of his description of her in *A Voice Through a Cloud*, one of his most telling portraits, an interesting facet of his own personality emerges. In conversation with her one day, when he said to her, '"I must leave the nursing home one day,"' and she responded, '"Yes, of course, but why spoil the ship for a ha'porth of tar?"' he reflected on the way 'hackneyed images and proverbs have always had the power to jump suddenly alive for me. There is a click and I see the needle in the hay, the stupid one crying over the spilt milk, the stitch in time saving nine. So now I was vividly aware of myself as an old hulk, leaky and sinking, swarming with rats and covered with barnacles. I saw the crooked shipwrights pretending to repair me but spoiling me, all for a ha'porth of tar.'

The next to assail his plans to leave the nursing home was Bill, telephoning from London. 'Now,' wrote Denton, 'the real joy of persecution possessed me.' After arguing futilely with his brother (he was not yet twenty-one, so had not reached the age of majority) he slammed down the receiver. 'I held it down firmly, as if afraid it would jump off its stand and begin answering me back again. I imagined a murderer holding a baby's head under the black water of a midnight pool. It gave me a pleasure to silence my elder brother, to treat him like a baby and hold his head under the water. If he rang again, the tinkles would be like bubbles coming up to the surface to be laughed at demonically.'

Resentment then took hold of him and he wrote a furious letter to his brother, blaming him for all his misfortunes. Bill, wisely, did not reply, though before long Denton received a letter from Lady Fox in which she reminded him of the pains Bill had taken over his comfort and welfare, and suggested that she should purchase for Bill 'a really good gold watch' on Denton's behalf. As he let the note 'flutter down to the breakfast-tray like an enormous blue snowflake', he day-dreamed of writing to tell her of his real feelings for Bill, but then began to reflect that advice such as hers must always seem impertinent and ludicrous, 'just because of this impossibility of knowing another's mind'.

One night, shortly before leaving the nursing home, he took it into his head to go out for a walk, dressed in his slippers and dressing-gown. In the morning the matron warned him that he '"might be taken up by the police"' if he insisted on wandering around in his pyjamas, and Dr Raven, who was again in charge of him following Dr Farley's departure, asked him if he would like any bromide. Denton protested that bromide was only for dogs that had fits, but the doctor assured him it was for humans too. '"I don't think I'll have any now,"' said Denton firmly. He wanted to add, '"I don't quite *fancy* it at the moment,"' feeling that the word 'fancy' had just the right touch of cosy vulgarity and dottiness.

The sudden appearance of Miss Hellier (Evie Sinclair), dressed in a fur cape and a little felt hat, and looking, as Denton remembered, the very embodiment of Winter, was to be the turn in the wheel of fortune for which he was waiting. Fond of playing pranks, she now announced herself to the nurse as 'Miss Wilberforce', so that her entry into Denton's room was a double surprise. They went out together into the town, and over tea she told Denton that her brother, who owned 34 Croom's Hill, had more or less given her the sack for what he saw as the extravagant way in which she ran the house. The thought immediately struck Denton that if Miss Hellier was free, why should she not keep house for him? Her response to the suggestion was, '"Of course, there is nothing I should like better in the world."'

After tea they went into an antique shop where Denton bought for 5s. a broken enamel box with an inscription on the top which read, '"Accept this trifle from a friend, whose love for thee will never end"', and gave it to Miss Hellier. Only after she had caught her train back to London did he realize that they had not talked about where they were to live. Since his main concern was to remain close to Dr Farley, who had moved to a practice in Tonbridge, he was soon house-hunting in earnest in that area.[5] Arrangements were made for him to meet Miss Hellier at Dr Farley's new house and, defying prudence, he made the train journey there unaccompanied. He took the precaution of finding a compartment to himself so that he could lie down on the seat, and if he was suddenly taken ill, no one would know. 'I could even die there quite quietly,' he thought.

Eventually they found a suitable flat to rent, on the ground floor of an early Victorian house in Tonbridge, 54 Hadlow Road (by an extraordinary coincidence his great-grandfather, Joseph Welch, and for a time his grandfather, too, had also once lived in Hadlow Road, in Loampits House).

Of the move itself, and of Denton's farewell at the nursing home, nothing is known, for it was at this point that his own account of events, given in *A Voice Through a Cloud*, came to an end; he was to die before he could finish the book.

5. Dr Easton, whose practice was at 42 Pembury Road in Tonbridge, had been appointed a consultant at the Kent and Sussex Hospital and also as the doctor to Tonbridge School.

SIX

Tea with Sickert

While Denton was still convalescing at the nursing home, Dr Raven tried to persuade a newcomer to the area, the venerable and volatile painter Walter Sickert, to call on his young and friendless patient. Sickert declined to put himself about, apparently with the sharp retort, '"I have no time for district visiting."' Shortly before Denton left the home, however, someone else managed to arrange for the student to be invited to tea with the master. Denton was to store the memory of this visit for some years, and following Sickert's death in January 1942 he submitted to *Horizon* an article called 'Sickert at St Peter's'. It was the publication of this article in August that year that was to launch his literary career.[1]

Just as he was preparing to set out for Sickert's house, who should turn up at the home but 'Mark', who in the article is given his real name of Gerald. Denton told Gerald that he was just going out and asked what he would do while he was away. 'He gave me one rapid glance,' Denton wrote, 'and then said firmly: "I'll come too."'

Denton was horrified. '"But you haven't been asked!"' he burst out.

'"That doesn't matter,"' said Gerald, '"one more won't make any difference."' Feeling in no condition to argue, Denton allowed Gerald to join him in the aged taxi that took them off to tea.

The house Sickert had recently moved into with his third wife, Thérèse Lessore,[2] was still being altered. The two young men entered through what had once been the cloakroom, and Denton was a little shocked 'on being confronted with a glistening white "W.C."' as soon as the door was opened. This visit was memorable, too, for a song-and-dance

1. The date of composition of the article, which was reprinted in *A Last Sheaf*, is not known. In his journal on 13 July 1945 Denton recalled having attempted to write a story some time in 1940, which may possibly have referred to the Sickert article.

2. By a strange coincidence, Thérèse Lessore had previously been married to the painter Bernard Adeney, with whose second wife, Noël, Denton was later to establish one of his most complex relationships.

routine performed by the seventy-five-year-old painter, and for Sickert's unnerving final blast as Denton and his uninvited companion left by the stable-yard door: '"Come again when you can't stop so long!"' he shouted after them. 'At these words,' Denton wrote with a rare trace of self-pity, 'a strange pang went through me, for it was what my father had always said as he closed the book, when I had finished my bread and butter and milk, and it was time for me to go to bed.'

On 15 July 1936, the year Denton left the nursing home to live in Tonbridge with Evie Sinclair, his grandfather in Henfield died at the age of ninety-one. Joseph Welch's four children inherited about £6,000 each, and the spinster Aunt Dorothy celebrated her new-found freedom by going off on a world cruise. Denton was now more alone than ever, though he still had his aunt Edith and her husband Thomas to turn to, and he spent the Christmas of 1936 with them at Leigh Vicarage, the house he had been making for when he met with his accident. The following year saw another major change in the family when his father remarried. Like his mother, his new stepmother, Ada Henderson, was an American, she and his father having met in Shanghai in the course of business. Denton was never to meet her, but after his father's death, by which time money had become a serious problem for him, he grew obsessed with the idea that his stepmother had made off with his inheritance.

Denton's fortuitous meeting with Sickert was to be followed over the next two or three years by a considerable broadening of his social horizons, when for the first time he made friends with whom he could talk freely and who would help him cast off the painful shyness and insecurity that had inhibited his adolescence. It was probably in 1937 that he first made the acquaintance of his liveliest correspondent, Marcus Oliver, a friend of Gerald's who seems also to have known both of Denton's brothers. Marcus lived in the Earl's Court Road in London and worked for John Haig, the whisky distillers. Though he liked to parade as a dapper lady's man, his true predilections lay in the direction of what Denton would have understood as rough trade, and over the next decade he and Denton were to exchange scores of letters full of camp gossip, tittle-tattle and scandal. An insatiable importuner of letters from the famous, Marcus was in many ways ideal literary material for Denton, but he only once turned up in a short story, as 'Angus' in 'Memories of a Vanished Period', published posthumously in *A Lost Sheaf*, a tale that recounts an evening of drinking he and Denton shared in London during the war.

One of their favourite subjects for gossip was an eccentric character by the name of Francis Streeten, who was a mutual friend and who may even have introduced them to each other. Streeten lived in Tonbridge and first met Denton, as he recalled many years later in a letter to a friend, 'around Christmas 1937' when, it seems, they fell into conversation one evening in the bar of the Angel Hotel; he had heard about a 'mysterious artist in Hadlow Road' who 'was said to roam the countryside making ambiguous approaches to young rustics', and after a while he realized that Denton and the 'mysterious artist' were one and the same.[3] Unlike Marcus, Streeten certainly did provide Denton with literary material, a fact of which he was well aware, since in the same letter he acknowledged 'the rather invidious distinction' of being portrayed in 'as many as four of [Denton's] short stories (including one unfinished one that has not yet been published). I say "rather invidious" because, as you know, his portrayals tend to be highly uncomplimentary.' In 'A Fragment of a Life Story'[4] he appeared as Denton's 'curious fat friend Danny Touchett', and in 'A Picture in the Snow',[5] a story in which his alcoholic mother also made a smudgy appearance, he was ruthlessly portrayed, for all his friends to recognize, in the character of 'Danny Whittome'. Prone to giving off delicate little titters in his piping voice, Touchett/Whittome had little rhinoceros eyes, a pug nose brown at the end with tobacco smoke, and wore stained, grey flannel trousers held up by an old silk tie.

Streeten's fairly chaste account of how he first met Denton contrasts amusingly with the version contained in 'A Picture in the Snow', in a way that illustrates Denton's facility for juggling with the facts. The story describes how, as Denton was coming out of the public library one day, deep in his own thoughts, he became aware of footsteps behind him. 'They seemed to be hurrying, then a shadow loomed over me and I looked up to see a very tall, very plump man of about thirty-five[6] passing close to me on the pavement. As soon as he was a few yards in front, he seemed to slacken his pace, almost as if he were waiting for me to catch up with him. He ambled so slowly that I did indeed

3. Letter from Francis Streeten to Benjamin Whitrow, 10 May 1976. Streeten also claimed that, during the war, Denton's country rambles had once resulted in his being arrested and questioned as a suspected spy.

4. Published in *A Last Sheaf*. An extensive first draft exists in the journals.

5. *A Last Sheaf*.

6. Francis Streeten, who was nine years older than Denton, would have been thirty-one in 1937.

draw level with him in a moment. Before I knew quite what was happening he had turned, bent down towards me with a tentative smile, and was saying in a surprisingly baby voice: "Oh – you look interesting; do tell me about yourself."'

Reviewing the differences between Denton's account and his own memory, Streeten wrote in the same letter, 'We must have got on quite well at this first meeting [in the Angel Hotel] as I remember that later that evening we went across the road together to watch the closing scenes of a pantomime, so it is rather curious that we did not see each other again till the following summer, when we met on a bus and he invited me to his flat. His first visit to my home a few days later he described with almost meticulous accuracy in his short story "A Picture in the Snow", though for artistic unity he represents it as an isolated encounter between persons previously unacquainted.'

The unpublished short story to which Streeten referred earlier in his letter was called 'Constance Lady Willet', a pseudonym for Streeten's mother.[7] The fourth story in which he appeared, yet again as 'Touchett', had no title and was not published until after Denton's death.[8] In it Streeten was described as 'hugely fat and babyish, with extremely bad teeth and rather winning ways'. He was also made out to be mean, which is odd since the story centres on his having won £15 on the horses and having treated Denton and two other friends to dinner – in reality, at The Leicester Arms in Penshurst. One of the other two, 'Markham', was in fact Maurice Cranston, later in life a philosopher and writer. Maurice, who was eighteen at the time and was living in Tunbridge Wells, was one of the young and lively set Denton met while living in Hadlow Road. He had been introduced to Denton by Francis Streeten, and he and Denton soon formed a warm attachment to each other. He remembers Denton at this period looking 'like the young Benjamin Britten, without Britten's solemn expression, but with sparkling eyes, a boyish smile and a fresh, excited flush on his cheeks, like someone very slightly and very happily tipsy'.[9] Although Maurice, who was never quite certain whether or not Denton really liked him in spite of their close friendship lasting a decade, was someone about whom Denton felt quite at liberty to be rude when writing in his journal (at one time he virtually accused him of plagiarism), he became one of the few intimates with whom Denton felt able to let down his hair.

7. Denton Welch Collection, University of Texas.
8. It was published in *Chance* in 1953.
9. Letter from Maurice Cranston to the author, 19 February 1984.

Within a few years of their first meeting, Denton was writing to Maurice to say, 'I am interested to know that your girlfriend would like to meet a real, live fairy. I suppose she only counts you as semi-demi and, consequently, is not sufficiently thrilled. I shall be dressed to kill, laying on my chaise-longue and I shall level the most terrible abuse at her, calling her a stinking female and other complimentary things.' He modified his tone somewhat when writing to confirm arrangements for Maurice and his girlfriend to visit him in his new home, The Hop Field, a modern house in the village of St Mary's Platt, some eight miles north of Tonbridge, into which he moved with Evie Sinclair in January 1940 and which he promptly renamed The Hop Garden. 'I've had such a dose of queens, veiled and otherwise, lately,' he told Maurice, 'that perhaps an honest-to-God female might be quite novel.' In July that year he addressed an amusing letter to both of them: 'My dear Maurice and Helga, I was so surprised at your strange news and am wondering what it can feel like to be married. Ever so goosy, goosy, goosy, goo I expect! I shall never pluck up courage enough to marry anyone – *male* or *female*. I shall have to content myself with light flirtations all my life.' He was, as it turned out, being unduly pessimistic, for in 1943 the much-maligned Francis Streeten was to introduce him to someone who was destined to prove him wrong, Eric Oliver, who was to become his closest friend and to live with him for the last four years of his life.[10]

At this period Denton seems to have been testing the limits to which he could stretch the boundaries of good taste, experimenting in dress and manners and observing his effect on other people. One day when he was living at The Hop Garden, shortly after he had taken to wearing a gold-rimmed monocle on a string, he invited a young woman to inspect a drawing he had done of a man in a bowler hat performing fellatio on a boy. He stood watching the girl, measuring her reaction, but she, completely ignoring the work and instead looking directly at him, simply said, '"Denton, you shouldn't wear that monocle. It makes you look such a cunt."' And he never wore it again.

In spite of his new circle of sympathetic friends and his excursions into the highways and byways in search of adventure, Denton's years in Tonbridge were not among the happiest of his life. While a patient in the Southcourt Nursing Home, frightened, lonely, and at twenty-one quite unable to handle his emotions, he had fallen in love with Dr Easton.

10. Eric Oliver was not related to Marcus Oliver.

When writing on 9 February 1944 to Eric Oliver, with whom he was by then very much in love, he was to confess, 'I don't pretend that I would ever have loved you as insanely and unreasonably as I loved J.E. – that sort of thing only happens when one is very young, very ill, very lonely and very inexperienced.' Only two days after Easton had moved to Tonbridge from Broadstairs, he and his wife, alerted by the sound of crying, had discovered Denton staggering around outside their house, scarcely able to walk. Easton arranged for him to stay in a Tonbridge nursing home for the night, and the next day put him on a train to Broadstairs. Within hours Denton had made his way back to 42 Pembury Road.

When Denton moved into his flat in Hadlow Road he would visit Dr Easton's house at all hours of the day and night. If Easton was not at home he would even hide in the house until his return, sometimes being discovered by Mrs Easton, to whom Denton's behaviour was profoundly annoying. Finding no response to his passion, Denton took to throwing tantrums, clinging to the banisters when told to go, trying to force a confrontation with the object of his love, and finally succeeding in making the doctor lose his temper. Eventually Easton was compelled to pass Denton over to one of his new partners, Dr Tuckett, which must have left Denton feeling more rejected than ever.

Physically, too, he was still in a bad way. On 23 June 1937 his aunt Edith was writing from Leigh Vicarage to her daughter Beatrice to say, 'Denton has not been very well lately and the doctor said he needed more rest and wanted him to stay in the nursing home. But Denton said a week there was enough and he could not bear the thought of lying up any more.' This indicates that Denton had returned to the Southcourt Nursing Home for a brief spell during 1937, and the reason he may not have cared to go back may have been because on his previous stay he had been confined 'in a small uncomfortable room quite isolated'.[11] During 1938 his condition continued to deteriorate, and early in 1939 he was back in Broadstairs, where he spent some months in a large and luxurious nursing home called Cliff Coombe, which was situated on the Eastern Esplanade and commanded views of the beach and the cliffs.[12] It was much more expensive than Southcourt (the fees may have been taken care of by Lady Fox), and Denton's stay there appears to have done him good, for in the untitled short story describing

11. Letter from Dr Easton to Eric Oliver, 28 March 1983.

12. Cliffe Coombe later became a private hotel, and in 1974 the building was demolished.

Touchett's win on the horses he recalled, 'I had been lying naked on the roof of a nursing home at Broadstairs for four months, so I was very brown and felt extremely well and lively.'

In addition, it seems that during 1938 the stress of his unresolved emotional conflicts, and in particular his continuing infatuation with Dr Easton, led him to seek psychiatric help. That he did so is indicated in an entry he made in his journal years later, in 1944, following a visit to a medical specialist in London. On 4 May that year he wrote, 'I remembered going to see the psychologist [Denton was always to confuse psychologists with psychiatrists] six years ago. The psychologist had a tiny room on the top floor; the urologist a large one on the ground floor.' Another record of these events is contained in an unpublished short story he wrote at the time, which stands as a landmark in his struggle for emotional maturity and in his development as a writer. 'Alex Fairburn', written in 1938, was the first entirely autobiographical work of fiction he ever completed. The narrator, 'Alex', is a woman of twenty-three whose marriage to a man named 'Jack' has come adrift. They had first met when 'Alex' was twenty-one, but she had behaved like a fool and only now did she realize just how big a fool she had been. 'When Alex left her husband she had gone to a psychologist and had been analysed. There had been the endless journeys to the little upstairs room in Wimpole Street.' Denton himself had of course been twenty-one when he had first met Dr Easton, and in 1938 he was twenty-three.

The year 1938 had been a critical one. Denton's persistent and embarrassing intrusions into the Eastons' home drove Dr Easton to write to him to say, 'I do very definitely say that I must see no more of you and that this business of seeing you occasionally is no good. You obviously cannot have me always and you must try and live your own life.' Writing in his journal on 2 December 1942 Denton recalled that in 1938 he longed and prayed to die before he was twenty-four, and it appears, if one is to take the record of events contained in 'A Fragment of a Life Story' literally, that he did make a half-hearted attempt to commit suicide just before his twenty-fourth birthday. The account was first drafted in 1942, but by the time Denton came to revise it some years later he had become a consummate story-teller capable of recreating the drama with brilliant comic effect.

The published version of the story describes how Denton made his way to his doctor's house, broke in through the french window, and was discovered as he crouched on the floor behind the drawing-room door. The doctor pulled him to his feet, holding him steady, for Denton was 'trembling violently with lust and fear'. After much shouting and swearing, Denton was told to go home, but instead he went round to the window to eavesdrop, to be rewarded with snippets of conversation about his parents, his money, his curious taste in clothes and his 'undirected sex life'.

Eventually the doctor and his wife persuaded him to leave. Denton decided to go home and try to kill himself. On the way home he contemplated jumping into the river, but decided against it as the doctor would not be there to see him do it. When he arrived back at his flat he found 'Touchett', sitting by the fire and looking 'exactly like a fat "doctored" cat'. He then remembered the Prontisil tablets which he had been prescribed (Prontisil was an early form of antibiotic). There were sixteen tablets in the box and he swallowed the lot. (He was meant to take four each day, so he must have known that sixteen were unlikely to prove fatal, though they might have turned him blue.) Rather than lie on his bed to await death in dignified privacy, he made the most of enjoying his last bowl of soup, accompanied by a glass of sherry. 'I must die happy and contented,' he thought.

Touchett considered Denton more drugged than dying, which only exacerbated Denton's sense of having been betrayed. 'He was clearly about to jump up and leave me. Those nicotined fingers, I thought, those dirty nails; those unspeakable teeth and your agile diverting mind, you are a wreck at thirty-four. You're craven and you'll one day be a lunatic.' Denton implored him not to leave him, but Touchett 'lurched to his feet like a frightened bullock' and told Denton either to go to bed or get a doctor.

As Touchett left the house, Denton swayed down the street after him, 'screaming oaths and blasphemy', but to no avail. On returning to the flat, Denton decided to burn some papers but then had to go for water to douse the flames. This brought 'Lydia' (Evie Sinclair) on the scene, and he told her to ring for Touchett's doctor. The doctor arrived and said to him, '"What's all this."

'He's just like a prefect who's discovered some peculiar goings-on in the disused cricket pavilion,' Denton told himself.

The worst Denton suffered was a headache, and next morning he realized that nothing had changed, either in the world or in himself.

Francis Streeten — 'Touchett' — was a prime example of the kind of person Denton cheerfully despised yet was fascinated by, largely because of his eccentricity. 'A close acquaintance of the author for many years,' was how Eric Oliver was neatly to describe him when he came to write an Introduction to *A Last Sheaf*. Streeten himself elaborated on this when he wrote in his letter, 'I knew him very well and in a sense we were quite close friends ... but it was what I would call a "detached" sort of friendship, with very little affinity of temperament or emotional warmth. (A psychoanalyst friend of mine once compared it to a friendship between a wasp and a bear!) Really it was based almost entirely on our mutual interest in observing and analysing the behaviour and psychology of the people around us, when we were living (or staying) in the same neighbourhood.' Certainly Denton's life remained thoroughly intermingled with Streeten's. In 1943, for example, Streeten wrote to tell him that his mother had fallen down in the street in Tunbridge Wells and was to appear in court charged with being drunk and disorderly; he thought Denton might like to go along and watch the proceedings. 'She of the large Edwardian Tudor house, the "Castle Careless",' Denton wrote in his journal on 26 July that year, 'with its butler and footman and page-boy, its silver tea-kettles and Earl Grey Blend, its greenhouses and lawns; she was now falling about in the streets, causing disturbances. I wanted to cry, seeing so clearly in an instant that everything goes from bad to worse. I wanted to back her against all the officious policemen, because she was well over sixty and quite lost and strayed. I marvelled at the amount of herself that she had managed to preserve, in spite of her lunatic life.'

Streeten's own life was scarcely less bizarre than his mother's. Again in 1943, Denton reported to Marcus Oliver that after having been pestered by Streeten for money to pay a fine, he had lent him £3 12s. 6d. 'The family is tragic, don't you think?' he wrote. Streeten once even landed in prison, for refusing on the grounds of conscience to do fire-watching in the Lake District. 'Poor Francis Streeten is about to be locked up I believe,' Denton wrote to Marcus on 5 October 1942. 'Did I tell you he wrote and asked me to lend him £70? Needless to say your friend was unable to meet this request! Hasn't his life been a ghastly muddle when you think of it?' Seven weeks later Denton was reporting to Marcus, 'Cecilia [Carpmael] says that Francis *likes* prison and that the warders are kind to him!'

At some time in 1938, amidst all the emotional turmoil and recurrent ill-health, Denton had met a lady who described herself as a former 'Edwardian beauty', May Walbrand-Evans, who was the widow of the vicar of Hawkhurst and who was to become one of Denton's many middle-aged intimates. 'Although she was a grandmother,' he wrote of her in his short story 'Brave and Cruel',[13] in which she is named 'Julia Bellingly', 'she often displayed all the bounce and gusto of a hearty schoolgirl. She retained that leathery quality. She would tell preposterous jokes, poke fun or wolf her food. But she also possessed a mature handsomeness that was remarkable.' May lived in a converted eighteenth-century pub called The Brown Jug in Hadlow, two miles from Tonbridge, and when in January 1940 Denton and Evie moved from Hadlow Road to The Hop Garden in St Mary's Platt they stayed for a time with her until their new house was ready to move into. 'There are nice people at Platt,' Denton told Marcus, 'and I think I shall really enjoy it when at last I get in. You must come and see it when it's ready. It's very nice staying with May Evans but it can't go on for ever.' With the break-up of his friendship with Dr Easton, Denton seems to have been searching for a new soul-mate and hoping that Marcus might fill the gap. Invitations flowed continuously from St Mary's Platt to London, beginning only days after Denton had moved into The Hop Garden. 'I was wondering whether it was worth your while to come down one day and see me here; I want rather to return some of my neighbours' calls by asking them to a little drinky, one morning or evening, and should love your moral support and active help; so would have them on the day you were down if you could bear it.' He was also longing to know what Marcus would think of the house, 'although there is tons more to do'.

The neighbours at St Mary's Platt were soon to become the focal point of Denton's life, and Marcus Oliver proved a popular local attraction. In July 1939 Denton had written to Marcus to say, 'Mrs Walbrand-Evans wanted to know who the young man like Ivor Novello was! I think she wished you to lie with her or something complimentary.' Shortly after this nonsense he was at it again: 'Mrs Bitch-Brennan told us that she thought you were rather too worldly and sophisticated for her taste – the sexy old thing loves young men that strip to the buff for a bout of fisticuffs, so what *can* you expect!'

Social distractions aside, however, once Denton and Evie were installed in The Hop Garden, Denton decided to write a book, a record of his life beginning at his birth. The idea was neither original nor was it at all promising, since the life he had lived scarcely justified a full-scale autobiography. 'Through the months of 1940 I plugged at it,' he tells us in his journal. 'Then it suddenly died on me.' With the collapse of

13. Published in *Brave and Cruel*.

the project came the inevitable writers' blockage, but 'in the autumn or the winter several tiny things suddenly crystallized into the determination, by hook or by crook, to finish a book that began with my running away from Repton and ended in China'. The seeds of *Maiden Voyage* had been sown.

SEVEN

'Catastrophe'

The inspiration to write an unorthodox autobiography – *Maiden Voyage* is, as its title implies, as much a travel book as anything – had come to Denton through reading J. R. Ackerley's *Hindoo Holiday*, and while recognizing that what he would write would be very different from that book, he knew he needed to learn from it certain commonplace devices which 'somehow made all simple, only leaving hard work and persever-ance to be cultivated'. He devoted most of 1941 to the task, working in bed, usually during the morning, and for up to four hours at a stretch. This regime gave him, he noted, a serenity he had not experienced since childhood, although he dared not read what he had written for fear of disgusting himself: 'All that mattered seemed to be that I should finish it, doing each piece as well as I could.'

On 15 August 1940, however, a major interruption had occurred. Denton had gone into Tonbridge to visit a friend, Peggy Mundy Castle, one of the many patrons he was to cultivate, with whom he allowed himself the luxury of an ambivalent relationship (she purchased one of his paintings, 'By the Sea',[1] yet he irreverently refers to her in his journal, on 27 November 1945, as 'Peggy Mundane-Arswhole'). While he was with her the siren sounded; it was their first air-raid. They heard gunfire and took to the cellar, but the charlady, still in the attic, shrieked out, '"One's gone down over there, or is it a bomb?"' They all ran to look, and saw a spiral of smoke in the direction of St Mary's Platt. 'I said gaily, "I expect it's the Hop Garden."' He cannot have been seriously worried though, for after leaving them he jumped into his Austin Seven (which his father had bought for him in 1937) and drove to the Angel Hotel in Tonbridge, where he 'fraternized with three cadets'. He stayed with them until late that night, and just as he was arriving home he heard 'a most extraordinary explosion'. When Evie met him at the front

---

1. Illustrated in *A Last Sheaf*.

door she said, '"Don't be frightened. A bomb has landed in the garden but none of your treasures are hurt."' (It was in fact a time-bomb, dropped earlier in the day during a raid in which no less than sixteen bombs fell in the wood behind the house.)

At this stage of the war bomb-craters were still a novelty, and the next morning a stream of visitors came to inspect the damage. Denton wrote excitedly to Marcus Oliver to tell him all about it: 'My dear, *the* most frightful catastrophe. A bomb fell eight yards from the house, right in the middle of the formal garden. Rooting up the pointed tree and smothering the whole place in mud and dust. It smashed all the panes in the downstairs windows and some upstairs, but do you know, not one bauble or ornament was smashed! I could have danced for joy when I got back, because there were all those glass lustres right in the window and they escaped completely. I wasn't in at the time but Evie was and she rushed into the telephone-box and was quite unhurt. It really is the most incredible escape – if it had been one second later the house would have been hit. I don't know who's going to pay for the damage or how it is going to be cleared up. The man is mending the window at the moment; he says it all has to be plate glass! But the garden is quite another cup of tea. It will require quite a lorry load of navvies I should think.'

The fright and the mess had in no way damped his sense of humour – or his love of gossip, for in the same letter he comments, 'Of course it's impossible to know why Gerald goes on seeing people if he finds them such toads. I shall never get to the bottom of that young man – not that I have leanings that way!' In another bulletin to Marcus, undated but probably written in September 1940, he reported that a letter he had written to Paul, who was then training with the North Irish Horse, had been returned by the censor. He went on, 'I've been reading rather a dreary book called "Twilight Men". Do you know it? All about what the author fondly calls "the intermediate sex". The hero was not at all my cup of tea and I think it's all rather badly put together.' Otherwise, he added, 'I've been having no adventures, except that I made a wrong diagnosis the other night and got the rather haughty answer that "I don't go in for that sort of thing". Frightful!!'

By June the next year, 1941, the first draft of *Maiden Voyage* was completed. Since he had never learned to use a typewriter himself, a friend called Freddie Beale ('Filthy Freddie' to Denton) offered to type the manuscript for him, and so new was Denton to the mechanics of writing that he even considered the possibility of dictating a revised version while Freddie typed. 'I thought that to revise my first writing would only take a few weeks,' he wrote later. 'I never dreamt that it was far the longest and most arduous part of the proceeding.'

His new life as an author did not, however, interfere too much with his social activities. Another letter to Marcus, written at about the same time, began, 'My dear, I'm having such a camp time,' and went on to describe meeting up with 'the queerest bunch of queers! An officer, a corporal, a doctor, a person who puts fuses in bombs and a Dutch boy with a headache!! I was quite overwhelmed. Today I've been to tea with two lesbians who asked me to meet what they described as "a charming boy with green eyes"! My dear, it was forty with huge gold teeth and a horrible leer. It kept on talking about guardsmen all thro' tea. It was really quite blush-making. I began to think that the whole neighbourhood is bewitched.' Additional excitements had been the discovery of 'an amazing magazine' called *London Life* – 'Have you seen it? All about various fetishes. High-heeled shoes, rubber sheets, spurs, short skirts and bloomers. Extraordinary the importance some people attach to accessories!' – and the news, 'I've had a weeny poem published in the Abinger Chronicle.'[2]

It was at this time that Denton, who was to become a formidable and persistent self-publicist in his own quiet way, began bringing himself to the notice of the famous. He started with Lord Berners, an eccentric peer and a gifted musician, painter and novelist. Denton had seen in one of Berners's books, *First Childhood*, a photograph of the author as a little boy, dressed as Robinson Crusoe in a shaggy goatskin with a macaw perched on his shoulder. He had decided to do a painting based on this photograph and he now wrote to Berners to tell him of the project. 'I should like very much to see the picture,' Berners replied on 7 September. 'If you have occasion to come to Oxford [he lived at Faringdon House, seventeen miles from Oxford] perhaps you could bring it – if it is not too large. Or could you have a photograph done of it? I don't think I shall be able to get to London in the next few months or I would suggest seeing it there.'

Before this promising lead could be followed up, however, a second

2. The poem was 'Jane Allen'. It was to be one of five of Denton's poems chosen by the composer Howard Ferguson to comprise his song cycle *Discovery*, published in 1952 by Boosey & Hawkes; the other four were 'Dreams Melting', 'Freedom of the City', 'Babylon' and 'Discovery'. All five poems were published in *A Last Sheaf*, and the songs, with the exception of 'Dreams Melting', were recorded for Decca by Kathleen Ferrier.

disaster was to befall The Hop Garden, a real catastrophe this time which brought Denton's two-year tenancy of the house to an end. He had in fact been thinking of making an offer to buy the house, and on 3 December Paul came over to discuss the idea. In the evening the two went to supper with a neighbour, Frida Easdale, and while they were there Evie rang to tell them that The Hop Garden was on fire. When they reached the scene they found flames in the kitchen and pools of water in the drawing-room. Denton dashed in to rescue a painting he had bought of the Nativity, which was already hot, and having taken it out into the garden he returned for more of his treasures. Suddenly he remembered that the painting of Lord Berners was still upstairs. He fought his way past soldiers, firemen and A.R.P. wardens, all of whom appeared to him to have come as if to a victory celebration, and, choking through the smoke, brought the sticky canvas to safety.

Eventually the fire was brought under control, but not before most of his mother's silver that he had brought back from China had been destroyed. Realizing this he 'gave a cry', and Paul said, '"So awfully sorry, Punky"'. When Denton came to inspect the damage he found the kitchen completely gutted. The fire seems to have started because of a fault in the construction of the flue (it had apparently caused a fire once before); Evie had smelt something strange and had opened the kitchen window to let out the smell while she went upstairs to have a bath, but while she was bathing the fire caught hold. She then lost her head, ran into the kitchen to save the first thing she saw gleaming – an electric kettle – and then rescued some old pyjamas and socks that were on the towel-rail. Meanwhile, Denton's precious silver was melting. Later that night, remembering the silver and the tea-set and the Georgian square-based glasses that had perished, Evie 'gnashed her teeth movingly'.

The destruction of his property must have had a far more profound effect on him than he let on to. 'His homes were furnished with things which he loved and which became a part of his own personality,' Maurice Cranston has written.[3] 'Each object in Denton's rooms was distinctive, and together they composed a most remarkable and original and beautiful environment. At Hadlow Road and The Hop Garden they were all set out with a certain stateliness. Denton had a wonderful sense of colour, and I think this is what enabled him to put together so many incongruous and startling things. Somehow the colours, all very mixed, of the curtains,

3. In a letter to the author, 19 February 1984.

the covers, the upholstery were so composed that the interior became an aesthetic whole, and as much a part of Denton's persona as the clothes he wore.'

As The Hop Garden was rendered uninhabitable, May Walbrand-Evans came to the rescue. She described the state Denton and Evie had been in when writing to Marcus Oliver (with whom she now enjoyed playing bridge) on 19 December: 'Of course you will have heard about poor Denton being burnt out & all his treasured possessions gone west & not even insured. He & Miss Sinclair, the latter badly burnt about the head, arrived here just over 2 weeks ago looking like a pair of tramps with black faces & sopping wet from the fire-engines & having had no food or sleep for 24 hours. I never saw a more pathetic pair. I kept them a week & we lived on the meagre rations of one person as it would have meant going to Malling to get all their cards [ration books] renewed. The poor Hop Garden will need £300 or £400 to make it even livable & this will not put it in original condition. The flames chased all round the walls & upstairs very rapidly as the fire-engine arrived in 7 or 8 minutes but the fire had got a good hold by then. It was simply frightful.'

The two refugees had then been offered temporary accommodation by another neighbour, Mrs Jane Gardener, in the front rooms of her house, Pond Farm, in East Peckham. 'After the first appalling thought of close proximity,' Denton ungratefully noted in his journal some time later, 'I steeled myself and accepted, for there was not a house to be had anywhere.' And on 10 December their surviving possessions were moved into what he described as the 'two bleak, dark front rooms' of the farmhouse. 'They looked unhappy, lost and cold,' he wrote, 'but I hung up the Louis Quinze cartoon to decorate the barrenness. It looked rather fine all across one wall. We borrowed what china and cutlery we had not got and tried to settle down.'

One of the treasures which Denton had managed to rescue from the fire was a sadly neglected eighteenth-century doll's house which he had acquired that winter when visiting a friend, Mrs Mildred Bosanquet, at her house in Seal. The doll's house had come to light when Mrs Bosanquet, in whose family it had remained since it was built in 1783, probably by an estate carpenter, was turning her cellar into an air-raid shelter. Denton had volunteered to take it off her hands and a carrier had brought it to The Hop Garden one morning while he was in bed, working on *Maiden Voyage*. He immediately began pulling away the Edwardian carpets and curtains. 'The moths' eggs,' he wrote, 'were as thick as fish-roe and the dust was like bat's fur.' By the time he had emptied the rubbish, there were only two pieces of Georgian furniture left, a mahogany Pembroke table and a small chest. The task of restoration, to which he devoted many months of detailed work, was to be interrupted when he left Pond Farm and had to put the doll's house into storage for a couple of years. He resumed work in the early weeks of 1945, when he 'suddenly had a passion for it again', and spent many more months over it, constantly on the look-out for miniature period furniture with which to replenish the rooms.[4]

Some account of events during the months he camped out at Pond Farm is contained in a letter to Marcus Oliver which, although it was written on headed notepaper filched from the Cliff Coombe Nursing Home, probably dates from March 1942. 'My dear,' he wrote, 'How are you? I often imagine your trials and tribulations. I had a perfectly horrible and outrageous experience the other day which I shall tell you about when we meet. I am still simmering about it. Fate really seems to play the lowest, rudest tricks ...

'I believe my Papa is safe,' he continued (at Christmas Denton had sent Marcus a card saying, 'I believe my poor Pa is interned', but this turned out to be a false rumour; Arthur Welch, who was still living in Shanghai, was not imprisoned by the Japanese until the end of 1942). 'Paul had a wire telling us not to worry. This is one relief. I only hope that the Japanese don't seize all his "rubber goods", raw and otherwise!!' Demonstrating that somewhat unpleasant streak of hypocrisy in his attitude towards friends he affected to dislike while making such use of, he informed Maurice, 'My novel has just been typed and I have been correcting the typing errors. Francis, Bogey-Man, Streeten is reading it for me and I'm waiting to hear his verdict.' Having earlier expostulated that 'Lord Berners, the old monster, has not answered my last letter so my picture is still without a purchaser!' he ended by hoping that his stepmother had not been raped in the Far East.

That 'last letter' to Lord Berners must have been a progress report on the painting, and before long Berners did answer it, writing, 'I am flattered that you should think my youthful portrait as Robinson Crusoe worthy of being made into a conversation piece. My hair in those days

4. The doll's house, beautifully restored by Denton, was presented seven weeks after his death to the Bethnal Green Museum of Childhood by Eric Oliver, who had inherited it. It is described and illustrated in *English Doll's Houses of the Eighteenth and Nineteenth Centuries* by Vivien Greene (Bell and Hyman, 1955).

was brown and my eyes also. Latter are still brown but my hair has more or less flown!' He added that he would look forward with interest to seeing the picture when it was finished. A viewing was eventually arranged in a room at the Randolph Hotel in Oxford, of which Denton wrote an account entitled 'A Morning with the Versatile Peer Lord Berners in the Ancient Seat of Learning'.[5] Lord Berners 'came in with a bouncing step and sank down on the bed in front of the conversation piece I had made. I thought as he sat there that he bore a very faint resemblance to Humpty Dumpty. He immediately produced a little gold box and began furiously to take snuff. I was not offered any, and I cannot decide whether this was rudeness or true politeness.

'"It's perfectly charming," he said, in a sort of amused, indulgent voice.'

Between pinches of snuff, little suggestions were made for alterations and additions, and after gazing at the painting for three quarters of an hour – Denton all the while longing for him to say he wanted to buy it, and yet dreading the idea – Berners merely said, '"You'll let me have a photograph when you've finished it, won't you?"'

'"Oh, yes, of course," I said gaily, feeling rather miserable.'

'Lord Berners's eye roved round the room. He looked at my ivory-topped bottles and brushes and then at my squalid little face flannel. It was ringed round with roses. I had found it in the toe of my Christmas stocking seven years ago, and had used it ever since.'

Lord Berners's eye at last came to rest on a bedside table where several books lay. 'I had purposely hidden his *Far From the Madding War* [published the previous year] under an old volume of Pope's pastorals which I had bought for twopence. It had seemed too fulsome to leave his books about bare and uncovered.' Berners, however, smelt it out immediately.

'"What did you think of that?" he asked urgently.

'"I enjoyed it awfully," I said, quite untruthfully. I thought it a trivial little book.

'"I'm so glad." He seemed to relax after my answer. I felt rather ashamed for giving him pleasure.

'"I've got more coming out after Christmas," he added with busy pride. And I understood, for I knew how easy it was to appear childish in one's enthusiasm . . .

5. Published posthumously in *Time and Tide*.

'As he was leaving he said, "Isn't this an extraordinary hotel? John Betjeman loves it."'[6]

Denton wrote repeatedly to Berners after their meeting at the Randolph. His first letter having gone astray, and because he was still hoping for a sale, he wrote in a second letter that his first had 'ended up rather peculiarly by saying that I'd like to give it to you as a present, if nobody else bought it. As I had no answer, I thought that you must be annoyed by the feeling that it was being rammed down your throat. Hence my last letter. I still mean what I said, and if you liked the picture at all when you saw it at Oxford, I will send it to you at once; as I really painted it for you.'

'My dear, what a fuss about the picture!' he later wrote to Helen Roeder from Pond Farm. 'I will bring it back one day [from the Leicester Galleries where it had been put up for sale] and come and see you.' He went on, 'My latest idea is that I shall get the job of *caretaker* to the W.V.S. depot which is just near here in a rather charming but huge old house. They want someone on the spot when everyone has left in the evening. I'd do anything for a house and it sounds a lovely idea, but do you think my sex will be a drawback? Perhaps you will have to buy me a beautiful pair of false bosoms from Wardour Street!'[7] Back on the vexed subject of the picture he added, 'Berners has written at last intimating that he has only had one letter from me since I saw him in Oxford. I thought it wise to pretend to believe this story and so negotiations have been opened again. I think I shall have to give him the picture!'[8]

The next celebrity to occupy Denton's attention was the Countess of Oxford and Asquith, widow of the prime minister Herbert Asquith. Denton had been reading her autobiography and now wrote praising it in terms, judging by her response, little short of sycophantic, while omitting to mention precisely which book it was that had so enthralled

6. John Betjeman, who knew Lord Berners well, commented on Denton's account of this decidedly strained encounter in correspondence with the University of Texas. 'Had they met more often,' he wrote, 'Mr Welch would have understood the shyness of Lord Berners. He was so shy that he could hardly bring himself to speak to someone when he first met them, and could never make a public speech. The first meeting, described here, to see an unsolicited portrait of himself as Robinson Crusoe, must have seemed to Lord Berners like a public occasion.'

7. Denton in fact became a messenger in the A.R.P.

8. In the event Lord Berners neither bought the picture, entitled 'Portrait of Lord Berners as a Child, Dressed up as Robinson Crusoe', nor accepted it as a gift, and as the Leicester Galleries failed to sell it – they were asking £40 for it – Denton eventually gave it to Helen Roeder.

him. She replied from the Savoy Hotel on 30 April 1942, in a note scribbled in pencil. 'You do not date your letter,' she wrote, 'and as I have been in the country I have no idea *when* you wrote it. You say that: Praise from a stranger may not be acceptable, but remember Denton Welch, you are *wrong*. I *love* praise, even from a "stranger"; and your letter was more than "acceptable". I do not deserve so much praise. Do tell me *which* book of mine you read. Was it "More Memories" or my autobiography? Or "Lay Sermons"? In any case, *none* of these deserves the praise you give them. I am a very simple person, and fundamentally humble ... Nevertheless I am proud of your praise.' And having promised to sign a book for him, 'when I get a proper pen,' she added, 'write to me again.'

This he did, several times, though ultimately to his regret; but all was well when on 19 June Lady Oxford again wrote from the Savoy, to say, 'I did not know that anyone did either *buy* or *read* my autobiography today. I am glad that you liked it. It would be very unwise of you to send it to me to write in it, as the posts are precarious. I never received the two letters which you say you wrote to me, or I would certainly have acknowledged them. To be "great and famous", as you say in your letter, is a difficult ambition, and I confess is one that I never want. To be wise and kind is better I think. Wishing you every success, I remain, yours sincerely, Margot Oxford.'

Meanwhile, things were going badly at Pond Farm between Denton and his benefactress, Mrs Gardener, as he related to Maurice Cranston when he wrote in May: 'How I wish I could dip into the "Well" too. But unless something urgently calls me to London I am tied to the spot by the turn events have taken ... The result is that Evie and I shall probably be on the streets, as this and every other neighbourhood seems to be stuffed to bursting with humanity.

'My only hope is that my eldest brother's wife's rich mother (this sounds rather involved and flamboyant!) will let us stay for the time being in her late Victorian mausoleum in South Kensington. If this comes off you must come and visit us in the dust-sheeted drawing-room!'

The move to a mausoleum proved unnecessary, however, for shortly after writing to Cranston, Denton and Evie had fled, 'after an absurd quarrel' with their landlady, to a house called Pitt's Folly in Hadlow, almost next door to May Walbrand-Evans's home and owned, since 1939, by Mary Sloman, the estranged wife of Harold Sloman, a former headmaster of Tonbridge School. (It seems likely that Denton had met the Slomans through his friendship with Francis Streeten, whose father, a stockbroker, was also a governor of Tonbridge School.) Adjacent to the house were rooms over the garage, and it was into these that Denton and Evie moved, for a rent of £78 a year, calling their own apartments Pitt's Folly Cottage.[9]

The move to Pitt's Folly Cottage, where he was to remain for the next four years, coincided with an important literary milestone in Denton's life, for it was here that he began to write his journals. Indeed, his very first entry, made on 10 July 1942, hails the beginning of a new era in recording the acceptance by Cyril Connolly, editor of *Horizon*, of the article he had written about his memorable visit to Sickert. It also reveals that from the very start of his literary career he was plagued with a dread of libel, for he records that he had received a 'rude little note' from Connolly asking if someone to whom he had referred obliquely in the piece was in fact the novelist George Moore. On 18 August Denton was writing to Helen Roeder, enclosing a copy of the article, to say that he was rather worried about a 'Mr Raven' he had mentioned in it, as he was a real and undisguised person whose brothers were pillars of Broadstairs society. 'I do hope they don't read *Horizon*,' he added. Six days later he was writing to Maurice Cranston: 'Do you think my remarks about Gerald were too malicious? Also I'm living in fear of an attack from the Mr Raven I mention.'

That first journal entry also describes a tea-party with 'Filthy Freddie' and his fiancée at The Leicester Arms in nearby Penshurst, where Denton 'played hostess and poured out' – an image of himself that was to be echoed by Helen Roeder when in 1958 she came to write an Introduction to *I Left My Grandfather's House*: 'He was a born hostess. He could make an occasion out of a cup of tea and a digestive biscuit.'

In no time at all the journal is offering evidence to support Francis Streeten's assertion that Denton had a reputation for roaming the countryside 'making ambiguous approaches to young rustics'. On 21 July, Denton records, as he was walking by the river, he saw a man and a boy working in a cornfield. 'They had taken their shirts off and their skin was beautiful and pale, like nacre, in the sunlight. Their brown throats and arms, grafted to their pearly bodies, were surprising.' He spoke to them, and the boy 'looked into me with that deep, sulky, suspicious adolescent look. His biceps and shoulders were like silky balls melting together. How I longed to be strong and lusty, not ill!'

9. It has been suggested that Denton chose the name in memory of his American ancestor, William Pitt Denton, but according to Mrs Brenda Cobb, who lived at Pitt's Folly with Mary Sloman, the Slomans had in fact renamed the house thus before Denton arrived there, its previous name having been Pitt's Water.

It is interesting that Streeten should have used the word 'ambiguous', for in Denton's accounts of his adventures that is exactly how they appear; yet his descriptions of these boys and farm labourers, many of whom he met while they were swimming naked, are on the whole highly erotic, leaving little doubt that his partial impotence, his essentially passive nature and his often-expressed fear of physical contact failed to damp his sexual enthusiasm. But whether his descriptions were inspired purely by a platonic appreciation of male beauty or even a sense of the contrast between their robustly healthy and his own sadly diminished physique, or whether they mask a deeper, sexual involvement, is left to the readers of his journals to decide.

The continuation of the same entry confirms, too, the strength of his determination to make a name for himself: 'Being ill made me think of being great and famous. They are always linked together in my mind. I must not be so ill that I cannot be famous.' Fame was, in fact, just around the corner. On 20 July he had received the proofs of his *Horizon* article, and when he had opened the envelope he 'just had a feeling of easy confidence, almost indifference'. The first thing he noticed was that his name had been misspelt; then excitement took over, and with Evie's assistance he spent the whole morning reading and re-reading the proofs, only managing to find two other mistakes.

His almost desperate desire for recognition had prompted him to send a photograph of his painting of Lord Berners to Sacheverell Sitwell, presumably hoping to extract from this eminent art critic and writer some endorsement of his own artistic talents. In the same post that brought the *Horizon* proofs came Sitwell's cool response. 'Dear Mr Denton Welch,' he wrote, 'Thank you very much for your most amusing portrait of Lord Berners. I can imagine it must have been rather fascinating to work upon. In the future (if there is one!) I shall look out with much interest for more of your work.'

If his first attempt to proselytize a Sitwell had failed to pay off, there remained Sacheverell's brother and sister, Osbert and Edith, still to approach. The success of this celebrated pair was to a large extent due to their assiduous self-publicity campaigns, though they were quite as well known for their championship of other artists — notably the composer William Walton — as for their own literary output. They courted publicity, knew almost everybody, and everybody knew them. Realizing, no doubt, that all three Sitwells would have known Sickert, and that they would be certain to read *Horizon*, Denton now decided to write to Edith, enclosing a copy of *Street Songs*, a recent collection of her poetry, with a request that she autograph it. It was a move that before long would pay a handsome dividend, but in the meantime he had to overcome the immediate difficulty of finding a publisher for *Maiden Voyage*. The going was to be rough.

The first publisher to reject the manuscript was Jonathan Cape (Denton made use of the rejection slip by drafting a poem on the back of it). But, as he told Helen Roeder, someone called Alex Comfort – 'he, I believe, is a medical student' – had sent him 'two very exciting letters' about it, and had 'pushed it off on to Arthur Waugh [a director of the publishers Chapman & Hall] who's promised to give his verdict in a week'. Alex Comfort was more than just a medical student; having published his first book, *The Silver River*, at the age of nineteen, and now being only twenty-two, he was something of a literary prodigy. Denton, without having met him, felt instinctively that here was another young writer who, unlike himself, already knew his way around the publishing world and would be sure to lend a hand. Indeed, he assured Helen Roeder that if Arthur Waugh did not take the book then Alex Comfort was going to take it to Herbert Read, a director of Routledge, and thrust it down his throat. 'Oh dear,' he added, his confidence suddenly waning, 'I do hope something happens!' He went on to tell Helen that Alex Comfort had suggested a meeting. 'If this takes place, will you come too?' he asked. 'I shall need a great deal of moral support to be able to confront a complete stranger who has read my autobiographical goings-on!'

Arthur Waugh, the father of Evelyn and one of the most respected publishers of his day, also declined to publish the book. Denton wrote on 22 August to thank Alex Comfort for his trouble, adding, 'I could get my other copy back from the "Fortune" and send that on to Read with your recommendation (if you'll give me his address).' He went on to ask whether Waugh had said exactly what it was he did not like: 'Was it the "tone" or the writing? Or did he think it not saleable?' When both the Fortune Press and John Lane of The Bodley Head also turned it down it was no wonder that Denton was writing to Maurice Cranston to say, 'I am almost in a state of collapse by the time the postman comes every morning,' and in another letter, 'Waiting for news about my book is reducing me to a jelly.'

Herbert Read, who was a well-known poet and critic as well as a publisher, now had the manuscript, and while waiting for a verdict from him Denton spent a weekend up in London with Helen Roeder. On the Saturday night they went into Soho, where everyone was 'gay and ready to be drunk'. They went first to a pub in Dean Street, as Denton reported to Marcus Oliver on 4 September, 'but it hadn't warmed up properly. There was only a negro, several rather dreary sailors and a little blondie whose sex I could not quite determine. So we went on to a Chinese restaurant stuffed with American officers. After that we landed up at the Café Royal where we saw (of all people) Captain Turner (Platt) and small son both eating [a] hearty meal. Wasn't it a queer place to take his offspring?

'It was rather dreary there too. Except for one or two amusing and obvious "cases" deep in conversation together. A family of Austrian (?) extraction next to us suddenly ordered a horribly expensive bottle of Rhine wine, which had the most rapid and disastrous effect on the two young men. They began a curious argument with much hand-waving and rolling of eyes. I could not quite tell whether they were quarrelling or being very affectionate.

'At last the old man (the father I suppose) took to running about the room in the most gay and inconsequent manner, whereupon the wife took the situation firmly in hand and bustled all her menfolk out!'

Eventually they returned to Helen's home in Notting Hill Gate. Helen took a bath and Denton, frustrated and excited perhaps by a rare night out in Soho and a glimpse, however dreary, of other people's sexual manoeuvres, went out for a stroll. 'It was getting late, after midnight,' he wrote in his journal. 'I went in at a door marked "Gentlemen", and found it thronged with stationary people. They were not going or coming, just standing in a sort of trance. I fled without more ado, feeling that I had intruded in some way.' He concluded this absurdly disingenuous narrative with the thought, 'I wondered if people were all night there, standing together in silence.'

On the Sunday afternoon they visited the orangery at Kensington Palace where there was an art exhibition for which Helen had helped Kenneth Clark, the director of the National Gallery where she now worked, hang the pictures. On his return to Kent, Denton wrote to Helen to say, 'I did enjoy our queer weekend of sight-seeing and raking over the muck heaps of Soho.' He added that he had decided to grow a 'common little moustache'.

He had meanwhile been busy distributing not only manuscripts of *Maiden Voyage* but also copies of his *Horizon* article, one of them to Lady Oxford, who responded with what he described as 'cold, almost coroneted objections to the Americanism "sensed" and the mention of W.C.s!' What Lady Oxford actually wrote, this time from her home at 44 Bedford Square, and admittedly with her countess's coronet on the notepaper, was, 'Dear Mr Welch, I thank you for praising my books, and for sending me Horizon. I have only read *your* review – Sickert at St Peter's – I shall read the others later. I think it an error of taste to write of "W.C.s", "passing water" etc, and I do not like the Americanism *"sensed"*. But I may be wrong, as I am an amateur in autobiography; and far *too* critical. Yours very sincerely, Margot Oxford.'

Her letter never ceased to rankle. 'I wrote a long one back,' Denton told Marcus Oliver, 'and I'm wondering if I shall ever have an answer, as I rather took a leaf out of her own book in the way of plain speaking, saying that I thought the mention of W.C.s was no more an error of taste than mentioning one's mother's lover (which she did in her autobiography)!! Rather strong meat don't you think? I'm afraid the old war-horse will retaliate with an icy silence.' None the less he did, surprisingly, take her remarks to heart, for he subsequently told Helen Roeder that he thought perhaps he would try to curb 'too many mentions of the W.C., for although this is probably the most innocent of the "bad taste" subjects, it is the one that seems to stick most in people's gullets'.

His inspired move in sending the copy of *Street Songs* to Edith Sitwell was now about to pay off. Just over two weeks after the weekend in London there came, on 16 September, what he called 'the day of miracles'. His post contained an offer to buy a picture, a letter from John Middleton Murry accepting two poems for the *Adelphi* magazine, proofs of another poem already accepted by W. J. Turner for the *Spectator*,[10] and the 'last final plum, jewel, diadem and knock-out', a four-page letter from Edith Sitwell.

Writing from Renishaw, the Sitwell family seat near Sheffield, where she was staying with her elder brother, Osbert, Edith expressed the greatest pleasure in signing the copy of *Street Songs* for Denton. She went straight on to praise his article on Sickert which, sure enough, had been shown to her one afternoon by Osbert. 'I cannot tell you how much my brother ... and I enjoyed your alarming experience with Mr Sickert,' she wrote. 'We laughed till we cried – though really in some ways it was no laughing matter. But one thing came out very clearly, and that is, that you are a *born writer!*' She returned to this theme later in the letter: 'As I say, we were full of admiration for the *writing* of your adventure. And my brother Osbert was going to write to Mr Connolly to tell him how very greatly we admired it.

'I do hope you have recovered completely from your terrible accident,

10. 'My House', published in the *Spectator* on 27 November 1942 and reprinted in *A Last Sheaf*.

and that you are able to paint,' she continued, indicating that she had made inquiries about him, for reference in the article to his accident is minimal. 'I hope, very much, that we shall meet one day. I'll promise not to sing, or to dance!'

Denton was over the moon. 'It was,' he wrote in his journal, 'such a beautiful, generous, deliriously exciting letter,' and two days later he was quoting great chunks of it in a letter to Maurice Cranston. Returning to his journal he went on rapturizing: 'I was childish with vanity, and still am, from its effects ... It is so thrilling to have such warm-hearted praise from a great genius ... Of course one would give all the screams of praise that Lady Oxford has ever uttered for one word from Edith Sitwell ... Oh, I have fed on her letter all day. It is perhaps what I live for, this sort of appreciation. I can never hope again to get quite such a generous dose, sent straight from the blue sky.' (It should perhaps be noted that no 'screams of praise' had ever come in his direction from Lady Oxford; quite the reverse seems to have been the case. And whether he would have regarded Edith Sitwell as 'a great genius' had she not lavished praise on him first we shall never know.)

Losing no time in seizing the initiative, he wrote to her again – before he had even found a publisher for his book – to ask permission to dedicate it to her. She replied, again from Renishaw, on 21 September. 'I was delighted to get your charming letter. And I cannot tell you [how] deeply touched and pleased I am that you should think of dedicating your book to me. It has indeed pleased me far more than you know, and of course I accept with the greatest pleasure. Thank you. I look forward to seeing it with eagerness.' She went on, Denton having referred in his letter to his state of health, 'Oh, I am very distressed to hear your health is so precarious. I do hope that you do not suffer pain ... I hope so much that you will recover from it, even if it takes a very long time. But it obviously is not true that you're not much use to anybody else, as you said in your letter.' She again expressed a hope that they would meet: 'Of course, it is singularly difficult in wartime. Still, we *will* meet, and, I hope, very soon.' And she closed her letter with a delightful flourish, quite forgetting grammar, style and any of the other literary niceties by which the Sitwells set such store: 'With best wishes, and *so many* thanks for the dedication, so very pleased and touched thanks.'

At last, on 25 September, Herbert Read responded with an 'encouraging' hand-written letter containing an invitation to lunch – always a hopeful sign coming from a publisher to an author. 'May lunch on Monday be successful and delicious,' Denton intoned in his journal.

'May he like me, may I like him. May the book be published with success. May I be paid and famous. My book is almost lovely. I know it. But for the cloud which is me in it, as well as the loveliness which is me in it.' With reference to his request to dedicate the work to his newly acquired patroness ('a sort of fairy-godmother', as he described her to Alex Comfort in January the following year), he added, 'Miss Sitwell has taken it for her present. I would write something fulsome and beautiful and florid at the beginning for her, but I may not dare.' In the event, it was she who was to write 'something fulsome', in a Foreword to *Maiden Voyage*, Denton's dedication reading simply, 'For Miss Edith Sitwell'.

From total obscurity Denton was rapidly coming to the notice of the famous. The day before he was due to lunch with Herbert Read he was invited to tea by Cecilia Carpmael, who had a studio in Cheyne Walk (later flattened by a bomb), in order to meet Graham Sutherland and his wife, 'she in black fish-net stockings, quite scarlet dress and bus conductor's satchel for a bag. He in good spirits and a curious shrimp-pink shirt and tie with what looked like surréaliste spiders all over it. Talk lapsing and chi-chi quickly and then righting itself in periods of silence. But a success, really a great success.'

He duly turned up next day at the offices of Routledge at 68 Carter Lane, and Read took him on to lunch at his club, the Reform in Pall Mall, though it was not until Denton took the opportunity, while Read was in the lavatory, of looking at the notice-board that he discovered which club he was in. Sitting at Henry James's old table, and without referring once during the meal to the purpose of their meeting, Read entertained him with anecdotes of the *beau monde*, telling him, '"I was in here with Eliot the other day. I was saying that I thought I would have to stop belonging to this club in order to save money. He answered in shocked tones, 'Don't you think that you ought to support it?'"' Read explained that he had himself never thought of a club in that light, as something one ought to support, but that it was typical of Eliot that he should, '"for he is a conservative in just that sense of the word – one who feels it his duty to support institutions that have come down to us from the past."'

When, after Read had paid the bill and the two had left the dining-room the subject of *Maiden Voyage* had still failed to come up, Denton, rather unfortunately as it turned out, produced his letters from Edith Sitwell. There was a moment of silence, and then Read said, '"I used to know her very well. I used to make omelettes for her."' Read explained that she had been good to him when he was '"young and provincial"', but that a coldness had grown up between them because he had not informed her when he became engaged to be married.

'"There was no reason why I should have told her; or Osbert,"' he said. '"My future wife was quite unknown to them and not literary."' Further trouble had been caused because an article had appeared in which the author, Geoffrey Grigson, accused Edith of plagiarizing some remarks on poetry from one of Read's own books. '"I can't go on saying that I don't believe a word of what Grigson wrote,"' he told Denton. '"You know what these things are. One can never put them right it seems – especially with the Sitwells."' There was a pause, and then, warming to his subject, he went on, '"Conceit isn't the word to describe their attitude. It's a sort of arrogance due, I think, to their loveless childhood."' (Edith Sitwell herself was obviously unaware of Read's current feelings, for when she next wrote to Denton, on 25 October, she commented, 'Yes, Mr Read is a most delightful, kind, and charming being. He was a shy and charming youth, and was part of the happy life of my youth, when I lived in London. We used to have large tea-parties on Saturdays, and Herbert Read and two others, sometimes four others, of our very intimate friends used to stop on afterwards, and help cook the supper. Herbert Read was a constant and delightful companion, and we always felt happy with him.')

Eventually, gossip exhausted, Read got round to talking about *Maiden Voyage*. '"Some people might call it precious,"' he told its author.

'"But then I suppose that's my personality,"' Denton croaked.

'"Exactly,"' Read agreed. '"It struck me in some odd way as very contemporary, or of your generation."' And as though he had still not come to a firm editorial decision, he went on, '"I'm not quite sure whether this is the best time to publish such a book, though; on the other hand there may be a feeling in that direction, a boredom with war and horrors."'

It had evidently been touch and go in the office, for two of the directors, including Read, had liked the manuscript, while two others had failed to understand what their colleagues found in it. '"I've had to explain rather patiently the merit I saw in it,"' Read said, but he assured Denton that, providing his firm's libel lawyer vetted and passed it, he could now take it that the book was accepted. What he had really wanted to meet for was to agree terms.

'"I know nothing about terms,"' Denton candidly admitted.

'"What a good thing I'm a poet as well as a publisher,"' Read replied.

Read offered an advance of £50, and then went on to discuss the jacket and title-page, suggesting that Denton decorate them with '"something rather elaborate and ornamental"'. After approving the title, which he thought good, he assured Denton that the book would be published the following February. (In the event it came out on 7 May 1943, and even that entailed an astonishingly speedy production schedule.) As Denton walked quickly down the steps of the Reform he thought to himself what 'a good lunch, a good day' it had been.

He was soon broadcasting to his friends every detail of his meeting with Read, writing to Marcus Oliver a week later, 'It is so nice to have a publisher who is also a poet and an art critic. About the libel. He seems to think that the mention of Repton will cause trouble. I should have thought that the public schools were quite used to anything by now!'

The libel lawyers, Oswald Hickson, Collier & Co., confirmed Read's fears when Denton, having received a letter from Read on 9 October telling him to make an appointment with them, rang them up. Within five seconds, so he reported to Helen Roeder, the lawyer was saying to him, '"My dear Welch, the Repton bits are a bit lurid to say the least,"' going on to assure him that they would soon be toned down.

'I felt that my book was mild as Mother's Milk, didn't you?' Denton asked Helen. 'Did K.C. [Kenneth Clark, to whom he had sent a copy of the manuscript] think it naughty or chi-chi and anything that could be objected to?[11] I suppose the chief trouble is in mentioning the school by name and using my true name as well. The English public schools deserve all the mud that is thrown at them. The only pity is that we still only dare to throw such very refined mud. Having bowdlerized my book so severely before it ever was set down on paper, I can't bear to have it emasculated again! Two severe operations in that region would be enough to kill anyone!

'I know the lawyer's a frightful man,' he went on. 'You could tell it in a moment. His first, rather sinister words were, "Welch, did you say. Oh, I know a lot about you from your book." Herbert Read must protect me and my book from this monster. I know that he will want

11. Kenneth Clark does not appear to have responded to receipt of the manuscript until Denton, nothing daunted, sent him a printed copy of the book on publication. Clark then replied, on 20 May 1943, saying that he had enjoyed the manuscript immensely and would now read the book again 'to enjoy the pleasure of your crystal eye'. He made further amends by congratulating Denton on his decorations, adding, 'What a ravishing book you could do if the times permitted fine reproduction.'

to make my work fit for inclusion in the Boys' Own Paper, and I must fight tooth and nail against being purified. Discussing the misdemeanours of schoolboys with Mr H. is going to be extremely embarrassing.' He asked Helen if on the fateful day – he had made an appointment with Mr Hickson at his office in Surrey Street at half-past two on 15 October – she would give him moral support by meeting him 'for a frugal luncheon together in some low bun-shop', though he ended up by suggesting that they meet at Fortnum's.

On 23 October, having run the gauntlet at the lawyer's office, Denton posted a copy of the manuscript to Edith Sitwell, who on 29 October idiosyncratically acknowledged its arrival by registered post: 'This is not a letter,' she explained. 'It is just to tell you the *MSS has arrived* ... It is a delight to me ... Yes, you are most certainly a born writer. Touch after touch, flash after flash, proves it. I am *full* of interest.'

She wrote more fully on 11 November, saying, 'It is obvious – as I've said so often that it is redundant to repeat it, and yet I must repeat it – that you are a real writer. Nobody but a real writer would get such exact descriptions.' She thought he had a particular gift for writing about horror, and advised him to write 'a dramatic, packed, short story with these sorts of atmosphere in it'. She went on, 'But apart from everything else, I find it an extremely *moving* book. I am, myself, very much moved by it. It has a touching and beautiful quality of youth and innocence about it, which has none of the silliness of youth – only a longing for experience, and a moving longing for warmth, as well as a sad loneliness.'

· Was Edith Sitwell herself being innocent when she thought of Denton as such? Winston Churchill's private secretary, Eddie Marsh, certainly thought so. After reading a review of *Maiden Voyage* in the *Sunday Times*, he wrote to the poet Christopher Hassall to ask if he had seen the review and to say, 'Someone was telling me about it [the book] in London. He said it was rather unfortunate, as the book was reeking with homosexuality, which she [Edith Sitwell] was probably too innocent to perceive ... The S.T. man says nothing about this aspect (unless he is hinting at it when he says, "It reveals, perhaps, at times more than the author intended"), and he praises it very highly. I think I must get it.'[12] It is hard to believe, however, that where homosexuality was concerned,

12. *Ambrosia and Small Beer: The Record of a Correspondence between Edward Marsh and Christopher Hassall* (Longmans, 1964). The *Sunday Times* reviewer was Gerard Hopkins, who also wrote that *Maiden Voyage* was 'just what the work of a very young man should be, fresh, assured, sensitive, alive in observation and in tone'. Denton thought this review 'a sensible one', as he wrote to his old schoolfriend, Basil Jonzen, on 16 June 1943.

Edith Sitwell did not have her eyes wide open; her brother Osbert, to whom she was devoted, was homosexual, living openly for many years with his lover, David Horner, and Edith herself fell hopelessly in love with a homosexual, the Russian painter Pavel Tchelitchew.

In her Foreword, a copy of which she posted to Denton on 12 January 1943, Edith Sitwell wrote, 'This is a very moving and remarkable first book, and the author appears to be that very rare being, a born writer. I have not seen a first book that produces this impression more strongly.' Reiterating her favourite phrase, she went on, 'Mr Welch uses words as only a born writer uses them. He never fumbles.' She concluded, 'I feel that Mr Welch may easily prove to be, not only a born writer, but a very considerable one.'

Enclosed with this panegyric was a letter suggesting their first meeting. 'I wonder if there is any chance of you being in London in April?' she wrote. 'My brother Osbert and I are organizing a giant Poet's Reading, on April the 14th, in aid of Lady Crewe's French in Great Britain Fund. And *after* that ordeal, I shall certainly be staying in London for a few days, so shall hope to see you, if you are there. It would be delightful if you are. *Before* the reading, I presume life will be one long hell of committees, arranging amplifiers, soothing the poets etc. So I suggest when the reading is happily over.'

Meanwhile, preparations for the publication of *Maiden Voyage* were occupying much of Denton's attention. While Herbert Read, as Denton related to Alex Comfort on 5 January 1943, had 'really been extremely nice and easy to deal with about everything', he had not been entirely businesslike over the matter of the advance. 'There is a slight fly in the ointment,' Denton had written to Maurice Cranston on 1 November, 'for I saw when I got it [the contract] home that it was for £30 not £50 advance. Also I am to be paid nothing for my decorations! I suppose the other hard-headed directors have countermanded Read's more generous offer!' Although still under the impression that he was not to be paid for the decorations, he continued his letter to Alex Comfort saying, 'I am so glad that Herbert Read wanted me to decorate it myself. The idea grew from my design for a dust-cover which he seemed to like. Now he has authorized me to do: endpapers, frontispiece, title-page, dedication page, full-length decorations to the three parts and an end-piece. I think the production will really be quite *lavish* for wartime!'[13] In the end, Denton

13. The frontispiece Denton designed was a charming self-portrait which later came into the possession of Mr Charles Monteith, senior editorial consultant at Faber & Faber, from whom it was subsequently stolen.

heard from Read ten days after publication that he was to be paid for his drawings after all; the fact had been 'omitted in error'.

In the midst of all this activity, Denton had again fallen ill and had taken to his bed. 'I could only think of things for a second,' he recorded on 24 November, 'before my mind switched in a painful dance to something else. All the time moving, jumping, thumping, aching; and strange visions of food that I could not rid myself of sometimes making me feel sick and sometimes tantalizing me.'

On 7 December he learned of the death of his father, though he seems not to have been told any details. (Arthur Welch had in fact died from lung cancer in Shanghai on 9 November, only a few days after being interned by the occupying Japanese army.) 'It was only the slightest shock,' Denton wrote on hearing the news, 'and there was hardly any grief with it at all.' He wondered whether his stepmother (who, probably unknown to him, had made her escape to America) and Bill were 'seizing as much money as possible'. He went on to note that he had always looked on his father as a rich man 'and a bulwark in some measure between me and the future'. He added, 'All that is left of my father is what he has left.' Like many emotionally deprived sons, Denton frankly coveted his father's possessions, hoping at least to be sent a cigarette case, cufflinks or a watch. 'I should like them chiefly,' he admitted, 'for what they are and only a very little because they were his.'

His father's death was not, therefore, one of the events of this memorable year which Denton chose to dwell on when writing his journal at ten to eleven on New Year's Eve: 'It has been damnable, on top of all my difficulties of temperament, to have that obscene accident. And I have been tortured enough. Something screams out in me that all is filth and devil-worship.' Then, in more sanguine mood, he rehearsed the year's successes, remembering that his painting of Lord Berners had been illustrated in *Vogue*, that another picture had been mentioned in the *Observer*, that half a dozen poems had been published, but above all, that *Horizon* had published his article on Sickert and that *Maiden Voyage* had been accepted for publication: 'This all may be only a beginning, but it means something and I must go on and on and on.'

EIGHT

Lunch with Edith

Like a spider, indiscriminate of the victims caught in its web, Denton used many of those who came his way as nourishment for his writing. Sometimes they were friends, sometimes mere acquaintances, sometimes simply those who had been rash enough to write him fan letters; their fate, as often as not, was to end up as characters in his short stories. His dependence on first-hand material became so notorious that many people deliberately avoided him for fear of what he would write about them, and others, suspecting that they had already been written about, would spend a great deal of time and energy in trying to discover, before publication, what had been written.

Late in 1942, however, Denton came to know someone who, after his death, was to turn the tables on him. She was Noël Adeney, who had trained at the Slade and was married to another painter, Bernard Adeney, a founder of the London Group. The Adeneys lived in London with their two children, Richard and Charlotte, and in addition to their home in Hampstead they also owned a holiday home, which Noël had designed herself, called Middle Orchard, in the Kent village of Crouch, near Borough Green and about six miles from Pitt's Folly Cottage. It was at Middle Orchard that Denton was to die in 1948, and before that his life was to become considerably involved with that of the Adeneys. After the war, Noël and Bernard even purchased and restored 34 Croom's Hill in Greenwich, the house in which Denton had lodged with Evie Sinclair when he was a student.

Over a period of six years Denton, a compulsive letter writer, wrote at least one hundred and thirty letters to Noël Adeney, and after his death she made use of them to concoct a highly fanciful 'novel' entitled *No Coward Soul*, which was published in 1956. Into it she crammed, under an assortment of paper-thin disguises, many of the people and places Denton had known. Maurice Cranston, who recognized every character in it without the slightest difficulty, recommended it for

publication to C. Day Lewis, a director of Chatto & Windus. Unaccountably, in view of the book's utter lack of literary merit, Day Lewis decided
to publish it, under the Hogarth imprint no less, on the condition that
Noël Adeney, to circumvent the problem of libel, would further disguise
the character based on Eric Oliver by making him female. (Although
Day Lewis already knew of Denton, having published one of his poems,
'Night in Wartime', in *Orion* in July 1945, it was not until Maurice
Cranston enlightened him that he realized Denton and his circle was
the subject of the novel.)

It was thus that Eric Oliver, whom despite her protestations to the
contrary Noël Adeney had disliked intensely, suffered the indignity of
being depicted as a vain, neurotic, dishonest, Fascist, clod-hopping land-
girl by the name of 'Gina Downs'. Even the name Gina was a calculated
insult, for it was the name of Mary Sloman's alsatian bitch. Two further
sex changes were involved in the process of disguising other characters:
Evie Sinclair became 'Ivor', and Helen Roeder became 'Denis', 'a young
businessman'. The rest of the cast is made up of Jack Easton (named
'Charles Essex'), Edith Sitwell ('Lady Olivia Standing'), the poetess
Dorothy Wellesley ('Lady Blank'), the biographer Hector Bolitho ('Victor
Tresco'), Denton's stepmother, Ada ('Alice') and his brothers Bill
('Stephen'), Paul ('John') and, strangely, a third brother who is not named
(it is therefore possible that Denton had told Noël about his infant
brother, Tommy, who had died). Denton himself became 'Merton', a
poet who has been injured in a railway accident.

The publisher's blurb states that Noël Adeney's first novel (it was,
mercifully, also her last) is about friendship and courage. It is actually
the product of a vindictive and jealous woman's desire for revenge on
her rival for Denton's affections, Eric Oliver. She was particularly
aggrieved because she believed that Eric had intercepted and destroyed
a letter which Denton, just before he died, had supposedly struggled
to the village postbox to send to her. Further resentment had arisen
immediately after Denton's death when Helen Roeder came to stay with
Eric at Middle Orchard and occupied herself, as Noël correctly deduced,
in typing up Denton's journals; Noël was convinced, with good reason,
that the journals contained unflattering references to herself. In an attempt
to smooth things over Helen wrote a letter to Noël which Eric placed
inside a book belonging to Noël for her to find, but this only made
matters worse.

Noël's own version of these exhausting events, along with much else,
is contained in *No Coward Soul*, the flavour of which is typified by its

description of Gina: she had 'kind but frightened eyes', a 'low, empty forehead' and a mouth 'grimacing with scorn or fear'. The narrator, 'Sydney', saw a face 'that changed from a bland smoothness containing no thought to an intense corrugation in an effort to have some, or to avoid it'. When asked for his reaction to the book, Eric Oliver very charitably replied, 'It is actually quite good in parts, although she made me out to be more rough and plebeian than I am. But it is better to be looked over than overlooked!'[1]

Noël Adeney first met Denton when, as she recalls in an unpublished memoir, she was taken to tea with him at The Hop Garden by a mutual friend at the end of 1940. She came away with the impression of a man only about 5ft 3ins tall (he was in fact nearer 5ft 5ins), with an appearance of 'uniqueness and urgency rather than beauty, heightened colour, a shrill, excited voice and with an uneasy walk that stressed a need for fulfilment and rest'.[2] She remembered meeting him several times in 1941 on visits to another mutual friend who lived near St Mary's Platt, but it is from September 1942, when she read the *Horizon* article on Sickert and wrote to him to say how much she admired it, that their uneasy friendship really dates. Denton reacted enthusiastically, as he often did to such overtures, and telephoned to invite her to tea (he was by then living at Pitt's Folly Cottage). At Christmas-time she in turn invited him to dinner, to which he turned up, she recorded, 'dressed very daintily in a beautifully made check suit'.

Her pursuit of him (as Eric Oliver has described it) can in part be attributed to a desire to get to know a promising young writer, but she was clearly also the kind of woman who enjoys the company of young homosexuals. On 28 March 1943, for example, Denton recorded in his journal a picnic lunch he had had with her: 'Lying in the Hurst Woods we ate our hard-boiled eggs and talked about homosexuality.' But, he added, 'her probe is so uncomfortable. She tells you just the things to ruffle you. And yet all the time she rather admires, or at least likes you.

'She ate my chocolate, which I resented [chocolate was, of course,

1. In conversation with the author.
2. Noël Adeney's son, Richard Adeney, who did not much care for Denton, has confirmed (in conversation with the author) that Denton spoke with an embarrassingly shrill voice. He also remembers him as a 'witty, gossipy, humorous, very vital sort of person, whom it was difficult to realize was an invalid'. Other friends found him essentially 'boyish', with a voice that, although often excited, had the musical quality of a light baritone.

rationed], although I broke off large pieces for her. Then Sir William Geary [the local squire] and Phyl Ford rode by on horses. I think they thought we were lying in the leaves making love. Wasn't that queer! Quite gruesome. She asked me if I talked to middle-aged women, like her, better than to younger ones. I found it difficult, because the moment one begins openly to talk about age with anyone, one always ends up by offending. Always one dates them just a little earlier than they expected, or places them unconsciously with the generation two years earlier.'

From time to time Noël and Denton were to get on each other's nerves. He, in the tiresome way that people so often do when in love, would often bore on at inordinate length in his letters to her about his new friend, Eric, while she tended to take too intimate an interest in the gory details of his accident and illness. This he resented, for he was genuinely revolted by being ill, and on the days when he was really unwell he seldom wanted anyone near him. In fairness to Noël, however, it must be stated that he did not always refrain from making it known to her and others just how unwell he was. Writing to her on 5 March 1943, he reported that he had meant to write the day before but after 'getting up and going about for a day or two, I have now had to go back to bed again! Isn't it maddening?' This particular bout of ill-health, he explained, had begun 'as a high-temperature attack' but now he had flu on top of it.

Evie, too, seems to have succumbed to the flu at the same time (Denton blamed May Walbrand-Evans for starting the epidemic), and to while away the time she was reading to him Alec Waugh's *The Loom of Youth* — 'of all things' — which seemed to him so dull that he could not think why it had been so popular.[3] Evie frequently read to him when he was ill in bed. *The Loom of Youth* was followed by Jane Austen's *Mansfield Park*, and although he had read it before, he told Noël that he had forgotten the end and was on tenterhooks to know what happened to Fanny Price. 'It is so nice to read about parsonages, and rolling parks, and pug dogs sitting on sofas with their mistresses, and eligible young men with ten thousand a year, when one is lying in bed, and feeling extremely sordid.'

He was particularly irritated to be stuck in bed again because he had

3. The *Loom of Youth*, written in six weeks when Alec Waugh was seventeen, was one of the earliest novels to touch on the subject of homosexuality in public schools. Its publication in 1917 caused such a rumpus that it was thought inadvisable for Alec's younger brother, Evelyn, to follow him to Sherborne, so he was sent to Lancing instead.

just started on a new painting – 'of a hermit outside his cave' – but he was soon cheered up by the arrival of a proof of the jacket of *Maiden Voyage*. 'It really has been printed very carefully,' he told Noël, 'and looks nice, I think.' On 11 March he was again writing to her to say, 'I'm still in bed, and last night I thought I was going to explode! My temperature seemed to be galloping away with me.' He thought it was 'pneumonia à la Churchill', but had not called in a doctor (Jack Easton was in Egypt with the Royal Army Medical Corps) as all the ones he knew in Tonbridge were 'rather horrible'.

These reports seem to point to a fairly serious relapse over this period and yet, incredibly, his capacity for work was undiminished. On 5 March he had interrupted the daily record of events in his journal in order to write the account of the walking tour he had enjoyed in 1933, which was to be published, after his death, as *I Left My Grandfather's House*, and in the course of two weeks – almost exactly the duration of his present bout of illness – he had completed some ten thousand words of it.

By 16 March he seems to have recovered sufficiently to have gone out of the house late at night and, in spite of the cold and his fear of becoming ill again so soon after recovering from the flu, to have made his way to May Walbrand-Evans's house on the main road by the iron gates leading to Pitt's Folly, where he loitered within view of the house in the hope that she would see him and ask him in. Instead he got into conversation with a passing Canadian serviceman, who thought Denton had been having a pee and asked, '"Did it get frost-bitten?"' The Canadian then began to boast of his sexual conquests (twenty times in ten days was his claim), but at last Denton shook him off, went home and felt a longing for his poems 'to be good; not smeary', as the Canadian's love-affairs had been smeary.

His poems, alas, were all too frequently 'smeary'. Poetry was the literary form he had tackled first, and while he continued to write it all his life he never mastered either form or expression in it. His poetic sensibility was to go, instead, into his prose. Indeed it is hard to discern any poetic model or discipline behind the lush sentimentality and sardonic flippancy of his poems, which more than any other artistic form he attempted illustrates his lack of opportunity to exchange ideas and criticism with his contemporaries.

A magazine called *Poetry* had accepted two of his poems back in 1941 but had ceased publication before they could appear. This disappointment would have been alleviated to some extent when Denton received 'an encouraging note' about his poems from Henry Treece, editor of *Kingdom Come*, for which Denton wrote to thank Treece on 20 June 1942, taking the opportunity to seek his advice about bringing out a collection of poetry. 'Should I begin by attempting to get a small book together,' he had asked, 'or should I content myself by trying to appear in periodicals? The Fortune Press have returned the few poems I sent them, saying that there were not enough to make a selection from. I feel therefore that I should like to appear with a group of other writers. I should like very much to know whether any anthologies of new poets are being made. Do you think this my best course of action?'

He ended his letter, 'If you have time to answer I hope you'll be able to give me some sort of advice as I know absolutely no other young writers and feel completely cut off and at sea.' His correspondence with Treece, which later broke down when Treece was rash enough to disapprove of the erotic subject-matter of his prose, revealed a good deal of self-knowledge in Denton about the inherent weaknesses in his poetry. 'I can't make out what is wrong with my poetry – something is,' he wrote to Treece on 14 May 1943. 'I have been writing poetry since I was nine years old, but I still don't know what it's really about. As a child I used to think that it was a rather pleasant magic process; but now I seem to have the greatest distaste for what I produce "in that line!"'

Thanking Treece for a letter of advice on 9 June the same year, he wrote, 'I agree with you in thinking that my poems are too narrowed down ... And I also agree with you that they need attention. But here I must admit that however much I try, I still find it quite impossible to formulate to myself what I am *trying* to do when I write a poem. I just want to do it; and consequently what comes out of me will probably be rather shapeless, rather sexy and probably rather trite. My critical faculty, after the event, will tell me of these things, but it hasn't given me much help yet in remedying the faults.'

His poem 'By the River' is a perfect example, chosen almost at random, of his 'sexy triteness':

> O Roger I shall yet remember,
> In the Winter's wet December
> I shall know your body's print.
> There in grass the satin dint
> Holds the shape of what you were
> Like a mould on Jupiter.

> And when the grass is dead and dry
> I'll still find where you used to lie.[4]

Another, called 'The Coppice', is even less successful:

> Walking close to the coppice,
>   Marching over the leaves,
> I catch the kiss and the coughing
>   The wind weaves ...
>
> Never again to touch him,
>   Know the silver of his tongue;
> This is the thought that strangles,
>   That seems to coat my lung.[5]

A number of Denton's poems were to be published by highly reputable journals in his lifetime, but they only amounted to short, occasional verse, and it is not too surprising that there was no rush to bring out a collection of his poetry.

Denton's first opportunity to meet Edith and Osbert Sitwell came to nothing. Osbert had rustled up some impressive royal patronage for the 'giant Poets' Reading' that his sister had told Denton they were organizing on 14 April 1943 at the Aeolian Hall – the queen and both the princesses were to attend – and on 2 April Denton was writing to Helen Roeder to tell her that he was going to see the Sitwells 'after the reading was over'. It is not clear whether he was planning to attend the reading and to meet the Sitwells the same day, or whether, as Edith had suggested, he was to meet her some time afterwards while she was staying in London. Either way, perhaps because of his ill-health, Denton's meeting with her was postponed, and he also had the misfortune to miss one of the more hilarious literary occasions of the war. T. S. Eliot recited from *The Waste Land*, Osbert read several of his eclogues from *England Reclaimed*, and Edith was the star of the afternoon, reciting in grand style her new poem, 'Anne Boleyn's Song'. Walter de la Mare, however, was unable to reach the gigantic lectern provided by Osbert (who was considerably taller than de la Mare), and one of Denton's editors, W. J. Turner, went on so long that he had to be silenced by the chairman. After the queen had left, Dorothy Wellesley, who had had too much to drink and who was, as Edith had told Osbert's friend

---

4. Published in *A Last Sheaf*.
5. *ibid.*

David Horner, 'beyond any words tiresome', struck Harold Nicolson with her umbrella and had to be restrained by Beatrice Lillie.[6]

Later in the year Denton was able to make up for having missed this jamboree by going, in company with Peggy Mundy Castle, to a provincial version, again attended by Dorothy Wellesley, in Tunbridge Wells on 2 October. The meeting was chaired by Vita Sackville-West, 'looking long-nosed, 1924 bobbed-hair a little frizzy, cold, very English country dowdy not-quite-brown tweed skirt and not quite red jersey, with long rather delicate legs'. She announced that Lady Gerald,[7] in spite of the recent death in action of her nephew, the Duke of Wellington, would after all be appearing, having decided '"that public duty should take precedence of private sorrow"'. Denton recorded that 'this little speech [was] delivered in a cold rather Lady de Burghish deadness with that blank completely unreceptive eye'. He added, 'One felt rather against this stuffed Vita.'

The reading began with the Irish poet Shane Leslie – 'bald and in battle-dress' – reciting from his 'Epic of Jutland' and then Rudyard Kipling's 'Mine Sweepers'. He also 'told an anecdote in a boring way of how his uncle in India was one of the first to see Kipling's Plain Tales of the Hills. He sent them to the *Daily Telegraph* who said that they were excellent but not quite up to the standard of their paper. Everyone laughed.' After a hiatus caused by the non-appearance of Louis MacNeice, who was due on next, the novelist V. C. Clinton-Baddeley read one of Dorothy Wellesley's poems 'in a heavy rather thrilling voice', and then Vita Sackville-West recited a poem of her own. Denton began 'to like her more – to feel that there was something rather nice and sad and quite quiet and feeling beneath the still English horse shell'.

When the reading was over, Denton had to restrain Peggy Mundy Castle from rushing up to Dorothy Wellesley with an envelope full of her own poems. The other poets 'stood about looking defensive', and

6. One account of this poetry reading is given by John Pearson in his immensely entertaining biography of the three Sitwells, *Façades* (Macmillan, 1978). A further, though second-hand, account of the fracas was retailed by Denton in a letter to Noël Adeney on 7 December 1943: 'Suddenly,' he had been told by his informant, 'a woman rushed up to Edith and the others and said, "Why wasn't I allowed to recite? I'll never speak to any of you again," and a great deal more. Tears streamed down her face and Edith burst into tears too! Harold Nicolson tried to calm D. Wellesley by putting a hand on her shoulder. Wellesley screamed, "Don't touch me, Harold." The scene was frightful – and the queen had only just left! Nobody knew what to do. It was awful.'

7. Dorothy Wellesley's husband was Lord Gerald Wellesley, who the day before had succeeded as Duke of Wellington.

the 'utter incompetent dreariness of the whole thing' was brought home to him, making him feel that the poets should have been ashamed to take part in such a squalid show. 'I vowed that I would never take part in that sort of poetry reading, if I was ever asked.'

A few days after the rather more dramatic occasion of Edith Sitwell's earlier in the year, Denton had been sent into a flat spin by the arrival of 'the well-known, exciting, thrilling, anti-climax yellow-orange envelope'; it was a telegram from Edith inviting him to lunch on 19 April. Although it was clearly addressed from the Sesame Club, that fearsome haunt of professional ladies in Grosvenor Street, Denton could not decide whether to reply to Renishaw or to Osbert's house in Chelsea. Eventually he dismissed the waiting girl 'without a tip (which I am told is quite rococo nowadays)', flew round asking everyone where he should send the reply, decided on the Sesame itself, sent a wire and then went to a telephone box to ring the club to see if Edith Sitwell was indeed in residence. (It is not clear how, having dismissed the girl, he first sent a telegram.) By this time his normally shrill voice had shot up several more octaves. 'The woman at the other end would insist on calling me Madam while I gave her my message,' he recorded in his journal the next day. 'I wanted to be quite sure that Edith was staying there.

'"Yes, madam," the woman said.

'"Don't call her," I shrieked. "I only want to leave a message."

'"Is it Mr or Mrs Welch?" the woman asked right at the end, still definite in her mind about my sex. I wanted to laugh.

'"Mr," I said. "Mr Welch."

'Was my voice fluty and high through nervousness?' he asked himself. 'I am not usually taken for a woman on the telephone.'

On the day of the momentous lunch he noted in his journal his feelings before setting off for London: 'Now it's happened, now I'm going up. It's rained in gusts; I've been reading *Street Songs* and eating breakfast with tickling contracting feeling in the centre of me. I think I will wear my blue suit. What will it be like?'

The train to London was so crowded that he was afraid he would become ill if he could not find a seat, and eventually he sat on someone's suitcase. When he arrived at the Sesame Club a sudden, irrational fear that he would not recognize Edith Sitwell overcame him. And then she appeared.

His description of her, written in his journal the following day, ranks among the most vivid she inspired: 'The tall figure dressed all in black, black trilby, Spanish witch's hat, black satin dress to the ankles and two huge aquamarine rings. Wonderful rings on powder-white hands, and face too powder-pearly, nacreous white, almost not to be believed in, with the pinkened mouth, the thin, delicate, swordlike nose and tender-curling nostrils. No hair, I can remember no hair at first. The rings, the glistening satin, and the kid-white skin.'

She immediately asked when *Maiden Voyage* was to be published. He told her that publication had been held up, but that he had heard it was over-subscribed before publication.

'"Isn't that wonderful,"' she said.

'"It's due entirely to your Foreword," I pushed out of my mouth. More nervousness. Hot, red.

'"No, it isn't. I think it's due to your article on Sickert." Here a laugh.'

They then moved into the dining-room where Edith, thinking to keep him out of the draught, placed him facing the window. (Denton, one suspects, would have preferred the light behind him.) As he watched her eat he realized that he had never thought of things going into her mouth, only things (poems) coming out.

She asked about his family. When he told her that his father had recently died, conversation, too, expired. He tried to get her to talk about Renishaw, but again, talk failed. At last they reverted to *Maiden Voyage*.

'"You really did like the book?" I ask.

'She flutters her hands in hopelessness.

'"Well, didn't I write to you all about it? No one could say more."

('Edith Sitwell,' he noted, 'does not often say so much.')

'"Now,"' she told him, '"I think it is time for you to do something violent and vulgar."

'"That's what I'm longing to do," I told her.

'"I will tell you what your danger is,"' said Edith, evidently warming to a theme. '"It is your ingrowing toenail. Everything in, in, in. It is perfect in that book, but you must not do it again."'[8]

Then the conversation turned to gossip about the royal poetry reading. Denton asked if the princesses had listened well. '"They sat

8. C. E. M. Joad, writing in *Decadence: A Philosophical Inquiry* (Faber & Faber, 1948), commented adversely on this very aspect of Denton's work, taking as an example of decadent fiction his short story 'Narcissus Bay' (published in the *Cornhill* magazine in 1945 and reprinted in *Brave and Cruel*). Joad regarded this as a work written under the assumption 'that any experience is significant and worthy of record, irrespective of the quality of the experience or the nature of the "object" of which it is an experience'. Denton himself found Joad's criticism 'absurd'.

very still in the front row,"' said Edith, '"and stared straight at one."' She added, '"The queen has a real interest in books."'

She talked about her favourite writers, saying how much she enjoyed Graham Greene's *England Made Me*, and recommended Kipling and Somerset Maugham 'as wonderful story models'. (The latter model failed to find favour with Denton, however, for three months later, having read two of Maugham's short stories, he described them in his journal as 'stupid'.)

After lunch Edith swept off to what Denton described as 'the forbidding, aquarium-dark drawing-room'. She seemed to be talking to herself and he wondered if he was meant to say '"What is that?"' or pretend not to hear. Suddenly he remembered that he had left his copy of her *Notes on Poetry*, which he had brought with him for her to sign, in the dining-room, so he went back to retrieve it. 'The other diners looked at me interestedly, I thought,' he recalled with glee. 'Nice, nice to eat with famous poet, lovely, magic.'

While they sat talking, 'a little old woman passes us, retraces her steps.

'"Miss Edith Sitwell, is it?" she asks so carefully, gently. As if one could mistake that black satin and those aquamarines!

'"Yes," the grave reserved answer – a little bow.

'"Would you be so good –?"

'*English Women* is thrust forward, open, ready to be written in at once. 'Edith Sitwell takes it.

'"But at your leisure, there is no hurry," she waves her hand, smiles, floats away, disappears.

'Edith Sitwell makes a face.

'"I suppose this happens all day long?" I say, feeling glad that I have not brought two books of poems.'

With his visit to the lawyer still engraved in his mind, he discussed with her the subject of censorship. '"The law, I think, is absolutely right,"' she told him. '"As Bernard Shaw said to me when we were all called to give evidence over the Well of Loneliness fuss, "Here I am, asked to say something about this pathetic book, and I don't know what to do because I know it's serious, unpornographic, but it's so bad as literature."'[9] And she went on, again exhibiting her curious blindness to Denton's own homosexuality, '"Let these poor people think or behave

9. *The Well of Loneliness*, a novel by Radclyffe Hall about lesbianism, had provoked a *cause célèbre* on its publication in 1928 by Jonathan Cape. Lurid publicity attended its court cases in the United States and Britain, where it remained banned for some twenty years.

like that, if they cannot help it, but don't let them write bad books about it. It is dangerous. In the hands of young people they might do great damage – not because of stimulation, but because of the terrible revulsion they might cause."' Denton, not certain what to answer, switched the conversation and then began to make polite noises about leaving, but Edith had a surprise in store. Osbert had asked his sister to keep Denton with her until a quarter past three as he, too, wanted to meet the talented young writer whose work he had spotted in *Horizon*. He duly arrived, and Denton was regaled with anecdotes, told 'with great skill and grace'.

Four days later, on 23 April, Denton wrote to Marcus Oliver: 'My dear, Terrific excitements! I had lunch with Edith Sitwell on Monday! And Osbert came along afterwards. I was reduced almost to a jelly, but they were both charming in quite different ways. Edith was magnificently impressive in black satin to the ground and aquamarines as big as lollipops. Really too queenlike. Her face is quite white, very smooth and her fingernails are after the mandarin pattern – one inch long!

'I think lunch went off well. We talked a lot and she gave me her new Poet's Notebook in which she had written Denton Welch from his friend Edith Sitwell! Osbert was quite another cup of tea. Full of anecdotes and would be naughty, I feel, with the slightest encouragement. Amusing. I must tell you all about it when we meet. Come over won't you when you can as before! Sleep on the floor! (poetry).' On 2 May he followed this up with further observations on the Sitwells: 'Have you heard much of Osbert in the past? He seems to be rather matey with the Queen, but is he also matey with queens in the plural do you think!' He added, 'I have not met anybody interesting except the Sitwells ... I think they are both going to be wonderfully helpful to me, because they both said that they must arrange for me to meet *other* people.'

Denton's letter of 23 April contained other titbits of camp gossip. Had Marcus heard of 'hulu's escape'? – a reference, apparently, to a mutual friend who had 'let her hair down to the very ground' so that the army psychiatrist had 'counted her out!' And he ended with the news that May Walbrand-Evans now had a schoolmaster as a lodger: 'He is rather nice and, I suspect, just a little pecu.'

Shortly after the day of the memorable lunch, Denton was able to send Edith Sitwell an advance copy of *Maiden Voyage*. ('The Maiden has not *yet* started on her voyage,' he had reported to Marcus Oliver on 25 March. 'Isn't it irritating? She is a dilly-dally! Apparently it all depends on the book-binders who hold everything up because there are so few.') On 26 April, Edith Sitwell wrote to thank him. 'My very real and warm congratulations,' she began, 'and all my most deeply felt good wishes for the great success of the book. I am *most happy* to have the dedication, and regard it with delight and profound satisfaction. It really *is* a good book, and you really *are* a born writer. I have said this so often that it is redundant to repeat it, but I must repeat it again.

'The designs are delightful, and the cover really beautiful, and very strange, and very satisfying.

'How exciting it is, when one's first book appears. No appearance that comes after can ever be quite the same.

'I regard this book as the birth of a *real* new writer, and I am very proud, as I said before, that the book should be dedicated to me. Actually, the passages in Horizon were the birth, but of course, a magazine, however much read, is a more limited thing.

'I look forward with excitement to seeing the reviews. They take ages to come, at this time, so do not feel despondent or flat if this is so.

'I read the book till very late (I reached the whisky episode, which made me laugh till I cried, all over again) and I find it every bit as moving, and as expressive as writing, as it seemed before.

'It is quite extraordinary, the way in which you are at home with words. It is like a jockey with a race-horse.'

She ended with her usual enthusiastic breathlessness: 'Strongly-felt congratulations – delight in the book – certainty of the quality of the book. All best wishes – and *thank you.*'

Four days after publication, Denton received a 'fine letter' from E. M. Forster, 'full of very *sensible* praise of the book'. It is possible that Denton himself had sent a complimentary copy to Forster, whom he admired enormously and with whom he was later to correspond on the subject of homosexuality and the law. Forster, however, may have been overstating his enthusiasm for the benefit of the author, for he also wrote, in an undated letter to William Plomer which probably refers to *Maiden Voyage*, 'Denton Welch is certainly easy to read, and he doesn't in this book tease anyone whom I think ought not to be teased. Anyhow he is the sort of writer I am always grateful to. They will never do any better, but that is their cul-de-sac, not mine.'[10] Denton also received

10. E. M. Forster made amends for this somewhat dismissive attitude to Denton's work when, after reading a manuscript copy of the journals, he wrote to John Lehmann on 17 July 1951, praising Denton's courage 'not only to bear his disasters but to *see* himself, so far as he can', and commending 'his sensitiveness, visual and tactile, and his occasional wisdom'.

a letter from Lord Berners, thanking him for a complimentary copy, which Denton most unfairly described as 'nice but not exciting'. Berners wrote, 'Thank you so very much for sending me your book, which I have enjoyed immensely. It is charmingly written and everything is seen from a strange and interesting angle. Edith Sitwell had already told me how good it was.' He apologized for not writing before, explaining that he had only just emerged from a nursing home after an operation, had found the book on returning home, and had 'read it in one gulp. I hope you'll write a lot more.'

The question of whether or not to send a complimentary copy of *Maiden Voyage* to Lady Oxford exercised Denton's mind a good deal. 'I can't decide whether to send one to Oxford or not,' he wrote to Marcus Oliver on 23 April. 'Do you think she's snubbed me too much! I don't want her to hang her copy on a string in the closet at Bedford Square!' It may seem strange that he should have even contemplated sending a copy to someone whose wholehearted approval he had singularly failed to obtain in previous attempts, but he had never been able to swallow criticism of his work in any form. Shortly after the war, for example, the novelist and critic Neville Braybrooke invited Denton to contribute to a quarterly magazine he edited between 1941 and 1951 called *The Wind and the Rain*. The story Denton sent in described a man entering a public lavatory, seeing a drawing of a nude on the wall and adding some pubic hairs to it. Braybrooke rejected the story as unworthy of Denton's talents, and by return of post he received a letter from Denton saying, 'Who the hell are you, and anyway, Peter Quennell thinks the story a work of genius.' If that was really the case, it seems strange that Quennell, editor of the *Cornhill*, did not in fact ever publish it.[11]

The truth behind Denton's dithering over Lady Oxford turned out to be that he wanted to rub her nose in Edith Sitwell's Foreword: 'I am still debating whether to send her my book or no,' he wrote to Marcus Oliver on 2 May. 'I am afraid she already thinks me an appalling nuisance; but I would like her to see Edith's Foreword, and just perhaps to dip into the book. I expect she would hate it, as she hated the Sickert article.' He must have made up his mind soon after sending that letter, for on 10 May Lady Oxford was writing a brief note from Bedford Square which can hardly have thrilled its recipient: 'Dear Mr Denton Welch, I thank you for your book. I am *not* a good person to give books to! I am too severe in my criticisms. Nevertheless, I would be very pleased

11. The incident described in the story was eventually incorporated by Denton into 'Leaves from a Young Person's Notebook', published in *Brave and Cruel*.

to have such praise as Edith Sitwell has given you in her "Foreword". Yours sincerely, Margot Oxford.'

Edith Sitwell, tireless in her determination to go on encouraging her protégé, was herself writing again on 27 May, to say, 'I do hope you are as pleased with the reviews as I am. I say "Pleased" – delighted would be the better word. In my own opinion, they really *could not* be bettered ... I can't tell you how delighted I am. I think you have every reason to be *really* delighted, and to feel that your career as a writer has begun splendidly.

'I long to know how the book is going. I hope the publishers are pleased with the book. They most certainly should be. I can't think of a first book that has had a better reception.' She promised to write yet again in a day or two, saying, 'This is only a tiny note. But I can't and must not let another day pass without telling you of my very real happiness that your book has been so splendidly received.'[12]

On 26 May Denton signed a copy of the book for Noël Adeney, and by the end of the month he had received his first fan letter, from 'an unknown admirer', as he described the correspondent on a postcard to Noël. 'I think he must be quite an *elderly* gentleman,' he told her, 'as he writes from the Athenaeum asking me to tea, saying that he read M. V. with such deep interest that he wants to meet the author in the flesh. He adds rather disquietingly that apart from finding the book a "work of real art", his professional interest as *psychologist* was also very much aroused!!' Having asked Noël's advice on whether or not to accept the invitation, he then wrote to Helen Roeder, on 31 May: 'Evie thinks I am being very ridiculous when I say that I don't want to go, but I have the fear that I shall be probed quite mercilessly by a sinister gentleman with hypnotic eyes.' He seems, however, to have made his mind up for himself for he ends, 'After all I suppose that one cannot come to much harm within the sacred portals of a building like the Athenaeum.'

His experience of London clubs – the Reform, the Sesame and now an invitation to the Athenaeum – had been due to expand still further.

---

12. Edith Sitwell – and Denton himself – had good cause to rejoice. The *New Statesman* considered *Maiden Voyage* 'the boldest kind of autobiography' and 'a work of outstanding originality and merit'. *Time and Tide* wrote: 'That Denton Welch in his very early twenties [he was in fact twenty-eight] should write a book which leaves a deep impression on our minds in wartime is an accomplishment not to be sneezed at.' The *Spectator* noted: 'He lives for us in these pages with an almost embarrassing vividness, his language is direct, sensuous and clear.'

A favourable notice in the *Daily Express* by James Agate resulted in an invitation from Edward Sackville-West, then working at the BBC, to lunch at Brooks's on 20 May. 'Oh, excitements,' Denton recorded on receiving this invitation; and knowing, surely, of the critic's lugubrious mien, he added, 'I must wear sober blue suit.' Ironically, word reached Sackville-West of the flamboyant style of dress in which Denton usually adorned himself when visiting London, causing him to decide not to risk introducing Denton to the dining-room at his club in St James's, but to go to the more raffish Café Royal instead.

Denton found Sackville-West 'rather small and quiet'. He spoke 'rather drawlingly, his face was pale, a little spotty, sad. He wore two rings on his fingers (rings that seemed innocent of devices or crests) and an identity bracelet.' In the fluster of cancelling his table at Brooks's, Sackville-West had forgotten to book one at the Café Royal, and as the downstairs dining-room there was full he and Denton ended up in the gallery. Denton ordered hors d'oeuvres, 'stewed in salt and vinegar', and having left much of it he was faced with a vol-au-vent, 'salt again to the point of horror'. When the éclairs arrived Sackville-West said, '"Oh, it's got custard in it!"' and began to scrape it all out. Denton asked if he had expected real cream and Sackville-West replied, '"I thought it might be that soya-bean stuff, which sometimes isn't so bad."'

The conversation proved difficult, Denton noting as its high point a moment when they both became excited thinking of the absurdities in *Maiden Voyage*, though Sackville-West soon grew sombre again. '"Sometimes your unpleasantness seemed quite gratuitous,"' he told Denton. '"A long pin comes out and in you push it."' He added, '"You'll probably hate it in a few years. But that won't make it bad, you'll just be like most of us, as we grow older – less willing to give yourself away on a plate."'

Suddenly, thought Denton, Sackville-West looked 'very staid and distant and rather primadonnaish'. '"When one is out of one's first youth," pause, "or perhaps out of any youth at all, one gradually gives less away. But that is what is so disarming about your book, the fact that you don't in the least mind making yourself out unpleasant or ridiculous."' He astutely advised Denton never to write beyond his own experience; this, he thought, was fatal.

Lunch had not been a particularly exhilarating experience. Afterwards Denton wandered down Piccadilly, where he saw copies of *Maiden Voyage* on sale in Hatchard's, and into Green Park. Some men were lying face down on the grass and Denton passed by them, 'looking at them furtively'. London, so full of sailors and American soldiers as it was during the war, made him melancholy. 'The pain of missing all this excitement in other people's lives is horrible. I feel the awful outpouring waste. I want to be back alone in the country as I cannot share it all.'

Twelve days later, on 1 June, he sent an account of his latest trip to London to his faithful correspondent Marcus Oliver: 'Edward Sackville-West was nice — his manner is a trifle languid, but he seems to show interest in my writing, and he has now taken three poems he says he's going to spout over the wireless with some others one night!' Like Noël and Helen, Marcus too was told about the fan letter and his advice sought on whether or not to brave tea at the Athenaeum. 'I don't particularly want to be poked and probed,' Denton wrote. 'One will have to wear one's spiritual chastity belt tightly padlocked on that day, I feel! The gent's name is Richard Armoral Howden. Do you know *anything* in connection with this name? If so tell me. You always know everybody!' He also told Marcus of another fan letter, from a Miss Jean Timbrell-Fisher, 'who sounds *quite* safe'. Later in the month, after endless indecision, he wrote again to report, 'I took fright and *didn't* go to tea with my elderly admirer last Monday! For one thing, I felt that it needed too much energy to go all that way only to gratify someone's curiosity, and I also felt from his last letter that he definitely required a blue-eyed house prefect, and I don't feel capable of playing this part!'

Marcus had purchased his own copy of *Maiden Voyage*. 'How noble of you,' Denton wrote to him. 'I only hope you think it's worth it. I am having such a spate of letters that you must not expect any sense from me. I really feel I'm standing on my head.' He added, 'I don't think May really likes the book. She shows more approval now that it seems to be having some success, but at first she was peculiar.' And borrowing Sackville-West's expression, he asked Marcus, 'Do you think I'm given away on a plate in it? I really *must* learn more reticence.'

It was fortunate for posterity that he never did; his second book, *In Youth is Pleasure*, was to be just as honest, painful and risqué an evocation of adolescence as his first.

NINE

'Almost a Corpse'

Just over a fortnight after meeting Edward Sackville-West, Denton began to wonder, despite 'letters and wires and lovely reviews', and Edith Sitwell telling him that, for a first book, *Maiden Voyage* had had the best reception she could remember, whether it could really be rated a success. 'How and when does one know?' he inquired in his journal. 'When the fat cheque rolls in? Is that what one is waiting for?'

While waiting for the fat cheque (which never in fact materialized) he began to see more of Noël Adeney at Middle Orchard. On 31 May he went there to supper and was given 'cold soup flavoured with claret, and fennel in long green shreds; then a sort of pilau of rice, onions fried, pimento excitingly scarlet like dogs' tools, and grated cheese. The tiniest new potatoes and salad. Afterwards plums, and creamy mild tomato cocktail to drink. A charming meal.' Afterwards she went rummaging for a pair of fishermen's red trousers which she wanted to give him, and she also lighted upon a tin of Earl Grey tea which she threw to him telling him to take it home. 'You see,' he remarked a week later, 'this is what goes on in nineteen forty-three, the year of the greatest war to stop all wars, if I have the quotation right.'

His attitude to the war can be judged from a letter he wrote to the Reverend Peter Gamble, an editor at the Readers' Union book club, on 20 January the following year, in which he related, 'Quite a well-known poet I will not mention wrote to me asking for my stories; then seemed to get v. annoyed about something and said I ought to stop my "narcissistic twitterings" and jump on to a 4-engine bomber and have my face blown off while flying over Berlin!!! Now all is restored to peace and politeness; but *aren't* people peculiar. Their reactions seem utterly unaccountable. If the war goes on much longer I feel we shall all become completely dotty and unreliable. I do hate this lunatic feeling in the air – or is it only my imagination? I think the brave new world is going to be quite exquisitely horrible!'[1] And on 11 April 1944 he wrote to Eric Oliver, 'I despise all this silly warlike muck. Nothing is worth anything except the goodness of individual people. To glorify the state is a mug's game.'

Much his most explicit statement on the subject of war was jotted down on a loose sheet of paper on 6 January 1943: 'I always remember the first war joke I saw. It was in an old Punch and I was a little boy in my grandfather's drawing-room. The Punch, unusual and therefore fascinating because it had no colour on its cover, I had picked out of the cupboard under the stairs. I took it with me and sat down in the bow window.

'Then I opened it and I saw the war joke. I think some wretched soldier in slovenly rolled puttees groped and slopped through the mud while Very lights or shells burst above him. Underneath was something incomparably British, middle-class, sordid, manly, and false – stinkingly false – something jolly and vomit-making.

'I stood up in amazement. It seemed horribly dirty and wicked to me – another example of the horrible devil-worship of grown-ups. I am not exaggerating, only the words are too flashy but there are no others.

'I was frightened and I always shall be at that sort of thing.

'Why don't they laugh and joke when the torture of the boot is applied – when the trap-door opens and the "last offering to Venus", so beloved of novelists, is made by the kicking victim? Why don't they laugh and joke in the hospitals when the patients scream and vomit? Why don't they laugh when the poor lunatics sit in trances of melancholy for days or when the homosexuals and other unchangeable neurotics weep and shout and build new facades even more brittle, more ginger-breadish than the older ones?

'Now this stinking broadcast shoots its obscene pantomime. Slimed over with this filth everything is Gilbertianly villainous and oh so good-humoured.

'This is what makes the war possible. We have such a wonderful sense of humour. So wonderful that it is quite grisly.'

He did not, however, dwell frequently on the war; distanced from it by his disqualification from taking any part in it, his attention was usually distracted by other dramas. He spent the Whit Saturday of 1943 by having tea with Noël, and afterwards they bicycled to a pub where

1. The poet was Henry Treece, to whom Denton had responded, 'Don't write to me again unless you can be civilized.'

Denton drank five gin-and-limes, 'and after each one grew a little more outward and demonstrative, but deep down was sorrow, pain, fear, death-longing, all crouching inside'. The next day he reported to Noël by letter — a letter he forgot to sign — that he was in bed 'with one of my peculiar high-temperature attacks'. He thought she may have noticed that he was 'more than usually disconnected yesterday, quite idiotic in fact! Today has been frightful, but this seems to be quite a lucid moment, so I am writing to say, do come on Tuesday, altho' I may not be able to go out. Will you come in time for lunch? Evie will do macaroni and tomatoes and cheese for us, or something like that.' He ended, 'I think I'm gradually simmering down now, which is good, for I've really felt all day that it was against all the laws of nature that I did not burst.'

When annotating in 1952 the letters she had received from Denton in preparation for writing her novel, Noël recalled that she had been apprehensive before Denton came to tea. 'We had been seeing much of each other; our friendliness was growing, but at the same time the climate had become too close.' She continued, 'I saw that he was tense, and, at once, with the utmost confusion and urgency he said; "I've *never* felt anything like it before, certainly not since Jack."' She took this as an affirmation of Denton's affection for her, and the fact that the letter was unsigned she took as further proof of Denton's necessity 'to withdraw the urgent words'. Denton, she noted, 'cannot trust. He could not trust my insight to place the words where they had a right to be, or to allow them to float away.' She ends her note: 'I must tell him plainly of my affection for him; make the same "mistake" that he had made.'

What is one to make of all this? The idea that Denton was in love with Noël, that his feelings for her were in any way comparable to those he had experienced for Jack Easton, is impossible to believe. A letter he was later to write to Eric Oliver indicates in the clearest possible manner that, on the contrary, it was Noël who had fallen in love with him. Was she therefore in some way trying to justify her own emotions by attributing them to Denton? The annotations were made four years after his death, just before the expurgated *Denton Welch Journals* were due to be published. Afraid that the *Journals* might contain unflattering references to herself, she was anxious, as her novel was to prove, to set the record straight as far as she was concerned. One cannot help noting that her annotations were made to appear as if written at the time of the events they refer to, though, in their confusion of tenses, if nothing else, the attempt is unsuccessful. Was she subconsciously trying to subvert the facts? The whole tone of Denton's letter is far too rational, not to say jaunty, to have come from someone experiencing the feelings Noël attributes to him. We only have Noël's word for it that Denton spoke of Jack Easton in the context in which she describes, while on the other hand we have proof, in a letter, that Denton compared his feelings for Eric Oliver with those he had experienced for Jack. The most likely explanation is surely that his remark was made to Noël at a later date, with reference to Eric, and that she brought it forward in such a way as to make it appear as if it had applied to herself.

Denton's true inclinations were meanwhile well on course. On 3 July 1943, as he was walking towards the river at East Peckham, he heard voices and then saw two boys 'on the opposite bank debating where to settle for their fishing. They came quite close to me and I heard them joking and swearing through the barricade of thick grass.' Later he saw that one of the youths 'had lain face downwards in the sun and forgotten about fishing. His back was naked and had turned a dull, rather creamy purplish-brown. A slight tremor passed through it every few moments, and then one saw the very minute drops of sweat glittering frostily between the shoulder-blades. I watched carefully until I had remembered the sight and then crossed the bridge and moved towards the weir. Three small, slightly ragged boys with braces, like a Wilkie painting, were fishing with a curious contrivance.'

Then, 'beyond, by the powerful, massive new locks', he saw 'a naked youth of about sixteen'. There follows in his journal an account of the conversation, artfully casual, which he had with the boy and his mate. After a time he got up to go. 'I hated to leave the happiness there. It made me think of Dorian Gray. (I suppose the youth–age business.) I thought of the boys in years to come. They would not be nearly so nice, quite horrible in fact. They had both talked about going into the services ... All the happiness would melt away.'

He had now been installed in his cramped quarters at Pitt's Folly Cottage for a year, and was beginning to feel restless. 'I am wondering if I shall not soon be on the move again,' he wrote to Marcus Oliver in an undated letter sometime in June. 'I feel that it would be folly in some ways to leave unless I found something awfully nice and not too expensive; but on the other hand I really would like to be in my own grounds, however small. Living here is really like living in the bosom of someone else's family. My ideal, I think, would be to have a tiny cottage on Ashdown Forest, but this is probably quite impossible to get. Do you know the names of any agents in Uckfield or neighbourhood? If so I might write in the forlorn hope of finding something. I've been here a whole year now, and it has really answered wonderfully well. I have been quite unmolested. I am just suffering, I suppose, from the slight feeling of constraint one has when on other people's premises.'

On 16 June he reported to his old prep-school friend Basil Jonzen, 'I am writing another book. I have really begun three! I don't know which will be finished first. I have been painting very little because of all this mad activity. I am now wondering what I shall do in the future – whether I shall paint chiefly to please myself, or whether I shall try to keep both things going almost equally. What do you feel about this? When you write, does painting fly out of the window, or can you hang on to it? There is something horribly depressing about being a painter in England, isn't there? People really don't seem to mind what one puts on the canvas or board, or why one does it. I think it must chiefly always be a private pleasure.'

Five months earlier, on 5 January, he had let fly on the subject of art critics in his letter to Alex Comfort: 'The standard of Art Criticism in our country is *fantastically* low. Just read Jan Gordon, or Earp or Clive Bell every week and you'll weep! They all seem to be suffering from the most curious blind spots and prejudices. And as for their knowledge [of] the actual *process* of painting – it seems quite non-existent.' He had continued his theme five days later in a letter to Betty Swanwick with a swipe at his own dealer, Oliver Brown of the Leicester Galleries, who 'covers his walls with manure because good pictures are so scarce'.

Denton never had a one-man show, and most of his sales were made through the Leicester Galleries, at exhibitions held for a variety of artists. His paintings at this time were selling for between £8 and £12, depending on size and subject, and critical acclaim for *Maiden Voyage* was helping sales. On 14 July 1943 he noted in his journal that he had heard from 'a Mr Julian Goodman', who lived in Gower Street (Denton noted that he had written on hand-made paper), saying he had liked the book so much that he had gone to the Leicester Galleries and had bought a painting of Denton's of a piebald cat. 'I knew this picture would sell,' Denton wrote in his journal, 'so it is nice to be proved right almost on the first day of opening. An absurd cat with a sleek, well-fed conceited look is really irresistible. I wonder what Mr Julian Goodman is like. Is he a rich Jewish financial gentleman? There is nothing nicer in the world than having one's production appreciated.'

Appreciation of *Maiden Voyage* was now on its way from an author and publisher whose literary judgements were respected throughout England and America. Frank Swinnerton, a contemporary of Wells,

Galsworthy and Arnold Bennett, had among much else been responsible for discovering Daisy Ashford's *The Young Visiters* and for recommending to Chatto & Windus Lytton Strachey's *Eminent Victorians*. He wrote to Denton on 15 July to say that Routledge had sent him a copy of *Maiden Voyage* in the hope that he would broadcast about it, but as he had no talk lined up for the present he had sent it on to another critic, Viola Garvin, 'in the hope that she will be able to speak of it'. He went on to say, 'The book is a great refreshment to a reader who is tired of all the second and third hand work which is being published, and I am sure it will be recognized by all who read it as new and very striking. Edith Sitwell says in her preface exactly what I should say about it, and I must thank you both for giving me such pleasure and for persuading Routledge to cough up a copy. I wish I had been able to give one more broadcast and praise it on the air.'

Denton replied by return of post, thanking Swinnerton for taking so much trouble, and mentioning a review that had appeared in the *Listener* which was, he said, 'perhaps the rudest; something in my temperament had evidently irritated the reviewer. It is a wonder to me that I have not irritated more reviewers. I am only just beginning to realize how personal, not to say egocentric, that book is. All the time I was writing it, I hardly thought of its effect on other people. I had never published anything before and didn't know if anyone would take what I had done when it was finished.'

Swinnerton must have responded to this with another letter, offering advice about the writing of *In Youth is Pleasure*, for on 19 July Denton was again writing to him, to say, 'Thank you for your most useful letter. It is what I need at this moment. You are quite right; one's second book *is* written with lost innocence. Far more frequently the questions crop up – Is this silly? – Will this shock? – Will this be misunderstood? One is far more conscious of the book in relation to other people. I think this tends either to make one stress and exaggerate one's particular characteristics, or to do the very opposite, to try to sink them in a more general formula.

'At present I am trying hard not to do either of these things, but to be as straightforward and natural as possible. The Lord knows if I'm succeeding!'

Unsolicited encouragement from such an established writer as Frank Swinnerton must have gone a long way to make up for Denton's infrequent contact with the literary world, barred as he was most of the time from travelling any distance or attending parties. Viola Garvin, to whom Swinnerton had passed on his review copy, was as impressed as he; at 4.25 p.m. on 22 July Denton dashed to his journal to note, 'I have just heard Viola Garvin cracking my book up on the wireless – saying that Edith Sitwell laid hands on my head like a priestess blessing a young neophyte or something. Very nice, very funny to hear one's name across the air. Lots of praise. I keep on wondering who was listening. She said people ought to listen when Edith says that she would not be surprised if I turned out to be not only a born writer but a very considerable one.'

Denton's other main lifeline from the outside world – gossip – was supplied at this time (as he recorded in the same journal entry noting the letter from 'Mr Julian Goodman') when Marcus Oliver came to stay for the night. 'We drank tea, then gin, then beer, then coffee, then port, then barley water. Wasn't it extraordinary?' It was indeed, and so was the news with which Marcus regaled him, 'all about the gaiety of Poole harbour where there are the dearest little pubs in which soldiers and sailors and civilians dance madly and feel awfully friendly. "Just like the South of France," he kept saying.' Marcus also told Denton about 'an earl of about sixty who had fallen in love with a schizophrenic youth down in Dorset'. Apparently the youth had gone into a coma after taking insulin, but had come out of it and was 'very prim and sober'. The earl had become so friendly with the boy's family he had been asked to stay. 'This,' Denton learned, 'puts the mother into a great flutter. Apparently they are all very peculiar, for the mother and air-force boy son sleep together in each other's arms.'

Denton had also received a visit from Francis Streeten, who had 'started baby talk and babble to show what a state he was in. He has no money, his mother has no money. At last I gave him two-and-sixpence to buy cigarettes with.'

'Mr Julian Goodman', far from being a 'Jewish financial gentleman', turned out to be the daughter of Lady Ottoline Morrell, half-sister of the sixth Duke of Portland, and a much maligned Bloomsbury hostess. Mrs Goodman (later Mrs Igor Vinogradoff) wrote to Denton on 15 July to say, 'I'm afraid my first name is very deceptive – I really am a woman. If I forget to put "Mrs" after my signature people are naturally misled.' She went on to explain that she had bought the painting as a present for her daughter's fifteenth birthday, but that she did not think she would be able to part with it.[2] 'I absolutely loved *Maiden*

2. Mrs Goodman did part with 'A Piebald Cat' as intended; it is now in the collection of her daughter Mrs Anne Gallon.

Voyage,' she added. 'If you're ever in London it would be very nice if you would come and see me. I've inherited a collection of pictures and china you might like to see.'

There followed a commission to do a painting of her pug, from a series of photographs because the dog itself was ill and in the country. Denton wrote to Marcus Oliver about the project on 17 August: 'Did I tell you that I sold a picture of a queer cat at the Leicester Galleries to a Mrs Julian Goodman, who has now commissioned me to do her pug? Isn't it amusing! I love doing the pug, whose name is Alex. The flesh and blood pug is not here, only a photograph. I think I am making quite a nice fanciful picture of it, with ruins and storm clouds in the background. The pug has a broken-hearted expression. Mrs Goodman sounds very nice, and rich. I am going to see her in September, when she gets back from Newbury.' (She had a cottage there which she later offered to rent to Denton.)

He duly presented himself, on 22 October as it turned out, at the 'brilliant scarlet door' of 10 Gower Street, the house into which Lady Ottoline and her husband, Philip Morrell, a Liberal Member of Parliament, had moved in 1927.[3] While he waited for his hostess he spotted a painting by Augustus John of Lady Ottoline. Her daughter, he decided when she appeared, was 'pretty with a very good nose'. She immediately lit a Turkish cigarette without offering one to Denton. He began to unwrap the painting of the pug, while Julian crooned, '"The darling. I must see the darling."' When he unveiled it 'she clutched her hands together and raved nicely'.

'"The only thing is, he doesn't wear a bow,"' she pointed out, and Denton reminded her that the dog had been wearing a bow in one of the photographs. '"Perhaps sometimes for parties or birthdays he wears one,"' she admitted. '"But it doesn't matter anyhow, as he's so virile that he can wear a pansy bow and get away with it!"'[4]

'"You're not a bit like your photograph in the Tatler,"' she told him. (On 7 July Elizabeth Bowen had reviewed *Maiden Voyage* in that magazine, and a photograph of him had appeared three weeks later.[5])

3. They had moved here from Garsington Manor, a Tudor house near Oxford, where between 1915 and 1927 they had entertained many of the leading writers of the time.

4. The painting was later reproduced in *Vogue*, on 20 November 1944.

5. On seeing the review Denton wrote in his journal, on 15 July, 'This gives me great pleasure. I have always been put off by the upper-middle-class snobbery in her books, but nevertheless I like to think that she it was who wrote that nice review.' As for the photograph, he noted, 'My picture in the Tatler today reproduced rather too small for my liking!'

1 Arthur Welch and his family,
photographed *c.* 1918. From left,
Rosalind, his wife, and his sons, Denton,
Bill and Paul

2 Denton (left) at the age of about five,
and Paul, aged about seven

3 Denton's grandfather, Joseph Welch, with whom he lived in Henfield, Sussex, from the age of eleven until he was sixteen

4 Dorothy Welch, Denton's aunt, who kept house for his grandfather

5 Denton (left) at the age of twelve, with Paul and three of the nine children of his aunt Edith Kane, at Leigh Vicarage in Surrey

6   Bill Welch at the age of about eighteen

7   Paul Welch, photographed when he was at Repton

8   Denton, photographed with a fellow student from the Goldsmith School of Art, Joan Waymark, when on holiday in Brixham, Devon, in 1934

Pond Farm
East Peckham
Nr Tonbridge

Hadlow 219.

My dear,
        How are you?
I often imagine your
trials and tribulations.
I had a perfectly
horrible and outrageous
experience the other day
which I shall tell you
about when we meet. I

am still simmering
about it. Fate really
seems to play the
lowest, rudest tricks.
They haven't touched
the Hop Garden yet, so
I'm still refugeeing here.
I believe my
Papa is safe. Paul
had a wire telling us
not to worry. This is
one relief. I only
hope that the Japanese
don't seize all his
rubber goods, raw and otherwise!!

Telephone: 28
Telegrams:

Cliff Coombe
Brooklands

I've just raked up this old
letter which never got posted.
Mary has told me your new
address. When will you be
coming down? I shall
want to hear everything!
Lord Berners, the old
monster, has not answered
my last letter so my picture
is still without a purchaser!
My novel has just been
typed and I have been

correcting the typing errors.
Francis, Bogey-Man, Streatham
is reading it for me and I'm
waiting to hear his verdict.
Have you seen Jimmy P
in London or anyone else I
know. I do hope you'll soon
get your commission.
I do hope my
step-mother hasn't been
raped in the Far East!
Love,
        D.

9   A letter to Marcus Oliver written in 1942 on the headed notepaper of the Cliff
Coombe Nursing Home, where Denton spent some months early in 1939

10-12 Three photographs taken during the last few years of Denton's life, showing his harpsichord, one of his baroque angels and his shells

13 Eric Oliver and Evelyn Sinclair, photographed when on holiday in Truro in 1946

14 Noël Adeney at the age of seventy-five

Opposite

15 Noël Adeney's portrait of Eric Oliver, painted in 1944 when he was twenty-nine

16 Denton cleaning one of his baroque angels at Middle Orchard in 1947

'"That made you look rather loopy and you're not."' They adjourned to the dining-room for tea, and here Denton was able to view Augustus John's devastating 1926 portrait of Lady Ottoline (he had painted three earlier, rather flattering portraits of her). Julian told him, '"I had an awful time getting it back from the Tate. When Daddy died it was on loan there, and John Rothenstein told me that it had been given to the Tate. I told him that people do not present valuable pictures to the nation without putting it in writing. There was quite a scene. In the end I sent a man in a taxi to fetch it. I felt awful. I felt as if I'd never get the picture into my possession again. It's all very well. I know that these things should go to the nation, but they're extremely valuable and I have three children."'

As a portrait of her mother, she commented, '"It's not a caricature, but it's cruel."' She spoke at length and with feeling about her childhood and her famous mother, about her belief that Lady Ottoline never wanted a child, and how she had made her play '"the sweet-tempered, rather brainless little girl part"'.

For some reason Edward Sackville-West's name was mentioned. '"Oh, Eddy would adore you,"' she said, and Denton told her they had already met. She described him as the most hypochondriacal person she had ever known, but that he was nice and kind and not really malicious, '"like so many of his temperament"'. She explained that his '"weight of sadness"' (well illustrated in Graham Sutherland's portrait of him) was due to the fact that there would be no heir to Knole, his family home. '"It's easy to say that he's probably reconciled to all this by now,"' she said, '"but still I'm sure that's what weighs him down."' [6]

On 27 July Denton heard from Routledge that there was a possibility of an American edition of *Maiden Voyage*, and on the same day he decided to write 'a short love story' for a magazine. He wanted to see if he was able to write 'what the average person thinks *is* a love story'. The result was 'The Fire in the Wood', one of his least successful efforts, in which he cast himself, most unconvincingly, as a woman named 'Mary'. The male protagonist, 'Jim', was a portrait of a woodman called Tom, whom Denton had met in 1941 and had invited back to The Hop Garden.

---

6. Julian Goodman's references to Edward Sackville-West's 'temperament' and to his lack of an heir (he was at the time forty-two and unmarried) were intended to imply that he was homosexual. There was, however, an heir; it was Edward's cousin, Lionel Sackville-West, who succeeded as Lord Sackville in 1965, Edward having held the title for only three years. While still a schoolboy at Eton, Edward had inquired of Julian Goodman's mother, upon their first meeting, 'What do you think of Gide, Lady Ottoline?'

'Behind the huge smoking bonfire I saw a half-naked man with a wide brass-buckled belt round his riding breeches,' Denton was to write in his journal on 25 May 1945. 'His shoulders were thick and broad, and his skin had turned to a tawny brown. His hair was all in his eyes and dusty with wood ash. He looked extraordinarily glowering and wild.' He was, none the less, 'gentle and strange', and he came from Yorkshire.

Whether the events recorded in the story represented reality or merely Denton's unrealized fantasies, one cannot be sure. 'I've been having a romantic affair with a woodman,' was how he had confided the matter to Marcus Oliver in June 1941, 'but now he's left the neighbourhood. I did a portrait of him. I'll show it to you sometime.'[7] It seems to have been Tom's return to the neighbourhood that prompted Denton to attempt his 'love story'. On 9 August 1943, writing in his journal in the afternoon at a favourite local picnic spot, Oxon Hoath, and seeing two freshly felled trees, he 'wondered if Tom was cutting the trees, and if I should suddenly come upon him, his skin a deep dirty brown, looking magnificent as he flung down his axe on the bark'. Denton seems to have been more haunted than inspired by Tom at this time, however, for work on the story was delayed for three years. 'The wood as I went through it today is full of memories of Tom,' he wrote in 1945, and it was not until 9 April 1946 that he recorded that he had been working the day before on his '"woodman" short story'. In it 'Mary' says of 'Jim', 'I want everything about him, his breath, his skin, his teeth, his bones, his hair.' Whatever Denton had meant when he told Marcus he was 'having a romantic affair', it is clear that he had been obsessed by Tom for as long as five or six years.

The events that were to furnish him with material for a far more accomplished short story, 'Brave and Cruel', occurred in August and September 1943, although the story as it appeared in print is set 'On a lovely late summer evening, soon after the end of the war'. The entire drama is described in precise and corroborative detail in his journal on 19 and 25 August and 2, 3 and 4 September 1943. Like everyone else in the story, the phoney fighter pilot, 'Beaumont', really existed, and it is clear that in real life he would have driven anyone but Denton frantic with his tall tales. Denton, though, savoured and nurtured anyone whose pretensions and absurdities might supply him with literary material. 'We have been having a most melodramatic time here,' he wrote

7. The whereabouts of the portrait of Tom, if it has survived, are not known. Denton also did a painting of Tom's cottage, which was bought by John Lehmann, editor of *New Writing*, and was reproduced in *A Last Sheaf*.

to Marcus Oliver, in a letter mystifyingly dated 16 September 1940, since it was certainly written in September 1943. 'A young man whom May got to know has been pretending that he was a pilot in the Battle of Britain, and got engaged to a nearby girl called Elizabeth Plummer. Just before the marriage takes place (by special licence) two detectives seize Francis de Montaigne (isn't this a wonderful name to choose?!) and cart him off to the station. He came up for trial the other day and was sentenced to three months hard labour for masquerading as a warrant officer. Isn't this a terrible warning to May not to befriend stray young men? I'd like to tell you all about it, by word of mouth. Francis de Montaigne, whose real name is *Bone*, has been in and out of gaol ever since the age of sixteen. I think he is slightly queer in the head, poor thing. He was rather likable in his way, the son of a farm labourer at Penshurst. He could [not] open his mouth with[out] telling the most fantastic stories. He told me that he went to Tonbridge [School] and after that to Christ's, Cambridge. Also that he was a direct descendant of the Montaigne of The Essays!! He was extremely dark and swarthy and did look undoubtedly foreign in some way.'[8]

An explanation for Denton's strange slip in dating this letter may be found at its opening, when he told Marcus he had been 'frantically busy and lately have been ill again and feeling like death! Today am much better, but still in bed.' The letter also provides further evidence of his desire at this time to leave Pitt's Folly Cottage. 'One of my aunts has moved in to a house at Ditchling,' he wrote (referring to his aunt Dorothy), 'and has divided two rooms, a bathroom and kitchen off, for someone else's use. I was half wondering about joining forces with her. Do you know it round there? Pretty I think, isn't it?'

More good tidings about *Maiden Voyage* arrived in the post at the end of September, with the news that the Readers' Union had almost certainly decided to publish an edition of six thousand copies. On 28 September Denton was writing to Peter Gamble at the Union to say, 'I am glad that you liked my book in spite of its faults. As you can see, I am not yet an experienced writer, but hope to be one day.

'It is interesting that you should think me influenced by Christopher Isherwood. I never read him till a few months ago when someone lent me "Lions and Shadows", which I liked very much. My own book had of course gone to press long before this. Perhaps there is sometimes

8. It seems that Mr Bone's escapades hit the national headlines. 'May's publicity in the News of the World galvanized the neighbourhood,' Denton reported to Marcus Oliver on 29 October 1943.

a similarity in outlook which has nothing to do with knowledge of his —works.'

Gamble's comparison was understandable, since Isherwood (who by coincidence had also been educated at Repton, a decade before Denton) is, like Denton, a writer whose work reads deceptively easily, and many of whose novels are autobiographical. Another writer whose works Denton had read, however, before setting out on his own literary path, was D. H. Lawrence, and if he was influenced by anyone it was surely by the author of *Lady Chatterley's Lover*, a book he read in 1938. During his first year at art school Helen Roeder had loaned him her copy of Lawrence's short stories, which was not to be returned to her until after his death. It is reasonable to assume that he read and absorbed Lawrence for the last sixteen years of his life.

The hope of at last making his fortune from *Maiden Voyage* was dashed when he learned that for his share of the 'Readers' Union spoils' he was to be offered by Routledge the grand sum of £20. But then thrilling news arrived about his favourite brother, for whose safety he had been anxious throughout the war. 'Isn't it fine, Paul has got an M.C.!' he announced to Marcus Oliver on 29 October. 'I have to go and buy a ribbon for him as the army has run out.'

Another exciting and quite unexpected event was soon to overtake Denton. Early in November he was lying 'ill in bed with high temperature and terrible headache', as he recalled in his journal three months later. 'Noël and May had been sitting in my room half killing me with their talk.' Just after they had left, and when he was 'trying to simmer down', he heard voices below. He had told Evie not to let anyone else come upstairs, but as the minutes dragged on his curiosity got the better of him, and he called out to her to ask what was going on. She said that Francis Streeten had arrived with a friend, and could they both come up for a minute. 'I consented and saw, walking into the room after fat Francis, someone in green battle-dress trousers, Wellingtons, and a jersey and white shirt, open, also white tops of pants showing above the trousers, large leather belt, face red-brown, with very good throat.' Describing the occasion on a postcard to Noël Adeney on 8 November, Denton wrote, 'After you left the other night, who should appear but Francis and a new hearty land-boy friend! The land-boy kept suggesting that I should get up and go out and have a drink with him! As I was almost a corpse by then, I could not oblige.' In his journal he recalled that he had felt so ill that he could not entertain them properly. 'I tried to be very bright; but it was an awful strain. They had been drinking in a pub and had come on to me later. They were still mildly redolent of the pub and beer.'

The 'new hearty land-boy' was Eric Oliver. He and Francis Streeten had met while working on a farm (because Eric had high blood pressure, and Francis was a conscientious objector, neither had been conscripted) and they were both living in a hostel in Maidstone. By 17 November Denton was writing his first letter to Eric, to say, 'Francis has just been in on his way back to Maidstone. I said that it was a pity I was ill when you both called, as it couldn't have been very amusing for you; but that I hoped you'd come in again another time. He seemed to think that you might like to, when you felt at a loose end; so I am simply writing to say, look in when you're passing. If you're doing nothing this *Friday* or *Sunday* and would like to come to tea, I shall be in both days.' Eric duly arrived, wearing a blue suit, and afterwards Denton lost no time in relating to Noël all the details not only of the suit but of the belt that held up Eric's trousers, of his sister who was an actress, of Eric's drinking habits, of his parents' having made a 'mixed class' marriage, of Eric's twice having run away from school and finally how, while manipulating Eric in the direction of the last bus, they had both fallen into a ditch in the dark.

Eric was the fifth of six children and the youngest of four boys. His childhood had been a strangely disturbed one. His three older brothers had all gone to Dulwich College, but Eric had failed the common entrance examination and had been sent first as a boarder to Ongar Grammar School, from which he ran away, and then to the cathedral school at Salisbury. At thirteen, in a fit of pubescent prudery, he had complained to his father about the other boys getting into bed with one another, and so had been allowed to leave. He never returned to school, going to work instead for his father who manufactured jewel cases in the City. Like many of his future occupations, this one lasted a very short time, and he soon began to drift from job to job, sometimes working on the land, more often frequenting race meetings and dog tracks.

Other news which Denton retailed to Noël may have leavened for her the tedium of having to read about a young man she had never met. Denton had a poem coming out in *Life and Letters* which was bound to be read by the other contributors, who included Edith Sitwell, Alex Comfort and Henry Treece. 'So,' wrote Denton, 'I feel absolutely hemmed in.' He continued, 'I think I must stop publishing poetry if I go on feeling so peculiar about it. There *must* be something very wrong with it. This poem is one of the worst for publication. Edith's hair will stand on end.'

He also reported that *In Youth is Pleasure* was driving him to distraction. Having got into a turmoil about it, he told Noël, he had written to Edward Sackville-West, 'as a comparative stranger', to ask if he would read and criticize it (Sackville-West had offered to do this when they had met for lunch), and he had received an answer that morning, 'very short, saying by all means send it for the "doubtful benefit of his frank advice"'. Denton added, rather gloomily, 'I'm sure I shall get it back with lots of blue pencil and sober comments. He somehow sounded dour and professorial; but I suppose that's what I wanted. He always managed to make me feel rather mudlarking schoolboyish. I suppose it's because he weighs his words and never says anything that could be misinterpreted. But perhaps that is just the person to vet my book. I probably shan't change what he says, only ponder on it. I'm working at the book madly to get it done.' He concluded his letter, 'I must stop now, I feel I shall have to work hours tonight on my book. Perhaps it will be all right. At any rate it isn't full of "loins" as Women in Love is!'

Eric Oliver's visits to Pitt's Folly Cottage continued, and so did the hair-raising manner of his departures. On 29 November Denton was writing to him to say, 'Hope you got home safely without a rear light. I saw a most enormous lorry pass me just after I'd left you. So nice to have you come over and so looking forward to seeing you again this Sunday. It is such a happy change for me to have someone to talk to after working most of the week.' This letter, which like the one to Noël Adeney he forgot to sign, crossed in the post with a letter and parcel from Eric. Denton wrote immediately to thank him: 'My dear Eric, I was so delighted this morning to get the book and your letter. It was very good of you to think of me and do what you said you'd do so punctually. As you can see, I wrote to you on Tuesday, but didn't post it at once. I also found another letter I wrote to you after your second visit here. I don't know whether I shall send it now or not; I'll see.[9] I also have the letter about Christmas Day here. I put it in my pocket. It seems to have annoyed you by its coolness and dullness, so perhaps I won't send it back to you either. Dear Eric, do believe me when I say that I *never* intend to be cold or dull to you. You are the last person in the world I want to be that to. It is just training that makes me matter of fact and bald in letters. I also don't care for the idea of other eyes than the ones intended seeing them, and I know you

9. The letter has not been preserved, whereas reams of other letters from Denton to Eric have. The assumption must be that Denton destroyed it.

have a naughty habit of leaving your letters about or showing them. Even the most boring letter of mine I don't care to have exhibited in this way. This is just my particular fad. There is also such a great deal that cannot be said in a letter; it is too difficult.

'Your letter to me I liked *so* much, but I could have wished that it had been longer. I think in some ways it *must* be a good thing that we met and became friends. We both ought to be able to help each other somehow, but just at the moment I feel so cut off, far apart from you, as if you were someone a long way off at the end of a long, long telescope. It makes me sad that we are such different people and so cannot share many interests; and yet I suppose what I like in you and admire are the qualities I lack myself. Perhaps one day, if neither of us goes and dies suddenly! we shall gradually gain common experiences which we can share. Perhaps not; perhaps we shall drift quite apart. *I hope not.*

'But whatever happens, know that I will always be your true friend, and that a part of me loves you and thinks about you as if you had been my brother. This letter is not supposed to be either dismal or sentimental. I only want to say what is in my mind. I shall love reading the book. Write to me again, saying anything you like. Your letter's privacy will be respected. My love, D.'[10]

At the time of writing this letter Denton had known Eric scarcely a month, had met him perhaps only three times and had written him no more than two fairly formal notes, one rather more intimate letter which he never posted and an invitation to Christmas lunch.

In the middle of another lengthy missive to Noël Adeney, dated 7 December, he was again retailing anecdotes about Eric, who had turned up at Pitt's Folly Cottage shortly after the house had been invaded first by May Walbrand-Evans, who had just escaped the clutches of the local squire, and then by Francis Streeten, 'in a maddeningly babyish mood'. Francis had had nothing to eat, 'so we all devoured toast and talked at cross purposes. It was terrible ... What *would* have happened if you had turned up too! I don't think you would have enjoyed it! As it was, May soon went back to her black-out, and Francis had to catch a mercifully early bus. So Eric and I were left by the gas fire.

'"I'm terrified of women like that, will she ever come again?" was all he said. Then we went out in the moonlight and posted two

10. Only one letter from Eric to Denton is preserved in the Denton Welch Collection in Texas. Eric Oliver has told the author that after Denton's death he destroyed his own letters because he felt they were not well written.

manuscripts of mine. Afterwards I showed him the wood, the summer-house above the pond, all in the moonlight. It was wonderful, somehow quite magic, like some night that had been caught in a trance for hundreds of years. Everything was utterly still, and everything had a halo. A mist rose up from the pond, and the moon shone through the mist.'

Denton gives a vivid portrait of Eric Oliver in a short story called 'The Diamond Badge', written as late as 1948, where Eric appears, thinly disguised, as 'Tom Parkinson'[11]: 'I knew him by his searching, rather anxious eyes. They were not the eyes of a man about to welcome wife, sweetheart or friend; they were too guarded, too ready to save the stranger from embarrassment. I liked at once his beaky nose, his tallness which was yet not overwhelming, the bank of dingy fairish hair flopping over his forehead. The sleeves of his open-neck shirt were rolled up and his beltless trousers seemed to hang on his hips rather precariously; they were slack round his ankles as if they dragged on the ground behind. I knew just what the hems would be like at his heels – caked with mud and beginning to fray.

'When we shook hands, I saw that he had tiny red veins under the tight brown skin on the sides of his arched nose; they were not in the least unpleasing, and the nondescript colour of his eyes soothed me. I guessed that we were almost exactly of an age, but I hoped, rather pointlessly, that he was the elder by a year or so.'[12]

On 13 December, having been invited by Denton to stay at Pitt's Folly Cottage, Eric turned up drunk. That night Denton had what he described as a 'wonder dream', in which a very good-looking chauffeur said to him, with reference to Eric and his intoxicated state, '"Am I going to be kept out till midnight again getting old Piss's luggage?"' Denton longed, in his dream, for Eric to be suaver, better dressed, more worldly-wise. 'Then I thought that all this snobbery about appearance was ignoble. I was annoyed that the chauffeur was so obviously only impressed with the opulent.'

Meanwhile, a temporary jolt to his literary progress had been administered by Henry Treece, in his capacity as editor of *Kingdom Come*,

11. 'The Diamond Badge' was published in full in *A Last Sheaf*, but the first half of the story, under the title 'The Visit', appeared in *Penguin New Writing* in 1949.

12. Eric was in fact six months older than Denton. For the first two years of their friendship Denton concealed from Eric his true age, maintaining that he was two years younger than he really was; and in 1948 he allowed Hamish Hamilton to state on the dust-jacket of *Brave and Cruel* that he was 'a young man still in his twenties' when he was really thirty-three.

who had rejected two of Denton's stories on the grounds that, although they were beautifully written, they were too amoral for publication. One of them, 'When I Was Thirteen', was arguably his finest short story. Referring to an incident recounted in *Maiden Voyage*, when his friend Geoffrey had kissed him in the station lavatory at Derby, an affronted Denton wrote to Noël Adeney, 'Tongues down throats and other things don't seem to worry Edith and Herbert Read. Why should they worry him! ... It makes me think that Edward [Sackville-West] will blue-pencil whole pages of my new book, but I shan't change anything until Herbert Read has seen it. I am *so* tired of all this absurd hypocrisy.'

On 17 December he made use of a Christmas card he had designed, decorated with a cockerel, to crow seasonal greetings to Treece. 'I can't resist telling you,' he wrote, 'that I have just heard from Cyril Connolly who says that he wants to publish the story which you thought was too amoral, in Horizon. I am so delighted; it is just what I needed. Your remarks really *had* shaken me a bit, and I began thinking that most of the things I wrote were unpublishable. I have also got a story in the New Writing which you may see.[13] I have just finished my new short book. I wonder if you'd think it very sexy!' It was Connolly who had launched Denton's career by publishing his account of taking tea with Sickert; by publishing 'When I Was Thirteen' he was now to ensure for Denton a considerable fan mail, mainly from male homosexuals to whom, in the restrictive climate of the time, the story of Denton's day out with Archer gave a licentious thrill. It also elicited a note of appreciation – of its literary qualities – from Edith Sitwell, who wrote to Denton on 20 April 1944 to say, 'I *do* enjoy the adventure in Horizon.'

Denton returned to the pleasure of lecturing Henry Treece on 8 January 1944: 'It really has been horribly difficult, all through childhood and adolescence, resisting the jokes and prods of parents, guardians, brothers and even friends; and now that I am independent I absolutely refuse to cloak what transparency and honesty remain to me in the conventional cloaks of heartiness, sophistication, irony and satire, which most people seem to find so very useful.'

The risks he ran in the cause of this honesty had been brought home to him the previous month when he had heard from Bill, in Africa, congratulating him on the success of *Maiden Voyage*. 'I feel so guilty,' Denton told Noël Adeney, 'because he hasn't read it and when he does he'll see how unkind I've been. He's probably getting a transfer and

13. The story was 'The Barn'.

coming back to England in a few months! I do hope,' he added naively, 'nobody will ever lend him a copy.'

His letter to Noël of 7 December 1943, recounting his sight-seeing tour with Eric in the moonlight, sheds light also on his current state of health. He told Noël that Dr Tuckett, the partner Dr Easton had handed him over to, had 'bounced in', said he had thoroughly enjoyed *Maiden Voyage* and had sent a copy to Easton in Egypt. Dr Tuckett also said he thought Denton ought to see a specialist once every six months. 'Doesn't this sound appalling!' was Denton's comment. 'He seems to think it quite serious that I have so many fever attacks now. (Incidentally I have one today and that is how I am able to write this long letter.) I am *so* enraged with it all. I seem to go to bed every fortnight or so now. It may just be a phase and I'll be better again. Tuckett says I must go to bed when my temperature goes up. Usually, of course, I can't do anything else. Today it's not too bad if I just lie in bed. Perhaps it will go tomorrow ... I hate falling to bits; it is so repulsive.'

Shortly afterwards, Denton had reported to Noël that he was battling with the last chapter of *In Youth is Pleasure*, and in doing so may have sown in her mind the seeds of her own notorious novel. 'You know,' he wrote, 'the more I think of it, the more I feel that you ought to write a kind of reminiscence book. I think you would probably *hate* mustering your forces to it, but when you were in the rhythm of it you would enjoy it. And these books always are nice to read – even if they're bad, which yours wouldn't be. I think you could make it very exciting if you were bold and didn't mind what you said. (This sounds as if I were prompting you to the most frightful indiscretions!) You probably would make money too, which is nice. It is curious that I should be saying all this to you, when my own book has driven me crazy this last week. Perhaps I want someone else to become equally insane.'

He had by now decided against sending the new manuscript to Edward Sackville-West for his comments. 'It's really like sending a bit of yourself in a parcel to undergo a nasty little operation,' was how he justified his decision to Noël. The letter ends with evidence of the stormy relationship that existed from time to time between Denton and his housekeeper: 'Evie has been appalling today. I'd like to put a chain and collar on her and fasten her up outside! It is hopeless to tell her to do anything.'

One of the points of contention between the two arose out of Denton's firmly held belief that Evie allowed her hair to fall into the food when she was cooking. He alluded to this when drafting 'The Fire in the Wood': 'Mrs Legatt [Evie] was busily cooking the supper. Mary [Denton] clung to this thought, picturing every detail of the electric stove, the pots, the pans, the wooden spoons, the thickly winking bubbles in the soup. Perhaps as Mrs Legatt bent low to stir, one of her hairs might fall into the soup. It *had* been known to happen, although Mrs Legatt would never admit it; the very mention of her hair made her furious.' Denton was eventually to fly at Evie with a pair of scissors to try to remove some of the offending hair. 'They fought like mad,' Eric Oliver reported. 'Denton thought Evie was dotty. Her cats were another source of contention, probably because of their hairs. Another thing that riled Denton was Evie's complete lack of any sense of time.' Evie's belief in Christian Science, too, came to madden him. She simply refused to believe that if he were to get up out of bed when he was feeling unwell that he would not be perfectly all right.

There is in 'The Fire in the Wood' a snatch of conversation between Mary and Mrs Legatt drawn straight from life: 'Mary told Mrs Legatt that the woodman was coming to sit, and asked her to prepare a good tea. Mrs Legatt looked at her as directly as she ever looked at anyone.

'"It's not often you want to do portraits from the flesh," she said in her rather strange, chanting tones; "you like to make things up, or do those fancy needlework horrors; I can't say I'd want one in a house of mine, if I had one."

'"You'd rather I tried to paint a straightforward portrait then?" Mary asked, wanting to talk about the woodman.

'"Well, that depends on what he's like; it's no good trying to make a silk purse out of a sow's ear, you know."

'Conversation with Mrs Legatt was always like this; after a plain statement, a warning, a proverb, she would slip away or lapse into silence. With her there was no continuation, no further step.'

One day sometime before Christmas, Denton decided to go up to London to find a suitable present to send to Edith Sitwell. She had long been famous for the aquamarine rings with which she adorned her beautiful Tudor hands (Denton had noted that she was wearing two when they had lunched together), and he decided to add to her collection. So, dressed 'with Edwardian elegance', as Noël Adeney recalled when annotating his letters, his ensemble including pale yellow gloves and a silver-knobbed stick, he made his way to Cameo Corner in Bloomsbury, where he found a topaz ring he thought would be apt. He received a letter of thanks, dated 22 December, from Renishaw: 'My dear Denton, I call you this, and hope you will call me Edith. I could not possibly express how much delight your *exquisite* present has given me. It is one of the most lovely rings I have ever seen. And I really think you *must* have second sight — for I have always longed for a pale topaz ring of that particular description and strangeness. But I couldn't have imagined this one, which has a singular exquisiteness of workmanship, imagination and colour. It really *is* a *beauty*. It fits the first finger of my left hand, as if it had been made for it. In fact it looks rather as if we had been born together. (Perhaps we were, several centuries ago.)

'I do not know which has given me the most happiness, your sweetness in giving it to me — or the intense beauty of it. Both seem part of each other.

'I haven't, in this letter, given the faintest idea of the pleasure it has given me. It is the one thing that has given me a feeling of happiness, that has happened for ages.'

She went on to tell Denton that Roger Senhouse of Secker & Warburg had written enthusiastically to her about *Maiden Voyage*: '*That* may be useful, in the long run. It is always as well to have two publishers on a lead.' She was longing to see the new book, and her letter was full of plans for Denton to meet Wyndham Lewis and to spend a day with her, having lunch first and then, in the afternoon, 'a giant tea-party'. Alas, when the time came, Denton was too afraid that problems with his bladder would result in an embarrassing accident, and so he did not go to see her. He and Edith were never to meet again.

On 21 December he wrote a note to Eric, inviting him to lunch on Christmas Day, 'if you've nothing better to do and if you don't mind meagre fare.' He warned him there might be nothing but Christmas pudding, adding, optimistically as it turned out, 'Noël Adeney and her son turned up here yesterday suddenly. If she turns up again at Christmas when you're there I think you will like her; but she may be in London with her family.

'Hope to see you Christmas Day. Love D.'

TEN

'Straining After Love'

The first Christmas Eric and Denton spent together was a disaster. Denton had made 'all the table pretty with china, glass, leaves and silver. The glass lustre shone, the red pepper looked pretty. Evie had made a nice meal with make-believe turkey, soup and plum pudding with hard sauce.' Beer and Algerian wine were ready to be opened, and Turkish and Virginia cigarettes had been put out, together with chocolate peppermint creams. All that was missing was the guest of honour.

At two o'clock Denton and Evie sat down to eat, 'looking out of the low window and commenting on the lateness, and the taste of things'. When Eric eventually arrived he was drunk. 'He bowed his head on his knee and groaned. It was quite real. He held on to one of my hands and didn't speak' — except to say, by way of explanation for his late arrival, that he had feared there would be someone else present and so had sought a little Dutch courage on the way.

After lunch Peggy Mundy Castle's daughter Rosemary dropped by, 'a little Christmas merry from drinks'. They 'talked hilariously and giggled', Denton remembered, 'and through it all I could tell how attracted Rose was to Eric'. After supper they all went down to The Rose and Crown, and when at last they came out again Eric said, '" Denton, I ought to see Rosemary some of the way home. You must be tired so I can do it alone."

'Of course, I knew exactly what this meant,' Denton wrote in his journal. 'I made rather unfeeling ironical comments out loud to myself, so that they could not hear unless they were very sharp. We bicycled along the road in silence. When we got to Pitt's Folly gates, I turned in at the drive and left them on the main road. I said "Good night" sharply and contemptuously. I was tired and I thought them both stupid and lustful. Rosemary's little lost "Perhaps Eric will see me to just where the houses begin" I thought ludicrous and dishonest. Of course, I knew what was going to happen the moment they were alone together.'

It was not until past midnight, shortly after Rosemary's mother had telephoned Denton, wondering what had happened to her daughter, that Eric returned. '"She's a passionate girl, isn't she,"' he said. Then 'he began to pour out all that had happened and all his own troubles and short-comings. He poured it all over me and I just sat back in the chair and listened and watched. Then suddenly I began to cry. Everything seemed so frightfully muddled and stupid and sad, and utterly hopeless. Eric understood. We were terribly morbid and gloomy and felt that we were both going to die.'

Eric spent most of Boxing Day in bed recovering from a hangover, but in the evening he and Denton cycled to a pub to drink beer, for as so often in the war, there was nothing else on sale. As they sat in the bar Eric said, '"Now, Denton, you feel as much out of water as I feel when you want to take me to tea with old ladies."' The pub was almost empty, 'and extremely dreary', and Denton soon left to go home for supper, leaving Eric on his own. At half-past eleven Eric came back to Pitt's Folly, covered in mud, having hurtled off his bicycle into a ditch. Denton tried to persuade him to stay the night but Eric insisted on making his way back to Maidstone, where he was living at 71 Allen Street. '"I won't come to see you again for a whole month,"' he told Denton, '"then I'll be good and sober again. I won't drink anything in 1944."'

Considering that Denton was by this time in love with Eric, and that Eric had behaved so badly, the letter he wrote to Eric on 28 December was remarkably temperate: 'My dear Eric, How I hope you got home safely after Christmas celebrations! I thought after you left that I should not have let you go; but in one way perhaps it was just as well, as yesterday I woke up with a particularly bad feverish attack and lay all day languishing with a most appalling headache. I'm better today, thank the Lord, but still rather groggy, and am staying in bed. Isn't it awful to be at the mercy of our bodies in this way! I do hope that *you* aren't feeling ill or worn out, too. You must drink less, Eric, else I feel that you'll absolutely ruin your health. You'd so hate to be invalidish. *Do* take warning. I feel so terribly sad about your drinking, perhaps there is no need, and you won't thank me for it, but there it is. I think, as you suggest, better not come over again for a little, as I would only be telling you this all over again, and the one thing I *will* not be taken for is a bore and a lecturer. It just isn't my line.

'We both, as very different people, have to muddle our way thro' life as best we can. I probably at times get messed up and in a turmoil just as much as you do. You know I would do whatever I could for you, if you ever get into any unpleasant jam, so don't feel too lonely unless you want to! Love, D.'

Thirteen days later he was again writing to Eric, to say he had thought this last letter rather preposterous and had almost decided not to send it, and then had thought it would be an antidote 'to the Christmas one which (although you may not remember) you told me at the time was chilly, indefinite, and altogether vague and unsatisfactory. I don't seem to be able to strike a happy medium, do I! For heaven's sake, if you haven't already torn the letter up, bring it with you when you come over. I will keep it here, if you want it preserved. I hate to think of your inquisitive landlady going thro' your pockets and cackling at my extravagances! and I won't have it, so please remember what I say!' He also told Eric that he was going up to London soon to see another doctor, 'but I think that very little can really be done about these high-temperature attacks. I must simply lead a very quiet life, then they are less frequent.'

A quiet life was, however, no more to Denton's taste than a sober one was to Eric's. The new year opened with momentous news, as we learn half-way through a letter Denton wrote to Noël Adeney on 16 January. First he told her that he had received a polite letter from John Lane of The Bodley Head to whom, among other publishers as well as his own, he had sent his new book advising that 'the auto-biographical fragment' should be handled by Routledge, who had handled his previous book 'with such success'. Denton told Noël, 'This in spite of being disappointing is perhaps the best solution to the problem. It would be difficult perhaps if there were arguments about publishing between Lane and Routledge. Nothing from Read yet,' he added. 'I supposed he's given it to the other directors to read. I shudder. I'm glad Lane seems to think there's no difficulty about publication, though.'

He continued, 'The Readers' Union offer's been accepted' (for *Maiden Voyage*), and then, 'I've begun a new book!' (This was to be his account of the accident, *A Voice Through a Cloud*, a book which was to occupy him for the next four years.) With no more ado he went on to tell Noël that Julian Goodman had written to him at length, enclosing no less than seven portraits of herself, with her pug in all of them, 'being kissed, petted, patted and generally manipulated', from which she asked him to paint her portrait. Although otherwise gratified by her letter, Denton was disturbed by the confession in it that Julian was £225 overdrawn at the bank and that he was not to expect to be paid for the portrait for months.

Noël was next informed that Eric, in 'altogether a very efficient and high-minded letter', had told him that he had not set foot in a pub that year. 'I think he wants to prove that he can do exactly what he says – about the drink and about not coming here for a month ... I *must* have been a governess at Christmas, to have impressed good behaviour on him in this way. I feel uncomfortable. I feel he'll turn up next Sunday in a starched collar.' More followed about his new novel: 'My book is agonizing to write. It will be awful if it's agonizing to read. I'm not going to tell anyone what it's about till it's finished, and I'm certainly *not* going to show it to Edward in M.S.! I think he's right about the one he read [Denton had had third thoughts about sending the manuscript of *In Youth is Pleasure* to Edward Sackville-West, who had advised him not to publish it]. It's obviously scatological in bits and it's obviously harping on one theme which also ran thro' M.V. The only thing is, am I to take these two things to be undesirable? If so, I must stop writing until I have a change of heart, which doesn't seem altogether likely.'

He told Noël that Evie had been making 'a great many unsuitable suggestions' about the dedication of *In Youth is Pleasure*,[1] as well as 'cynical remarks about wills not always turning out as one expects them to' – a reference to Denton's hopes of inheriting a large sum from his mother's friend Mrs Carpmael.

On the same day that he sent this long letter to Noël he wrote also to Eric, announcing that Rosemary Mundy Castle had visited him the previous day with her mother. 'She was rather self-conscious and hardly dared mention your name. This amused me. I think she thought I'd be thoroughly annoyed and put out,' a remark which clearly indicates that Rosemary knew of Denton's feelings for Eric and therefore of his homosexual inclinations – as, indeed, did most of his friends and neighbours. 'Marvellous about not going into a pub this year,' he added. 'You really seem able to do what you say you'll do, when you've made up your mind. Next Sunday it will be exactly a month since we've met, as you arranged. Looking forward to seeing you for lunch if you can manage it. Much love. D.'

On 18 January Eric, anticipating the month by a few days, turned

1. Denton eventually dedicated the book to his dead mother.

up unexpectedly when Denton was out. He left before Denton got home, and in the evening Denton wrote to say, 'So sorry to miss you this afternoon. I've just come in and Miss Sinclair's told me that she came back and found you looking very nice in a grey suit! And that you were very polite, and apologized for rowdy Christmas behaviour. You evidently went down *very* well with her!'

At last, good news arrived from Herbert Read, in a letter Denton described to Noël as 'a masterpiece'. Read wrote, 'I have read your book with the greatest possible interest. There can be no question that it fully maintains the brilliant qualities which distinguished your first book, and any reservations that we may have are not strictly speaking of a literary or critical kind, nor for my part are they in any sense ethical. I confess to a certain disappointment in that it is a continuation of the theme of your first book and does not yet show your ability to go beyond the autobiographical medium. But the real trouble — and here I agree with Sackville-West — is one which is personal to you and which you must decide. The picture of the hero you present is one which most people will find perverse and even unpleasant, and however unjust this may be it will undoubtedly affect the attitude of the public to your future work. I would suggest, therefore, that you give this consideration very careful thought, and if you are still of a firm and settled opinion that you would like to proceed with the publication of the book we on our part are perfectly willing to agree. It may be that in the interests of the sales of the book two or three phrases may need amendment or deletion; but this is a question that need not raise any real difficulties.'

'I wonder,' pondered Denton in his next letter to Noël, 'if they think the book will be successful financially, or whether they just think it will stop a gap until I write something more possible?' Part of the truth may have been that while the directors of Routledge, and perhaps Read himself, had more serious qualms about publishing the book than Read's letter suggests, they recognized that, after the extraordinary success of *Maiden Voyage*, there would be no shortage of other publishers ready to take it off their hands if Routledge did not publish it. However that may be, Denton lost no time in writing to Read to say that he was happy to go ahead with publication, 'and if people make rude noises after me in the streets they must do so and I must put up with it'. Later he had his doubts, and again asked Noël's opinion. 'Do you think I will get known as the scatological monger, and be forbidden to all the genteel libraries?' he wondered. 'Do you think I am unwise?'

John Lehmann had also written to Denton, in connection with

publication of 'The Barn' in *New Writing and Daylight*, suggesting that they meet when he was next in London. 'What's he like?' Denton asked Noël. 'Do you know?'[2] Unaware that Denton had already reworked the story twice before sending it in to him, Lehmann had suggested that it could do with 'a little rewriting and pulling together'.[3] Denton, unperturbed, replied that he would go over it again if Lehmann really thought it necessary, but he asked, 'Do you think its lack of very perceptible shape is due to its being, almost completely, a plain statement of fact? Whether this is a good thing to attempt or not, I tried very hard to keep it only to this; and consequently I may be a little more inept in some passages than I would otherwise have been. I do hope you will use it, for although I too thought it was clumsy, I still liked it for some reason; that is why I sent it to you.'

Lehmann replied that he did not want Denton to change the story again if he was not convinced that it could be improved. Denton, conscientious craftsman that he was, did look at it again, and two weeks later sent in a slightly revised and improved version with a covering letter saying, 'I did not like one or two sentences and adjectives, they did not really express my true feeling. I could, of course, have changed it a great deal more, but I resisted this temptation, as I knew that it would make it into something quite different and perhaps worse if I persisted.'

On 23 January Eric arrived as expected and stayed overnight. The next day, in spite of the time of year, he expressed a desire to swim in the river, so they set out, Eric borrowing Evie's bicycle, which he managed 'wonderfully' while calling out to Denton, '"Go slower, that's how you wear yourself out going at it hell for leather"'. They ended up, however, at The Chequers in Crouch where they ate a picnic lunch in front of a log fire in the bar. 'I realized,' Denton recorded in his journal the next day, 'that this was something I had wanted to do all my life – to eat a picnic meal by a fire in an olden room with Eric while the rain beat down outside.'

Denton intended to take Eric after lunch to Middle Orchard to meet Noël, though he 'was afraid that he would jib at the last moment. He has a horror of middle-aged women, thinking that he appears as nothing but an oaf to them. I cannot understand this, as they usually, I think, must like him. He seems only really comfortable and natural in the

2. The two never did meet, though after Denton's death Lehmann temporarily housed a quantity of Denton's furniture for Eric Oliver.

3. *I Am My Brother* by John Lehmann (Longman, 1960).

company of men. He can get on with any sort of men.' Denton's next diary comment on Eric was more revealing: 'He treats me with a mixture of thoughtfulness and solicitude for my precarious health and an almost cynical realism about my thoughts and feelings. All my actions are put down to very mundane motives. This may be all quite true, but it is a shock. I could do the same for him, but I don't.'

As they were preparing to leave the pub the landlord's wife said, '"You two hiking?"' and Denton pretended that they were. 'I suddenly wanted to be hiking and hearty and pre-war and pre-accident,' he wrote, 'everything young and careless.' He continued with a thought which was to become a recurring theme in his journals and letters: 'I wished that Eric and I had known each other when we were both eighteen and that we had walked miles together every day and slept every night in haystacks. I longed for it quite bitterly, and I felt the desperation that everything was dying and decaying and that Eric and I who were just made to be young and gay for ever together would go down getting sadder and older and more entangled every moment of the day.'

Middle Orchard was just around the corner from The Chequers, and eventually Denton persuaded a reluctant Eric to accompany him there. Both Denton and Noël have left accounts of the visit. According to Noël's, which appeared first as an annotation to Denton's letters and was then made use of in *No Coward Soul*, Denton entered the house first, 'looking as if he were dragging by a rope a dark aquiline young man whose head was deeply bowed, arms hanging far out from the sides of a large torso, which was stretching apart a light grey jacket; with his short legs shambling, he reluctantly followed. Denton and I chatted; the young man was dumb. I noticed his kind blue eyes, his low empty forehead, his small mouth. I saw a face too large for the head; a face that changed from a bland smoothness containing no thought to an intense corrugation in an effort to have some, or to avoid it. It was as if he had within him some perplexity or reflection which he feared to acknowledge. I wondered if his aggressive torso, his small tight hands as he held his pipe, his arms so lavish in gesture, as they handed me cigarettes, were always ready to do battle with this inner foreboding.'[4]

According to Denton's account, Eric 'hung under the porch, waiting out of sight, nervous'. Once inside, Denton decided to go upstairs in order to leave Noël and Eric alone together, feeling that it was 'much

4. Noël Adeney's description of Eric as an ape-like figure contrasts markedly with that of others who knew him, who testify that he was good-looking, with just the kind of manly figure that would have appealed to Denton.

easier for two strangers to talk alone than to have a mutual friend making it easy for them helpfully'. But his tact was in vain, for when he came back Noël left the room and Eric turned to him, 'desperately', and said, '"Denton, how long have we got to stay?"' He was 'imploring, like a child'. He told Denton, '"I want to break the room down when I'm stuck in a bloody chair like that."' As they were leaving Eric suddenly turned to Noël and said, '"Good-bye, thank you so much for the tea and I'm sorry I've been so disappointing."' Once outside and on the road again, 'Eric let out terrific sighs and puffs of air, as if he were recovering from some terrible strain. I said, "It's good for you. You can't be so anti-social and boorish."'

Back at Pitt's Folly, having been drenched on the way home, Eric changed into an old camel-hair dressing-gown and Denton put on a priest's cassock he was fond of wearing. They sat by the fire, and Eric rested his head on Denton's knees. Then he took Denton's head 'carefully between his hands and began to massage it as he had been taught, behind the ears, the nape, the temples. I let him do it. It was soothing, rhythmical, and I liked it. He did it very carefully. I felt grateful.'

Evie brought them soup, bean pie and apple pie, then they dressed again and went out to wait for Eric's bus. After it had gone, Denton felt 'nothing but all the sadness and parting and dying and diseases in the world. All the accidents and hate and the long, long everlasting going-on-ness of it all. I thought that I and Eric and all people living were nothing but the reflection of all the thousand million who had gone before, and I thought that in a little time, almost no time at all, we would all be gone again and swept away.'

Within a week Eric was back again at Pitt's Folly, and on 30 January Denton sat down to write a long letter to him: 'Dearest Eric, You have just gone and I am sitting over my supper, waiting to go in next door [his landlady, Mary Sloman, and Brenda Cobb, who was living with her, had invited him to come in to meet a guest who was visiting them] and listening to "I will give you the Keys of Heaven" on the wireless. I want to say so much and I don't know where to begin.'

He then went out, and on his return continued the letter: 'I have just come back from next door. My God, Eric; I feel just like you did at Noël's; blown out and completely fuddled. The conversation – like half-witted pea-hens screaming. They *would* talk in what they imagined to be a sophisticated way, and the result was painful in the extreme. Oh my dear, I really feel as if I'd been beaten all over. It makes me feel so ashamed and hot and cold when other people talk complete balls for two hours. The only nice thing was [when] one of the women said, "I only caught a glimpse of your friend, but I did think him extremely handsome"!! This is *you* (when you were pumping Evie's bike last week) in case you don't know! It pleased me so much that she said this. I expect she wanted to hear a lot more about you which was *not* forthcoming.'

As for the other guest, 'The man I was asked to meet was appalling; about 20ish and so vapid and conceited that I felt uncomfortable for him. An actor going out to near East and Italy, just like your sister. I loathed him – and she [it is not clear to which of Denton's hostesses he is referring] thought he was one of my persuasion and we'd get on so well! I can't stand those egoistic buggers. He could do nothing but cap everything that was said by repeating some ghastly made-up story about his own exploits.

'They are playing lovely Mozart now on the wireless. It is such a relief after all that bloody silly talk. I wish you were here. You have a soothing effect on me and I feel all rubbed up the wrong way. Don't mind if this letter's gaga. I'm drunk without wine, as Evie says. And a little "with" too, I think.

'I have written three poems for you. May I, later, if I publish them, put your name or initials at the top? Tell me if you don't want me to and I won't, but I would like to. I would like to dedicate my new book to you; but perhaps not, as I think it should really be dedicated *publicly* to some highly respectable and eminent woman! Besides, you may not like it as you haven't read it yet. I want to write all about you, so that years afterwards people will read it and think about us. They'll read how we had tea together or went for a walk in the moonlight wood. When we're in our cold, cold graves, they'll be sitting cosily by the fire turning the pages! I'm always thinking of this. I want people to read about us 500 years from now.

'If you want me to look after any things for you, bring them next week (if you come next week). I will take great care of them. But don't come next week if you don't want to (even if you aren't going to your brother's). It would be *awful* for me if I thought you came without particularly wanting to. All that month you stayed away it seemed perfectly right to me. I don't know why it did, and I don't know why I didn't miss you *much* more, consciously, but there it is – something seemed to make it quite right. I suppose you felt so too, else you wouldn't have done it. I wish I knew why exactly you did. I hope you didn't think I was thoroughly fed up with you, because I wasn't. I was only tired and I felt everything was *hopeless* and I got sadder and sadder. In the drive when you said, "Shall I come back in a month" and I didn't answer, I thought, "Better not ever see him again, nothing's any good. Everything gets in more and more of a muddle." I felt that you'd always be tight and I'd always be maddeningly sober and this made me terribly sad. I felt I couldn't reach you at all and you were killing yourself. It makes me wish I'd never met you. Everybody's life is so sad — yours is — mine is — we're all falling to bits. One is young for so short a time and it all rots away. I get this on the brain sometimes and I get so alone feeling that I could burst.

'When you were tight at Christmas, you brought this all out in me. Because I wasn't tight too, it worried me. I thought it was so terribly bad for you and you'd probably get run over and killed pedalling about in the dark. Oh Eric don't get killed — don't booze too much — and know that I'll always do anything I can for you.

'This is a drunken letter, but I'll send it to you with my love.

'PS. Come Sat. and spend the night and we can go out the next day; or come Sun. if you prefer; or don't come at all if you're going to your brother's; or you need a change of scene. I'll understand perfectly.'

On 7 February Eric moved to a hostel in Appledore, seven miles south-east of Tenterden in Kent and some thirty-five miles from Denton's cottage. The day before he moved he came to see Denton and the two went out for a picnic, calling at a pub for several gins first. They found a spot in some woods to sit down, and lunched on hard-boiled eggs, toast, coffee, biscuits, apple tart and blackcurrant purée. Eric drank beer. They lay back 'against the tree trunk, close together', Eric having put his coat round Denton to save him from the cold. 'I knew I would remember it afterwards and always,' Denton wrote later. 'It was too sad to forget.' Eric, seeing how gloomy Denton was becoming, had kissed him. 'We both felt then, I think, how doomed we were, how doomed everyone was. We saw very clearly the plain tragedy of our lives and of everybody's.' As they were leaving the wood they had left their eggshells on the ground. 'I think of those terribly sad eggshells lying in the wood now. I feel that I shall go back to visit them.'

That night Eric, taking up Denton's offer to look after his things, left with him his signet ring and snuff box because he was afraid they might get stolen in the new hostel. He wrote to Denton from Appledore almost straight away, 'a charming letter, really straightforward and poetic mixed in one', as Denton described it to Noël Adeney on 9 February; 'but he needs must spoil it at the end by stupid troublesome heart-searchings about "love" – whether it is ever possible for two people to say they *really* love each other – isn't it better simply to say that they have a certain fondness for each other's company?' It reminded him of 'Lawrence's and Middleton Murry's sordid wrangles, in the letters, as to whether they really loved each other or disliked each other heartily'.

He went on, 'Since I have never mentioned the word love to Eric, or ever expected him to love me in the fanatical all-embracing sense he mentioned, I became furious and wrote what was probably a very unwise ten-page letter. I expect he will now think me quite unaccountable and hysterical, but I became so annoyed with this silly search for absolutes that I did not mind what impression I gave. How does a person of his divided personality expect to find complete love with anyone, whether man or woman? Will he find it with the Rosemary Mundy Castles of this world? Will he find it with me? Will he find it with the youths he works with, or the innumerable landladies' daughters. It seems extremely doubtful to me.'

Denton's 'very unwise ten-page letter' ran in fact to twenty pages; and he was being less than honest when he asserted to Noël that he had never mentioned love to Eric, for although he may not have used the word itself, the whole sum of his behaviour can hardly have left Eric in any doubt as to his feelings. The letter that so annoyed Denton was, unfortunately, subsequently destroyed by Eric, though its message is easily deduced from both Denton's reply to it and his further comments on it to Noël. Eric's well-meaning attempt to draw attention to the obvious imbalance of feeling between them touched a raw nerve in Denton. 'I suppose,' Denton rampaged on to Noël, 'I should have liked his plainness and simplicity in thus explaining his doubts and his misgivings as to his true feelings towards me, but I didn't; I found his openness both burdening and insulting. I really find these measuring rods of affection horribly clumsy instruments; they seem to inflict awful wounds on the affection itself. It was as if all feelings below a certain level were counted as nothing, and that every effort were being made to force unnaturally one of the feelings over the level so that it could be called love.

'I really am exhausted by this straining after love and this wailing over the lack of it. It is a false god and it swallows its victims up mercilessly, so that they become nothing at all.

'You must be bored with all this about Eric and me, but I have told you just to show how impossible situations become when they are dragged forcibly into the open, there to be thrashed out mercilessly.

Now I suppose I am an obscurantist; but I think that really is the thing to be in human relationships. Of course it is not always easy to rest content in that state at all; a part of one is always longing to have every-thing clear-cut like a diamond; but efforts in that direction only seem to make confusion worse confounded.'

There is a good deal in this letter which, although ostensibly concerned with Eric, may have been intended also as a comment on Noël herself and her relationship with Denton. Noël, for her part, when annotating the correspondence, maintained that this letter of Denton's in fact referred to another he had written to her 'which was surprisingly insensitive and obtuse', and which, as she had been uncertain how to reply without giving pain, she had simply handed back to him the next time they met, 'saying I did not want it and that he should have more insight than to be blinded and misled by other people's idiotic remarks'. It was presumably in response to that that Denton had begun his letter to her with 'Just a note to say that in spite of my letters I really must not be mistaken for one of those insufferable people who are always imagining themselves to be the objects of other people's desires. I think this is the sort of vanity I suffer from least. I *know* that I am of the physical type the least desirable, the most uninspiring to women. (I don't like this last sentence much, but don't know how else to put it.) It has always seemed to me *so* impossible that I should ever get into difficulties of this sort that I have never bothered to think of them seriously.'

The combined effect of his ill-health (did anyone realize just how unwell he was, or take account of it?), the emotional strain of his feelings for Eric and now, it seems, an absurd confusion in his friendship with Noël Adeney, must account for much of what Denton dashed down in his 'very unwise' letter to Eric that day. 'My dear Eric,' he wrote, 'How right and truthful you are. Your letter is *good*. I am *quite* conscious, I think, of the true nature of your feelings for me ... You find the barrier of our different temperaments much more insurmountable than I do. It is just because you *are* different that I like you. You wouldn't touch my imagination in the very least if you approximated more to my type.

'But apart from this difference, I think there *are* some points which should bind us together, and I think they would, if you would allow them to. You seem so distrustful of your emotions and feelings that you appear to tear them to pieces every now and then ...

'I can quite truthfully say that, apart from Jack Easton (for whom I had a quite overpowering obsession) I have not been as fond of *anyone* as I have been of you over the last few months. But I think this feeling would die in a moment if I thought you didn't really care a damn for me. In fact let me explain once and for all, dear Eric, that it is not your lusty body that is your chief attraction (I have seen many as lusty or lustier and they've not been of the slightest interest) but your essentially good nature. Your real self is surprisingly honest, generous, sensitive and affectionate. I could also reel off a list of your faults, but what is the point? You know them all, and they are not so important. The important thing is what is good in you, and what is good in you shines out very clearly. *I mean this.*

'It would be unspeakably sordid to me, if you only came to see me or kept up with me because you thought I expected it of you. The whole idea of your trying to please me against your own inclinations is quite *disgusting*; and you would do it *so* badly Eric, because you're so truthful, so please don't ever try.

'I have the unpleasant fear that you may have tried, while you've been here ... I assure you I am a very realistic and unsentimental person, and quite willing to believe that I am not in the *least* desirable or inspiring to you or to anyone else. It's easy for me to see that I'm probably quite grotesque in some people's eyes. This doesn't worry me. I have lived for so long without love – or rather without love of the right kind from the right person (there has been plenty of love from the wrong person) that I am quite capable of going on living for the rest of my life without it. In some moods I would quite ruthlessly sacrifice all the lovers in the world to my work. I want to get something done, and shall do, I hope, if I don't die. From this point of view it can be seen that love is probably not so overwhelmingly important to me as it is to some people. But in other moods, I am just as much in need of it, of course, as anyone else. But it seems to me that the most natural thing is to be devoted to one's work and yet be able to have great friendships as well.

'But if nobody is capable of loving one, one must simply go without, and work instead. This is my philosophy. So don't ever think I'd go crazy for lack of love. One cannot force what isn't there, and it's no good my screaming at you or anyone else "Love me!" if it's impossible.

'I don't pretend that I would ever have loved you as insanely and unreasonably as I loved J.E. – that sort of thing only happens when one is very young, very ill, very lonely and very inexperienced (besides, you wouldn't have liked it at all!) – but I do know that I would have been capable of loving you pretty deeply, if you had wanted it ... All I want to say is, I wish you'd just be happy and gay if you've enjoyed knowing me *at all*, and not *bother* whether you *love* me or not. It ought to be quite obvious by now that I have felt love for you; but I also felt love for my Siamese cat and have got over it now that it is dead!

'Christ, if you told me you loved me, when you didn't, I should be sick. If I hadn't felt any love for you, I just wouldn't have taken any notice of you. I don't care a fuck for most people; they're just like so many peas in a pudding to me. Casual acquaintances, I feel I never want to see again too.

'I am very annoyed with you now, because I think you are utterly shallow and not worthy of any deep feeling at all; but perhaps this is just because my vanity is piqued, who can tell?

'You have humiliated me; but you like doing that, and I can stand it, if you really have *any* feeling for me behind this surface cruelty; but if you haven't, for God's sake bugger off somewhere else. I have enough difficulties, emotional, physical, mental, on my hands without the added worry of a totally one-sided affair. I go quite hot with shame to think that you may only have come to see me because you thought I wanted you to. And there was I, fussing and arranging, and scrounging food and drink because I thought *you* liked coming! It is too ludicrous, like one of those silly plots for a farce or musical comedy.

'Don't be annoyed if I appear to abuse you in this letter. I am really abusing myself (don't laugh). You will realize it is not the letter to leave for a seventeen-year-old to see or anyone else. Please destroy it at once, or put it in this envelope and send it back to me. You needn't trouble to write yourself.

'I am unable to put "Love", "Yours ever" or any of those things. They seem to mean nothing at all for the moment. I don't even particularly want to sign my name, but no doubt if you're very clever you'll be able to guess who it's from ... The rain is pouring down in great gusts and it's getting dark and I'd like to knock your teeth down your throat, if I knew it wasn't such an impossible wish.'

ELEVEN

'Good Night, Beloved Comrade'

A stage had now been reached in the relationship between Denton and Eric in which Eric was being expected to shoulder burdens for which he was clearly ill-equipped. Denton tended to intellectualize his emotions whereas Eric simply took life at its face value. Denton revelled in the use of words, whereas Eric found articulation an extremely difficult exercise. Though Denton flirted with the idea of promiscuity he was in reality a more naturally monogamous person than Eric, and there was also in Denton a streak of cruelty and a desire for sophistication which was in marked contrast to Eric's essentially gentle, unjudgemental and sensitive temperament. Eric had never met anyone as gifted as Denton before, or so certain of his attitudes and aims, and to be battered by lengthy letters full of neurotic anguish must have been for him a new and unnerving experience.

Denton, however, was quick to recognize when he had gone too far. Within three days of his hysterical outburst of 9 February he was writing, presumably in response to a letter from Eric, to ask forgiveness for 'the insolence and rudeness' in his last letter 'if there was any, and I feel there must have been.

'I suppose,' he added by way of explanation, 'I was a bit upset because you didn't seem to care about anything at all. Perhaps you are right, and it's really bloody silly to make a fuss about love and friendship and everything else; but just sometimes one has the feeling that it's awful to go through life so absolutely alone, and one longs then to be in contact with another human being.

'I think you make a mistake when you feel I can't understand your different states of mind. You must remember that I have had a great many different states of mind to deal with myself since my accident. I have been terribly ill, and nearly dead, and terribly unhappy, and feeling that I'd go quite dotty with it all ... If I talk very little about illness and appear not to notice your quick changes of mood, it isn't that I'm blind, it's simply that I feel we've all got to behave as normally as possible to get on as best we can; otherwise we might all sit down and go quite cuckoo.'

He continued, one suspects without great conviction, 'I don't think I'll write to you any more after this, as you must find it an awful curse feeling that you have to answer. You can't be very fond of writing in your spare time.

'Once more let me say how sorry I am if you found my last letter a silly and unwanted and rude outburst. I just felt a bit frustrated; as if you'd treated me rough and thrown my feelings back in my face, because you thought they were bogus.

'I can't help thinking of you a bit now; but I don't suppose I'll mind a bit soon.' As if to hedge his bets, he ended, 'Good-bye for now.'

Two days later he wrote again: 'Dear Eric, You won't feel far away, unless you want to, will you? The flea-bag's always here for you, so just come and use it when you get fed up with your hostel and want some peace, or a change of scene. I *shall* enjoy hearing your news. Yours ever, Denton. P.S. I'm always here.'

Meanwhile, the arrival of a letter 'from the libel lawyers' about *In Youth is Pleasure* must have come as a welcome diversion. They were 'very reasonable and sensible this time', Denton reported to Noël, 'confining themselves entirely to business, no literary or moral criticism thrown in. Always do things by post! Much the best plan.'

On 11 February he cycled to Penshurst, and on the way back, passing a pub Eric used to frequent, his thoughts turned again to his friend. 'Curious to think,' he wrote when he got home, 'that all this time while Eric worked on the farm, hated it, was utterly lonely, got tight as often as possible just for something to do, I was only a few miles away in Tonbridge, walking the streets in my restlessness, trying to make myself iller and iller by any foolishness, wanting to die. And we never met and all the years in between, seven, eight, we knew nothing of each other, they all melted away and wasted.'

Another letter came from Eric, whose conscience seems to have been disturbing him. 'Dear Eric,' Denton replied on 18 February, 'For heaven's sake don't fuss! Your letter made me cry *literally*. I can't bear you to spoil everything by all this worry. What *does* it matter if you pinch anything of mine or not! I give it to you beforehand. So if you want anything just take it as a present. Remember you can't ever lift anything of mine because it automatically turns into a present.'

It would appear that Eric had in his letter suggested that they break off their friendship, and Denton clearly saw the need to repair some of the damage he had done in his outburst of nine days earlier. 'I make absolutely *no* demands on you at all,' he continued. 'You don't have to be fond of me, write to me, or pay me any attention at all, unless you feel like it. And I understand completely when you *don't* feel like it ... I would gladly swop all my circle of friends for you, and if you really don't ever want to meet my middle-aged women you needn't. It gives me the greatest pleasure to lock them out and be only with you.'

He went on to assure Eric that their friendship did not interfere with his work, 'Unless, as at the moment, you make me thoroughly unhappy and muddled by your seeming to want to cut me off from you completely. There seems absolutely no reason for this (unless of course you find me utterly boring and distasteful).

'Life is so terribly short. We *must* love each other and trust each other a little, else what's the good of living at all? And think of the long time when we'll be dead and utterly alone.

'Do please *think* before you decide to cut yourself off from me in this ruthless way. If you do decide to, I suppose I shall just have to submit to it, but it seems to me *terribly* unnecessary and cruel, and I would never be able to forget it.

'I know I love you. I'm not beglamoured or silly about you, I just love you and accept you, just as I accept and love my brother Paul, or anyone else I'm fond of.

'Dear Eric, don't let's be so tragic and gloomy about our affection for each other. Our lives are already much too full of unpleasant possibilities and problems. Can't we snatch just a little pleasure for ourselves, and not think of tomorrow or the next day? Circumstances will probably be only too ready to divide us and keep us apart. Isn't it for us *not* to be destructive and critical? Shouldn't we at least try to have some moments of understanding and gaiety? Neither of us need demand or expect anything of the other. I don't demand or expect your love or any part of it.

'Christ, Eric, please don't spoil everything so wilfully. It really breaks my heart (whatever that phrase means).

'I swore never to burden you with this sort of letter again, nor would I, if I felt I did not have to make my position absolutely clear. You owe nothing to me, and I fully realize this. We are two separate persons. But does this mean that we were never to meet or find any enjoyment in knowing each other? Must we really be absolutely lonely all our lives?

'If you care anything for me at all, won't you make some sort of effort to see me fairly soon, or tell me what effort you'd like me to make, so that we can talk instead of writing all these terribly frustrating letters. Do come to see me very soon, this weekend, or next, or any time, if only to get this thing settled. Now that I've written this, it looks as if I'm trying to make you do what I want. You will of course only do what *you* want. I am powerless to influence you and wouldn't want to, even if I could. You must only do what your heart wants.

'At any rate you know now what I think.

'I love and trust you, Denton.'

Denton's continual denial of his need for Eric's love has to be taken with a pinch of salt. He must have been well aware of his physical limitations as a lover, and of Eric's feelings of emotional inadequacy. Rather than drive Eric away by making plain his attachment to him, Denton tried to underplay his own needs in the hope that Eric would come half way to meet him. He also realized the danger of continuing an unsatisfactory correspondence much longer with someone for whom letter-writing was a burden. The ploy worked, and beside himself with pleasure, Denton was writing to Eric again on 23 February to say, 'My dear Eric, I was so *delighted* to get your letter. Yes – do come on Saturday, as soon as is convenient to you ... I'm so happy to think you're coming that I can't write any more. It seems ages since you went, although it's not yet three weeks.

'On Monday I was in The Chequers at Ightham drinking gin all alone. It was terribly gloomy. The gin reminded me of you, for some reason, and I thought you'd disappeared for good. But it wasn't true after all. I shall see you Sat. Meanwhile, my love, D.'

Eric duly arrived, staying the Saturday night, and much gin was consumed by the pair of them. Less welcome visitors were soon to follow. On 4 March Denton was writing to Eric to announce, 'Someone is coming to see me tomorrow whom I don't particularly want to see. To keep the person at bay I shall have to be very bright and talk a lot and sit rather a long way away; unless I get Miss S. to chaperon me. However I don't know that I should be mentioning this to you, since you always think I'm so silly in suffering people when I don't want to. This can't exactly be avoided tho', as I've just had the letter announcing the visit.' He gives no further details of this particular visitor, though in his journal on 2 April he mentions that as a result of his photograph appearing in *Vogue* he had been plagued by 'absurd fan letters', one from a Free-French Volunteer girl, another from a man who had offered to nurse him and a third from someone who wanted to paint his portrait. 'I shall keep them all at bay,' Denton wrote, 'feeling terrified of their disillusion if they should know me.' Often, however, there was no avoiding them. The French girl turned up without an appointment and Denton, after cursing and swearing beforehand, treated her to tea and supper, took her to the woods to pick primroses, and signed her copy of *Maiden Voyage*. As he was escorting her to the bus stop, May Walbrand-Evans put her head out of her window and offered the girl a bed for the night. May later told him she had thought her a nice girl for him to marry.

In the same letter to Eric he apologized for the 'weak-kneed' state he had been in on the Sunday of Eric's visit. His generally depressed state continued, and may have been responsible for the sentiments he expressed when again writing to Eric on 7 March: 'I suppose (if I must tell you the truth) I was unhappy last time we met because I felt very fond of you and yet not much good to you. I had the feeling that you'd probably much rather be with another, different type of person, and I was just rather a strain and a nuisance. I felt that you couldn't really like me, and I wanted you, like anything, to like me.

'I suppose too I was in that state because, as you say, I pity myself sometimes. I feel that all my youth since nineteen has been wasted because of being ill and getting a little better and being ill again. It's made everything such a terrific strain and effort. That's why I'm jittery and nervous and self-conscious.

'And I wish like anything that this wasn't so and that I could have enjoyed myself and done a lot of silly things like anyone else. I feel that all my earliest days, which should have been the best, have been spoilt for me; and I lie down and wallow in it sometimes! However, I don't mean to again to you, if I can help it! I should hate to repay you in that way for being so kind to me.

'I've never had a friend like you before and I don't suppose I ever shall again ... I don't know what I'd do if you walked out on me. I suppose I'd just go on living as I do now, but I know I'd distrust people more and more and I'd think that things were worse than they are ...

'Oh God, Eric, I always seem to get so gloomy and full of the state of my own feelings when I write or talk to you, and all I really want to do is to amuse you or make you feel happy!

'Come Saturday; it will be *fine*. Shall I expect you sometime in [the] afternoon? I shall be here all the time so just turn up. Lovely! I will get some beer in. The sod who came to see me on Sunday drank some of the last lot. God! and wasn't I bored and disgusted with him! I suppose

I was comparing him with you all the time, which didn't exactly work out in his favour. He didn't seem to me a real person at all — just a lump of dough.'

The letter ended on a note of panic: 'My eldest brother, Bill, the one I'm rude about in the book, is coming home! I hope he won't bring a libel action or come down to Pitt's F.C. with a revolver or anything. If he does, will you come and be a thug for me and help me put him on the mat?!

'"Good night, Beloved Comrade". (These are the words of a Negro song I heard.) I like them. They say what I want to say to you. D.'

When Eric arrived at Pitt's Folly on 11 March he found Denton in bed with a temperature of 104°. 'He put his hand on my stomach and we lay contentedly talking and I began to feel better,' Denton recorded three weeks later. 'He had a restful, good effect on me.' The next morning, however, Denton was up again and off with Eric on his bicycle, to a pub called The Volunteers, where he decided to get drunk and started ordering double gins. 'Eric frowned. I think he thought it rather hysterical.' At closing time, they made their way to the wood where they had enjoyed their last picnic, and were rewarded by the sight of 'those blessed eggshells lying there still. Eric marvelled, as I hoped he would.'

Denton was 'much drunker this time after five gins' — by this he may possibly have meant five double gins — 'and when we sat down at the foot of a tree in the delicate warm sun I suddenly burst into tears. Frightful, but true. And this flood set us talking, talking, talking about friendship, love, hate, fear of death, on, on, on.' They stayed out, talking and walking, until six o'clock.

One of the things Denton discovered about Eric's past during these searching conversations was that he had attempted suicide when he was eighteen. 'When Eric tells me things like this,' Denton wrote, 'life seems so terrifying that I want to die. And I long wildly to have known him all my life. I know it would have been different if I had. Perhaps not better, but different, less mad.' He imagined Eric in the years before they knew one another as 'Sweet and kind, terribly young, foolish, generous, utterly without guidance and judgement', and he added a sentence that gives the central clue to his love for Eric and his desire to live with him, for in Eric he saw someone who was as vulnerable as himself: 'Again I say how I long to have known him then, to have seen what was gnawing at him all the time.'

The next letter he wrote to Eric, on 14 March, appears to be a continuation of their conversation in the woods. He wrote that he was glad he had drunk the gin, 'for I think it made our talk in the woods more possible – and the talk was a good thing, because it helped me to talk about what gnaws at me rather – the fear I have that it is absolutely impossible for you to find anything to like in me at all. I feel so lonely and deserted when I have this fear that I'm at my very worst. I'm sort of defenceless then and that makes me try to cling on to you too desperately.

'When I'm bad like that, if you could just reassure me a bit, as you did in the wood, you'd put me right.

'I'm so conscious of the quality I lack – you've no need to tell me – it hits me in the eye every day when I wake up. And this knowledge makes it difficult for me to believe that you can care anything for me at all. I feel awful, and absolutely left out in the cold, if I can't believe that there's just some little bit of me somewhere that might vaguely resemble your cup of tea. I suppose I should not allow you to see this longing for a tiny little bit of affection. Worldly-wise people would certainly tell me that it is the very worst possible way of going to work; but it seems that I have to be *quite* truthful with you. I even have to admit it when I have told you that I am nearly twenty-seven when I am really twenty-eight. And for me to have to confess that I've told a silly, petty, pointless, vain lie like that is *very* difficult. I have also had to tell you things about my accident which never ceases to give me pain, humiliation and embarrassment.

'I can't tell anyone hardly about these things, and I try to go on from day to day pretending to everyone that I'm really perfectly all right. It puts a pretty good strain on me, and I sometimes feel fit to bust.

'The fact that I used to be so hardy and free from all that sort of thing makes my present messed-up state very hard to bear with a good grace. It's given my conceit and pride a smack which it won't ever forget, and I have to use quite a lot of will-power sometimes, not to feel rather dotty and hysterical about it.

'I know that the faint possibility that I just might be well-known one day (if I don't die) doesn't cut any ice with you at all. I would hate it if it did. It's all much to me, compared with the feelings I have for you. (Please don't think it vain of me to talk about being well-known in that open way. It doesn't look too good now I've written it down.)

'I'm absolutely unused to being with anyone else I like, and so it gives me a sense of responsibility. I also want to look after you, because

I think you don't take proper care of yourself. You may think this all very feminine and unnecessary, but there it is. Just put up with it, or tell me to shut up.

'I must too say I'm sorry for trying to thrust money on you in that impulsive, vulgar, offensive way. That too is part of my anxiety neurosis about you. I feel that you may really be needing the money, and it seems awful that I should have it here lying idle. I haven't much money now that my Pa's dead and his estate all unsettled and buggered up by the Japanese, but what I have and what I can earn I would always want you to make use of, if need arises. If you ever wanted anything, I'd love to get it for you; if I had the dough.'

On the subject of his work, Denton told Eric he had been correcting the proofs of 'When I Was Thirteen' all that morning. 'I think it's awfully peculiar and don't know *what* the Great British Public will think. I hope it will shake them and send electric shocks down their spines. I feel awfully sadistic about the reading public. Don't you think they ought to be woken up? I shall probably get myself locked up for "obscene reference". You will have to come and feed me thro' the bars then.'

Denton's next letter, written on 21 March, was concerned once again with his health, which was in a particularly bad state at this time. 'My dear Eric, I don't mind if you poke fun at tubes [a reference to the catheter he was obliged to wear]; I can take it — from you. You never worry or offend me as many of the women I know do. This weekend Noël and Frida Easdale came to see me and made me feel like an addled egg. I wish I could have swopped them for you. I understood absolutely what you mean when you say that women are affected and you wish they would stop talking.

'I had begun to think that it was quite impossible — that a person like you could have understood or feel interest in a person like me. The fact that you can, even a bit, has really made me much less pessimistic.'

He went on to report there had just been 'two colossal bangs! — bombs I suppose; which reminds me that I am not really brave, as you suggest. I suppose I have the quality which makes people salvage as much as they can from the wreckage! I've certainly had to do that with myself after my accident; but I don't think that's bravery; that's just making the best of a bad job.'

Denton told Eric he always wrote too much to him 'because I don't know how to stop. I ought to stop now because it is getting quite late. The aeroplanes are droning about, the All Clear has gone. I sit here under the wooden angel's wings [a baroque angel was one of Denton's prized possessions] and with the lamp all shaded and draped with newspapers. Miss S. is fumbling in her room going to bed. I wish you were here with me now, when it is utterly quiet and still and peaceful. I want to tell you all my thoughts.

'It's fine knowing a person like you. It's made a terrific difference to me.

'Good night, sleep tight (only in the best sense of the word, of course). You know how much regard I have for you, so I need not say any more.'

Denton's high temperature on 11 March seems to have been a prelude to a new development in the general deterioration of his condition. 'As you saw, things haven't been going very well with me for the last week or so,' he wrote to Noël on 25 March, 'and they finally came to a head while we [he and Noël] were having tea in the haystack. I began to feel very peculiar, and when finally I did rush home I was in quite a bad state. I went straight to bed and in the morning my temperature was 102°. I stayed there all yesterday and felt frightful. It's gone down to 100° this morning, so I feel better, though still very achy and floating.

'I'm afraid I shall have to stay in bed in spite of Eric's arrival, but I am not worrying about this, as he is not restless, and if he does get tired of sick-rooms and beds, he can go out on his own.'

Noël herself records, in her annotations, that during their picnic Denton had gone round the corner to relieve himself, and on returning said. "'It *can't* be right, there's so much blood, great dark clots of it."' Dr Easton was still away on war service, and although appointments were made through one of Noël's sisters for Denton to see a specialist, he refused to keep them; although he acknowledged that he was in need of more medical help than he was receiving, he feared that a consultation would result in his return to hospital.

On 29 March he celebrated his twenty-ninth birthday — 'quite the nicest birthday I've had for a long time, and this in spite of my guts'. Noël gave him 'an exquisite' eighteenth-century watch 'with a lovely disc of gorgeous blue glass at the back', which Denton played with all afternoon but then had to send back to the jeweller as it yet had to be made to work. 'I *do* hope he'll hurry and that he won't touch it or maul it in any way,' Denton wrote to Noël the next day. 'I'm longing to polish it myself.' His birthday held in store another surprise, not at all a welcome one. His brother, just back from Africa, had sent a wire from the Conservative Club. 'Do you think Bill will arrive?' Denton nervously inquired of Noël. 'This is pure horror to me.'

Eric also remembered Denton's birthday, and Denton wrote to him to say he must not spend any money on him, adding, 'I can't repay, too, things like your goodness to me when I'm ill. Instead of sitting down and reading, and then going out for a drink, you stay with me and do all to ease my discomfort and pain. This made an enormous difference at the weekend. I wouldn't have been nearly so well on Sunday if you hadn't behaved as you did. No one else has ever done this for me, either.'

He told Eric that one of his aunts had sent him £1 and another 'her kind regards'. As for the news of Bill's arrival in England, he wrote, 'Isn't it frightful. He'll be down here any day now, because I've written to say I've not been well. He read both my new book and the Horizon article ['When I Was Thirteen'] which comes out in April. This worries me far more than it ought to, I suppose. I feel very guilty about maligning him in print. I think it will hurt his feelings more than it was ever meant to; I felt that he would be out of the country and that he'd never read anything I wrote.'

This was Denton at his most disingenuous, and the passage highlights the ambiguousness of his relationship with Bill. Like a naughty schoolboy, he had known perfectly well what he was doing when he was writing about Bill in the novel and the short story and was determined to get a good story into print regardless of the pain it might cause his brother. Moreover, it is obvious that he had himself sent typescripts to Bill of both the article, which was not due to appear until the following month, and *In Youth is Pleasure*, which was not to be published until the following year. Whether he was half hoping that his strapping elder brother would come storming down to confront him, and was enjoying the thrill of fear this brought, or whether he had simply been required by Herbert Read and Cyril Connolly to obtain his brother's approval to publish both works and had reckoned on dealing with the consequences by post, there is no knowing. Whatever the truth, all credit must go to Bill for the generosity with which he was to turn a blind eye to Denton's literary indiscretions.

Denton continued his letter to Eric with the news that Evie had been 'a terrible bitch all day. I suppose I've insulted and offended her and she wants to get her own back. I hate her like anything when she's like this. It's especially awful when I'm ill.'

In this letter, too, he touched on the subject of suicide: 'I think I talk to you too much about popping oneself off. It's only because I think I'm going to have a very sticky death, and so I want to be able to do myself in as bearably as possible, before I have too much lingering and languishing. Anyhow, perhaps I'll live for years, in spite of all my imaginings and premonitions. Tonight I don't feel as if I would though! I feel as if everything is falling to pieces, and I'm the chief piece of garbage!'

He finished writing this letter a day later, after spending all morning working on the decorations for *In Youth is Pleasure*, 'but now I'm a bit ill again and am lying on the bed. I really feel stricken down this time by a much longer bout.' He was also apprehensive about the arrival of Bill: 'I am living in fear and trembling of finding my aggrieved brother standing on the doorstep. I wonder what he will look like now, I haven't seen him since about 1937.'[1]

Five days later he was well enough to go out on his bicycle. 'It was really lovely in the sun by the river,' he wrote to Noël, 'but I felt very depressed for some reason. No brother Bill has turned up yet, which is a relief. Do you think he'll come for Easter with Anne?' Having already mentioned to Noël his plan to send some poems to the *Cornhill* magazine he commented, 'I want to know what a lot of different people think about my poems. Edith doesn't say a word! Perhaps you have to publish a book before anyone even knows you write them.' (It is possible that Edith Sitwell thought it kinder not to comment on those of Denton's poems she had read.) As usual, his letter was a mixture of information about work in progress ('I've been trying to do another small picture of a woolly dog sitting near a rustic seat and tickling its ear with a sunflower'), of news about everyday domestic matters ('Evie says Friday is Good Friday and she will make mock Hot Cross Buns'), of gossip about neighbours ('What *is* going on in May's head all day?'), and titbits of slander ('There are two fair-haired small boys staying here and I wish I had Gerald with me so that he could enjoy them; but perhaps on second thoughts they are not quite the public-school age yet. It must be awfully upsetting to have *such* a narrowed-down age group'). He ended on a note of horror so typical of him: 'The cat caught a baby rabbit and left, very appropriately, its hind quarters in the lavatory. This was too much for me. I keep thinking of it.'

The same day, 5 April, he wrote to Eric, to say, 'You don't have to feel sad about my precarious health, nor do you have to come and see me when I'm ill. It must be very boring for you to watch me lying in bed. I must admit it cheers *me* up a lot, but it can't exactly be *your*

1. Denton had spent two days in London with Bill in February 1937 shortly before he and his wife, Anne, sailed for Shanghai.

idea of pleasure!' He quoted a review in the *Spectator* mentioning his story 'The Barn' in *New Writing and Daylight*: '"Mr Welch has produced another tremulous and sexy story in the manner of his Maiden Voyage, all about a fat woman in stays, and the contrasted beauty of a tramp who comes to sleep in the barn." Pretty steep this, isn't it! It made me laugh. What *will* they say about my new book!' He went on, 'I suppose you were born kind, for you've certainly been very good to me. Jack was good to me, but then it all ended in the most frightful mess, and that made me think that all friendships go down the drain in the end. I never thought that I'd have anything but the most passing acquaintanceship with anyone again.'

All the while that Denton had been concentrating on sorting out his relationship with Eric, it appears that his friendship with Noël had again been drifting into a dangerous muddle, as he revealed to Eric in a letter on 11 April: 'Noël was here yesterday and we sat on the river bank drinking tea in the sun and she said suddenly, "Does Eric know how much I love you?"!! I didn't know what to say and felt terribly embarrassed. This sort of thing is a bit confusing, isn't it. I suppose I'll get used to it soon. Nothing ever quite works out as it should, does it?' He ended his letter, 'Come soon won't you. I get impatient. I want to be as happy as I can while I can. In spite of being a Storm Trooper in Jack Boots [a reference to Eric's professed admiration for Mussolini and Hitler] you have a pretty good slice of your friend Denton's love!!!'

When one considers how frequently and debilitatingly ill he was at this time, the amount of energy he was able to summon up not only to cope with invasions of all kinds into his life but to record everything that happened at such length, is cause for amazement. Sometimes, as on 13 April when Eric rolled up late at night, 'plus another land-boy, Peter Clements (sticky-out ears, large, smooth-faced, rather pug-nosed baby looking)', he would send off one version of events to Noël, another to Marcus Oliver and then write it all up again in his journal.

Eric and Peter had descended on Denton after missing their last train to Appledore, and he, in sheer desperation, as he told Noël, 'began to get awfully social'. In order to put them up for the night Evie dismembered her own bed, 'and soon the floor was strewn with mattresses, palliasses, flea-bags, army blankets and ragged pillow-cases. My room became a complete doss-house, and after long, long talking into the night, we began slowly to go to bed.

'Eric and Peter both snore and there is no possible sleep for me so I just lie and think and the moon slowly rises until it's shining right on my face and then a nightingale (a quite real nightingale) warbles and tremolos and weeps for the rest of the night.'

When he came to write to Marcus Oliver on 19 April to tell him about this episode, he had much other news saved up: 'I've been meaning to write and explain away my rather distant earlier letter to you.[2] Truth to tell, "Little by Little" [Eric] had been causing me a certain amount of anxiety and I had him on my mind so I just meandered on about it to you. Hope you weren't terribly bored. It must have been rather uninteresting. We have been seeing each other about every fortnight. It is fun really and I enjoy it, but Eric is naughty and *will* not leave the booze alone. The other night he turned up at 10.30 with another youth and demanded beds, as they'd been dog-racing and pub-crawling and had missed the last train to Appledore!!

'Can you see your friend getting out the mattresses and turning the upper chamber of Pitt's Folly Cottage into an elegant doss-house? My dear, they both snored their heads off and I lay sleepless listening to the nightingale.

'I wish I was up to this wild picnic sort of life. I have a terrible nostalgia for my very early youth before I was a crock. It is great fun, isn't it, to live on impulse; and here I have to live in such frightful and careful retirement.

'I really have been rather groggy for some time, and am trying to decide who to consult about myself. I wish I could find a decent doctor or specialist. I hate them all, and feel that I shall probably fall entirely to bits before I go to see another one.'

He did not mention to Marcus that Eric had returned two days later on his own, and that they had quarrelled with each other. 'How we quarrelled,' he wrote in his journal, 'and how terribly unhappy I grew, and how hopeless.' In the long silences Eric drank bottle after bottle of beer and Denton smoked cigarette after cigarette until his fingers were brown. 'And then Eric made it up with me and sat on the stool and took my feet (which were already on the stool) on to his knees. So we sat in this curious position and made friends again, and I felt I would forgive him almost anything.'

It was after two in the morning before they went to bed, 'but for a wonder we slept well. Only once or twice I woke up to see the moon on Eric's face, making it look like lean, lovely, hollowed sculpture, and with the sound of his breathing was mixed the wonderful nightingale

2. This earlier letter has not survived; the reference to Eric indicates that it had been written some time in February.

which never stopped. And I felt so much better and less worried by my body that I rejoiced, and could not resist telling Eric how eased I was. And it seemed a miraculously pleasant end to our trouble and unhappiness.

'I thought that it was always easy to be friends with Eric and difficult, terribly difficult, to keep up a dignity and grievance ...

'I don't know what will happen in the future to our friendship, but now it is good to keep it alive all I can.'

TWELVE

'A Madness Grows'

One day sometime during April, Denton was out with Noël Adeney when they met two friends of hers and the four of them repaired to a nearby pub. Noël allowed Denton to buy a round and later, as she recorded after his death, 'feeling responsible for the exchange of drinks, especially as Denton, at this time, never drank anything himself', she sent him a postal order to cover the cost of the drinks. Her remark leads one to wonder just how much she knew about him at all, since at precisely this time he was drinking gin by the gill; and her action elicited an interesting response from Denton. Returning the postal order to her on 27 April he wrote, 'You really mustn't worry about me, and money, and buying drinks and things. "Without wishing to appear vulgar" (this is the new phrase that Evie and I throw at each other in our peculiar badinage) my supplies really are more than adequate for my needs. In fact at the moment, what with one thing and another, I feel quite rich!'

Apart from thus avoiding any obligation to Noël, his feeling of relative wealth may have been prompted by having recently received a cheque for fourteen guineas from Cyril Connolly for 'When I Was Thirteen'; and for the short story 'At Sea' he was expecting £15 from *English Story*. Cyril Connolly had also written telling him that Hamish Hamilton had expressed an interest in publishing a collection of his short stories. Allen & Unwin, too, had written to Denton after seeing the story in *Horizon*, asking him 'to submit books to them', and two of his paintings had been bought by a Mrs Serocold. 'It is happiness to have things liked,' he noted in his journal on 21 April, 'but when I'm ill as I was on Wednesday and other days everything pales to nothing and I want to die more than anything on earth. I think all I can do is to keep my work going as long as I can. And if I can no longer, then I will die.'

'I had a hell of a time battling with my body in the early part of last week,' he wrote to Eric on 27 April, 'and now am feeling much better, thank God. I hope this will last over the weekend. It certainly should do. I am going to see Mrs Easton [Jack Easton's wife, Caterina, was also a doctor] on Friday evening to see if she can suggest anything to bring about an improvement. I expect she'll tell me that I must go up to London to be poked and prodded by some more horrible specialist. If she tells me to do this I have decided that I will, because life, on and off lately, has been pretty unendurable.'

On 2 May he was writing again to Eric to say, 'I have just heard that I have got to go and see the specialist tomorrow in London and I'm afraid I am dreading it. I wish you could come too, to give me moral support.

'I saw Mrs E. yesterday and she pumped out some blood and put it in a bottle to be tested. As you say, it hardly hurt at all. She also wanted to examine me, so my trousers remained at half mast for several minutes. I didn't mind this. I don't know whether you would. You seem to have a prejudice against women doctors. I think she is very good and understanding and she seems now quite to like and trust me.'

The reason for Mrs Easton's change of heart was no doubt due to the fact that Denton was obviously no longer emotionally dependent on her husband. She had found his persistent visits to her house in Tonbridge an irritation, and his infatuation with Jack an unwelcome intrusion. Whether Denton ever appreciated how embarrassing his attentions to Jack had proved is doubtful.

Denton kept his appointment with the specialist, at 3.30 p.m. on 3 May, at 26 Brook Street in Mayfair. 'As I expected he had nothing new to suggest,' he wrote in his journal the next day. Afterwards he had called on one of the new fans he had acquired in April, a man named Guy Allan – who had written offering to nurse Denton when he was ill. 'He said it was an art, like everything else,' Denton had reported to Marcus on 19 April. 'I secretly agreed, but thought that perhaps it would be wiser not to surrender myself to his tender care. It would be awkward if he got too artful, wouldn't it.' He was also a Christian Scientist, and he had revealed in his letter that God had sent him especially to succour Denton. 'I wish he'd begin his work,' Denton wrote with a touch of sarcasm. 'I should love to be succoured.'

He located Guy Allan, a painter, in his studio in Glebe Place, just off King's Road. 'Stacked in masses,' he noted as he went inside, 'were Guy's and his boyfriend's canvases. They were really a little better than I thought they would be.' He quickly became fascinated by Guy, who talked of the Bohemian life and of hob-nobbing with the aristocracy, telling Denton, for instance, 'that the Duchess de Choiseul's daughter was once very fond of him, and her Belgian husband became so incensed that he nearly killed them both in a car crash by mistake on purpose'.

On returning home, Denton wrote to Eric to say he was going to be X-rayed in Tunbridge Wells, 'just to see if anything more can be discovered; but I suppose I'll have to go on stewing in my own juice'. He went on, in pessimistic mood, 'They don't seem to take any interest at all. Perhaps they do when you're actually on the point of death. I felt it was all rather a waste of time and money bothering with them at all. It's made me angry and frustrated, as you can see. I suppose I had a sneaking idea that he might be some use and make helpful suggestions; in spite of all I've said against doctors. However I'm going to try and give up bothering about it now.'

He went on to tell Eric that no less than four publishers had approached him recently. 'I begin to feel mildly in demand,' he announced with justifiable pride.

The rest of his news concerned a distressing turn of events in his relationship with Noël, who when he had last seen her had burst into tears. 'It really was terrible. I felt hot and terrified and helpless. I am wondering what I should do now. I have nearly decided to write and suggest we don't meet for some time. I do seem to have a fantastically painful effect on her and her scenes shock me, because one sees how much upset and distress each person unwittingly inflicts on another. It's all a perplexing muddle. I wish very much Noël wasn't fond of me. It puts a burden on me, and I want to throw it back on to her. I've never had this problem quite like this to deal with before.

'Noël's passion for me is amazing, don't you think!' he continued. 'It has been going on now for over a year. And she wanted me to go to Middle Orchard to live with her, and drive Bernard out into the streets!! I suppose I respect it, like I respect anyone else's passion, but I can't understand how she ever *allowed* herself to get into that condition of loving, or obsession, or whatever it is. I suppose I'm not one to talk when I think of how I behaved with Jack; but I was very young and also very ill, which makes a *tremendous* difference to your behaviour.

'Now that I have written all this about Noël I feel rather ashamed and mean; for after all, it is *very* rare to have people to love one in that intense way, and it has certainly never happened to me with someone I could have loved in return. But I can't understand how my coldness, my frank explanations, have had no effect. All along she has known how utterly alien all this sort of stuff is to me. I feel this ought to have put her off quite a lot, but it doesn't seem to have; it seems to have goaded her on! I hate possessive people more than anything on earth. I wish I had been more reserved.'

On 16 May, having evidently decided what he must do about Noël, he wrote to her as gently as he was able: 'I wonder if you will think it quite wrong-headed and rather peculiar of me if I suggest that we don't meet for a little time? I seem to have become slightly diffused and dissipated lately, what with one thing and another, and I feel that I *must* brood and dwell on my new book in a lean and lonely period. Of course paying all this attention to my body is disintegrating – but also I seem to have been talking so much and saying so little! If I want to get anything done, I have really to cut myself off, at least in snatches, I have decided.

'I don't really think that you want to change me, but I think that being such very different types of people we are bound to react rather badly on each other sometimes. But I don't think that matters if one just takes it all in one's stride.

'I'm afraid,' he added, taking responsibility for the situation on himself, 'this is one of those meandering, dotty letters, that leap from one layer of consciousness to another – a true reflection of me at the moment!'

Noël appears, if her subsequent annotations of Denton's letters are anything to go by, to have attributed Denton's desire for a 'lean and lonely period' entirely to his being bothered about Eric – which, as it turns out, he was, having written in his journal on 8 May, 'When you long with all your heart for someone to love you, a madness grows there that shakes all sense from the trees and the water and the earth. And nothing lives for you, except the long deep bitter want. And this is what everyone feels from birth to death.'

On 15 May he had gone into Tunbridge Wells to be X-rayed, and several days later he heard from Mrs Easton that nothing further had been discovered, but that the plates had been sent to the Brook Street specialist for examination. 'I don't know if he'll have anything more to suggest,' Denton wrote to Noël on 23 May. 'I suppose it really is all rather satisfactory, except that I am still left with my unpleasant and mysterious spasms! However, they've been much better lately, and I hope they won't return!' He also told her, 'So far from having a peaceful lonely time, I have had Eric here from Saturday to yesterday evening! And there have been such mental upsets and turmoils and difficulties that I now feel as if I'd been smacked all over! However I suppose it is all my own fault. I seem built to make human contacts go wrong.

'All last week before Eric came I worked rather well and felt contented and unfussed,' he continued. 'Of course there is loneliness as well, in seeing no one and having no one to talk to, and I don't know how long that sort of life is good for one.'

Taking up the theme of his previous letter to her, he added, 'But I don't know if it is a good thing for you and me to go on seeing each other. We talk and amuse each other and the hours pass quickly and pleasantly enough (if there are no hitches!); but surely underneath there is something deeply unsatisfactory which will always be making itself felt in the most awkward and muddled way. Do you agree with this? Or do you think that I am just making difficulties, and trying to tidy everything up more than it ever *can* be tidied up?'

On the same day he wrote this letter he also recorded in his journal: 'The postman has just come to take the appalling letter that I have written to Eric. I hear the slam of the car door and the starting of the engine, and now I know that he will really get it. It is on its way already down the drive, to the road, to the office, to Ashford and at last to Appledore. The face at the other end, as it reads it – what will it be like?'

The studied drama – if not deliberate childishness – of this entry and, indeed, of the letter itself, can only be understood in the context of the accumulated strain of visits to doctors, emotional entanglements with Noël, his nagging fear that his love for Eric would never be returned, and finally the weekend of 'mental upsets and turmoils'. The letter to Eric began: 'Better call it all off. Now that you've gone and I can think all round the subject and say what I like on paper without thinking of your feelings, I see how mad and weak-minded of me it is not to have stopped seeing you some time ago. My only excuse for ever beginning anything so stupid is that I was utterly bamboozled by you. You are indifferent to me ... I realize it now, only too well – and of course much too late.'

Recriminations and abuse pile one upon another for a full twenty frantic pages: 'You could not have treated anyone more cruelly than you have treated me ... You have hoodwinked and cheated me ... You have hurt me, insulted me and made use of me ... Whether you realize it or not, you have behaved abominably to me ... Please don't show [this letter] to Peter or any other lout; at least I must trust you that far. I hope you will tear it up or burn it, which is really the right fate for it ... Good-bye. It will certainly not be my fault if we meet again.'

While he waited in a state of panic for a reply from Eric, the fan letters continued to arrive, one from a schoolboy in Sheffield ('I only wish I had Gerald here to pass him on to!' Denton told Noël, from whom he found it as impossible to break off relations as he did from Eric), and one from 'a Peter Cromwell who lives in Mount Street, who says he was "thrilled and enchanted" with the Horizon story and wants me to go to lunch'. Ill and out of sorts as Denton must have been, he nevertheless decided to 'counter-attack' by inviting Cromwell to lunch with him. A date was fixed for 5 June, and Denton gave him prawns, lettuce hearts and partridge eggs, macaroni, plum flan, peppermint creams, coffee and apple juice. 'He knows Connolly and Toynbee and all those people,' Denton noted in his journal, 'and he'll tell them all about me. Awful.'

By 26 May, having been thinking 'all the time of Eric at Appledore', he could bear the suspense no longer and that evening telephoned Eric. The next evening he telephoned again and then wrote to apologize. 'Forgive tonight, but I was tight. You have made me so unhappy. I feel beside myself just at the moment, to think that you can never again give me the mildest tenderness, because for some reason you have decided that I am utterly unattractive to you. Heaven knows, I probably am ... Have I meant nothing to you since you knew me?' he asked. 'I don't expect you to love me like Cleopatra! I feel my demands on you have been almost nil; but when you seem to find even kissing me repugnant, I suppose things are indeed pretty hopeless.' Feeling rejected both physically and emotionally, he was now talking seriously, both in letters and in his journal, of suicide. 'If I don't die soon,' he continued to Eric, 'I shall certainly try to do myself in properly. It is always cheap to talk about suicide, but I simply can't go on coping with everything and this added horrible frustration, upset and humiliation. I certainly have no vanity now. You have knocked every scrap out of me. You have knocked everything out of me but bitterness. And I can't understand why you have done it.'

The next morning (it was in fact Whit Sunday), still in the grip of depression, he was writing in his journal, 'Every night now comes over me the terrible restlessness just before bed, which I thought would never come again. And I feel that I must tear the walls down. I must go anywhere out of the house to wander in the lanes on my bicycle. I cannot keep still. And the thought of Eric haunts me like a ghost. After I said that I was sorry, I made everything much worse than it was before. Now I am just waiting to telephone again, and I am going up to London if I can [Eric was staying there with his mother for Whitsun] to try to settle something.

'This whole week has been such drab monotonous pain. And nothing to hear or see. No letter. My work has somehow died to nothing, and I think of nothing but dying or killing myself. I could kill myself so easily with tablets, no other way. The right time and place really only remain to be found now. How nasty the talk of suicide, yet how inevitable it sometimes seems.'

By the afternoon of the same day he was sitting with Eric under a plane tree in St James's Park. 'Talking there under the tree, I really thought that we had decided only to be friends and not quarrel,' he wrote in his journal after his return home, but somehow things had gone wrong at the end of his visit. In the evening he and Eric had gone off to a public house in Dulwich and had got very drunk. They then went back to Eric's mother's flat and in the morning Eric applied ice packs to Denton's head. 'To live this way is death,' Denton wrote, 'and I know it, for me, and yet something extraordinary for me seems to come out of it.'

As soon as he was home, on 30 May, he was writing to Eric to say, 'Please forgive my behaviour, and going off like that ... I'm not usually as unpleasant as that, but as you say, I'm a bad loser. I simply cannot get used to the idea that someone one's become really fond of no longer finds anything to love in me. You will understand that this is a terribly hurtful experience ... You have been in so many ways the friend that I have longed for, that I can't bear to think that I have come to mean absolutely nothing to you.' Yet he found it in him to end his letter, 'Thank you for the weekend and for really, under the circumstances, being as charming to me as possible. From your true friend, Denton.'

An optimist of phenomenal tenacity, he was writing again to Eric on 1 June, 'I absolutely refuse to quarrel with you.' He suggested that they should not see each other for some time, but he still argued that it would be stupid for them to break for ever. The following day he received a letter from Eric, to which he replied by return: 'Just let me say at the beginning that I have gradually been led into being *terribly* unwise with you. As you say, it means death when one tries to make someone love one. No one knows this better than myself and I am ashamed of being guilty of this weakness with you ...

'Oh my dear don't make excuses ... You have of course never been under *any* obligation to come here and you need never come anywhere near me again if you don't want to. The matter rests, and always has rested, *entirely* with you ... I'm sorry I've pestered you, sorry I've

bothered you, sorry I've been too fond of you. Can anyone say more?'
He could, and did: 'I have written you another long letter, but what
is the good of sending it? You are so obviously *insisting* on being out
of sympathy with me. There is no need. I shan't worry you again.'

On 6 June Denton learned that the invasion of Normandy had been
launched, and during the night he heard 'the continuous scream of
bombers ... going to battle, and the whole world seemed more wicked
and mad than seemed bearable'. On 10 June, however, all thought of
both Eric and the horrors of war would have been driven from his mind
by the arrival of the first batch of proofs of *In Youth is Pleasure*. 'The
story looks funny in print,' he wrote to Noël, 'with the chapter headings.
Evie has just said that it is readable but unwholesome, and artists can
be *just* as interesting if they'd only be wholesome.' There were, though,
other worries: 'I must say now that my qualms grow and grow when
I see what I have written about my brother Bill.' Even more pessimistically
he continued, 'I think everyone will hate the book. It really *is* going
to be an orphan.'

Four days later, as though his rows with Eric were not wearing enough,
he reported a minor skirmish with Evie. 'Only this morning,' he wrote
to Noël, 'she asked me why May had my French coffee pot on her
cabinet and when I said, "Because I swopped it with her," Evie said
in her grudging whining voice, "*You* think they don't but *I* know women
try to get hold of you. I can't understand how you're so blind." So
you see, she is going through a phase of thinking that she is the wise
virgin and I am the gullible fool. She doesn't usually say silly conventional things like that to my face. She will be better again.'

He went on to tell Noël that he was expecting his Christian Scientist
admirer, Guy Allan, to visit him that day, and that he was thinking
of wearing 'green battle-dress as an antidote to so many scarves, ribbons,
pompoms, sandals, tassels and Etruscan rings'. When Guy arrived Denton
heard from him how he had lunched the day before with Nina Hamnett,
a talented but alcoholic friend of Sickert who had a studio in Maple
Street and a cosmopolitan circle of artistic and Bohemian friends. Guy
had asked her whether she had read *Maiden Voyage*, whereupon she
had thrown up her hands and said, '"Have I not! All the homosexuals
in London have been shrieking at me, wanting to know how anyone
could write a book like that. They're furious with him."' Denton later
inquired in his journal, not unreasonably, 'I wonder why?'

On 27 June, having heard no more from Eric since the beginning
of the month, Denton wrote to him to say, 'Just a line to ask if you're

still alive!' and to give him belated news of Peter Cromwell's visit: 'I quite liked him, but found him a little languid. I think he would depress me if I saw a lot of him.' He ended what was by his standards a brief letter, 'I *am* so sorry about Whitsun, Eric. I have never consciously wanted to force myself on anyone, but I was so terribly unhappy then; and I felt so deserted and exhausted and ill. The drinks at The Greyhound took away my last shreds of good sense and consideration. I could think of nothing but myself. I have such a terrible sense of urgency at the shortness of life when I am like that. It makes me quite desperate. Please understand ... I knew how stupidly I was behaving but I could not stop myself.'

Batches of proofs of *In Youth is Pleasure* were 'flowing in', Denton told Noël the following day, 'and I hate the book as I read it. I've turned against it. I hope it's chiefly boredom. I'm ploughing on with the new one fairly contentedly now again, thank goodness, after the very hopeless-feeling Whitsun period.'

The title of the book being proofed, as he told Marcus Oliver when writing to him on 27 June to bring him up to date with his news, was 'really the title of an old pre-Elizabethan poem by Robert Wever', of which four lines were to be incorporated in the frontispiece he designed for the first edition:

> Methought I walked still to and fro,
> And from her company I could not go –
> But when I waked it was not so:
> In youth is pleasure, in youth is pleasure.

Denton's house was on the direct flight path across Kent for the German V1 flying bombs aimed at London, and every effort was being made to shoot them down before they reached their target. 'My dear,' he continued to Marcus, 'the spook-buggies (as the doughboy called them) are *frightful*! One's just been shot down over the Hadlow Rose and Crown not 200 yards away. Quelle Vie!'[1]

Things were getting so dangerous that Noël and her husband had decided to live temporarily in Hertfordshire, and they told Denton to move into Middle Orchard should he be blown out of Pitt's Folly Cottage. 'The only thing that can be said is that one hasn't been brought down on the house yet,' he reported to Noël on 3 July, 'although it shakes nastily when they burst.' He noted that three of the doodle-bugs,

1. The first flying bomb of the war had fallen in Kent just two weeks earlier, on 13 June.

as they were immediately nicknamed by the public, had exploded only a few hundred yards from the cottage, 'and one at Tonbridge has mucked up all the tiles and window-panes for miles round. Nothing is broken here yet, the house just jumps.' He told Noël that if he did have to move to Middle Orchard he would promise not to read any correspondence or open any drawers or cupboards. 'I've grown strangely conventional in these respects now,' he assured her.

Having still not heard from Eric, he was growing anxious. 'What *has* happened?' he wrote to him on 4 July. 'Are you dead? If not, do drop a line to let me know how you are; otherwise I shall be worrying so much, thinking that the doodle-bugs have got you. They really are getting frantic now. They've been bursting all round here.' Three days previously, he had spent a rowdy evening at The King's Arms in Tonbridge, and he had noted in his journal when he came home, 'In the drink and the closeness of so many other people, my love for Eric seems to have died away. So real a love to die away into love for everyone, for the whole world.' Writing now to Eric he suggested, 'It is perhaps a good thing to have a little gaiety and friendship before you're dead, isn't it? I have only just begun to see that human relationships are the *only* really important thing on earth. Nothing else means anything without them. I have so often turned away from them, thinking that it was a good thing to live in isolation; always criticizing, despising, seeing through people, thinking nobody good enough for me. But I know now suddenly what all egoism leads to. It leads to death, negation, nothing. It is as if one were still alive and yet had committed suicide. If one does *no* good, gives *no* happiness, goes out to *no* one, what is the point of living at all?'

Too impatient to wait for a reply to this letter, he telephoned Eric's hostel the same day only to find that there was no answer. Thoroughly alarmed, he tried to ring Mrs Oliver, but she also was out. It was not until a few days later that he was put out of his misery, when he received a letter from Eric indicating at least that he was safe. Denton was 'so dislocated what with relief and pleasure', as he told Noël, that he at once wrote to Eric asking him to come to stay for a week and enclosing £1 for the train fare. Eric's letter, which had in fact been written on 2 July but had somehow been delayed in the post, appears to be the only extant letter from him to Denton:

'My dear Denton,' Eric wrote, 'The hostel was bombed the Friday before last; it happened in the afternoon. I was working on the hill, a mile or so away. I saw it come down and guessed it must have fallen very near, it made me feel quite sick for Peter had taken the day off and I thought he'd been killed. However, when I got back he was safe and sound. He had spent the day in Ashford. He makes me very unhappy. We went to Maidstone on Thursday but he left me to go to London. I'd have gone with him, but realized how pointless it would be. I saw him to the station, wished him a good time and did my best to look as though I didn't mind. Afterwards I wandered about Maidstone feeling very much alone and unwanted. I sat waiting for the bus. I thought of you; that I was being paid out for the unhappiness I'd caused you. An old woman came and sat beside me. She began telling me her troubles. She had been very rich but had lost her money in Singapore. I swopped the American cigarettes she had (and didn't like) for some of mine.

'We are isolated here, the nearest buses and trains were miles away, thank God. The place we moved in was a lovely old house before the Army (and now the KWAEC[2]) moved in. Most of the inmates have gone away for the weekend. Peter hasn't come back yet and I'm half hoping he won't ever.

'It was nice hearing from you again – your adventures and bombs ... I've never heard the new bombs called the things you call them. I just think of them as a weak reply to the ones we call 8,000lb Block Busters and drop on Berlin.

'Thanks for the poem. I'd like to see it, only you must never take me seriously again. I've got four of your letters, they are safely locked away.

'I hope your new book has lots of success.

'Please remember me to Miss Sinclair.

'All the best, Eric.'

The tone of this letter leaves us in no doubt about Eric's current feelings for Denton, and the fact that Denton was at last becoming adjusted to the position is shown by a letter he wrote shortly before receiving Eric's. 'Dearest,' he wrote to Eric on 5 July, 'I want to say something quite simply to you, and yet I am afraid of appearing excessive. Anyhow – here goes. It is quite obvious that I am really devoted to you, else I never would have stood some of the things you've said and done to me. I will not deny that you've hurt me and wounded me till I felt almost mad. And lately I have been so unhappy that everything has appeared utterly worthless and I only wanted to die.

'But in spite of all this I *know* that it is right for us to be friends

2. The Kent War Agricultural Executive Committee, by whom Eric was employed.

and I *know* that I can help you and comfort you in your unhappiness over Peter or any of the other things that life does to one. Just as Noël with her devotion and *real love* has helped me when I felt deserted, kicked off, despised. In a way I have learnt an awful lot, thro' having such a painful, agonized time with you. And the chief thing I've learnt is that the love and friendship of other people whoever they are is *all important*, and one ought *never* to cut oneself away from it, as one is tempted to do, when things go wrong.

'I know,' he continued, 'that you have not a tenth of the feeling for me that I have for you, and I *do not expect it*!; but I think that you have a kind and *deeply understanding* heart, that you wish me well, even believe in me a little as a writer; and I think from all this comes a wish that I should have a little happiness before I pop off, which you also know might happen rather suddenly.'

THIRTEEN

Middle Orchard

Eric accepted Denton's invitation and came on 7 July to stay with him. 'All has gone swimmingly, and he is here for a week,' Denton announced triumphantly to Noël four days later. Then the idea came to him to take up Noël's offer of the use of her house, even though Pitt's Folly had so far escaped the flying bombs. 'May we (if we one day climb the hill) go to Middle Orchard?' he asked Noël on 9 July. 'We will *absolutely* promise not to touch or disturb or investigate *at all*, but just sit and rest and have a change of scene for an hour or two.' He added, 'If you would rather we didn't go in, we'll just have our picnic on the veranda and then go on perhaps to Trosley[1] or somewhere.'

Four days later, having received no response from Noël, he wrote again: 'Did you get my letter asking if Eric and I could pay a visit to M.O.? We have a mad scheme now of taking a roast chicken (which we have) and some tins of Heinz soup and other eatables and having a grand evening picnic there. May we? And also, if we got benighted or felt tired could we roll up in our sheet flea-bags on the studio divan or one of the others? If this is utterly repulsive to you or Bernard you *must* say so in *no* uncertain terms. Anyhow, we might feel it too much effort to plan the night away and take all the things, but at present we are toying with the idea of a night in new surroundings, all alone, which would have the double advantage of giving Eve a respite and allowing us to escape from her for a little.' Anticipating, perhaps, that while Noël would not mind him staying in her house on his own, she might be less keen to let Eric, whom she could never bring herself to accept, he added, 'Eric really is *perfect* in the house and I can absolutely guarantee that there will be no boozings, bangings, or pryings or breakages. You can be quite sure of that.'

He went on so persistently that Noël could hardly have refused

---

1. Phonetic rendition of Trottiscliffe, a village eight miles north of Hadlow.

without causing offence: 'Do tell us what you think of this scheme. It would be for Saturday night. We think it is lovely at the moment, but as I say, we might not get ourselves together enough for it, and of course you might forbid it!'

Noël capitulated, and on 14 July Denton wrote to thank her. 'Just had your letter saying that you'd like us to go to M.O. This is lovely, thank you *so* much. Eve is now cooking the chicken and stuffing it with May's herbs, and I am going to make the bread sauce myself at M.O. – that is, if the stove's in working order and if I may use it. Eve is going to cook everything else here. Roast potatoes and salad then raspberries, I think, and cake.'

At the same time that Eric came to stay, Denton had also been expecting a visit from a 'golden hair youth' named John Bloom whom he had met one sunny day in June by the river. The boy had been sunbathing naked, and Denton had been so taken by him that he had written two long descriptions of the encounter, one in his journal and one in a letter to Noël. 'I wonder if he'll meet Eric here,' he had written to Noël when he knew Eric was coming, as if she had not already heard enough about his emotional affairs. 'I can't think of the weekend, and yet I can't think of anything else.' John Bloom came as expected, and the three seem to have got on well. 'Eric and John Bloom are sitting here talking across me as I write on the bed,' Denton reported to Noël on 13 July. 'We have all been down to the river, but it kept raining, and after hiding in pillboxes we decided to come home. I am hoping John is not staying to supper, but am afraid he is.' The lad appears to have been especially in need of company, for at the end of his letter Denton told Noël, 'Poor John Bloom is shaken to the core, because he saw a bus have its roof removed by a bug and the people sitting up in it, still dead!'

The next day he was telling Noël, 'As you will know, this week has been something completely new to me. Eric said at the beginning, "By the end of this week you will hate me and be telling me to get out," but that hasn't been the case at all. Nothing has gone wrong, except one night I made myself rather ridiculous which I shall tell you about, perhaps.' He decided to tell her straight away: 'It was the first day John Bloom was here (he had been Wednesday and Thursday, once with a bunch of roses, which for some reason tickled Eric very much – and once with a bag of gooseberries!). We went to The Artichoke before supper (I drank *barley* water) but Eric *would* buy pints which John could hardly get into his small inside.

'After supper, when John at last got up to go, Eric also jumped up and said, "I'll bicycle some of the way with you." Remembering Christmas and Rose and the bushes, I said good night very abruptly and left them at the top of the stairs. I was seething with fury.

'I was very surprised when Eric returned in about ten minutes' time. I thought he might be away for hours – but I was still *very* angry and not entirely reassured; so I began banging about the room doing the black-out and yelling at Eric, "Have you no loyalty, consideration, even ordinary good sense? You *can't* ride home with *every* single person you meet here – man or woman!" I think Eric thought I was dotty at first, then he began screaming with laughter and I felt a great fool. I suppose I was overcome by the similarity of circumstances. It seemed so very plain to me; but I knew at once, when he began jibing at me, what a mistake I'd made.'

He was writing again to Noël on 18 July, 'Just to tell you how much we're loving it at M.O.', and to confess to having broken the handle of a soup cup.' So ingenuous was he that admitting to her what a fool he had made of himself with Eric came no less naturally to him than confessing to the breakage, or, indeed, to something she need never have known, that John Bloom had moved in to her house too. John turned up, he told her, just as he was cooking supper. 'After supper, if you please, he said, "Do you think your friend would mind if I curled up in one of her chairs? I don't fancy the ride back to East Peckham tonight." I was hoping and hoping that he would go, because I wanted to be alone at Middle Orchard with Eric, but what was I to do after this direct question? He had evidently worked it all out in his mind when he heard Eric and me talking about our expedition on Friday. Of course he stayed, and did nearly all the housework (very well and efficiently) on Sunday ... Before he left he said longingly, "I *do* hope your friend lends you her house again." He seemed quite entranced. He slept in the living-room on the bed you'd put there.'

Unsparing of Noël's feelings, Denton went on, 'Eric and I quite shamelessly use your bed, which is lovely. *Do you mind*? I wondered and wondered before deciding, but all the other beds are far away from each other and narrower, and now we feel wonderfully safe with the doodles whistling overhead and the balloon barrage pimpling the sky all above Middle Orchard. (Did you know it was here now?) All the crews are camping in the fields about.

'Do you feel, Noël, that we have turned M.O. into a bear garden and that I should have driven John Bloom away? I hope not, but I have slight qualms about making such complete use of your place. I can't remember enjoying myself so well before. Now I am going to stop as I want this to get the post and Eric wants to put a tiny note at the end.

'We are having all our meals in the garden and only going in to sleep at night. Eric wears no clothes at all.'

Eric's tiny note read: 'Dear Noël, Thank you for letting me stay at your house with Denton. We are having a really good time. I hope you're enjoying the change just as much. My best wishes, Eric.'

The idyll was shattered just two days later, however, when Noël paid a visit. Although Eric 'was in a stuck pig mood and *wouldn't* say a word', he nevertheless went off with Noël to The Chequers and there, it appears, talked complainingly about Denton. She advised him that should he decide to break with Denton he should do so gently. After Noël had left, Eric began to have second thoughts and repeated to Denton everything she had said. Denton took her to task when writing to her on 22 July, his letter showing how rapidly he had progressed in his handling of relationships: 'I had hoped that if ever you talked to him you would try to point out all that you thought was good or worthwhile in me — if you think anything is good or worthwhile — especially what was good and worthwhile in me for *him*.

'I have not the slightest intention of letting him break away either quickly or slowly, and he just hasn't a chance of doing either while I am in this frame of mind! I am not saying this arrogantly, but it is simply true. I would see that we did not lose touch.

'Couldn't you have told him that nothing but good for him could come of his knowing me, instead of allowing him to ramble on about boys, or girls, or goats, or whatever his particular fancy of the moment was? He can have those too. I don't interfere. I am tired of being told how his love falls short of mine and is *quite* different ...

'I am *perfectly* happy to be with him as I have been this fortnight with no wrangling or probing; but it was terribly destructive to have everything raked out as on Thursday night. Would you, if you ever talk to him again, just accept the situation that we are friends and expect to remain so.'

He went on to tell Noël of a minor fright they had had, when 'a doodle with only one wing was turning over and over and nearly descended on the house', and to reassure her, 'It really is so lovely here.

We *are* grateful! But you must let me pay for electricity and things won't you, since we have been here a whole week now.'[2]

He ended, 'I hope I don't sound upset about your talk with Eric. I'm not. I'm only upset by its unforeseen effect. I know you said nothing that should be regretted at all.'

Nor does it seem that anything Noël said did any permanent damage, for on 8 August Denton – by this time ending his letters to her with 'love' – wrote, 'Isn't it extraordinary that Eric and I can live together for five weeks in spite of peculiar moments. I can't get over it. What will happen next!'

Things were going so well that he was now beginning to forget his own needs in favour of Eric's. Writing again to Noël two days later he told her, 'What I want to do is look after him and to make his life as pleasant as possible. This may be considered domination of the worst kind, but I can't help that. It is so obvious that in all ways he looks miles better thro' staying with me. You've said it; May's said it; Evie has. Three *very* different persons!'

He went on to tell her the news that Guy Allan was expected from London, 'with his German boyfriend' (a nineteen-year-old called Vernon), and that they were planning to camp in May Walbrand-Evans's garden. 'We are expecting Guy to have the most incredible camping outfit, tassels and bells and chiffon flags hanging from the corners of the tent, and inside, incense censers and artificial water-lilies floating in black bowls. I suppose we will be disappointed and he will come down as practical as a boy-scout!'

A book of poems had arrived from Edith Sitwell, 'with love', and a 'Sheffield schoolboy', having seen 'When I Was Thirteen', had sent a poem about Pompey the Great, asking him to 'criticize stiffly', together with some rather inept criticism of his own of the *Horizon* story. 'I wonder what sort of boy he is, don't you?' Denton asked Noël.[3]

One reason that Eric had been happy to accept Denton's original invitation to stay for a week was because his friend Peter Clements had left the area after the hostel had been hit by a flying bomb, and he had been reluctant to move into new accommodation without him.

2. Still at Middle Orchard at the end of the month, and having done 'frantic mental arithmetic, trying to find out how much bread and milk and electricity we have used', Denton sent Noël a cheque for £6, part of which she returned.

3. Denton's fame had spread far beyond Sheffield: 'I have heard too,' he recorded in his journal on 13 September the same year, 'from someone in Australia and from the editress of the *Laundry Record!*'

The week had stretched to a fortnight, and a fortnight to six weeks, and on 13 September, while the two were again staying in London with Eric's mother, Denton recorded in his first journal entry since 11 July, 'Eric and I have lived together now since July at Pitt's Folly, in Middle Orchard (Crouch) and now at Streatham. And in some ways it is the strangest thing in my life – to share almost my whole existence like this. I have not even written in my journal, yet alone at my book.'

Denton and Eric had discovered, more or less by accident, that they could exist happily at close quarters with each other, and from now on they were to live together permanently. It would appear that Noël had warned Denton that Eric would prevent him working, for in July he had written to her to say, 'You are quite right about work, and if I'm good for *anything*, that is the thing; but this long time with Eric has been so unplanned and so unexpected that I have just given myself up to it without thought. It is true, I suppose, that Eric in some way does destroy my urge to work, especially when he's out of sympathy with me. Living like this now, I don't realize things as I do when I'm alone, and because he does not get or comprehend a part of me it seems to hide away, and lose importance in my own eyes.

'I know that it would be a stupid life for me to go on indefinitely doing nothing, but I don't feel for a moment that I should ever get into that state. I think that sooner or later I shall be thrown back again entirely on myself, and then if I don't work there is nothing for me at all.'

Back at Pitt's Folly, Noël having meanwhile returned to Middle Orchard, plans were being laid by Denton for her to paint Eric's portrait. No arrangement in this ménage was without its subterfuge, and on 22 September Denton was writing to Noël, 'I couldn't say much on the phone as Eric was at the top of the stairs, and I didn't want to appear to be talking him over with you. However, afterwards I told him what you'd said and then added, "You'd hate to sit for Noël, wouldn't you?" to which he replied rather shortly, "I wouldn't mind it"!! That was surprising to me and I felt that my wiliness had really been rewarded, for always before so many objections had been raised to sitting. He asked, "Will Bernard be there?" I said, "I don't expect so." I said this to make things appear easy. Perhaps you can fix on Bernard's London days.

'Eric said, "Does she want me to pose naked?" I said, "No, in the red shirt." He said, "I saw Noël looking at me and I thought she was thinking, 'There he is in another of Denton's shirts.'"!!

'I then said, "No, she wasn't, she was thinking that you looked good in it." Was that the right thing to say? If you still feel like doing it, do write to Eric a little note. He might try to back out of it, when he comes to the point, but try it and see. I told him you'd asked if I could not have a moment's peace thinking of all his indiscretions to you. But that made him laugh.'

Within twenty-four hours of sending that buoyant letter Denton was lying 'sick and ill all day', as he recorded in his journal; 'So ill that I couldn't eat or think, only lie in pain, waiting for the next wave of sickness to come over me. And Eric looked after me wonderfully, staying with me all day, watching me, making the bed, and putting the cold towels on my face. I thought it would never pass; all life seemed an agony of sickness. But even then it was wonderful to have a friend near you, to help you all he could. The desolation of sickness was lessened somehow. In the night I woke up much better, and I turned the light on and read poetry, with my creeping, hardly recovered eyes; and I looked across at the stripped-pine eighteenth-century mantel in front of me, and I thought of all the beautiful rooms I could make in a house of my own. Always with sickness come these reveries.'

He reported his state to Noël next day, telling her that Eric had now returned to his mother for a week; 'So I am rather enjoying the queer feeling of having all the day to myself. Life seems more luxurious for some peculiar reason. Is it the absence of the necessity to adapt oneself at all? Perhaps I like the feeling because I know I shall be glad to see Eric again at the end of the week. I hope to do quite a lot of writing. So far I have only washed Eric's trousers and sent off some awful poems!'

He went on to tell her that Eric was going to write to her from London about sitting for his portrait, and that he seemed quite acclimatized to the idea. 'If it comes off, I shall be interested to see what you make of him. He should be good to do, don't you think? If he flattens his hair out, you must push it up on his forehead; but I have told him about this, so perhaps he'll have it wild.'

While Eric was away Denton wrote to him frequently. In his first letter, addressing him as 'Dear Hero', he reported that Noël had been looking after him all afternoon; in his next he wrote, 'If your mother wants you there and you want to stay, you won't come back to me, will you? I'm quite content flogging my brains (not what you thought)'; and on 3 October he reviewed the conflicts created by his need to work: 'All this week I have been writing every day, but it is such a plaguing and worrying job. I begin to feel quite addled, but I hope something will emerge. Do you think I'll be able to write properly and not be too moody and peculiar when you are here! I hope so. Let's try anyhow and see how it works – that is, if you want to, really. I think you sometimes know more or less how I feel about the general situation, but I am never quite sure what surprise you will have for me up your sleeve! And so I get the idea that it is hopeless to plan anything.

'It would of course be quite crazy for us to live together for any length of time if you were continually champing and chafing and feeling a fish out of water. Although you say I will never face facts, I can see as well as anyone that it would be murder for me as well as for you. Selfish or not, you must believe me when I say that I would like you to be happy, quite apart from any consideration of my own.'

With thoughts of food seldom far from his mind, he asked if Eric's mother would let him return before the weekend as 'Eve has got a chicken which will need eating'. Returning to his main theme he added, 'Dear Eric, I really am so fond of you; but I don't think I'll ever drive you crazy again unless my fussiness does this time! You must take a chance.' Flippant now, he ended, 'You can always pack up and fly. The only thing you can't do is to bring a buck-negress home. It would make the Ladies [Mary Sloman and Brenda Cobb] jealous. Gina [their dog] pines for you, I think.'

On 10 October, after Eric had come back from London, he and Denton went into Sevenoaks to visit the dentist. They had lunch on the way at Aplin's in Tonbridge, 'in the draughty, barn-like, hideously Tudorized room. Welsh rarebit with tomatoes for me, baked fish for Eric, then awful buns and imitation cream and coffee.' Afterwards Denton spent 18s. on four broken Derby and Worcester plates. In Sevenoaks they called on an uncle and aunt of Eric's, Harry and 'Jum' Barnett, who lived in Uplands Way in what Denton described in his journal as a 'right, tight little house'. The uncle was 'antagonistic to me and rather rude to Eric, gradually thawing into a bore', though the aunt was 'nicer, more sensitive and delicate and genteel'. When she learned that Denton had received encouragement from Edith Sitwell she said, 'It's not surprising at all. Artists aren't jealous, not if they're big.'

The next day Eric had his first sitting for Noël's portrait of him, and while they were thus occupied Denton worked on his new novel. In the post that morning he had received a 'very queer, meagre letter' from an 'unknown gentleman in Chingford' who had bought from the Leicester Galleries one of his paintings, a 'Gothic flower piece', and wanted to know more about it. 'I must write [a] very nice, delighted letter back,' Denton decided. 'It made me extraordinarily happy to know I'd sold a picture when the news came at breakfast.'

At lunch-time, taking a picnic and wearing a 'fine sweater from the Hebrides or some islands' which Noël had given him as a present, he went to Oxon Hoath to read, but then 'the rain suddenly beat down, and I was reading Dorothy Wordsworth's diary until the page was soaked and almost falling to pieces'. In the evening he and Eric were invited next door for coffee, and Denton took peppermint creams and 'wore the new sweater, to cause talk to flow'. Describing the evening to Noël two days later he wrote, 'My sweater caused a sensation at the Slomans' on Wednesday night. Brenda was apparently particularly taken with the shape under the armpits. Mrs Barclay [another neighbour] and Sloman also doted, and I was fingered all over. There was a large log fire and you can guess how roasted I was, but I loved wearing it. I've worn it ever since.' He had had to drag Eric to Mary Sloman's 'almost by force', he told her. 'I said that I had come to the end of my excuses, and if he didn't go this once, they would imagine that I didn't dare produce him. It went off quite well, tho' Eric kept saying afterwards that they thought him nothing but a fool.' He added, 'When we left, Gina jumped up and licked Eric's face, and Brenda said, "Oh, isn't it sweet, aren't they lovely together."'

The difficulty of reconciling the state of mind required for work with that induced by the presence of Eric in the house became more acute as demands upon Denton as a painter and writer began once more to flow in. Having been commissioned by *Vogue* to write and illustrate an article on ghosts and dreams, he pondered the problem in his journal: 'I wish it would all come in a flash, but it won't, and I must begin to evolve something. Always the actual subject before stimulates and then flummoxes. In so many ways it is lovely to have Eric living with me here for the winter in this tiny garage cottage with only this one room, but I find myself getting swallowed up only in living with him. It changes all my feelings about work. I want to work so much now. But I haven't yet readapted myself.'

On 18 October, news obviously having crossed the Atlantic that he was at work on a third book, he received a letter from the New York publishers Doubleday & Doran, who had admired his stories in *Horizon*, asking him to submit the book to them. One of those stories, 'When I Was Thirteen', was to be a source not only of praise but of some embarrassment, as he discovered when eight days later he received 'the most extraordinary letter from someone in Sheffield who has written to me before about my book and story in Horizon. It can only be described as a very uncomfortable love letter, and I am wondering what on earth to reply.' He had less difficulty in deciding what to reply to another letter, from King's College, Cambridge, inviting him to deliver a lecture on contemporary literature. 'Delightful if I could be persuaded,' he noted in his journal. 'What would I feel like, talking to and looking at the undergraduates? Imagination falters. They say nothing about lodging me or anything of that sort. Do they ever get any writers to go, I wonder?'

That journal entry was followed immediately by another containing one of his rare descriptions of his method of painting: 'I am painting a new picture, which I have done first of all in pencil outline, carefully then with turpentine to darken and strengthen the line. Now I put on, rub on, colour very gingerly, very little. The board is whitened and rubbed down so that the mahogany shows a little in places. Now I think that in some ways I have found the technique for my painting, direct, simple, permanent and utterly unlike what is usually understood as oil painting.'

On 24 October he went up to London with Eric to take some new paintings to the Leicester Galleries, to buy pyjamas at Swan & Edgar's and to deliver to Julian Goodman the portrait she had commissioned from him.[4] They found 10 Gower Street in a sad state of dilapidation, having been bombed and broken into and now 'quickly becoming a slum'. Julian showed Denton an eighteenth-century snuff box, big enough to hold cigarettes, and he found himself wishing that she had 'the sense or the generosity' to give it to him in exchange for his portrait. She also told him that when the doodle-bugs had begun to fall she had 'gone down to the country with an Augustus John under each arm, which she hopes are worth a thousand pounds apiece'. Altogether, 'the whole meeting was a little wrong and dislocated', and he could not forgive her the snuff box. 'I still thought about the old silver gilt snuff box,' he wrote later, 'and decided that I should like it very much.'

On 9 November he had one of his wisdom teeth extracted, and the next day he heard that Maiden Voyage was to be published by Fischer in America. By the middle of the month Noël had completed her portrait of Eric, and Bernard Adeney brought it over to Pitt's Folly Cottage

4. Julian Vinogradoff (formerly Goodman) recalls that the portrait, a three-quarter-length study painted from photographs, was done in deep greens and blues that made her face look 'gruesome'. Its present whereabouts are not known.

on 23 November. 'You have changed the shape of his face a little, haven't you?' Denton commented when writing to Noël. 'I like the inscription arabesquely in the air. May came just after Bernard and said, "Oh, I think it's like him," rather grudgingly! It *is* nice to have it.' He then told her that he had received jacket proofs of *In Youth is Pleasure*, and he added, 'I have also had the yearly collection of stories called "English Story" with a story of mine in it. It is shaped from an incident on board ship with my mother, a strange nervous man and a Bourbon princess woman who, I hope, is not really recognizable or well known in England. I have never heard of her from that day to this, lest she is the woman Hitler removed from her husband a few years ago from the South of France. Anyhow, I don't think it matters as I have not been libellous, only personal. I wish I didn't have qualms. I suppose everyone does, when they write. It is the most giving away thing there is, don't you think?'[5]

Eric had meanwhile gone up to London to stay with his mother again, and Denton wrote to him on 25 November, having three days earlier had a temperature of 103°, to say, 'I'm still in bed but doing things – writing my book and writing letters – really very contented and busy, so you won't hurry back on my account, will you? There is so much for me to do. Of course I didn't mind you going to your mother's. It was quite the right thing to do. These temperatures just have to go off of their own accord – and anyhow it's good for me to be on my own.' After asking Eric to let him know if he needed any ration coupons he signed off, 'From the Bearded-Queen-Bee'.

Denton was proud of his new beard. 'It is so nice and simple and somehow what God intended,' he told Noël when writing on 28 November to thank her for suggesting that he and Eric should again stay at Middle Orchard (she had been concerned about the damp in Pitt's Folly Cottage). 'Do you think I will be sinister?' he asked her. 'May keeps calling me Rizzio. The only person I don't want to look like is D. H. Lawrence.' He continued, 'It has been very nice here quite alone in bed. I have written a short story, done some of my book, a lot of letters, and have been reading Boswell's "Life of Johnson". It seems all a dream that I've been living in this room with someone else. I look at Eric's shoes and wonder.

5. The story was 'At Sea', and about twenty-two years had elapsed since Denton and the princess had met. The same issue of *English Story*, which had been founded in 1940 by Woodrow Wyatt, also contained work by Elizabeth Bowen, Rex Warner and Henry Treece.

'Eve,' he confided, 'has returned to an earlier personality in some way, and is running about getting meals and then reading "Bleak House" to me, until I can't bear the grotesqueness any more, and then she switches to Persuasion which I have read three times already. We have secured a chicken for Christmas, if nothing else. I'm going to drive her to begin the plum pudding when she comes up with the tea.'

At 6.10 p.m. on the evening of 30 November Denton noted in his journal that he had received a letter from an aircraftsman in India who was researching his literary and artistic works, 'even down to little poems in queer magazines!'. It made him feel, he wrote, 'as if I had been preserving myself on a top shelf for years, waiting to be discovered. As if I were dead and done with, and watching some future person ferreting me out.'

At the same time he was also trying to sort out his thoughts about living with Eric. 'When Eric was away and I lay in bed so still with books, my thoughts, the pretty things I have collected, I thought that all I really wanted was to be alone, to think and to dream in a daze about work I shall do. But now that he is asleep on the bed, I find I can still think and dream, and I even feel better physically because someone is there if I should not feel well.

'There is always this question with me, to be alone or not. Really, to be alone is my nature. If it were not so, I would not have been alone as much as I have.

'Is reverie really what people live for, and do they just do things to feed their reverie?'

On 4 December, a day of sunshine and frost, Denton and Eric set out to cycle to Trottiscliffe. Before setting off Denton wrote in his journal, 'I don't feel as well as I did when I woke up,' but, characteristically, he did not allow that to stop him going. By the time they reached Middle Orchard, which was on their way, Denton was feeling much worse and was rapidly developing a high temperature. They went into the house – the Adeneys were away in London at the time – and Denton flopped down on a couch in the drawing-room. Eric wrapped him in an eiderdown and lit a fire, and as Denton was now too ill to move, they decided to stay the night. When the Adeneys returned home the next evening they put Denton to bed in their daughter Charlotte's room where he stayed, constantly nursed by Noël, for the next eight days. Eric, too, remained at Middle Orchard, making the fires and breakfasts, washing up and sawing wood. 'I've never known anyone so willing to take on the work like this,' Denton wrote on 11 December, having got out of bed for the first time the evening before. 'It makes me think of Cinderella.'

It was while he was recuperating that Noël took the opportunity of pointing out to Denton one of his more amusing, if embarrassing, eccentricities. 'I sometimes say just what is in my mind,' it appeared, 'after I have said some politeness that completely clashes with it. Several times she has caught me doing this and I am unconscious of what I have done. When she asked me if I'd stay here a day or two more and try to do a little work, I was very polite, and then I added, "I'll see if I can stand it"!! Eric says I asked John Bloom interestedly all about his life in London, then turned away and said, "Oh, I wish you'd go."'

This spell in bed had been one of Denton's longest since his accident, and he was now more concerned than ever about his condition: 'The laziness that creeps over me in a strange environment is like an animal that ought to be fought, but is just looked at and then turned away from. I have been wondering too all about my health, how much of the rest of my life is going to be lived lolling about, waiting to feel well enough to do something. And I think that I really cannot have a great deal of time to do anything, and that even if I do not write in my diary, I shall regret it.

'Is it in Montaigne that I have just read that the way to know what to write about is to think of all the things you wish writers in the past had mentioned? I wish that people should mention the tiny things in their lives that give them pleasure or fear or wonder. I would like to hear the bits of family or intimate history they knew.'

Forty-eight hours later, safely back at Pitt's Folly Cottage, he was writing to Noël to thank her for looking after him: 'I have the feeling now that I shall be well for some time. I feel full of schemes for getting things done, which is a good sign.'

At Christmas-time, however, he was ill again, though he managed to dress in order to go for a walk with Eric 'in the sunshine in the frosty wood' before lunch. In spite of his being ill, this Christmas was altogether a happier occasion than the Christmas of 1943, as can be gauged from one of Evie's rare letters, written on 'flimsy brown toilet paper' to Noël on Christmas Day:

'Dear, dear Mrs Adeney, Thank you again & again for your present.

'I *knew* it would be something exquisite! But what a lovely present! And you have evidently made it yourself. I shall treasure it & prize it & wear it with great joy.

'Puss Denton very quickly noticed the antique Georgian silver buckle which I think is adorable & enhances it in one's estimation tremendously. I shall want to take it off to show people the beauty secret. All the little hinges are so pretty.

'You will be glad to know that D got up today to Christmas lunch-dinner which we all three had or commenced in the early afternoon (Eric came back last night not much the worse for wear). During the courses May Walbrand-Evans walked in on her way back from having her Christmas lunch-dinner at Mrs Littleton's & stayed to coffee. You know Mrs L. D calls her a lump of dough & her mother Mrs Pickering who Capt. Littleton used to call a few fancy names!

'D's room today has been a bower of scent & flowers. The result of your scent & little B [Brenda Cobb] gave him a flowering begonia in a pot.

'I can never thank you enough for all you do. The extra milk is wonderful to have. The eggs you sent have been so exactly right for D during these last few days.

'And now in conclusion, as Mrs Carlyle used to say (she is supposed to be a relation of D's although she spelt her name Welsh), Yours faithfully & sincerely, Evelyn Sinclair. P.S. Thank you once again for the lovely present & all the beautiful ideas & designs.'

Six days later, Denton wrote in his journal, 'Now we are by the gas fire here on New Year's Eve — Eric sleeping on the bed, me writing my book, trying to pick my own brains.

'All the years are too short — over before they have lost their newness. Nineteen forty-four still has a novel flavour, but it is going into the grave.

'This year has taken a stranger turn than any I expected. If someone had told me at the beginning that I would share everything before it was out, I would never have believed it.

'It had seemed something so impossible for my temperament that I would have laughed.

'In my wall is the mouse that scratches and dances. It seems as immortal as we are, and it is all a painted lie. No mouse or man after a hundred years — no cottage in the trees — only the earth, the water, the dripping woods and the low sky for ever.'

FOURTEEN

'Many Marvellous Things'

On 8 January 1945 Denton celebrated the beginning of the new year with a lyrical passage in his journal: 'My life is a great unfoldment of many marvellous things about it. I would not have thought that I would be damaged and ill so soon (twenty) or that so comparatively late (twenty-eight and a half) I should find someone with whom I could live in almost complete peace. All of life before that had seemed quite necessarily a solitary affair – and so it still is, but with an utterly different quality of solitude. In my heart are hung two extraordinary pictures: one is called "Accident and Illness" and the other, exactly opposite, tilted forward as if to meet it, is called "Love and Friendship".'

From now on he was to be as content when Eric was with him as when they were apart. Together they had learned to accommodate each other in the confined space of Pitt's Folly Cottage, and when separated for short periods they each remained at ease. On 22 January Denton was writing to Eric, who had gone to stay with his sister in London, to say, 'Dear Tunyer (which is my new way of spelling it),[1] I nearly didn't get your letter this morning. The Harlot [Evie] swore that she had looked and there was nothing for me; then a little later she came up with your letter, saying that it must have gone into the Ladies.

'No Lady, thank the Lord, has yet come in here ... Mrs Adeney also has not appeared. She has a cold and sent Bernard with the milk and a note. He said, "How are you? You look rotten." People ought to be gagged if they say these things.

'I've been trying to work quite a lot, but my brain goes dead in the evening and I wish some very nice interesting people lived next door so that I could go and talk to them.' He added the news that he had decided to do away with his beard on the first spring day – 'I think Francis is quite right, my line is to try to look boyish, not dignified'

1. 'Tuna' was one of the many gastronomic nicknames Denton invented for Eric at this time.

– and that he had been reading a book by J. B. Priestley, 'who sounds an awful man. It's all about the industrial north and the Potteries. Not exactly me, but it has a perverse fascination.'

The following day he drove Evie to the bus stop so that she could catch a bus to Tonbridge. 'She seems to hold it against me that buses wait for no one,' he wrote to Noël when he came back and was installed in bed with three sweaters on. 'Has anyone been born with less sense of time?' He reported that with Eric still in London, Evie out shopping and 'the Ladies' attending a wedding in London, the whole of Pitt's Folly was his. 'It is a lovely feeling – the snow makes it even more isolated. I hope Eve takes hours and hours to do the household shopping. For once she can be as snail-like as she likes and I shan't murmur.' He also told Noël that he had sent off articles and pictures to *Vogue*, 'though dissatisfied with both'; his new theory was 'that one must not have work hanging about. One must do it somehow, and then shunt it off.' At that point he was interrupted, and when he returned to the letter it was to announce: 'The mad Eve has just come back and said that the bus didn't stop for her! She's now set out on her bike.'

He continued with a complaint against his publishers for what he regarded as their dilatoriness in setting a publication date for *In Youth is Pleasure*: 'I wonder if protests to Routledge would make my book appear any sooner. I feel now that it is really more than a joke. Most books can't have had to wait quite so long as this.' Routledge had accepted the book towards the end of January 1944 and were to publish it in February 1945, involving a production schedule of just over a year which, especially in wartime, was not unreasonable. Yet it does appear that Denton had been led to believe that publication would take place in 1944, and that for some reason a delay did occur, for both the title page he designed and the publisher's imprint page in the first edition carried the date '1944'; when Routledge reprinted in May 1945 they amended the date of first publication to 'February 1945' and had Denton alter his title-page accordingly. His impatience may, in addition, have been exacerbated by new domestic worries: 'I have had no talk with Sloman yet,' he told Noël, referring to some upset with his landlady. 'I am hoping she dreads it as much as I do. I wish she'd just written a little note, either to say all was all right, or voicing her complaint. Perhaps she will descend tonight, primed with champagne after the wedding! I wish E. and I could find perfect cottage in perfect position.'

In spite of all this, and the damp in Pitt's Folly Cottage, which seems to have been getting worse, he did not lose his sense of humour. On

6 February he wrote to Noël, 'All the cigarettes have grown mould, Eric has put currants into the cider to turn it into brandy, Eve is chopping something on the kitchen table – perhaps we shall each have a nice helping of parsley.' Referring to a book Noël had sent him containing photographs of exotic foreign lands he continued, 'I don't think I shall move to Bali just yet. Just a little too much jungle and undergrowth. I think I must stick to my cottage in England, in spite of these awful winters which look like finishing me off. I felt spring was really here too, but today it pours.'

In Youth is Pleasure had at last been printed and Denton was now busy sending out complimentary copies. On 20 February Edith Sitwell telegramed that she was reading the book with delight, and three days later she followed up with a letter saying that she thought his new book had 'all the quite *extraordinary* vitality' of *Maiden Voyage*; 'Don't be depressed because you yourself have "taken against" it. One always does, with one's second book. It's a well-known fact.'

On 25 February he received further flattering letters, as he informed Noël, including 'one very buttery one from Berners. I'm *so* pleased I didn't send him a copy. It is nice to get unsolicited testimonials!' Lord Berners had written: 'I must write to you a line to say how intensely I have enjoyed your book. It has caused a sensation in this house.

'In these days of so much turgid "new writing" it is delightful to read anything so clear and limpid, so exquisitely written, so vividly exciting, so psychologically convincing. It will continue to haunt my memory and is one of the books I shall often re-read.'

The one person whose reaction to the book continued to cause Denton anxiety was his eldest brother. 'I have written to Bill,' he informed Noël, 'telling him that it *must* be taken as fiction and that I myself would not like to be taken for the central character!' His faith in miracles must have been absolute if he seriously expected Bill to believe that; even had his exclamation mark not given him away, there is no mistaking Denton in the character of 'Orvil Pym', just as there is no mistaking Bill in 'Charles', Paul in 'Ben' or his father in 'Mr Pym'.

Other reactions to the book, meanwhile, were generous beyond Denton's hopes. On 6 March Frank Swinnerton wrote to say, 'I must apologize for my delay in writing to you about In Youth is Pleasure. I have been ill. It seems to me that you have done extraordinarily well in preserving just that precise and delicate beauty of recording which distinguished Maiden Voyage!! Taken in conjunction with that book, this one represents something extremely original, which nobody else could have written, and which, in this kind of writing, will not be surpassed. There is no sign at all, to me, of that bad sort of self-consciousness which we spoke of before; and the book is a complete success.'

He went on to warn Denton: 'I don't think you will be able to go on repeating the same success – however, you may equal it in quality – because readers so soon grow querulous. Therefore I could wish that you might gradually move away from Orvil and into other and different minds which would give scope for richer displays of your talent. But I do not urge this, because you will chiefly be guided by knowledge of what you can and can't do, and I expect you will get too much advice. So as every writer can supply loads of material for his own self-distrust I shall repeat here and now that "In Youth is Pleasure" is extraordinarily good and that you have done something splendid in making your second book (the most difficult book of all) so perfect a companion piece to your first.'

The pleasure and peace of mind that should have been Denton's reward for the unexpectedly warm reception to the book – it had, like *Maiden Voyage*, been sold out before publication – was soured by renewed demands on his emotional and physical stamina. On 18 March he was writing to Eric, 'Dear Tunia, from your Dublin Prawn; I'm in bed because last night I began a temperature; not too bad tho', and today it's been scarcely up at all, so I'm hoping I've nipped it in the bud.

'Noël appeared yesterday while I was putting the fan light into the doll's house. I hadn't shaved and looked frowsty, but she sat and watched me working and it went fairly well to begin with; but after a bit I seemed to dry up and I rather wished she'd go.' In the end she persuaded him to cycle with her to Stallion's Green, three or four miles north in the direction of St Mary's Platt, 'and then she would insist on sitting on the side of the road for hours. I became surlier and surlier and she asked me why I had "gone so far away". It was awful. At last I got up to go and when I arrived home I knew I was ill. Eve read to me and afterwards I tried to go to sleep, but it was rather a bad night.'

The Germans, too, refused to leave him in peace. 'Early this morning,' he continued to Eric, 'there was the biggest rocket noise of all.[2] I thought windows or beams were going to crack. It seemed to go on for some time, like an earthquake. I'm wondering if it was in the Crouch direction.

'I've been doing nothing all day for fear of bad results. It is disappointing that I've had an attack, as I thought I'd beaten them down.

2. A reference to one of the new German V2 long-range rockets, the first of which had fallen on Orpington in September the previous year.

'The Ladies came home last night and had forgotten their key so they called up to me to let them in! I ran down and all was very smooth and affable. I hope there'll be no more difficulty.'

On 29 March he celebrated his thirtieth birthday, which became, he noted, 'almost a festival'. Eric gave him 'a charming, solid seal-top spoon', an apostle spoon and 'a tiny bottle of Benedictine with all the labels on'. Evie baked a simnel cake and gave him 'a broken cup, with scarlet and black flowers on it'. An aunt sent £1 and, 'quite by chance', a smock-frock in blue and white cotton arrived from Guy Allan. Noël also gave him a birthday cake, as well as some 'tiny glasses' which, Denton told her the next day, 'are quite miraculous. We have all been crooning over them, including May, who bounced in, just after Eric had returned [he had been to Crouch to collect milk] with rhubarb I'd asked her to get. She didn't know it was my birthday, but she had to be told, since there were two birthday cakes confronting her. She promptly gave me the rhubarb as her present! And then Mrs Sloman sent up two bars of chocolate and a cherry blossom!'

News came from Routledge early in April that W. H. Auden had reviewed *In Youth is Pleasure* in *The New York Times* (when Denton saw the review later he thought it the 'most sensible' of the American reviews) and that the American edition also had sold out, necessitating a reprint of five thousand copies.

Mary Sloman's 'smooth and affable' behaviour turned out to indicate only a temporary armistice, for on 1 May Denton was writing in his journal, 'There have been upsets and troubles with Sloman, our landlady. She was insolently trying to make use of Evie and Eric. Evie was violent and told her not to dare to interfere with my morning's work, and I got so disturbed by it all that I wrote a note to say that we could not look after her dog and her house while she was away. I did not think that I ought to pay any more rent[3] and that Eric could not help her in her garden for "pocket money" and that it had, of course, not been meant seriously and therefore I must not be annoyed.

'After this terseness I thought that there might be an explosion, for I had never been so frank and plain like that before, always wrapping things up in butter as she has done. But instead she and her friend Brenda came into coffee with me, and were quite tamed, pouring flattery and charm all over me, saying that they tell everyone that for as long as I like it is "Denton's Cottage" and that I am not to worry.'

3. Denton eventually agreed to increase his £78 a year rent to £93.

Nevertheless, he had already decided that he would have to leave Pitt's Folly, if not because of Mary Sloman then at least because of the damp, and had been writing to friends to see if they could suggest alternative accommodation. Julian Goodman offered him the cottage she owned at Garsington, but the rent, at three guineas a week, was more than he could afford; the cottage was in any case still occupied, by a colonel and one of Lady Ottoline Morrell's former parlour-maids. Edith Sitwell, to whom he had also mentioned his domestic problems, wrote on 2 May to say, 'I *wish* I could help you about a house, but I know of none, and what is more, I feel pretty certain that they are extremely difficult to find.' She continued in her best Lady Bracknell manner, 'I dare say your landlady is being tiresome because of war strain. It is having a most unfortunate effect on a great many people.'

After advising him that as far as his literary affairs were concerned he should get himself an agent, recommending her own agents, Pearn, Pollinger and Higham at 39 Bedford Street ('Ask to see either David Higham or Ann Pearn, and say I sent you. They are admirable agents, and take a lot of trouble, and are very nice people'), she went on to console him with the revelation that being a writer at Renishaw was not without its difficulties, too: 'Poor Denton, I am sorry to know that you are working under such wretched conditions. I can tell you, if it is any comfort, that my life here is much the same. Our beloved aged retainers fight with *everyone* unremittingly. I do not mean that *your* house is at fault – it is surely the other way round. But I mean we have to try to work with everyone squabbling round one – floods of tears, accusations, departures, hints, threats, screams, doors banging!!! The deaf replacing those who are not deaf, and consequently more shouts!!!

'If I hear of a house I'll wire to you and then write. Meanwhile, for goodness' sake don't throw away your house in a panic.'

Once again it was Noël Adeney who came to the rescue, if only offering a temporary refuge. On 7 May Denton was writing to her to say, 'We should *love* to stay for a day or two at M.O. if it really isn't a nuisance and added complication.' She was not to make any beds as they would bring their own sheets, and they would be leaving Evie behind so that she could get on with some belated spring cleaning. 'I did too much carpentering [on the doll's house] yesterday,' he added, 'but I am husbanding my resources and expect that I shall be all right for climbing the hill on Wed. or Thurs.'

Denton and Eric moved into Middle Orchard on 16 May, by which time it had been agreed that they could extend their stay to ten days.

The weather was unusually fine – it was 99° in the sun – and on the first evening they had supper out of doors. Denton spent the next day wandering from room to room, 'wondering how I would furnish it with my things', though three days later the novelty had worn off and he found himself prey to pessimistic thoughts. 'Today,' he wrote in his journal, 'I feel as if my talent was nothing, coming from nothing, turning into nothing with infinite pain and labour. Everything buzzes in me, my tongue, my eyes, my face, and my thoughts. They are the greatest buzzers of all. I wrote a page and a half of my Chinese story[4] this morning, and a letter to N. Adeney, and then this afternoon I tried to paint Eric with humiliating results. It is clear that I have no idea how to begin a straightforward portrait. I can only contrive and tickle fantastically and that only sometimes. But that would be good, and what I want to do, if I could rely on myself body and mind, but I can't.'

In the middle of May he heard that there was to be a Swedish edition of *In Youth is Pleasure*, though he complained to Noël that the 'advance royalty' of £20 which he received for it from Routledge did not seem very much, 'so I think I must go to that agent. It is getting too complicated for me.' Indeed, as he wrote in his journal on 25 May, 'It seems that a little literary success is not connected with more than a little money, for I now have a book in Sweden, a book in America, and two editions here, and what I have to show for it is two hundred and thirty-eight pounds.' To add to his despondency, he had been sick all day on 23 May, 'and it seemed as awful as if I were dying ... I thought it would never stop, but it did towards evening, and Eric looked after me and did everything. So yesterday seemed easy and calm after the horrible threat and the melting of every rock.'

Denton and Eric had been joined briefly at Middle Orchard by Evie, when she had completed her spring cleaning at Pitt's Folly, but on 20 May she had gone off in a fury, as Denton reported to Noël the next day, 'downing tools because I threw her sandals away (they were mended with cardboard and safety pins) so don't be surprised if we are standing on our heads when you arrive. To cap it all, the Vicar called in the middle of the Atmosphere!' Evie had, moreover, taken all their money with her, 'so I can't buy scrubbing brushes or *anything* but Eric is just going to Pitt's Folly Cottage to collect things'. Two days later a postcard arrived from Noël inviting them to stay on at Middle Orchard if they wanted to, and it was Eric who wrote to thank her, 'because today Denton

4. 'The Coffin on the Hill'.

woke up not feeling well with sickness, headache and a low temperature, but don't worry, as these attacks, although pretty bad at the time, soon pass off. So in the meantime I'm keeping him warm with hot water bottles. He hasn't been able to eat yet except for a sip of tea, but later on I shall make some Bengers. It's rather disappointing as up till now he's been rather well.'

Eric continued, 'Denton has taken a great fancy to M.O. and is wondering if ever you thought of moving, how much it would cost and if it would be more than £2,500.[5] It seems he's made up his mind to leave Pitt's Folly Cottage.'

By 30 May Denton had shed all despondency about the nature of his talent, reflecting in his journal, 'When I read about William Blake, I know what I am for. I must never be afraid of my foolishness, only of pretension. And whatever I have I must use, painting, poetry, prose – not proudly think it is not good enough and so lock it inside for fear of laughing, sneering.' As he was cleaning his teeth that morning he wondered what had become of a short story, 'The Judas Tree', which he had sent to John Lehmann, and soon afterwards there arrived in the post a letter from Lehmann accepting it for publication.[6] In the same post was a letter from Routledge informing him that Bonnier, the Swedish publisher of In Youth is Pleasure, was now contemplating an edition of Maiden Voyage.

On 14 June a letter arrived from the biographer Hector Bolitho, saying that an American magazine called Town and Country had commissioned him to write a feature on Denton and asking if he could come down to see him as he 'wanted to make it good. He said he wasn't very good at that sort of thing, so I must help him, if the idea didn't depress me too much.' Denton, now back at Pitt's Folly Cottage, promptly invited Bolitho to lunch two days later, noting in his journal that Eric was going to rustle up strawberries, asparagus, light ale and cigarettes 'so that we can give him a little something after his journey'. For Denton to receive any visitors other than neighbours or inquisitive fans was a rare occurrence, and he never attempted to conceal from them his eager-

5. It later became clear that Noël Adeney had no desire to sell Middle Orchard, and that in any case she thought it worth double the figure suggested in Eric's letter. For the rest of his life Denton longed to buy the house, though it is doubtful whether he was ever in a position to raise enough capital to buy a house of any kind; when he died he left only £5,578 6s. 6d.

6. 'The Judas Tree' was first published in Penguin New Writing in 1945, and was reprinted in Brave and Cruel.

ness to meet them. In his excitement he devoted pages of his journal to Bolitho's visit: 'We are wondering what he'll be like, and whether it will be a pleasant day or agony. I hope he won't ask embarrassing questions. Nothing could be worse than that.

'I have often heard his name but I don't really know what he writes. Is it history, at all? Or am I mixing him with Philip Guedalla? The name so harsh, Byzantine, has always stuck in my mind, because I have never been quite certain how to pronounce it, and I have wondered what nationality it was.'[7]

By arranging the interview to take place so soon Denton had at any rate ensured himself no more than forty-eight hours of worry. 'It is so difficult to explain to a stranger the state of one's health,' he wrote. 'One either says too little or too much. If he wants to know why I have to be so careful, I shall just have to tell him, I suppose, that I was once riding on a bicycle, when someone ran into the back of me and fractured my spine. But I hate to. I shall feel as I did the other day when Noël Adeney started a hateful conversation about me. She just wallowed in "death beds", "stricken deer", "tragedy", "the hurry to get work done". I am not a spectacle for curiosity, hers or anyone else's. I will not be dramatized. No one has been so blatant as she has been. She is truly sentimental, because she plays with her feelings, so that they shall excite her.'

Noël had, at least, made herself useful now by briefing him on Bolitho with information culled from *Who's Who*. 'It is nicer to know a little about one's visitor, isn't it,' Denton wrote to her on 15 June. 'I too thought he was a historian. I am sure he is quite quite the wrong person to write even the smallest snippet about me, but it will be interesting to see what his impression will be, just because of this unsuitability.'

Bolitho arrived early for lunch the next day as Denton recorded afterwards in his journal, 'while Evie and I were still getting things ready. I had lain the little marble-topped chess table with my mother's very flat, delicate Italian lace mats, the small squat cut-glass tumblers, the old straight-sided white-and-gold sugar-basin in the middle with the poppy, a marigold, briar roses, cat mint and some magenta star flowers on it.

'The 1740 silver christening spoon, the big salt cellar, and the urn-

---

7. Hector Bolitho, whose name amused Denton so much that he parodied it as 'Hector Bolithiero' in his short story 'Brave and Cruel', was in fact a New Zealander who had come to England as a result of meeting and travelling with the Prince of Wales. Thereafter he established himself as a biographer of the royal family, writing lives of Queen Victoria, the Prince Consort and Edward VIII. Philip Guedalla had died the previous year.

shaped pepper pot were making the table look pretty. I was just putting the crispbread in the Gothic toast rack on the table when I heard the taxi draw up. He was a long time telling the man when to call for him again, so I wandered backwards and forwards uncomfortably and Evie went round the corner and then retreated. We both hated the moment before the encounter with the stranger.

'At last he was walking up the dark stairs. I switched on the light and saw a small tubby man with large heavy rimmed glasses and a rather square "German" head with bushy white-grey hair.

'At once it was really very easy, ordinary. I curled up on the bed and he sat in the armchair. I offered him a cigarette and he began to tell me that he was just out of the Air Force.' The light ale for which Eric had been dispatched does not seem to have materialized, and Bolitho was offered cider instead. The asparagus duly appeared, however, followed by new peas, hard-boiled eggs, sardines, new potatoes, salad hearts and then a strawberry shortcake — 'the pastry really beautifully made by Evie. H. B. after his second helping said, "I feel like an overfed schoolboy"' — and during lunch he regaled Denton with anecdotes about the famous. He also 'spent a lot of words on his desire to have money, his willingness to be a "hack" as he called it, to earn enough for comfort and luxury.[8] He seemed to treat me as someone who would never behave in the same way. It is difficult to know whether people are really complimenting you, when they take up this attitude, or whether they are just thinking you a poor incompetent. They are doing both, I suppose — praising and blaming your supposed unworldliness.'

After lunch they went for a walk in the wood, and when they returned they were joined by Eric for tea. Bolitho commented to Eric, when Denton left the room for a moment to speak to Evie, that it was nice to meet someone unspoilt by success; and to Denton himself he said, '"Your vocabulary is so unpretentious."' ('What did he expect!' wrote Denton afterwards.)

When the taxi at last arrived, 'we took him out to it, and he pressed both our hands with a meaning look. Something most understanding — put on, of course, but likable, for in spite of all the little insincerities, that even a great person can't entirely weed out, he seemed to wish one well, "to want to live and let live" as Eric put it.

8. In this Bolitho succeeded, becoming known for his generous hospitality in his Brighton home. Among his eccentricities was a habit of dropping pennies in the gutter for the pleasure it gave him to imagine children finding them; another was in ordering a taxi to convey him to dinner in the next street.

'Eric said, the moment he was gone, "Well, that went off like a house on fire. What do you think he'll write? Something pretty good."

'And we talked about it all, and I suddenly felt quite exhausted.'

Twenty-two years later Hector Bolitho reworked his original *Town and Country* article for publication in the *Texas Quarterly*, giving it the title – on the strength of one meeting – 'My Friendship with Denton Welch'. In it he reveals his colonial snobbery in describing Evie as a 'servant' and Eric, whose relationship with Denton he understood perfectly well, as a 'housekeeper'. Denton's harpsichord, a Dolmetsch, he described as a spinet. Apart from these details, his observations contain much sensitive reporting. With reference to Denton's room, crowded with bed, easel and angels, he wrote, 'One absorbed some of the claustrophia of his life, and the self-analysis such a pattern encourages. But there was absolute tidiness. I realized later when I watched him cutting a cake with the timid precision of a surgeon that the talent for tidiness in his words and his painting, the delicate music of the spinet, the bird-like caution of his movements, the gentle kindness in his manners were all one talent. Each word, each movement, each pencil line, each striking of a match, each time he filled my glass with golden cider: all grew out of his inability to be clumsy or vulgar, in mind or movement.'

Bolitho also caught nicely Denton's unaffected use of slang: '"Have a cig," he said, which surprised me. Then, "Oh golly," and of a woman we both knew, "She's a bit dotty."'

On 2 July Denton wrote to Bolitho to thank him for sending a copy of the article he proposed to submit to *Town and Country*. 'I have absolutely no criticisms to make. I like it all very much. Perhaps it has made me too equable and controlled, but I am very pleased you have. I should hate the readers of "Town and Country" to learn everything.'

By nature Denton was never entirely 'equable and controlled', though he was now growing more so through the stability he derived from his relationship with Eric. Certainly he was growing less and less inclined to tolerate tantrums either in himself or in others. 'What *is* wrong?' he had asked Noël Adeney in a letter on 19 June. 'What cause is there for resentment? Or am I misunderstanding your mood and imagining that it is to do with me when it isn't?' The latest friction arose ostensibly over a domestic arrangement they had made, but it clearly went deeper than that on Noël's part. 'You should not have dashed over with the milk like that,' he told her. 'We both admit that it *is* irritating for you, if it is not collected at the right time – but it really is "our funeral", isn't it! And anyhow, we can always make cream cheese!

'But it is silly of me to dwell on the milk question, which has no real significance. It is lovely to have it, but if it is any bother, nuisance, irritation, bore, just *stop* it. We can manage now, with care, because there is more milk in the summer.

'I'm afraid nothing will persuade E. to fetch any more at the moment! He can't bear "atmospheres" and just seems to evaporate in them. I tell him that he need not feel involved, but he does, and he hates it.

'I too hate them now. They either make me feel perfectly dead and miles away or else caged up in a madhouse, where disembodied wills raven around, trying to devour other wills. Nothing could be more demonish than that. One just retreats behind high blank walls.'

Trying on this occasion to spare Noël's feelings he added, 'This may be all very smug, but it is also all very true.' Then he crossed out the sentence and wrote, 'I have crossed that out because it sounded even smugger.'

Noël was still on his mind on 21 June when, Eric having gone away for a few days, Denton wrote to him, 'Dear Tu, Eve has just got up from her siesta to make tea, and I hope to do a little work this evening as I have done nothing so far. I hope the little Mrs A. won't come crashing on me tonight.' This was followed the next day by a progress report on his new book: 'Dear Lobster, I wrote rather well this morning and didn't feel agitated, but I'm afraid the book may sound awfully peculiar and I expect nobody will like it. I must finish it tho', as I myself like it best of all.' Two days later he wrote again: 'My dear Tu, I can't write much as I am ill again. Isn't it a curse. I began this morning, but I haven't been sick or anything so it may go quickly. I went down to the river yesterday. That may have started it. I can't tell you how morbid it makes me feel − sort of death in life! But it's only passing, I suppose. Eve has been reading to me to while away the time. Wish my head would stop aching. I always have the feeling it never will again.' He ended, 'You be *very* careful of yourself, won't you.'

On 26 June, Eric this time being his 'Dear Piece of Fruit', Denton reported, 'Noël suddenly appeared yesterday and stayed from lunch till 10 o'clock! But she was fairly good on the whole, and I smoothed her down as much as possible. Once, I *think*, she tried to make trouble between you and me, but I took no notice, so nothing came of it ... As mildly as possible I tried to point out what made her difficult to get on with, but it is not much good; only a bald statement would get thro', and then she would make too much of it and dwell on it for days. She wants to know if you and I would like to go there [to Middle Orchard] for a week on about July 7th. I said, "Did they really not mind lending the house" and she seemed to want to, very much. I can't really tell what I ought to do, for I hate to be churlish and I hate to appear to get involved in an unsuitable way. All this we can rake over later! and you can say what you'd like to do.'

He also reported that Hector Bolitho, who had taken away with him on the day of their lunch a pile of Denton's press cuttings, had now returned them beautifully mounted 'on virgin pieces of paper. They look too good to be true.' He ended, presumably referring to his life-long pursuit of sexual adventures, 'I'm quite all right now and am going to be very wise. As you say, my scouting days are over.'

On 4 July he was sending Noël 'Just a hurried note to let you know we hope to go to M.O. tomorrow evening. It depends on my state, but I am cosseting myself tremendously, so all should be well.' In the same letter he revealed, 'We were hoping Jack Easton might appear and give me wonderful new treatment or drug but he hasn't.' (For some reason Denton was three months premature in his expectations; it was not until 5 October that Dr Easton, released from army service, wrote to him to say, 'Just a line to let you know I am back at work. Dr Ramsden spoke to me about you and suggested he had a word with you as to who you want to call in when you are in need of medical help. From my side I am perfectly willing and would like to be your doctor – our relationship would be the same as before and more mature I guess.')

Their stay at Middle Orchard lasted about twelve days, during which time Denton read Ivy Compton-Burnett's *Elders and Betters*, and he and Eric voted in the landslide election which brought Churchill's post-war government to an end – 'and of course did everything wrong and began to chat in those secret horse boxes, so that a man rushed round and said, "You can do what you like at home, but you mustn't do it here!"'

Shortly after returning to Pitt's Folly they received a visit from two Australian fans which was to inspire, on 22 July, one of Denton's most vicious journal entries: 'Ted Nichols and Robin Cornell arrived for lunch – late – and Robin, in his pathetic, arrested-development way, had to explain that they were late because they had drunk too much the night before, and that had made them sleep late and miss the train. It was sordid. And all through the afternoon we had to listen to his disgustingly commonplace titbits about his own fascination and charm. (He had one of those fish faces and underwater eyes which *always* are trimmed with thick horn-rimmed glasses.) This sort of person should be smacked and put to sleep – for ever, but I suppose they live longer than most people and burden others for years with their extraordinary pretension and mental squalor.

'I will write no more about them – except to say that we had thistle artichokes and melted butter, cold fried fish, peas, carrots, lettuce and Eve's sweet salad-dressing made with condensed milk, then cherry flan – coral-coloured cherries, stoned and bottled by Noël Adeney. Afterwards we smoked Dunhill cigarettes and chatted and shouted, till anyone who was listening must have thought that we doted on one another's company.'

At the same time Denton was pursuing his house-hunting in earnest. On 26 July he and Eric went over to Trottiscliffe to see a small house called Ivy Cottage which belonged to Mrs Carpmael and which she had offered to them for 14s. 6d. a week – 'amazing rent for nowadays', as Denton remarked in his journal. Unfortunately, he found it 'squalid after the last derelict old father and daughter had left it', and felt, as it was also semi-detached and was right in the middle of the village, that it would be foolish to move there. Things seemed to be looking up, however, when on 3 August he wrote, 'There really seems some chance now that I may be able to build a tiny house, and I keep seeing in my mind exactly what I want. A long room downstairs with three french windows from floor to ceiling along one wall, a fireplace and an old mantel at one end, and at the other a blank wall for my tapestry cartoon. Upstairs three small bedrooms and the bathroom.' Nothing, alas, came of this plan, and the dream house was to remain a dream for ever.

The rest of the month was to prove on the whole dull and unhappy, since for two weeks of it he was confined to bed and was feeling too unwell to work. He had been prescribed M & B tablets (a sulphur drug manufactured by May & Butler which was widely prescribed before the advent of penicillin), 'which, I suppose, made me feel even worse – black, dead, inhuman as a boulder – telescoped into myself till nothing could come forward', as he wrote in his journal on 26 August. The high point came on 23 August when his brother Paul came to see him. 'He looked very well, I thought, and not battle-worn at all,' Denton wrote to Noël two days later. 'It is a relief that he is quite all right,' though he seemed very restless, 'and wanted to pick everything up and look at it, so that I had the feeling that there was a caged animal in my room'.

To pass the time while he was in bed Denton had been reading a travel book by Norman Douglas. 'I have never read him before,' he told Noël. 'He is half boring, and half rather pleasing, I think.' His only activity otherwise had consisted of doing a small drawing for the cookery page of *Vogue* of 'succulent morsels. This time it is pastries and pies, which rather lend themselves, don't they.'

On 2 September Paul paid another visit. He was planning to go to China to help Bill sort out their father's business, and he told Denton that 'if we get nothing else, we will eventually each get eighty shares in Wattie & Co., and if the firm gets going again and is moderately successful, we should each get about three hundred pounds a year. But there is the mystery of what has happened to all the rest of our father's money. Did he spend it all? Will our stepmother be able to throw any light? It is all peculiar and just what one would expect, I suppose. He had about four thousand pounds a year in director's fees alone.' (Writing to Noël a year later, on 17 July 1946, Denton disclosed that his stepmother had sold everything, even his brothers' clothes, and was very disappointed that her husband had left less than she had expected. Although she had made a Will 'leaving everything to us that was not already tied up', Denton was 'sorry that Paul could not even salvage some of our possessions, for I might have been able to have some more of my mother's family things'.)

With his health failing him more and more frequently as time went on, Denton must have realized that his cycling days were numbered. Determined to remain mobile, and having sold his father's Austin 7 early in 1943, he now set about buying a car from May Walbrand-Evans. At the same time his energies were also bent on again trying to persuade Noël Adeney to part with Middle Orchard. 'I am wondering what you have decided about the house – whether to plunge or draw back,' he asked her on 22 September. 'It is terrible to have to make up one's mind, isn't it. It seems so much more natural to hover and ponder eternally.' After a long description of another house he had taken a fancy to, he ended poignantly, 'It makes me long to have an old house to restore and live in.'

Things cheered up, though, when he had a visit from Helen Roeder, who told him 'two plums: one that Eddie Marsh approved of my books, and the other that K. Clark who hadn't approved came up and told her that her naughty little narcissus had written another story and the strange thing was that he was a poet! Doesn't Helen know what titbits to feed to one.' He added, 'We played "drawing consequences" which became awfully rude and funny.'

Another boost came shortly afterwards in the form of a letter from one of the joint managing directors of Routledge, Murray Ragg, dated

28 September: 'The new and lively French publisher, Le Sagittaire, have agreed to publish [*Maiden Voyage*] and we have given them an option on In Youth is Pleasure. They are to pay an advance of £30 against a royalty of 7½ on the first 3,000 copies and 10 per cent thereafter. It will however, I fear, be some months, if not a year or two, before the French edition is out, as the shortage of paper and labour is even worse there than it is here.' But, he continued, 'The news of the American edition is not, I fear, very good. Fischers printed a second edition but have got stuck with it as the demand for the book has apparently ceased. We have, however, taken steps to ensure that the printed copies shall not be wasted and have ordered 2,000 copies of them for ourselves for sale in this country, so don't be surprised if you see the American edition knocking about over here. It's a pity it's not a more beautiful edition but it would equally be a pity to have it wasted entirely.'

It was on 4 October that Jack Easton eventually surfaced, when he called not on Denton but on Mary Sloman next door, though he wrote to Denton the next day to offer once again to act as his doctor. Denton was relieved that Easton had not called on him that day, as he told Noël Adeney: 'We had Francis sitting on our faces on Thursday, so it was a very good thing really that Jack was too involved with the Ladies to come in. Francis would have stared so, and said such things in his piping treble.'

Denton had again been ill during the first week of October, and had dated the onset of this latest bout to 2 October, when he had been visited for lunch by an eighteen-year-old schoolboy named David Carritt. 'But,' he wrote in his journal on 9 October, 'I only put it down to the exhaustion due to his froth and nonsense. (He is humorous.)' Denton had found Carritt 'nice really ... and rather clever. He played the harpsichord well and I gathered he was a very bright boy at Rugby – a precocious conversationalist, with a few spots on his face, excitable movements. He loved mentioning the names of minor old masters – obviously cut out for a museum worker.'[9]

Denton's next visitor was one whose appearance he had long been dreading. On 10 October he wrote to Noël, 'I have just heard that Bill and Anne are driving down on Sunday to see us! Isn't it frightful. I can't think what it will be like. The two of them together is more than

9. David Carritt many years later joined Christies, discovered a number of immensely valuable paintings and became, in the words of Hugh Leggatt, 'one of the few geniuses in the fine art world'. He died in 1982.

I had bargained for. Bill is going to China "to rescue some of our bread and butter" as he puts it.' Denton's anxieties turned out to be groundless, since Bill could not have behaved more smoothly when he arrived. Indeed, Bill never stored any resentment for the things Denton wrote about him; on the contrary, both he and Paul became proud of their younger brother's achievements.

'My brother has grown grey hair at the sides and he told me all about our father's latest Will,' Denton wrote in his journal afterwards. 'It appears now he has left everything to my stepmother unconditionally. She is sole executrix too. This, which seemed so very bad on the surface for us, is apparently not quite so bad, as Bill thinks that the whole thing can be settled, if he offers her an annuity on condition that she gives over half the shares to our keeping. At present she is staying in Shanghai and swearing that she is going to run the firm herself. It is just like the wicked stepmother in children's stories. Bill says that in a good year, when all is in running order again, the shares should bring in a lot and that in a year or two we should all have quite a comfortable amount. But I suppose Ada knows this too and so I can't help feeling that she may be very difficult.

'There is also,' he continued, 'the question of money of our own mother's that may now go into her pocket. For our father sold the house (bought with our mother's money) for about £15,000. This should really have been divided between us instead of going into our father's estate. Bill says that he will rake this up if Ada will not agree [to trading her inheritance for an annuity]. I suppose money is so fascinating, so repelling and so tiring because it has the power to draw all forms of ingenuity out of people.'

Bill had surprised Denton on his birthday by sending him £100. 'I still can't believe it,' Denton told Noël, 'and the cynical part that is in all of us keeps wondering what prompted him to do so; I really am *very* grateful and only hope that any criticisms I have printed haven't worried him at all.'

Another panic seized Denton not long after Bill's visit, as a result of a commission from *Harper's Bazaar* for a short story. On 26 October he wrote to Eric, who was then staying with his mother in London. Addressing him this time as 'Dear Tuna', he asked if Eric could postpone his return for a little while as he would not mind 'another couple of days of brooding solitude for I am battling with a short story for Harper's Bazaar in America. I am in rather a state about it and trying my hardest to get it done, so feel afraid of being distracted from it. But if you've fixed up for certain to come tomorrow, do come and I can just shut myself up even if you are here ...

'Two catastrophes have happened since you've been away. First one of my tooth stoppings has come adrift, and next the car got a puncture just as I came home on Wednesday! I haven't even attempted to change the wheel, thinking of my weak and dithering state. So will have to try and do it together next week. How I wished you'd been there to cope. I had just come back from seeing that house at Little Hawkwell. They want over £4,000 for it and the rain was pouring through the roof. It was very gruesome all alone in it. I sort of enjoyed my own horrors. At one moment I thought I saw a ghost out of the corner of my eye.'

Where Denton thought he was going to acquire £4,000 for a house, with or without the rain pouring through the roof, is hard to imagine. Yet so anxious was he to leave Pitt's Folly Cottage, and so great was his désire to own his own home, that his fantasies were now running riot; he even told Noël Adeney that he had just heard from Helen Roeder about a house for sale in, of all places, Ladbroke Square.

FIFTEEN

'A State of Siege'

Whatever exactly it was that had prompted the suggestion that Denton's 'scouting days' were over, there were times when the recognition that they indeed were was painfully brought home to him. On 26 October, as he described in his journal that evening, he had gone into Tonbridge and, towards dusk, as he was pushing his bicycle through the town, he had seen on the other side of the road 'another shadow walk'. Someone was following him. 'I walked very calmly, slowly, so that it should pass me under a lamp-post. And then I saw that it was quite a young sort of gypsy country boy.' The boy asked him for a light. They fell into step, and talked about horses. 'Then unaccountably, I left him.' Agonizing over the incident in his journal he wondered whether it had been a sense of his own inadequacy that had overcome him, or whether he had been put off by the impossibility of real contact between them, 'the complete hollowness of casual bonhomie – built on a lie – the lie of pretending that one feels no deeper. One pretends to be a dear little machine, when one is a devouring flame.'

After parting from the boy Denton had then done some shopping, but before long had thought he saw the boy again, 'and my heart was all jarred and jumping'. This time he avoided contact and went towards the river to sit down. There it had been 'suddenly quite easy for me to see that I should go home at once to supper, not go on over-tiring myself and making myself ill, as I used to do so often in the past because of the thing that was eating me. It was all clear that I should never wander and grope about and gaze, that I should always make for something and do it, that I was lost if I did not make a pattern for myself. When I go back into formless days, feel stifled with my lack of ability, feel that everything is smeared and smudged, I have the vision of true madness. Not melodrama madness but just dithery madness.'

'What has happened to my heart tonight' were the words with which he opened his account of this incident, and they clearly reflect the sexual longing he still experienced in spite of his partial impotence. Nowhere else in his writings does he more explicitly indicate the struggle he had to preserve his creative balance and the self-discipline required to overcome the frustrations and anguish caused by his condition. The degree to which he did achieve a balance can not be better judged than in the considerable frankness and restraint he was able to command in his telling of the episode.

Frustrations of quite a different order were attending his plans to move house. On 16 November he went to Crouch 'to find out what was really happening', only to discover that the Adeneys were not after all about to move. 'So,' he noted in his journal, 'we won't be able to move to Middle Orchard. I am very thwarted, impotent-feeling, as if we shall never have a house and garden.'

The disturbances in his routine work must have continued for some time, for on 20 November he was writing in his journal that he still had his story to complete for *Harper's*, 'another for Kingdom Come, my Vogue drawing to do in four days, my book to finish, pictures to finish for the Leicester, and two for the Arts Council. How much of this will get done soon? I am a snail worker turning out about four paragraphs a day and messing with my pictures till they are an obsession.' On 25 November he again brooded on his inability to forge ahead: 'So nothing-blank in me tonight after sickness and flu. All day touching at my drawing with my black pen, turning away from the writing always, because drawing soothes and lulls, and should do so, else there will be no good picture.' He reflected, 'It is lazier to be a painter than a writer, but only if you are both. If you are only a writer, then you are lazier, because you waste your hands. Only if you copied out your books most exquisitely you would be better.'

He had been visited the same day by Maurice Cranston, who had come to tea and had told him of seeing a copy of *In Youth is Pleasure* on a bookstall in the Charing Cross Road, 'labelled boldly and baldly "Of Interest to Students of Abnormal Psychology". He thinks I should tell Routledge to object, but I don't think it matters at all.'

Two days later he recorded encouraging signs of activity at Middle Orchard, where he had paid a visit that afternoon. 'We hope like anything that Noël is going to buy 34 Croom's Hill and move there. It will be funny if she does.' More to the point, it might also leave the way open for Denton at last to buy the property. On returning home, 'May came out of her house screeching at Eric like a fishwife-parrot, and when I followed him I found her all draped on the Recamier sofa with sticking-plaster over her eye and burnt-brown-red dripping down her face and dabbed all over the towel that was covering her full-front.

'It appears that she trod on a brush in her kitchen and threw herself down on the brick floor. She had felt gruesome and so she had posed herself and waited till we brought the car back ... She was like a sinister waxwork – she had that added touch of falseness which is much worse than the blood and the towels.'

The purchase of 34 Croom's Hill by the Adeneys was attended by complications. Although Evie's brother was the true owner of the house and was trying to secure a sale to a woman who had put in an offer before the Adeneys, the title deeds were in Evie's name and she refused to cooperate with her brother if the Adeneys were not to have the property.

Denton soon had something far worse to worry about, however. On 20 December, 'just before Evie came up to read ... something seemed to shift delicately in my eye and there was a slight swimming of which I took little notice'. Before long he had developed double vision, 'seeing two teapots, two Evies and two lamps', and when he went into the bathroom to examine himself in the mirror he 'saw there that my lid had dropped down and the pupil underneath was huge, velvet black, almost swamping the tiny coloured rim. The other pupil was normally small. The whole effect of my face was wickedly languorous and lopsidedly un-me.'

He settled down to what he described as 'a night of deep pain in the heart of my head like a tight little walnut', and in the morning he found 'the lid and the eye on my left side all seemed to be sinking down to the left – everything left, hooded, wilting'. Dr Easton was summoned. 'He came up the stairs without Evie saying anything to me, and I was not perfectly certain that I had not deluded myself until he opened the door and stood there. He was more or less the person that I had first seen ten years ago in the garden of the nursing home at Broadstairs.'

After examining Denton he 'walked up and down in the way that might be so annoying in someone else. I knew that if there was anything terrible that had to be said, he would say it more delicately than anyone else I knew; but still I did not care to wait for his verdict. It was a trying moment. I darted my head from side to side and smiled restlessly as if everything in the world was as trivial as could be.

'Then he told me that he thought it was a temporary paralysis of the third nerve, and that it would get better but would take some time.

First he said a few days, then six weeks or perhaps two months!' In the meantime Denton was to wear a black patch over his left eye to stop him from seeing double.

By the end of the year Denton knew for certain that he was going to be able to leave the cramped, damp conditions of Pitt's Folly Cottage and move into Middle Orchard as Noël Adeney's tenant. He had been 'waiting to hear the final word' before dashing into Tunbridge Wells 'to use all our coupons on yards of material' for new curtains, and on 31 December things were settled enough for him to be writing to Noël to suggest an annual rent of £100. 'This would still be, I suppose, quite a lot less than the rent you might get from someone else today, but it is as much as I ought to spend, and as you have said, you will still have the use of a little bit of the house.' He went on to fidget about who was to play the wirelesses where, who was to pick apples from which trees, whether the lease should last for two years or three, and at the end of it he asked, 'Is there anything else to discuss? I can't think of it, if there is. The thought of leaving here at last is most exciting.'

The discussion of details was not to be relinquished so lightly, and the new year was scarcely three days old before Denton was writing again, presumably in reply to a letter from Noël in which she had offered to accept less than £100 a year: 'Naturally,' he wrote on 3 January 1946, 'it would be nice for us to save all the money we can, but I don't quite see why we should do it at your expense! Shall we compromise and agree to make the rent £96 – that is exactly £24 a quarter, so it will be nice and neat. I of course don't want to make life too expensive for myself, but you will see that I fully realize that you'd probably get a much higher rent today from someone else, even with the arrangement of your keeping the studio and hut for yourself. Perhaps soon something will be arranged about my Pa's affairs, and then if things are easier for me, and if it seems right and proper, we could make a little adjustment.'

As for his health, he told Noël that he had been in bed with a temperature for the past three days, and that his eye still troubled him. 'It's improved, but it isn't completely right, and I can't really use it in conjunction with the other, because it is just a second too late with everything, and so I still see double.'

By 16 March his vision had improved sufficiently for him to be able to drive Noël over to her new home – his old lodgings in Greenwich. Not having been there since the day he had stopped to collect his belongings on his way to the Southcourt Nursing Home, his thoughts now went back to the very first time he had gone there, when Evie had opened the door to him 'and been as moony and as unattached as she still is. Strange to think that from that day to this she has been somewhere about the place. First I lived in her house, now she lives in mine. And she is as inhuman as ever.'

Two days later his past must again have returned to him, this time triggered by a letter from Geoffrey Lumsden, the Repton schoolfriend who had inspired one of the characters in *Maiden Voyage*. Geoffrey, now in Bombay, had been inspired after reading Denton's book to attempt a book himself, and he enclosed the beginnings of it together with a dedication to Denton. He explained that he had been particularly excited by *Maiden Voyage* because 'I know you and because the book is the product of a brain that I know and knew when, like mine, it was young and developing and which at the time contained the seeds of *Maiden Voyage* and no doubt so much more, and here is the first blossom, and more and greater will follow. Many congratulations.'

The move to Middle Orchard – planned for 25 March – for some reason does not seem to have found favour with Evie. On 21 March Denton wrote to Noël at her new home: 'I meant to write sooner to ask how you were getting on, but of course I have been in bed again, and then at this difficult time Eve has been kicking up perhaps the biggest fuss I've yet known. All last night there was muttering, calling out of the windows, closet-flushings (time and time again), door-slammings and wild accusations. We took her up to M.O. in the morning and she was able to help with some cleaning, but after about $\frac{1}{2}$ hour she fled and, I suppose, walked home. All is perfectly calm this morning and she's better than she's been for years.' Nevertheless, he had already decided that Evie needed a change of scene, and since she had recently heard of two sisters in Cornwall who wanted a housekeeper, 'E. and I have encouraged her to go if she possibly can, since it is so clear that she needs an entire change ... What is so amusing is that today she is smiling and cooshy. She is bringing me things in bed, and even answering when I talk to her! It is a pity that such an improvement could only be brought about at the end of her time here.'

He continued with an account of the redecoration of Middle Orchard. 'They have begun on the kitchen and the ceiling pink looks awfully nice. They are going to do the living-room eau-de-Nile. It is a paler, prettier colour than I had intended, but they have no grey-green, no yellow and no grey. They are going to do the landing and hall after we get in.' He had tried cleaning some paintwork himself, 'but it does me in too much ... I think I shall have to do almost nothing myself, if I'm to keep going at all. It is maddening, but there it is.'

The day after moving in to Middle Orchard he announced to his new landlady: 'Here we are! painters still in the house – Evie exhausted, but in a very good temper – Eric bathing, and I husbanding my energies on the bed in your room. It is looking really very pretty with the new curtains and the doll's house.' Evie was planning to stay on with them for a month before having a 'holiday' of indefinite duration – a trial separation, in effect – in Cornwall with the two sisters. 'I'm afraid they would not have her if they knew how frivolous she was about staying any length of time!' he continued to Noël. On 1 April he wrote again to say, 'I am already very fond of your room. I find that I am always wanting to retreat to it. E. says that I must learn to eat *downstairs* so that there will be less laborious tray carrying. My doll's house looks beautiful up here. I keep staring at it from my bed.' They had been pleased when the painters left, he told her, 'for we felt that we were always attending to them – giving them beer and cups of tea to keep their strength up. They were very nice, and they helped to bring my secretaire upstairs. They heaved it with ropes over the balcony; there was nearly a most horrible accident.'

There were, however, financial details which still needed pinning down: 'I am not absolutely certain, after re-reading our agreement, whether you would like me to send you my cheque at the *beginning* of the quarters or the *end*; I am sending it now to cover this quarter, till June 25th; but if you prefer it at the end and not the beginning I can change after that. I am trying to think of all the household things I can do without getting out of bed. I can only think of cleaning the glass lustres!' So ignorant of business practice was Denton that he was unaware not only that the quarter day fell on 24 June but that rent was customarily paid in advance. His ignorance no doubt accounts for his obsessive worrying about these details, and on this occasion, as indeed on many others, Noël must have found him just as infuriating to deal with as he sometimes found her.

On 7 April he had a haemorrhage. 'I bleed inside,' he wrote in his journal, 'and when it comes out of me, almost fascinating in its disgustingness, I feel full of snarling that I am spoilt. To have always to do every fragment of work with the gloves of sickness sheathing each finger, to have that added! The glove of flesh is thick and deadening enough, without the bewildering adventure of illness never-ending.'

The very next day, he was out driving again, and only a mile or two from Middle Orchard, at Wrotham, he found a place where he had walked when he was eighteen, on a 'pilgrimage from Winchester to Canterbury. Remembering it, I had a spear in me for my spoilt ease and strength of body. I whined for what appeared to me that suddenly taken away beauty of ease and agility. How I loved my lightness, springiness, endurance, tautness! I thought, "I shall always be this spring-ing, dancing-wire taut person," then in two years I was flat on my back with the fear of no walking any more and the certainty of illness till the grave. Yet how amazingly my body has put up with it. I must look more worn with it than I should look; but it is not dramatic. It is horrible when the ill look dramatic. It throws every friend into confusion.'

The friend who had most noticeably been thrown into confusion when Denton, not long after his accident, was looking his most dramatic, had been his art-school friend Gerald. Gerald had been abroad for most of the war, and on 16 April he came to visit Denton, 'fustulating, fabricating his flash trash – all tinsel from India, Cairo, Pretoria,' Denton wrote in his journal. 'His endless stories pouring out, and he sitting on you from one o'clock till ten at night. Bullying insistence of such a talker and squatter, and underneath his sly snake eyeing you. Extraordinary innocence of his conceit – every story concentrating on himself – and what a transformed self, quite unrecognizable.

'I suppose the terrible flaw in him is his lack of any brooding, sulky depth. He is a music-hall man recording his funny self for ever on a wearing-out gramophone.

'He says he does love to meet all sorts of people, including well-known ones. Here he reels off his list of names. Wavell, Mountbatten (Lady), Auchinleck, Turkey princes, Greek princesses. Again it seems endless – everything was endless.'

Yet Denton had been fascinated by him ever since they had first met in 1933, writing constantly about him to Marcus Oliver, often complain-ing about him but never dreaming of throwing him off. 'I'm wondering if you've had an irate note from Gerald saying that he didn't want to see you any more,' he had inquired of Marcus back in 1940, 'as I told him in a fit of pique that you also found his manner difficult to deal with on occasion. He spent a week down here and was altogether too much for me. He seemed to belittle everything and everyone, to make himself feel big...I do hope I haven't made trouble between you two but when he said that I was the only person who found fault with his behaviour, I couldn't resist mentioning your remarks about him.

I do wish he'd get over his wretched inferiority complex and simmer down.'

On 7 May Evie at last left for Cornwall, dressed 'in new coat and skirt, peaked cap (maroon) and fur hat', as Denton reported to Noël. 'She looked very trim, and although I think she dreaded it a little, there was excitement too. It still seems extraordinary that she should have done all her shopping and that she should have gone – quite miraculous.' He added, 'I hope she will save her mad scenes for many months to come. E. thinks she will be quite normal with strange people.' The farewell was recorded in his journal: 'She came in to say good-bye while I was eating breakfast in bed. I wondered what would happen. She made two little running darts at me. It all melted away. I wanted it to be all drifting away in gaiety. I ran out afterwards in my cassock to wave them off. The wind blew the skirts of it. Evie was almost hilarious, to cover the good-byes.'

Reflecting on their dozen years together he continued, 'How strange it is to think that after all this long time she is gone. It is so good for her really that we both hope she will stay some time, though we feel that she is almost certain to return eventually. How many violent quarrels there have been between her and me. What extraordinary behaviour there has been sometimes. Yet I suppose she is what you would call quite devoted. This does not mean that she would in any way comply in small particulars, but that she would always protect and guard. She has a streak of madness, of course, and that often makes her touching, infuriating and tragic.'

Within a month Evie had quarrelled with her Cornish employers, 'and threatens to come back to us,' Denton noted on 11 June. 'But it has been such calm without her that I shall do all I can to get her some other place. Never, for anything at all, live in a house with brooding blackness and unreason, though the person may have devotion and a hundred other virtues as well. The black bile seeps everywhere in everything.'

In May a letter arrived from New York from the magazine *Harvard Wake* (later renamed *Viva*). The editor, José Villa, who was planning to devote his August issue to Edith Sitwell, had written to Edith herself asking her to send a story, and now wanted Denton to contribute an article about her on the lines of his *Horizon* piece on Sickert. Denton then wrote to Edith to ask her permission to do an account of their lunch together, and on 15 July she replied, 'I am filled with a mixture of really *extreme* delight and some trepidation at the thought of your describing that lunch party for two. (Trepidation remembering your description of Mr Sickert. But at least I did not, as far as I remember, dance or sing. Oh, how Osbert and I laughed over that description.) Well anyhow, trepidation or no trepidation, I am *enchanted* that you are going to do it, and look forward to it very greatly.

'Of course I trust you to do exactly as you feel about it. I would love to see it if you have a spare copy, however, just for the sheer pleasure of seeing it.'

She went on to say that she was planning to come to London on 2 September and that she hoped Denton would lunch with her again. 'Also we *may* be doing Façade, and it would be great fun if you would come to that with me. But I am not certain yet if Constant Lambert can find a suitable conductor. He simply won't pay attention. Willie Walton can't conduct it, as he is busy with King Lear.' For all her seemingly relaxed attitude at the prospect of being written about by Denton, she was clearly apprehensive, ending her letter, 'Do just for the sheer fun of it let me see your description of our lunch.'

Denton began on his new commission straight away, but soon ran into problems. 'It is so difficult to write this article,' he wrote in his journal on 15 July, 'for so many things cannot be repeated. Edith said she thought Vita Sackville-West and Rosamund Lehmann poor writers. Dorothy Wellesley also. These names I have to wipe out. There was all the amusing part about the Dorothy Lady Gerald Duchess of Wellington that is, arriving drunk at the poetry reading and not being allowed to recite. I long to travel over this forbidden ground. But all the time I have to think if my words will cause mischief between these people and Edith.'

He worked on the article solidly for the next few days, 'and made myself ill'. On 20 July Jack Easton 'came to see if he could suggest anything to make me better ... He seemed to like the house, and said, as he often does, "You are lucky, how I envy you, being able to live as you like."' Still unwell a few days later, Denton nevertheless consented to a '"fan" from Colchester', Peggy Kirkaldy, coming to visit him and staying the night at Middle Orchard. 'I decided to say "Yes" in spite of temperature. I did not know what else to say. There seems a time when to plead ill-health any longer seems disgusting.' When she arrived he was pleased to find that 'she had brought food with her and towels and scented soap, the perfect guest'; he also found her to be the perfect subject for a short story, and she makes her appearance, alongside Eric and Denton himself, as 'Susan Innes' in 'The Diamond Badge'. In this story Denton ruthlessly portrays himself as a cripple named 'Andrew', a character seen through the eyes of the female narrator, 'Susan Innes'; Denton was, of course, as anxious to know how he appeared to other people as he was to record his impressions of them, and as an experiment in self-portraiture alone the story is of interest.[1]

In August, relations between Evie and her employers were settled enough for Denton and Eric to consider spending a week with her in Cornwall, but in the end Denton decided that the journey would be too much for him. He went to the station on 8 August to see Eric off, and he 'could not help thinking, "What if I should never see him again!" My mother had been swept off like that, not in a train but in a car. I just saw the waving hand, the little corner of face; then they were gone and I never saw them again.' He wrote to Eric the next day at 57 Daniell Road, Truro, to tell him that the *New Yorker* had asked him for a story, 'as they like When I Was Thirteen in the American edition of Horizon short stories, so it does look as if the story has been reprinted, though again, I suppose by the owners of Horizon so perhaps I don't get paid again.'

His financial state was still on his mind the next day when writing in his journal: '"Maiden Voyage" has come out four times here – that is including six thousand copies printed for Readers' Union Book Club. Twice in America. Once, so far, in Sweden, France, Italy, Germany and Austria (soon). I used to think in my simplicity that to be published in many countries meant much money for the author. But of course it does not follow. I don't think so far that all the publications of "Maiden Voyage" have earned me more than £500, certainly not more than £700.'

Commissions of all kinds were flowing in fast. A magazine for adolescents called *Junior* had asked him to illustrate a story by Katherine Mansfield entitled 'The Voyage', and the *New York Post* had invited him to send them a contribution. 'It would be lovely,' he wrote in his journal on 9 August, 'to have the health and vigour to do all these things one after another smoothly, in the moments that I spared from the book. I have always the tantalizing picture of happy busyness to goad me.' He must have been amused to receive also a letter from the *Sunbathing Review*, telling him that Bernard Shaw, Laurence Housman, Naomi Mitchison, Vera Brittain, A. E. Coppard, J. C. Flugel, Robert Gibbings and C. E. M. Joad had written for it, and asking 'will I write

1. In his Introduction to *A Last Sheaf* Eric Oliver incorrectly stated that one of the portraits reproduced was of 'Susan Innes'; so far as is known Denton never painted a portrait of Peggy Kirkaldy.

too – a likely theme, the value of nudity in schools "as a means of countering the unhealthy practices with which anyone who has been educated at a boarding school is familiar"! I think the only thing I can truthfully say in reply is that I feel that nudity would increase the "unhealthy practices", whatever they may be, perhaps set a fashion through the whole school for them.' The articles in the magazine, a copy of which was enclosed with the letter, he found 'very like the tracts Evie's sister brought me from the Bible and Tract Society. God and Jesus are replaced by Sun and Naked Body.'

He had also received a letter, he told Eric on 13 August, from Michael Ayrton, 'the guy sometimes on the Brains Trust', who wanted him to exhibit with sixteen other painters at Heal's in a show of pictures priced below £40. 'He said he hoped we'd meet, as he is an admirer of my work! I was pleased to have this letter, but I didn't like him at all on the wireless – a sort of smug conceited tone. But the wireless must be a terrible ordeal to face.'

The upshot of Denton's efforts to write about Edith Sitwell was an article entitled 'A Lunch Appointment', a copy of which he must have sent to her for on 30 August she was writing to say, 'I am *so* grateful to you for what you have done, writing this article for José Villa's paper.' But, she added, 'The little wretch has now disappeared from my horizon – not a word from him. So I haven't seen the essay yet.' The essay she referred to was presumably a piece Villa was writing about her; as for Denton's article, no trace of it has survived. She continued, 'Can you A come to a lunch-party, and B stop on for a large tea-party on Wednesday the 11th [September], at the Sesame Club. Lunch at 12.45. And if you are going to be in London on Monday the 9th, do come to Façade. It really is great fun. I do look forward enormously to seeing you.'

This seems to have been the last letter Edith Sitwell wrote to Denton. On 11 September he noted sadly, 'This is the day that I should have gone to London to have lunch with Edith Sitwell, and afterwards to be with her at what she called a big tea-party! But I could not face going in my precarious state. This is the first day – except for the dentist on Saturday – when I have been out of my room for three weeks or a month. I wish I could have gone to Edith Sitwell's.'

The appearance in close succession of three eccentric letters from a navy chaplain, the Reverend Richard Blake Brown, brought into the open at last a fan of whose existence Denton had been aware for some years. The first letter was 'written in three different coloured inks, in enormous letters on two different coloured papers with different stamped headings (violet green and scarlet) and little whimsy pieces, such as "No telephone on purpose". A photograph enclosed too'; the second, written 'on vivid blue paper with a mustard yellow seal', contained a picture of Queen Mary; and the third, again different, was decorated 'this time with an enormous bishop's mitre, seal of turquoise wax and red-and-green initial "R" on the envelope'.

Brown was an Anglo-Catholic dilettante who wrote novels of a sub-Firbankian kind. His connections with Denton were in fact so numerous and so close that it seems odd that the two had never met. Not only was Brown connected by marriage to Francis Streeten, and was an old acquaintance of Cecilia Carpmael, but he had also corresponded – at least since 1934 – with Marcus Oliver, who must in turn have gossiped to Denton frequently about the chaplain and his outrageous lifestyle. Certainly by the end of 1942 Denton knew all about him, for he wrote to Marcus on 24 November that year to say, 'I should so like to meet R.B.B. Apparently he is not on speaking terms with Cecilia now!' The link between Brown, Marcus and Denton is all too easy to understand, for Brown, too, enjoyed corresponding with grand people. Like Denton, he wrote to Lady Oxford, and he was also a friend of the queen's dress designer, Norman Hartnell, and of Mervyn Stockwood, later Bishop of Southwark. His devotion to Queen Mary was fanatical – his lavatory contained a pop-up portrait of Her Majesty – though when on one occasion he was summoned to preach before her while she was living at Badminton, the sermon he delivered was so outré that he was not invited to take sherry with her after the service. His marriage, to a lady he had occasionally condescended to take to dinner at the Ritz, was equally disastrous; their honeymoon lasted ten days, starting at the Savoy and ending at Claridges, and to Marcus Oliver he described his wife as the one person who '"ever since I married her has bored me almost more than any other human being I've ever known"'. This would have come as no surprise to Marcus, to whom he intimated that a steady supply of German boys was the true focus of his attentions. Although Denton did eventually meet Brown, he seems, surprisingly, to have passed up the opportunity of immortalizing in literature one of a dying breed of thoroughly dotty Anglican clergymen.

Michael Ayrton's invitation to Denton to exhibit at Heal's resulted in two new paintings which Eric delivered on 25 September. One of them, 'The Coffin House', was purchased by the novelist Rose Macaulay, who at the beginning of the following year wrote to him about it: 'I have bought your Coffin House, which I like more and more. I see you haven't signed it (nowhere that I can discover, unless it's worked in among the fauna and flora somewhere). I wonder if any time you are in this direction you would let me know, and come in and sign it – I suppose it would have to be on the glass. It would add yet another distinction to a distinguished picture, if you would do this some time.'

Denton's reply elicited a speedy and witty response. 'Thank you so much for your letter,' Rose Macaulay wrote on 10 February 1947. 'I have found the signature in the top left corner; quite legible; but the one on the leaf in the bottom right corner seems to have got overgrown with leafage and acorns since you did it, and though, helped by your drawing of the leaf in your letter, I searched diligently among the undergrowth, I couldn't be sure I had found it, tho' I saw one or two possibilities. If ever you are able to come here (which I very much hope, and am sorry to hear that you are house-tied for the present) please identify it for me. I find the picture more and more fascinating, as I knew I should when I failed to resist it at the Leicester.[2] The detail is so exquisitely mortal and corrupt, the robin singing against it with such brave larger-than-life protest. I especially like the blind white hare pawing the toadstool; and the clawing tree-trunks, like dendrofied ghosts or dragons reaching for the sky. Your pen-work is so beautifully precise and strong; and all the colour is good. I should like some time to visit the scene myself. When or if I do (perhaps when there is petrol again) I shall certainly let you know, and come and visit you if I may. The picture almost smells of fungus and a damp wood; I know the smell so well. It must have been exciting to do. It seems to me unusual to be able to do two things so well as you do, writing and picture-making.'

The frequency of Denton's bouts of ill-health now made it imperative, should Eric ever be away for any length of time, to have someone else there permanently to help with the house. Evie had paid a brief visit to Middle Orchard in August, and Denton was trying to persuade her to come back. 'I was,' he wrote of that visit in his journal, 'at my worst while she was here and could see her hardly at all; but she had her sister Mildred to stay the night, without telling me, and they talked and laughed and clattered over the box floors till late at night!' On 11 November he was writing to Noël to say, 'We have been in a state of siege here – both in

2. It would appear that the painting (reproduced in *A Last Sheaf*) had failed to sell at Heal's and had therefore been transferred to the Leicester Galleries. Its present where-abouts are not known. At about the same time, Denton sold his painting 'The Woodman's Cottage' to John Lehmann. This is now in the collection of Mr W. H. Boomgaard.

bed at the same time; but now we're better and E. has gone to do some shopping. It grew so gruesome last Sunday that we sent a telegram to Eve, but luckily she was away in Bath so was not disturbed, and E. got quickly better the next day. But we have since asked Eve to come back at least for a little time at Christmas and she seems quite keen. We are going to work it this time very firmly with strict days off and holidays away, so that she remains linked up with the outside world. It is all to be written out for her, before she returns!'

For practically the whole of November Denton was laid up in bed, venturing out only towards the end of the month for a picnic in the car and to find a christening present for his brother Paul's godson. 'To preserve me as much as possible, we only went to one shop, the Malt Shovel, and there I chose a little cream-jug, George II, 1759, eight pounds ten shillings.' On 4 December he reviewed the past year in his journal: 'Lying here, able to do nothing, I have realized that all the year has been a sinking into bed and a painful rising out of it – only to be dragged down again before I could draw breath or spread my arms.' Even keeping his journal up to date had been too much of an effort, and it was not until this entry that he recorded, 'I have not said yet that Evie came back on the eighteenth of November, and has been cooking really delicious meals for us. She does make life easier, and I have got beyond worrying over her eccentricities. In spite of bad beginnings over time – everything late and the clock looked upon as a useless ornament – we now feel glad that she is back.'

Still brooding over his father's estate, he was worrying more than ever about his financial prospects. 'I keep wondering if I shall receive anything,' he wrote. He speculated, too, about Cecilia Carpmael's Will: 'I wonder what she has to leave. Sometimes I work it out contentedly at anything between fifty thousand and eighty thousand pounds;[3] and I go through her possessions too, remembering the few nice things, the Georgian silver teapots and Persian rugs.'

His Christmas post contained a letter from Hector Bolitho, sent from the Mayflower Inn in Washington, Connecticut, enclosing his *Town and Country* article which the editor had entitled 'In Welch is Youth'. 'The article is buttery,' Denton noted with approval in his journal on 17 December, 'and they have reproduced, quite well, my pen-drawing fancy portrait of myself. I have also had a Christmas card from Julian Goodman, but with her new name Vinogradoff on it – nothing more. So

3. Denton's lower estimate of Mrs Carpmael's wealth was not far out; she was to leave £51,557 2s. 6d. when she died the following year.

she is properly remarried. Every time I have a card from her I feel a little piqued, I suppose because I gave her the picture I painted of her instead of selling it and have ever since expected a beautiful present – an eighteenth-century silver-gilt snuff box or a tiny Chinese Mirror painting. Don't give pictures away, you will always begrudge them, or feel that they are not properly appreciated.[4]

'The most surprising card of all was the one that came on Saturday, forwarded from Pitt's Folly and accompanied by one from Mrs Sloman – this makes me think that Mrs Sloman first peeped at it. It was a long card with a distressing picture of a sort of out-house and star crosses in a black sky that shaded down into spots and dots and stripes – a sort of madness of cross-hatching. I opened the book card and found on the left page in a rather bulgy, flowing writing – From the Duchess of Wellington (Dorothy Wellesley) Xmas 1946 – just like that, brackets, Xmas and all.'

On Christmas Day Denton and Eric entertained a twenty-one-year-old German prisoner of war, Harry Diedz, to lunch. Like so many of Denton's guests Diedz was to end up as a character in a short story, in one of the shortest Denton wrote, entitled 'The Hateful Word'.[5] Indulging once again in literary transvestism, Denton cast himself as 'Flora Pinkston', a 'county' type of woman in whom Denton obviously saw himself mirrored. The story describes her meeting with Harry:

'"You going my way?" she asked in her casual, brassy voice. "Can I give you a lift? Masses of room."

'She waved a hand, indicating the empty car. It was characteristic of her not to modify the superciliousness of her tone, to use phrases like "masses of room" which he would probably not understand.'

With poignant effect, the story also reflects Denton's constant mourning for his lost health. Flora, we are told, 'moved with long, easy strides, as if lazily conscious of an elegant, well-dressed body.' By the time Denton wrote those words, his walk was slow and painful, and he was so thin that his clothes hung loose over his body. Nothing short of supreme determination was keeping him going at all.

---

4. Three years earlier Denton had, nevertheless, made a gift to Julian Goodman of a charming miniature painting of a cat, which he had inscribed on the back, 'Julian from Denton Christmas 1943'.

5. Published in *A Last Sheaf*.

SIXTEEN

'Torn Apart by Wild Apes'

The year 1947 opened for Denton with a request from the freelance broadcaster and editor of the magazine *Triad*, Jack Aistrop, for Denton to write a five-hundred-word script about his work for a programme on him being prepared by the French section of the BBC. The idea, it seems, was for Denton to read his piece in English: 'They do the translation and one only has to record the thing which although fairly frightening isn't as bad as doing it directly,' Aistrop assured him. Whether or not Denton was really daunted by the idea, however, there was in any case now no question of him being well enough to travel to London to do the broadcast, and he devoted himself instead to the task of completing his third novel, writing short stories and struggling to maintain his journal, increasingly preoccupied as it was with financial disappointments and chronic illness.

He spent the first three weeks of January in bed, 'able to do nothing'. England was in the grip of one of its most severe winters, and the cold, on top of post-war exhaustion and the scarcity of food and fuel, was depressing the entire nation. 'The snow has been falling for days,' he wrote on 28 January. 'It is falling now; there is a great layer on the roof. The wind bites through the apple trees and round the corners of the house.' Later that day he wrote, 'In all the illness I have had the horrible sensation that the tables, chairs, lamps and confusion of books near me were writhing into life and becoming extensions of myself, like new limbs, utterly unwanted, but insisting on living and doing my bidding.'

The next morning there were 'frost flowers' thick all over the panes and the milk was frozen. 'The pipes were frozen too, and the snow thicker than ever. I have not got out of bed, and will not till I hear the pipes thawing. I have been writing here, then eating chocolates as a reward.' On 2 February he recorded, 'The snow is still thick, and it falls fitfully, the flakes floating down, or driving more fiercely mixed with a little rain. As I lie in bed, only getting up twice a day, I feel that I shall never walk about again. The effort seems tremendous. My legs sway and my head swims.' Prompted by the publication of one of his poems in *Orion* he wrote, 'I wish to have stories and poems in many magazines. I want to finish my story[1] and my book and get them to the publishers. I want to be a sausage machine pouring out good sausages, savoury and toothsome, delightful, desirable. I want pleasure and interest to flow from me.'

On 13 February he was complaining, 'The bitter weather, the snow and ice, never disappear. If there is a thaw, it freezes all the more afterwards to make up for it. All the bathroom taps and plugs are frozen now, in spite of our having the electric fire on all night. And now with the electricity cuts, we have no current between nine and twelve, two and four. Eric is sawing wood in the snow. Evie is bumbling about in the kitchen, waiting for the current to go on so that she can cook lunch. My hands are so cold I can't write smoothly or easily.'

A bitter blow came on 3 March when he learned that his mother's old friend Cecilia Carpmael, who lived a few miles away in the Oast House in Trottiscliffe, had died without leaving him a penny. She had fallen and broken her thigh and, good Christian Scientist that she was, had refused medical attention. It appears that she had until recently assumed that Denton would have been well provided for by his father, but when she had discovered that this was not the case she had omitted to do anything about it in her Will. Denton devoted many pages of his journal to his grievance over this, and if there was one grudge he carried to his grave it was surely against Cecilia for not leaving him a sizeable slice of her fortune.

Partly as a result of Mrs Carpmael's death, as Denton reported to Noël Adeney on 9 March, 'Things have been in rather a turmoil here, for not only has Eric been fetching and carrying nearly every day for the Oast House, but Evie has been cooking them fish pies and apple tarts; and on top of everything Evie has thrown a cup of hot tea at Eric and been thoroughly spanked for her caprice. She is still in a towering rage, swearing that she will "have the law on him". She bangs doors all the time and kicks E.'s shins when he has the tray in his hands, and E. only turns round to say that next time he will take her trousers down! in true macabre low comedy vein. It is all quite grotesque and peculiar, really like a Punch and Judy show.'

On 5 April Denton recorded for the past two days he had been working on a watercolour of a large-eyed girl wearing a hat. 'I must have

---

1. The story Denton refers to was probably 'Brave and Cruel'.

begun it some years ago,' he wrote. 'I suddenly came upon it in a cupboard, and in spite of not feeling well, I was so pleased with it in some way that I began at once to make all sorts of little changes and additions.'[2] He had been feeling well enough the same day to have gone out, taking a picnic lunch, to Cobham where in the parish church he had come upon a boy and a girl, 'quietly staring, withheld, serious, sexy; the youth with a satchel slung on his shoulder and grey-blue smoky skin round his eyes, giving him rather a beautiful, made-up look. They were both short, and I thought of them as pleasing, stumpy dolls.'

His hopes of a legacy from Mrs Carpmael having been dashed, Denton was once again preoccupied with the prospect of receiving something from his father's firm. Noël made inquiries on his behalf in the City and on 9 May Denton wrote to thank her: 'It is just that one gets over-anxious when one is ill; for after all there is still something to live on in the bank and I have Routledge's statement at the end of this month, together with one or two cheques due for articles and drawings.' The royalties from Routledge came to over £100. In addition his brother Bill, as he told Noël on 4 July, had been 'extraordinarily good. In his last letter he offers to send me "a few hundred pounds" as he puts it, whenever I need it; and he also wants to know what it costs to keep E. and Evie and me, so that if I am ill again for a long time and not much coming in, he can come to the rescue, and I won't feel that I might have to delve into my capital.' It was at this time that he also learned, to his shame, that the £100 he had received on his birthday the previous year had been his brother's army gratuity.

On 22 May Denton went to see an oculist in Tunbridge Wells, 'to see if those queer headaches were anything to do with my eyes', as he explained to Noël, and shortly afterwards he was back in bed, being injected with penicillin every four hours by Eric. Within a few weeks he was able to fend for himself again, and in July Eric took the opportunity to go up to London to visit his mother – and, to judge by Denton's letters, to escape from 'atmospheres'. On 7 July Denton wrote to Eric, complaining first about Evie and then turning to Noël: 'Isn't she insanely petty? I really think we are all as nice to her as can be expected, taking our different natures into account. I hope no upsets get too unmanageable.' Referring to the Quarter Day the following year, when his tenancy agreement would come up for review, he went on, 'I've told her we must have

2. This painting, which became known as *A Beauty Waiting in the Fields*, was reproduced in *A Last Sheaf* and in 1954 was purchased from the Leicester Galleries by Mr Geoffrey Parsons.

a more businesslike arrangement in March. I wish they'd sell.' He wrote also to Noël herself the same day to ask, 'What do you mean by "lively hostility"? This really is nonsense. I am completely free from such a feeling. It would be very extraordinary if I was not.' With reference to the mysterious feud between Evie and Eric, he admitted that she was 'a difficult woman' but that Eric was 'the very *last* person to want to make trouble'.

On 13 July Woodrow Wyatt, the editor of *English Story* to which Denton had contributed in the past, wrote to say, 'I am not quite happy about the two stories Evergreen and Leaves From a Young Person's Notebook. I am most anxious to put another of your stories in the next series of English Story, but whilst I am still considering these two stories I should be most grateful if you could send me any other stories you have finished. You did mention that you might finish one fairly soon.'[3]

It is hard to imagine how, in spite of ever more frequent and more painful bouts of illness, Denton managed to keep up the flow of work. On 7 August the pain was so severe that morphia had to be administered. After the doctor had left, 'the killing pain lost its grip, became playful even, nagging a little, jabbing, dancing, settling down at last to a comfortable thrumming'. He was out of action for four days, writing on 11 August, 'Now I want to do nothing, yet hate idleness. I have to push my pen through wads of cotton-wool, and outside the men are emptying the cesspool.'

Relations with Evie, having steadily grown worse, reached such a pitch in October that it appears she simply upped and left. Did Eric and Denton goad her? Noël Adeney believed they did, and when annotating Denton's letters she wrote, 'I was surprised she had not gone before. I remember one afternoon in Denton's room, he and Eric pouring out abuses at her to me; the door trembled for some moments, then Evie burst in. "It's all lies, lies, lies, Mrs Adeney," with such passion and tears and pain, that I followed her downstairs, risking a rebuff. She was standing by the french window, shaking and desolate. I touched her arm.

'"Evie, I'm sorry."

'"Oh, Mrs Adeney, you don't know. Eric doesn't know *how* to behave."'

'No word from Evie yet,' Denton reported to Noël on 19 October. 'I do think she is the most split in half person I know. I am just making another Will, and I can't think what to do about her. It seems now almost

3. Woodrow Wyatt in the end rejected both 'Evergreen Seaton-Leverett' and 'Leaves From a Young Person's Notebook'.

as if I'd never known her. She seems to infect one with her own inconsequence.'

In the Will he was about to invalidate he had left everything to Jack Easton. He may have pondered for some time on what to do about Evie, since the new Will was not signed until 4 March the following year, and in the end he left her £500, describing her – for she still had not returned by the time he signed it – as his 'former housekeeper'. To each of his brothers he left £150, thinking that they might object to the bulk of his estate going outside the family, while the new residuary beneficiary was to be Eric. Jack Easton now got nothing. It is interesting to note, in view of his preoccupation with the special value of possessions, that Denton did not leave a single memento to anyone.

For the next six weeks he was consumed with illness and pain. Late at night on 22 October he was writing that he longed bitterly for his strength and health, 'nothing more, just the old things I had lost and am almost too ashamed ever to write about'. Early on 4 November he was sending up a prayer: 'Oh morning, build up into goodness, so that I can eat, think, work, enjoy.' But it was a prayer left unanswered, for thirteen days later he recorded: 'Awful days and nights since I last wrote. High fever all the time. The first night of this new attack, I was in so much pain that Eric gave me a morphia injection ... Every day after that I was just drowsy, aching in a high temperature for more than a week.'

On the last day of November he was sufficiently recovered to be able to write to Noël with the news that he had broken with Routledge and had moved to Hamish Hamilton. Having taken Edith Sitwell's advice to sign on with her literary agents, he was now reaping the rewards: 'In spite of a slight pang, I think I'm pleased about it. Hamilton sounds very nice and I shall certainly have a bigger advance and much higher royalties.' Hamish Hamilton was planning to bring out a collection of his short stories, to be called *Brave and Cruel*, 'But the great trouble of the last few days,' Denton told Noël, 'has been that Hamish thought that the story which deals with Monte was libellous. He doesn't think so now, if I make some small changes.' This was the title story of the collection, describing the phoney air-ace, 'Micki Beaumont' (in real life he was known to Denton as 'Monte'). Also immortalized in it was Denton's neighbour, May Walbrand-Evans. 'I hope,' he continued to Noël, 'May won't mind my picture based on her. It really isn't *her*, but obviously founded on bits of her. It will be a nuisance if she is hurt. Don't mention it at all, will you. I'd much rather she found out after the book is out. It probably won't appear for months, and then she might not even come across a copy. It is difficult using living characters. One seems almost bound to give offence. I suppose I must learn to wrap myself more and more in fictional clothing.'

In popping May into a short story and hoping she would not notice, he was being quite as naive as he had been over his brother Bill. She had known Denton for nearly ten years and had taken a close interest in his books; even if she did not receive a complimentary copy of his new book from him, she could hardly fail to see someone else's. As far as Monte was concerned, however, it was Denton himself who had raised the question of libel, as his journal entry for 17 November reveals: 'All through this time the agents were fixing up an agreement with Hamish Hamilton, my new publisher, about my book of new short stories. They had it all beautifully arranged, then I went and spoilt it all by saying that I thought the longest story, "Brave and Cruel", libellous. Hamish Hamilton agreed, and now it all hangs fire, with me still in bed, able to do nothing properly and wondering what to begin on.' Thoroughly depressed, he added, 'I don't want to think of writing any more. It is a deadness and a worry.'

The next day brought some reassurance. 'Hamilton writes that he doesn't want to sacrifice "Brave and Cruel" since it is such a good story and adds so to the bulk of the book. He seems to want to get round the libel difficulty somehow. I felt heartened; but I still don't know what he is going to do. If it's libellous to describe Monte's being sent to prison, I suppose it will always remain so. Short of writing a quite new story, I can't really disguise the present one at all.'

The Leicester Galleries also had been active, inviting Denton to contribute to a New Year show of nineteenth- and twentieth-century artists they were planning – 'this in spite of not selling anything of mine this summer,' he wrote. 'Again I felt heartened. I don't know why because writing and painting both seem impossibly difficult to me at the moment. I feel wrapped in a deadening blanket, just able to eat and think dully. I spell words wrong and muddle them up and feel unbelievably tired after writing one letter.' Nevertheless, by Christmas Eve he had finished two paintings for Eric to take up to the gallery for him, and in the meantime he also managed to find the energy to design an intricate invitation card for the private view.

His state of health had fluctuated as erratically as ever. In his letter to Noël of 30 November he had announced, 'Jack seems very pleased with me. The blood test agreed with the sudden mysterious lowering of my blood pressure. He thinks I will be much better now, if I get stronger. He has given me another of those dreadful foods to take. This one is called

Hepavite. I haven't had it yet, but he says it is not nearly so bad as that diabolical beef-tea-bone-manure. It would be nice if I could be up and about again as I used to be.' He also reported, 'No more news of Eve. It would be funny if you met her on the heath one day. We are wondering if she will just turn up for Christmas as if nothing had happened.'

On 19 December he was worrying again about *Brave and Cruel*, even though it was not due to be published for another twelve months. 'I don't know at all how my short stories will be received,' he wrote to Noël. 'They aren't supposed to be nearly such a money-making concern as a full-length book.' The 'full-length book' he was thinking about, which he had begun to write in 1944, had not been touched for months. 'I am busy now reading thro' and changing my long book which has been left over a year,' he told Noël. 'It gave me rather a shock at first, but I'm getting more used to it again. I can't think what it will sound like to other people.'

On Christmas Day, after lunching on tinned turkey sent from America, he and Eric went for a drive — 'my first time out since October'. From New Zealand, following a mysterious letter from the Mayor of Auckland, they were expecting a parcel containing two tins of dripping, one tin of sheep's tongue, one tin of pork luncheon meat and one tin of steak-and-kidney pudding; which, the mayor hoped, would bring relief to Denton in his present hardship. It was not until another letter arrived, from Hector Bolitho explaining that he had given the mayor Denton's address, that the mystery was solved.

Early in 1948 a second attempt was made to persuade Denton to take part in a radio broadcast; this time the approach came from Rayner Heppenstall, who wrote inviting Denton to contribute to a feature programme for the BBC Third Programme. Denton invited him to lunch at Middle Orchard on 30 January, and two days later described him in his journal: 'He seemed slow, almost drugged. He had the sort of composure that puts one at a disadvantage, if one is afraid of gaps in the conversation. One rushes in with trite things, with anything to break the dreadful, imposed, uneasy Buddha calm.' Heppenstall smoked all the time, and Denton noted that 'the bony fingers of one hand looked scorched, as if he wore a glove which had been in the oven too violently'; and his eyelids 'seemed often to be sliding down, like rather sluggish drops of porridge'.

At the end of the month Evie at last manifested herself, in the form of a parcel of butter and a letter saying that she would 'probably' send her address later. At the same time Denton also heard that there had been a fire at Hamish Hamilton's offices. 'I'm hoping my M.S. has already been sent to the printers!' he wrote to Noël, referring to *Brave and Cruel* in a way that indicates that the libel problems had now all been solved. On 6 February he ventured out with Eric in the car, 'the fur-lined coat round me, the rug over me and my feet perched up on a cushion on top of the picnic basket', as he wrote in his journal the next day. 'I felt delightfully comfortable lying there, gazing out at the country. It was strange and wonderful and new to be doing something like this again, to be dressed in my Donegal tweed suit, a new grey roll-neck sweater and a yellow scarf. The only thing that reminded me of illness was the difficulty I had in moving. Ever since Jack's lumbar puncture last year I've had to move about with painful care. If I don't, terrible pains shoot through me. He ... tells me that the aches and pains are probably due to the original accident, when I fractured my spine...I only wonder when I shall be able to walk again with comparative ease...I should feel easier if I thought it was melting away, but it isn't. It has been there for about nine months and it is still fiery torture if I sneeze, cough or move about suddenly. And of course to be sick is quite out of the question – one just feels as if one was being torn apart by wild apes.'

Some light relief was on the horizon, however. It appears that a gentleman named Joe had been telephoning Denton's great-aunt Blanche, the sister-in-law of his grandmother, Edith Welch, to inquire 'What colour knickers you are wearing, or perhaps you're not wearing any knickers today', and Aunt Blanche's housekeeper had telephoned Eric to see if the calls had been coming from Denton. 'I suppose,' Denton wrote in his journal on 11 February, 'my aunt still thinks of me as a boy, capable of preposterous tricks. The housekeeper told Eric that she thought it might be me, because I had been so ill. If the telephone was near my bed, I might easily do silly things to while away the hours of the night.'

Whiling away the hours had rarely been a problem for Denton, though he now seemed to be finding it harder and harder to concentrate. 'I have done a tiny bit of revision which nagged at me all yesterday,' he recorded on 25 February. 'Why does the mind go limp and soggy when confronted with two sentences that are not as they should be? Why can't one shake one's head and begin anew? It is almost as if the words were strangling one.' Two days later came a revealing reflection about the journals themselves: 'In Gide's Journal I have just read again how he does not wish to write its pages slowly as he would the pages of a novel. He wants to train himself to rapid writing in it. It is just what I have always felt about this journal of mine. Don't ponder, don't grope – just plunge something down, and perhaps more clearness and quickness will come with practice.' Seldom satisfied with his own achievements, he wrote on 16 March, 'How I am aware of the thinness, the affectation and strain of what I write! Revising, correcting, is hateful, fishy, shaming. I would knock the posture out of words, bash them into shape, iron out their obstinate awkwardness.'

On 28 February he heard from his agents that they had sold his short story 'The Trout Stream' to the *Cornhill* magazine for a suggested fee of 'about twenty guineas'. Two days later he learned that May Walbrand-Evans had died. Now, at least, he would be spared any worry about her reaction to 'Brave and Cruel'. She left a dozen books to Eric and to Denton she left 'her lovely Queen Anne mirror'. 'What pleasure it gives to be left something in this way! It has never happened to me before,' he wrote when the news reached him.

His relationship with May had been typical of so many of his friendships, for although he was undoubtedly fond of her he was often extremely rude about her. In 1943, for example, he had complained to Marcus Oliver that he had been cleaned out of copies of *Maiden Voyage* by 'vampire-bats like May', and he echoed the sentiment in 1946 when he wrote to another friend to thank him for some eggs, adding, 'I hear May had two off you on the way up! She is a blood-sucking bat!' On a postcard to Marcus sent on 22 February 1943 he wrote, 'May is getting coarser and coarser. She sniffs now like a char.'

Not long after May died, Denton had another visit from perhaps his favourite butt of derision, his art-school friend Gerald, who was now teaching art at Eton and swimming around in royal circles. On a visit the previous June Gerald had told Denton 'of his visit to Buckingham Palace to see the queen about the pictures she is probably commissioning, of some old servants, I think'; now it transpired that he was shortly to attend a service at Windsor Castle for the Order of the Garter. The service was later broadcast, and Denton listened 'to the commentator's absurd inanities over the wireless and thought of Gerald sitting in a dark corner, wearing the expression of a self-possessed but slightly hostile mouse, drinking in the sights and sounds, silently rolling the names over his tongue; Princess Elizabeth, the Duke of Edinburgh, Montgomery, Portland, Devonshire – to say nothing of the king and queen. Tomorrow he goes to stay with the Wavells at Rinwood. Eric says he hopes he makes his bed there instead of leaving it all tousled and frowsty as he did here.'

Towards the end of May, Eric was obliged to telephone Jack Easton for some 'mysterious but effective headache remover', and on 26 May Denton wrote in his journal that he was now finding it a strain to talk to visitors, 'although it used to be a joy of life'. On the other hand, he wrote on 8 June, 'With a high temperature these last few weeks I can read for long stretches, a thing I have not been able to do for months and months, but I do not seem able to write at all.' He was, nevertheless, still full of plans for the future. On 6 July he wrote to Noël to say, 'We have been hoping for a long time that Evie will come back within the next two weeks so that E. can go to his mother ... I do hope Eve makes an effort to turn up. I'm longing for her to do a little house cleaning. I have had to make a new curtain for the front door, since the Chinese gauze is so old that it's rotted. The new net, 2½ yards, cost 19s. 9½d. Can this be right? When I bought it, I thought the man meant seven pence something a yard – not seven shillings. It is quite nice but ordinary. Is net always expensive? I thought it would be as cheap as butter muslin. All this took place yesterday when I went to the dentist. I have finished the curtain now and it certainly looks quite dainty. What I really want to write to you about is to ask if you still would entertain the idea of selling me a bit of the bottom of the orchard ...'

Still dreaming of building a house, and aware that he could not stay at Middle Orchard for ever, he even started house-hunting again. Meanwhile, on 6 July he had a visit from Maurice Cranston, who brought 'titbits from Oxford and other places', including a message from Lord David Cecil to the effect that he had found *Maiden Voyage* to be one of only two books that had moved him in the past seven years. On 9 July Evie had reappeared. 'She is staying at least a week, so she says,' Denton wrote to Noël the following day. 'E. and Eve went out shopping hours ago and there isn't any lunch, but I don't mind, since I can write in peace. Eve seems to fill the house.'

On the last day of July Denton went out in the car with Eric – 'the first time for weeks' – to see a stable and coach-house which was 'suitable for conversion'. In August he announced in his journal, 'I have a new doctor.' It appears that Jack Easton was thought to have too far to come in the event of an emergency, even though he lived only seven miles away in Tonbridge. The new doctor could not match up to him, however. 'I can't say I take to him,' Denton wrote. 'Wooden, caricaturish face, a sort of sparse-haired, golliwog effect. When I told him of my accident, he began to examine me rather as if I were a doubtful kipper at the fishmongers. He seemed to find me just as unappetizing as he suspected, for he said suddenly, "Have you been told anything about a tubercular condition or not?" I shook my head. The word had a funny sound. I thought of cows and udders and children with crumbly bones like the ones found in tinned sardines.' On 10 August, brooding no doubt on the new doctor's gloomy diagnosis, Denton wrote, 'Death seems so far away; it recedes and becomes more and more impossible as one grows iller ... The horrible thing about it is its utter silliness.'

While lying in bed with a temperature of 103°, he received a second visit from David Carritt, who came bearing an invitation from the two eminent and aristocratic writers who lived twenty miles away at Sissinghurst Castle, Harold Nicolson and Vita Sackville-West. 'I don't suppose I shall ever get there,' Denton lamented on 18 August, 'but I should like to see the house amongst the castle ruins.' He added, 'I have a little sneaking silly hope that there might be some tiny place near there for us, if we have to leave here in March.' The thought had evidently been prompted by a visit that very afternoon from Noël – 'rather jerky and witchlike', according to her tenant. 'It is clear that she cannot really decide what to do about the place. She would like me to go on living here, would like to sell it for an enormous price, and keep it herself all at the same time. A division of desires in a person's face is curious to watch. The features seem to lose themselves. It is as if the nose, the eyes and the mouth were hunting for each other.'

As luck would have it, a brief respite from his illness allowed him after all to go on 27 August to tea at Sissinghurst, the romantic jumble of Tudor and Elizabethan buildings which the Nicolsons had bought in 1930 and which they had immediately set about restoring, creating in the process perhaps the most magical garden in England. Denton's journal entry for 31 August, describing this outing, was one of his longest, and it was also his last. On the day of the great occasion he spent the morning trying 'to do nothing at all, husbanding all my resources for our visit to Sissinghurst in the afternoon. We started rather late, because the realization that we had all day made us dawdle over everything, including lunch and our final dressing. I put on my Pekin grass-cloth shirt, my Donegal tweed suit and old "patinated" shoes with lolling tongues. The back of the car was filled with two velvet cushions, gold and terracotta, and the green-and-black Nairn tartan rug Paul brought back from fighting in Italy. I lay there with my feet up, preserving myself frantically.'

It was already half-past four when Denton and Eric reached the village of Sissinghurst, and on approaching the castle they spotted 'a tall woman, whom I took at once to be Vita', saying good-bye to a man in a car. (Denton had seen her before, of course, at the poetry reading in Tunbridge Wells.) 'She wore cord riding-breeches which disappeared into tall laced canvas leather boots.' On her head was a large straw hat, 'floppy and flimsy'. Her manner seemed to him 'a little withheld, a little torpid. It was not quite social or bright enough to make a first meeting really easy.'

As they sat down on a bench in the garden Vita offered them 'crumpled cigarettes' and tried to make conversation. At last Harold appeared.

'"Is tea ready?" Vita asked, with a trace of petulance or anxiety.

'"Yes," said Harold, "it is waiting."

'Now,' Denton wrote, 'began the stickiest part of our visit.' They had to walk across the garden, down the yew walk to the Priest's House, 'and neither Vita nor Harold seemed to be able both to manoeuvre their guests and talk to them easily at the same time.' It does not seem to have occurred to him that the Nicolsons may have behaved awkwardly because of an entirely natural embarrassment at his frail condition; by this stage he was walking slowly and with extreme caution, and it was obvious to anyone who saw him that he was desperately ill. Their shyness became all the more noticeable when they were joined by a house guest, the society hostess Lady Colefax. 'If I had felt, before, the awkwardness of Harold and Vita,' he wrote heartlessly, 'I was now made doubly aware of their shortcomings; for Lady Colefax at once began a sprightly conversation about nothing in particular.'

He found the tea-table 'only laid with a large farmhouse cake and cucumber sandwiches, but there was an air of richness and profusion'. In no time at all his hosts began to discuss the man whom Vita had been seeing off just as Denton and Eric had arrived. 'This dismembering of the just departed guest in front of the but lately arrived ones struck me as stimulating but perilous,' Denton observed. He went on to record more of the tea-time chit-chat, and concluded his account – and his journals – with these words: 'In writing down our conversation, flatly, quickly and rather clumsily, I am very conscious of its inanity and purposelessness; and yet in reality it had another character. Lady Colefax made it bright, quick-moving; Harold and Vita were beginning to feel at home again in their own house; Eric was enjoying his cider, and I felt warmed and protected by the richness of the room. Almost everything stopped short at the seventeenth century. For once it was refreshing to see nothing from one's own favourite eighteenth and nineteenth. Taste which is not one's own is a sort of holiday. One criticizes but enjoys. I wished I could be left alone to look about me. Even now, as I write, I' –

Harold Nicolson, too, wrote up the visit in his diary. His entry for 27 August read simply, 'I have a slack day – just pottering about with my book. Sibyl [Lady Colefax] comes down for luncheon and remains till

Monday. The French Government have fallen over Reynaud's Finance Bill. Denton Welch and Eric Oliver come over.'

After Denton's death the Nicolsons remained in touch with Eric for some years. When Denton's last novel was published in 1950, under the title *A Voice Through a Cloud*, Harold reviewed it in the *Observer* on 12 March that year and wrote to Eric five days later: 'I am very glad you liked my review of Welch's book. It is certainly an unforgettable work and will, I hope, have a considerable sale. I should like to feel that he was remembered by this book above all the others, since I think it shows far greater power and assurance. You may be interested to hear that my review has led to several people writing to me and saying how much they themselves suffered in hospital from the same sort of callous treatment.

'John Lehmann wrote to me the other day and mentioned the diaries. Evidently he is afraid that Denton Welch's occasional asperities would cause great offence. I feel myself that it would be a pity if the diaries were not published since, if they are anything like A Voice Through a Cloud, they should be of the utmost interest. I have written to John Lehmann, but am not sure whether I shall persuade him.

'Of course I realize there is a difficulty, since people are extremely touchy and much resent sharp remarks about their failings being given to the public. On the other hand it is very unsatisfactory not to give real names, and either to disguise them or to represent them with a dash. One method would be to leave out the more insulting passages by dots to indicate that an omission occurs. This creates grave anxiety, as you may well imagine, but is at least quite defensible. You yourself would be somewhat disconcerted if you read in a published diary "Eric Oliver came to dinner ... He did not leave till 2 a.m. and left his raincoat behind."'

At Christmas-time Denton had sent an advance copy of *Brave and Cruel* to Vita as a present, for which she wrote to thank him on the very day he died, 30 December 1948. She read of his death in *The Times* the following morning, and wrote at once to Eric: 'I hope you will allow me to say that I can realize what this must mean to you, as far as one can ever realize the full meaning of grief to another person. I had so hoped that you and he would come here again next spring, and now it is not to be, though if ever you cared to come by yourself you would be most welcome. It is dreadful that so brilliant a talent should be lost to the world. I know how good you were to him, and what care you gave him.' She added a postscript: 'I wish I had known him better! We all took to him so instantly, that day.'

She wrote again on 4 January 1949: 'I fear you must be feeling dreadfully lonely. Please don't resent my saying this!' A few weeks later Eric sent her a copy of Denton's last journal entry, though it was not until 8 April that Vita was able to respond. 'Oh, I have been ill and was unable to get over to my sitting-room where I had put it away,' she wrote. (Her sitting-room was in the Elizabethan tower and was strictly out of bounds to everyone, including her own family.) 'It was good of you to send it, though I must say I was rather horrified to see how completely we had failed to put Denton at his ease; I was under the impression myself that we had got on rather well. Well, one lives and learns. How terrifyingly observant he was, down to the smallest detail.' She remarked, nevertheless, 'How I wish it did not break off just where it does.'

When the journals were eventually published in an abridged edition in 1952, Vita Sackville-West reviewed them in *The Times Literary Supplement*. She wrote to Eric on 27 February that year: 'It pleases me so much that you of all people should approve of my review. I had felt some diffidence about it, because, after all, my acquaintance with D.W. was so very slight, alas; and somehow one feels impertinent trying to interpret so complex and remarkable a personality.'

During the few months left to Denton following his visit to Sissinghurst, death had continued to seem far away. On 27 September his brother Bill wrote to say that he would send a food parcel for Christmas. 'What do you especially need?' he asked. 'Fats, I suppose.' On 29 September, still house-hunting, Denton informed Noël that he had seen 'a rather awful bungalow at Trottiscliffe', though when he next wrote to her, some time in October (he was again forgetting to date his letters), he had taken a turn for the worse: 'I'm afraid it has been a most frightful time ever since you left. I feel completely flattened out − as if I couldn't pull myself together again; but I suppose I shall. I'm beginning to eat, after five or six days of having nothing at all, so something is reviving. Lovely sun and frost today.' Another undated letter, written in November, reported, 'My latest problem is a most unpleasant gasping for breath. Can it be asthma? A thing I've never had in my life. One night was very disturbing, but since then I only wheeze like a pug dog. I sit in a howling wind and that makes it better.' He also reported that Evie, 'apart from one set-to, has been excellent. The trouble was caused by her ranting that I would be perfectly all right if I got out of bed and dressed. We both [Eric and he] grew so wild that we began bellowing at her. Why is it so difficult for rather a simple person to grasp that another is ill? I mean quite apart from Christian Science. Is it just lack of imagination? I do believe Eve thinks I could go out and garden, if only I'd make the effort.'

On 1 December Hamish Hamilton sent the advance copies of *Brave and Cruel* along with a letter informing him, 'It would have been disastrous to publish in mid-December when booksellers will not look at new books and literary editors are tearing their hair, so in the interests of us both I am holding back until January.' In the event the book, dated 1948, was published on 7 January 1949, two days after Denton's funeral.

On 3 December Denton signed a copy for Noël Adeney. Then, remembering no doubt the 'unsolicited testimonial' he had received when *In Youth is Pleasure* was published, he sent one also to Lord Berners. Berners, absent-minded in the extreme, responded fulsomely in a letter postmarked on 31 December 1948 but dated by him 1 January 1949. It was sad that Denton should not have seen the letter, for Berners wrote, 'Thank you a thousand times for sending me your lovely book of stories which I have read with the greatest delight.' He had recently been to see John Betjeman, 'whom I found very enthusiastic about the book. I persuaded him to lend it to me and when I got back I found the copy you had sent me.' Berners ended by inviting Denton to stay with him some time after 7 January.

On 14 December Eric sent a copy of the book to Hector Bolitho, enclosing a letter explaining that Denton had been unable to write himself 'since he has been ill for months, and it has left him with heart palpitations if he does anything at all'. None the less he added that Denton would be delighted if Hector would call again, for lunch or tea.

On 15 December Denton renewed his driving licence. He was struggling to finish *A Voice Through a Cloud*, though progress was painfully slow. Eric's next report to Hector Bolitho, sent on 28 December, informed him that Denton was still having morphia every night, sometimes twice, 'so that he asks me to explain that he is in rather a dopey condition'. He added a postscript: 'Denton is on the last two or three chapters of his long book, so if his health improved the book should be finished at least in the next few months.'

Denton was closer to death than Eric — perhaps even Denton himself — could know. *A Voice Through a Cloud* remained incomplete, though by a smaller margin than Eric suggested in his letter, since there can be little doubt that it lacked no more than a dozen pages. Fifteen manuscript books lay beside Denton's bed, a living testament to his courage and tenacity in the face of death. So many times had he seemed too ill to survive any longer, yet so many times had he rallied again, that both Eric and Evie grew used to his permanently critical condition. Even on the day of his death, 30 December, he seemed in the morning no better and no worse than he had been for many months past.

'He had just kept himself alive by will-power,' Eric has said. 'He'd recovered so many times that the only time I realized something was seriously wrong was when I tried to lift him up, and he was a complete dead weight.' It was two o'clock in the afternoon. Denton had died, aged thirty-three.

An Epilogue

The aftermath of Denton's death was not without what he would have described as its dotty moments. In anticipation of a funeral service packed out with literary celebrities, a fleet of hired cars was dispatched to the railway station at Borough Green, but none of Denton's influential patrons turned up. The service, held on 5 January 1949 at the parish church of St John the Baptist in Wateringbury, near Tonbridge, was attended by less than two dozen people, among them Evie Sinclair, Lady Fox, the Adeneys, Maurice Cranston, and two women whom none of the others present had ever seen before; claiming to be long-lost friends of Denton's mother they insisted, in the absence of any relatives, on being treated as the chief mourners, installing themselves directly behind the coffin and in front of Eric Oliver, who had held the dying Denton in his arms.

The order of service informed the congregation that Denton had 'passed on' at the age of thirty-two. (His death certificate also held him to be thirty-two, while Eric, when he came to write a Foreword to *A Voice Through a Cloud*, even asserted that he was thirty-one.) Afterwards the coffin, draped with a red Aldermanic gown Denton used to wear when writing in bed, was taken on to Charing where Denton, dressed in the priest's cassock of which he had been so fond and in which he had lain on view since his death, was cremated.

Back at Middle Orchard, where coffee and sandwiches were served (Noël Adeney appears still to have been labouring under the illusion that Denton disapproved of alcohol), the solicitor added his own bizarre twist to an already incongruous occasion by starting to read out Denton's first, invalid, Will, in which Denton, before having met Eric Oliver, had left everything to Jack Easton.

On 4 February Eric wrote to Hector Bolitho to tell him that Hamish Hamilton was 'more than eager to see the novel Denton was not quite able to finish, and thinks Edith Sitwell would very gladly write an

Introduction for it'. Edith herself had been in New York when she heard the news of Denton's death and had written to John Lehmann on 6 January: 'Poor little Denton, I am filled with sadness about him. Not thirty ...' In the event, *A Voice Through a Cloud* was published not by Hamish Hamilton but by Lehmann himself, in 1950, though without any Introduction. In 1951 Lehmann also published a new collection of short stories, poems and paintings under the title *A Last Sheaf*. The following year Hamish Hamilton brought out *The Denton Welch Journals*, edited by Jocelyn Brooke, consisting of about half the total manuscript journals. A further selection of poems, edited by Jean-Louis Chevalier, was published in 1976 by the Enitharmon Press under the title *Dumb Instrument*.

In the years that followed his friend's death, Eric allowed ties to lapse and Denton's possessions to disperse. Indeed, he distributed valuable mementoes like confetti. Maurice Cranston received the Louis XVI secretaire. John Lehmann was given one of Denton's most brilliant paintings, 'Cat', which he reproduced in *A Last Sheaf*. Hector Bolitho was sent 'The Animal-Doctor should put you to Sleep', also illustrated in *A Last Sheaf*, as was another painting, named 'Nina' by Eric because it reminded him of Nina Hamnett, which went as a gift to Cyril Connolly's wife, Barbara Skelton. Connolly himself, after reviewing the *Journals* in 1952, and although he had never met Denton, received from Eric a cheque for £5 in appreciation. Vita Sackville-West received a cigarette box, and even Osbert Sitwell, who had known Denton for perhaps twenty minutes, was given an expensive pair of cufflinks. Other possessions were sold off cheaply or were given away at various times, and the only keepsakes Eric possesses today are a cigarette case and the urn containing Denton's ashes.

Many of the letters Denton had received from famous people were sold on Eric's behalf by Hector Bolitho to an American dealer, who in turn sold them to the University of Texas. Not appreciating the potential value of the copyrights in Denton's writings, Eric was persuaded to part with them by an alcoholic antiquarian bookseller by the name of James Campbell, who promptly resold them to the University of Texas. When Campbell later went bankrupt he declared the copyrights among his assets and the Official Receiver sold them in good faith to Faber & Faber. The deception was discovered and Faber were reimbursed.

Denton's favourite brother, Paul, never married and died in Hong Kong in 1954. Bill was divorced from Anne, married Judy Lambert in 1947, and died in London in 1965. Aunt Dorothy lived to the age of eighty-seven, dying in Ditchling in 1972. Noël Adeney died in 1978, as did Francis Streeten, who ended his days, as Denton had predicted he would, in squalor, in St Leonards-on-Sea. Marcus Oliver retired in genteel poverty to two rooms over business premises in Gloucester Place in London, and in 1982 he dropped dead in the street, leaving neither relatives nor a Will. The only treasure he possessed among an indescribable muddle of theatre bills and third-rate bric-à-brac was a collection of forty-two letters from Denton, which was discovered hidden beneath a cushion in his sitting-room.

But by far the strangest turn of events had occurred shortly after Denton's death, when Eric Oliver, despite his professed dislike of middle-aged women, proceeded, in the bath, to divest the fifty-five-year-old Evelyn Sinclair of her virginity.

Bibliography

Listed below are the principal published writings of Denton Welch:

Brave and Cruel and other stories (Hamish Hamilton, 1949)
The Denton Welch Journals, ed. Jocelyn Brooke (Hamish Hamilton, 1952)
Dumb Instrument, ed. Jean-Louis Chevalier (Enitharmon Press, 1976)
I Left My Grandfather's House (Lion and Unicorn Press, 1958; Allison & Busby, 1984)
In Youth is Pleasure (Routledge, 1945; Oxford University Press, 1982)
The Journals of Denton Welch, ed. Michael De-la-Noy (Allison & Busby, 1984)
A Last Sheaf (John Lehmann, 1951)
Maiden Voyage (Routledge, 1943; Penguin Books, 1983)
A Voice Through a Cloud (John Lehmann, 1950; Penguin Books, 1983)

Index

297